Truth, Love & Clean Cutlery

Truth, Love & Clean Cutlery

A guide to the truly good restaurants and food experiences of the

USA

Introduced by

Alice Waters

Associate Editor Gabriella Gershenson

Contributing editors

Erin Byers Murray
Osayi Endolyn
Devra Ferst
Rebecca Flint Marx
Paula Forbes
Mindy Fox
Dara Moskowitz Grumdahl
Adrian J.S. Hale
Joy Manning
Lara Rabinovitch
Chandra Ram
Hanna Packin
Laura Shunk
Rachel Tepper Paley

Blackwell&Ruth.

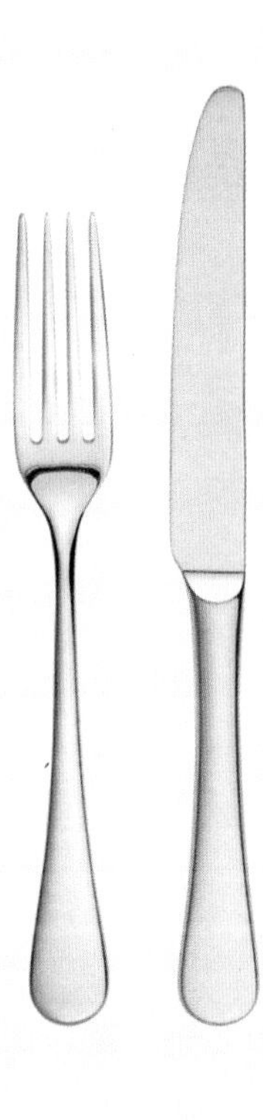

Of all the qualities that distinguish a truly outstanding restaurant or food experience, perhaps truth, love and care are the most important. A passion for creating food that is so good that it will never be forgotten, an environment that makes that extraordinary food taste even better, and a care for the ground or water from which that food is derived and the community in which it is served.

Restaurants that care about these things aren't just good, they are exemplary. **Truth, Love & Clean Cutlery** was conceived to identify and shine a light on these inspiring exemplars so that the rest of us can find, support and enjoy them.

Geoff Blackwell and Ruth Hobday
Publishers

A note on navigation

We have tried to make this guide as simple as possible to navigate. With this in mind, the restaurants are listed first by region, followed by state. Within each state, the restaurants are listed first by major city, then alphabetically by county. We hope this enables readers to easily find the wonderful restaurants near them, so that they can celebrate sustainable, ethical and simply good food.

Contents

Introduction 11
Our Mission 16

THE WEST COAST, ALASKA & HAWAII 21

Alaska 23
California 27
Los Angeles 28
San Francisco 47
Greater California 61
Sonoma 79
Hawaii 87
Oregon 91
Portland 92
Greater Oregon 100
Washington 101

THE SOUTHWEST & ROCKY MOUNTAINS 107

Arizona 109
Colorado 117
Boulder 120
Denver 121
Greater Colorado 129
Montana 137
New Mexico 141
Nevada 149
Texas 151
Utah 161
Wyoming 167

THE MIDWEST & GREAT LAKES 171

Illinois 173
Chicago 174
Greater Chicago 179
Indiana 181
Iowa 185
Kansas 189
Michigan 195
Detroit 197
Minnesota 201
Minneapolis 202
Greater Minnesota 212
Missouri 217
Kansas City 218
St. Louis 223
Greater Missouri 227
Nebraska 233
North Dakota 237
Ohio 239
Oklahoma 245
South Dakota 253
Wisconsin 257

THE SOUTHEAST 265

Alabama 267
Arkansas 273
District of Columbia 281
Washington 282
Florida 295
Georgia 301
Atlanta 302
Greater Georgia 306
Kentucky 311
Louisville 312
Greater Kentucky 319
Louisiana 321
New Orleans 322
Maryland 329
Mississippi 333
North Carolina 339
Asheville 340
Greater North Carolina 348
South Carolina 355
Tennessee 361
Nashville 362
Greater Tennessee 370
Virginia 373
West Virginia 379

THE NORTHEAST 383

Connecticut 385
Delaware 389
Maine 391
Massachusetts 399
New Hampshire 413
New Jersey 417
New York 423
Brooklyn 424
New York City 432
Greater New York 463, 468
Pennsylvania 479
Philadelphia 480
Greater Pennsylvania 484
Rhode Island 487
Vermont 491
Chittenden 492
Greater Vermont 495

Our Good Things 503
Farmers' Markets 504
Hero Producers 505
Social Enterprises 512
The Edible Schoolyard Project 513

The Editors 514
Index by location 517
Index by restaurant name 520
Acknowledgments 527

Alice Waters

When I started my restaurant, Chez Panisse, in 1971, I wanted it to be a little French restaurant where my friends could come gather around the table, eat delicious food, and discuss the politics of the time. My friends and I were all part of the political counterculture, but sustainability was not yet on my mind; taste was what brought us to the doorsteps of the local organic farmers. We realized that the farmers who were growing the most delicious ingredients we could find–flavorful heritage varietals of fruits and vegetables, picked in season at the height of their ripeness–were also the people using traditional, sustainable farming methods, treating their farm workers fairly, and taking care of the land for future generations. In time, I came to understand the paramount importance of these foragers, fishermen, farmers, ranchers, and dairymen, and the values they brought into the restaurant.

It began in the mid-seventies with lambs from Dal Porto Ranch in Amador County. As we built our relationship with the ranch, we learned we could only get the lamb in the spring, when it was at its most tender and succulent; we discovered what the spring lambs ate and how they were cared for; we learned how to butcher them so that every part of the lamb could be used; we experimented with different ways of cooking spring lamb to best bring out its delicious flavor. That was the beginning of our edible education, and through the years we have had those sorts of revelatory moments time and time again as our network of suppliers came to define our food and our philosophy at Chez Panisse. In the beginning, we used to tell the farmers what we wanted them to plant; now, it's the farmers who give us the ideas for what we should cook. They are all dedicated to sustainable, regenerative agriculture–they know the land and the crops and the seasons better than anyone.

Fast food already had a stranglehold on the United States when I first opened Chez Panisse. And over the past forty-seven years, its influence has continued to grow. I believe that in today's world, fast food culture is still the invisible moral structure underneath us all, guiding us all subconsciously and affecting everything we do–from the way we look at the world, to how we see ourselves, to how we do business. It influences the way we set up our homes, our schools, our politics. When you are eating in a fast food restaurant, not only are you malnourishing yourself, you are also unwittingly digesting the values of this fast food culture. Those values become part of you, just like the food. These fast food values tell us that everything is disposable; that time is money; that our natural resources are limitless; that seasons don't matter, and everything should be available year-round; that uniformity and cheapness should be valued above all else; that 'more is better'; that work is drudgery.

Fortunately, there's a powerful counterforce to fast food culture–a slow food counterculture, if you will. And this counterculture has its own set of values: sustainability, equality, patience, justice, nourishment, empathy, stewardship, beauty. These values–the values that *Truth, Love & Clean Cutlery* are upholding and championing with their set of criteria–are part of our very natures, but have simply been deadened by the fast food culture. These are the sorts of basic values that give us our humanity and have defined our way of living since the beginning of civilization. Returning to them is not hard. It can be as simple as taking a bite from a beautiful, perfectly ripe Suncrest peach from Masumoto Family Farm at the height of summer. It is why I often refer to this as being a delicious revolution–there is so much beauty in the biodiversity of the earth, and once you open yourself up to it, you can't return to the hollow, empty values of fast food culture.

What *Truth, Love & Clean Cutlery* understands is that the way restaurants operate can make a tremendous impact on our planet; restaurants have the power to be ethical anchors for their communities, all while serving delicious food. Last year at Chez Panisse, we fed five hundred people a day. We buy directly from the people who produce our food, and instead of money going to the middlemen, it goes straight to the source. Last year, two and a half million dollars went directly to our producers. And we are just one small restaurant. This is the kind of mutually beneficial relationship that can exist all around the world between restaurants and farmers. For it is a two-way street: the values of these farmers are introduced into the restaurant and absorbed by every diner, effortlessly. These values are absorbed, too, by the staff who work at the restaurant–the cooks and the servers, the dishwashers and the bussers.

Truth, Love & Clean Cutlery provides a roadmap to restaurants that understand the importance of operating morally and sustainably; that treat their workers with compassion and humanity; that value the health and well-being of their customers, and that help us all to become good citizens of this planet. It is more critical than ever that we identify these sorts of restaurants around the globe. Because we vote for the sort of world we live in not just when we go to the ballot box; we vote for it every time we come together around a table and sit down to eat. Every time we pay for a meal, we have the opportunity to directly lift up the restaurateurs who are out in the world doing the right thing, helping to reinvigorate their communities. We all need to lend our support in every way we can.

Mapping this movement is something I have wanted to do for a very long time. And what excites me is knowing that we have not found every restaurant yet. Each day new businesses are opening that hold these sorts of values dear: little bakeries, cafés, taquerias, neighborhood spots. This movement is growing, and I know there are so many more people out there doing incredible work, ready to push us forward. This is just the start–and I am so inspired that we are all beginning to gather together.

“Every place we list serves delicious food. That’s a given. After that, our guiding principle has been the care taken by the people who run the restaurant. Care in sourcing the food and how it is produced; care in dealing with its staff, customers and community; and care for the environment, in terms of energy, waste, and water.”

Jill Dupleix

Jill Dupleix

Truth, Love & Clean Cutlery is a new, kinder, dining guide designed to identify the restaurants and food experiences that go above and beyond great food and wine in the ethical and sustainable ways with which they run their business.

For the past decade, chefs and restaurateurs have been shifting their priorities to support sustainable and ethical practices by farmers, producers and wine-makers, placing a greater value on health, community, conscience and care. They are working harder than ever to cook with seasonal, locally sourced produce, reduce their carbon emissions and minimize their waste.

At the same time, more diners want their money to go to good restaurants with good food run by good people. This guide aims to bring everyone together at the table.

Every place we list serves delicious food. That's a given. After that, our guiding principle has been the care taken by the people who run the restaurant. Care in sourcing the food and how it is produced; care in dealing with its staff, customers and community, and care for the environment, in terms of energy, waste and water.

Establishing a clear criteria and rigorous auditing process hasn't been easy–and will never be flawless–but ultimately it comes down to everyone being open, transparent and respectful. Our editorial team is made up of some of the most experienced and talented food writers in the world. To assist them in their roles of identifying those restaurants most worthy of inclusion, each restaurant answers a rigorous survey–a self-audit if you will–citing examples of the sustainable practices and ethical principles that inform how they run their business.

This combination of experience, research and 'gut feel', validated by information from the restaurants themselves, can best be described as eighty percent due diligence and twenty percent leap of faith. It's a decision we have made to trust the process and trust the people.

We want to know if their seafood is sustainable, their waste minimized and their staff nurtured. We cover things like energy usage, community and collaboration, seasonality of ingredients, and respect for the local region and its people. We put a value on things like accepting imperfections in produce and in people,

"At last, the deeply held beliefs of both diners and chefs are beginning to align and reconnect."

producing one's own food, optimizing energy efficiency to reduce carbon emissions, reducing chemical usage, encouraging a happy and diverse workplace, working creatively to use what's readily and immediately available, menus that provide alternatives to meat, and owners who consider the health and well-being of their diners. Being nice, tick. Being fair, also. Not being a bully, definitely. It's basically 'best practice' for restaurants, encouraging change towards a more ethical, sustainable food–and dining–system.

We want to eat where we can tick as many of these boxes as possible: where the food is seasonal, which supports local farmers and reduces waste; where there are healthy alternatives to red meat, deep-fried stuff, and mayonnaise; where the fish and seafood are as sustainable as possible.

We are deeply respectful of how hard it is to run a profitable and sustainable business in the highly competitive world of hospitality, and we are in awe of everyone who uses their business as a force for good. That's why we want the world to know about them.

Truth, Love & Clean Cutlery is, we hope, a step in the right direction, helping diners choose a place to eat based on something beyond good food and wine. By choosing restaurants that have a clear mission to improve their sourcing, seasonality and sustainability, diners are endorsing ethical behavior. By encouraging diners to spend their money on people who are trying to have a positive impact on the planet.

We value good food and good friends. We value time over money, community over celebrity, and empathy over ego. We value the seasons and the rhythm of nature, and people who work with them rather than against them. And we value being able to dine together and to work together to shape the world we live in.

The restaurants you will find in *Truth, Love & Clean Cutlery* are ones we believe in; great places that are trying to do the right thing; where the act of dining is joyful, and the enjoyment of good food is amplified and intensified by the obvious care taken from paddock to plate.

We live in a changing world, where our choices now dictate the future. At last, the deeply held beliefs of both diners and chefs are beginning to align and reconnect.

"These restaurants aren't just good … they're **good**."

Bamboo Sushi (p. 92)

21

The West Coast, Alaska & Hawaii

Alaska	23
California	27
Hawaii	87
Oregon	91
Washington	101

23

Alaska

Fresh Sourdough Express

Homer

What
Proudly serving local & organic food since 1982

Who
Donna & Kevin Maltz, owners

When
Breakfast & lunch, daily

Address
1316 Ocean Drive, Homer, AK 99603

+1 907 235 7571

freshsourdoughexpress.com

Bookings
Phone

Price guide

What they say
"At Fresh Sourdough Express, we believe in serving peace and love in the form of food. We make an effort to educate our staff, suppliers, and customers about the interconnection and impact our ingredient choices and food system have on the health of the environment and personal well-being. Sustainability is a top priority in all aspects of our business practices, from sourcing produce to light bulbs. Some of our founding principles from 1982 were never to use toxic Styrofoam, recycle everything possible, repurpose all we can, donate food waste to farmers, hire, buy, and serve locally, make goods from scratch, and use organic produce whenever possible. We have witnessed how our commitments have made a difference and proudly donate to environmental organizations."

Signature dishes
Alaska sourdough pancakes; rhubarb cobbler; reindeer grill.

What we say
You might not personally know Fresh Sourdough Express owners Donna and Kevin Maltz, but I'm guessing you've come across their AH!LASKA brand, the nation's first organic chocolate syrup, which kids and adults have been enjoying since 1992. It got its start here. The couple have been environmental activists since they opened up shop in 1982. They were way ahead of their time. In 2007, they were active in founding Sustainable Homer, an organization to heighten awareness of the pressing environmental issues. In 2010, the couple was honored the Small Business Owners of the Year in Alaska, lauded as socially responsible "green pioneers".

Froth & Forage

Anchorage

What
Casual restaurant featuring locally sourced produce, meat & other goods

Who
Zachary Reid, chef/owner

When
Breakfast, lunch & dinner, daily

Address
27635 Seward Highway, Indian, Anchorage, AK 99540

+1 907 653 1009

frothandforage.com

Bookings
OpenTable.com

Price guide

What they say
"We rely heavily on locally grown produce that is available year-round: local hydroponic farms grow greens year-round to provide a fresh variety of greens; other seasonal farms store root vegetables in root cellars for year-round availability, and we use a variety of preserving methods for what we're not able to get through the winter months - pickling, curing, smoking, blanching and freezing."

What others say
"Inventive comfort food that often pops with color and flavor."

The New York Times

What we say
Chef Zachary Reid and, his wife and business partner Michelle McIntyre met in high school and have been working in the restaurant industry ever since. With a menu that features interesting local ingredients such as reindeer caribou and foraged blue oyster mushrooms, and fresh, Alaskan seafood from sustainable local fisheries, their focus is on unprocessed, locally sourced fresh food, with real ingredients that speak for themselves. Their dedication to support local food even has them currently working on building a community food hub where locals can bring and exchange backyard produce and other homemade products with one another.

Ludvig's Bistro

Sitka

What
Rustic Mediterranean fare fresh from the Alaskan oceans

Who
Colette Nelson, chef/owner

When
Lunch & dinner, Monday to Saturday

Address
256 Katlian Street, Sitka, AK 99835

+1 907 966 3663

ludvigsbistro.com

Bookings
Phone, walk-ins

Price guide

What they say
"Ludvig's Bistro is a seasonal spot in Sitka, situated on the gulf of Baranof Island, a skip away from Juneau. We serve sustainable wild seafood directly from the, clean Alaskan waters, purchased 200 yards from the bistro. There is something so special about walking the docks in the sea air, and picking out a fresh king salmon or live king crab, and thanking the fisherman face-to-face."

Signature dishes
Tuscan scallops: Weathervane Alaskan scallops with prosciutto, Marsala, truffles, and caper berries; Katlian special: fresh local sable fish, king salmon or halibut served with asparagus tip risotto and local lemon sorrel sauce (honors Chief Katlian of the Tlingit Alaska Native tribe); Alaskan paella *mixta*.

What we say
Ludvig's Bistro not only sources all their seafood responsibly from right outside their door, but they help the local fishing community in other ways, too. The chef works with the Sitka Conservation Society teaching a program called Fish to Schools. She teaches school-aged children the importance of sustainable fishing and the health benefits of eating fish. Then, they get to cook recipes together that become part of their school lunch program. Many of their dishes use hyper-local ingredients inspired by people and places from their world travels.

27

California

Botanica Restaurant & Market

Los Angeles

What
A restaurant & market devoted to vibrant, creative, vegetable-centric cooking

Who
Heather Sperling & Emily Fiffer, owners

When
Breakfast, lunch & dinner, daily

Address
1620 Silver Lake Boulevard, Los Angeles, CA 90026

+1 323 522 6106

botanicarestaurant.com

Bookings
Resy.com

Price guide

What they say
"We are passionate about what we refer to as nourishing hospitality. We believe that healthful eating and cooking can be vibrant, abundant and satisfying, and this philosophy extends to everything we do at Botanica: our warm and welcoming service, our natural wine list, our herb/fruit/vegetable-based cocktails and, of course, everything on the plate. We see the future of food as delicious, balanced and fulfilling, emphasizing vegetables, fruit and grains. We use the best possible products to create food that is colorful, creative, exciting and nourishing - food that makes you feel good!"

Signature dishes
Grilled lamb kabobs, kofte-style with spices galore, herb salad, and dill-sumac yoghurt; crudités and dips: beet-walnut muhammara, whipped tahini and dukkah with market vegetables, and Bub & Grandma's cornmeal focaccia; morning mezze with almond-red pepper romesco, smashed potatoes, caramelized leeks; heirloom tomatoes and cucumbers, six-minute egg and salsa verde, marinated olives, and Bub & Grandma's bread.

What we say
Botanica's food celebrates the bounty of Southern California, with fresh, healthy dishes that are packed full of flavor. The menu is dictated by what is available at the local farmers' markets, and all fruits, vegetables, olive oil, tea, and coffee and are sourced from within California. "Our biggest goal is to provide nourishment and abundance on the plate using California's most beautiful vegetables (and smaller doses of sustainably caught and raised seafood and meat)", say owners Heather Sperling and Emily Fiffer. Vegetables are the stars of the show at this Los Angeles restaurant.

Botanica Restaurant & Market (p. 28)

Baroo

Los Angeles

What
Named after a bowl that Buddhist monks use for their meals

Who
Matthew Kim & Kwang Uh, co-owners/chefs

When
Lunch & dinner, Tuesday to Saturday

Address
5706 Santa Monica Boulevard, Los Angeles, CA 90038

+1 323 929 9288

Bookings
Walk-ins

Price guide

What they say
"We use the name Baroo - 'Buddhist's bowl'- as a metaphor for embracing and respecting Mother Nature. Eighty percent of our menu is plant-based, and we source from farmers' markets and vendors that prioritize fair-trade and environmentally friendly ethics. We grow nasturtium, lemon verbena, and some of the other aromatics and herbs used on our menu. We also reduce food waste by using food scraps (e.g., for stocks and seasonings) or experimenting with fermentation (e.g., homemade kombucha, pickles, kimchi)."

Signature dishes
Noorook, made primarily with Job's tears, roasted koji beet crème, fermented kamut and farro, flavored with finger lime and rose onion pickles; kimchi fried rice made with pineapple, microgreens, a sous-vide egg, and roasted seaweed; *bibim* salad, made with asparagus, heirloom carrots, fennel, celery, and baby radish and flavored with *gochujang*.

What others say
"If it's true that the Inuit have 53 words for snow, anyone eating at Baroo should get to invent at least a few new synonyms for umami. There simply is no better way to describe what makes each dish here so compelling."

-Julia Kramer, *bon appétit*

What we say
Baroo is a thimble-sized, lab-like restaurant located within an unmarked storefront of a forlorn Hollywood strip mall. It serves boundary-defying "Korean-American" grain bowls and salads, as well as handmade pasta that would make any Italian nonna proud. Kim and Uh's profound respect for nature is seen in their meticulous attention to detail and in the flavors they coax from it.

Broken Spanish

Los Angeles

What
A fresh take on modern Mexican cuisine

Who
Ray Garcia, chef/owner

When
Dinner, daily

Address
1050 South Flower Street, Los Angeles, CA 90015

+1 213 749 1460

brokenspanish.com

Bookings
Website, phone

Price guide

What they say
"Broken Spanish draws on the city's rich cultural diversity, the wealth of Southern Californian produce, and Chef Ray Garcia's classical training combined with the powerful influence of his Latin upbringing. We locally source all of our produce direct from farmers or through foraging, and we use sustainably sourced fish and seafood as well as responsibly raised pork, beef, chicken, and lamb. Corn is central to our menu and our masa (for hand-pressed tortillas) is ethically sourced, providing a fair living wage for farming families in rural Mexico. We also actively source wine from Baja California, one of the closest growing regions to us."

What others say
"Ray Garcia is here to elevate the Mexican-food situation ... I taste a tostada that rips my head off my neck. It's a plate of 'shrooms tossed in a black-garlic sauce with *chile de árbol* and set over a grilled masa cake, familiar yet brand-new."

-Dave Holmes, *Esquire*

What we say
Broken Spanish combines the traditions of Mexican farming and heirloom maize culture with the modern influences of Los Angeles. Be sure to stop in for delicious hand-pressed tortillas, spinach tamales or flavorsome chicharróns.

Dialogue

Los Angeles

What
An intimate restaurant featuring an extensive tasting menu

Who
Dave Beran, chef

When
Dinner Tuesday to Saturday

Address
1315 3rd Street Promenade, Suite K, Santa Monica, CA 90401

dialoguerestaurant.com

Bookings
Resy.com

Price guide

What they say
"Dialogue is about telling a story through food. We craft a menu in a manner that is intended to build upon a single idea. Each dish is not necessarily a complete thought as much as a stepping stone to bring the diner to the next. Our passion lies in finding and offering a unique perspective on food, one that the diners can (we hope) relate to and find a bit of themselves in. Food can be so much more than just something to satiate cravings. It is emotional and has the opportunity to connect so many levels. Dining is an experience and we are pushing to add another layer to that, one that people can relate to on a more intimate and personal level."

Signature dishes
Parsnip with crab, coconut, finger lime, chili, sesame and shallot; lamb with nasturtium, fermented strawberry, and wild herbs from Topanga canyon; thirty-day dry-aged ribeye with charred watermelon and smoke.

What others say
"A Dialogue meal tends to be closer to a conversation between chef and patron than to a culinary tour de force."

-Jonathon Gold, *Los Angeles Times*

What we say
Dialogue offers a highly conceptual and multi-sensory modernist experience with a laser-focus on Southern California seasonality. Taking the concept of slow food seriously, this Santa Monica restaurant pays special attention to seasonality. If you can handle ten-course or eighteen-course menus, this is a must-visit.

Kali

Los Angeles

What
Fine dining restaurant with a focus on California cuisine

Who
Kevin Meehan, chef/owner

When
Dinner, daily, lunch Monday to Friday

Address
5722 Melrose Ave, Los Angeles, CA 90038

+1 310 503 8393

kalirestaurant.com

Bookings
Phone, website, OpenTable.com

Price guide

What they say
"Our restaurant is a California-inspired fine dining and contemporary experience rooted in the best local ingredients, with a zero-waste philosophy. Our tasting menu changes with the seasons."

Signature dishes
Black garlic and barley risotto; charred avocado salad with kale meringue; gelato with sugar-cure yolks.

What others say
"If you were to judge it from your Instagram feed alone, Meehan's cooking would seem much more avant-garde than it actually is - much of the food here aims for comfort rather than shock. Take a half avocado charred on the grill and served with a raw salad of shaved vegetables. Rather than offset the avocado's natural creaminess with hits of acid, Meehan doubles down on unsaturated fats, topping the lush green fruit with pistachios and a heavy drizzle of olive oil."

-Garrett Snyder, *LA Weekly*

What we say
Kali represents the cutting edge of modernist California locavore cuisine in a fine dining setting. Each dish is created to showcase the best of what this region has to offer, including the extreme localism of sourcing from a nearby garden in their Larchmont neighborhood in Hollywood.

Gwen

Los Angeles

What
A restaurant with a butchery servicing both the kitchen & customers

Who
Curtis Stone, chef/owner & Luke Stone, managing owner

When
Brunch & dinner, Monday to Saturday

Address
6600 Sunset Boulevard, Los Angeles, CA 90028

+1 323 946 7513

gwenla.com

Bookings
Walk-ins, phone, OpenTable.com

Price guide

What they say
"Our European-style butcher shop is the heartbeat of Gwen. We use primitive fire-cooking methods over the in-house fire pit and *asador* to prepare pasture-raised, hormone and antibiotic-free meats (many of which are local). We also create charcuterie, seasonal vegetable, and pasta dishes. We reduce food waste through our whole animal butchering, using every part, and we purchase 'dual-use animals' from ranchers (e.g., ewes that have already provided dairy and wool). We hire through Chrysalis, a nonprofit that gives jobs to low-income and homeless men and women, and we have worked with the National Young Farmers Coalition and AdoptTogether."

What others say
"The charcuterie might include a rich 'nduja, the spicy spreadable salami that's all the rage with meatheads these days, as well as light feathery fiocco, pork leg cured with pink peppercorns and rosewater that gives it a hint of floral funk at its edge. The multiple vegetable dishes that come as salads and sides are deceptively simple but always reveal a trick of technique or creativity that makes them shine."

-Besha Rodell, *Eater LA*

What we say
Gwen, a world-class butcher shop and fine dining restaurant by Chef Curtis Stone and his brother Luke Stone, aims to deliver the best-in-class for quality, taste, and service. Curtis brings a careful sensibility to his fine temple of meat, from the sourcing to the plating. Not to be missed.

Holbox

Los Angeles

What
Casual Mexican *mariscos* restaurant, using local & sustainable seafood

Who
Gilberto Cetina, chef/owner

When
Lunch & dinner, daily

Address
3655 South Grand Avenue #C9, Los Angeles, CA 90007

+1 213 986 9972

holboxla.com

Bookings
Walk-ins

Price guide

What they say
"We are inspired by the Yucatán but we build our menu daily based on fresh, local seafood purchased from local fisherman co-ops using artisanal methods like short-line, and limited to Baja California, Southern California and Central Coast catch, preferably 'best choice' or 'good alternative' according to Seafood Watch. We also focus on eco-friendly proteins like bivalve aquaculture and zero-waste initiatives like using the entire fish, including head, carcass, and scraps. Chef Cetina also regularly leads cooking demonstrations, including how to butcher and use a whole fish."

Signature dishes
Pulpo en su tinta (braised and fried octopus, calamari ink *sofrito*, handmade corn tortilla); *almeja preparada* (fresh-shucked giant surf clam with homemade ketchup, *chili costeño, chili guajillo*, fresh orange juice, and lime juice); *ceviche de kanpachi* (sustainable Omega Blue Baja kanpachi, tomato, red onions, cilantro, arbol-guajillo sauce, avocado).

What others say
"One of the best shrimp cocktails in the city - plump, crisp bits in a purée-filled sundae glass crowned with a single steamed prawn. The blood clams surpass what you've had at the famous Baja street stands. Is transcendence too much to ask from a seafood tostada? That I'll leave up to you."

-Jonathan Gold, *Los Angeles Times*

What we say
Cetina's Holbox is a love letter to the Yucatán and to the treasures of the sea. Don't miss it.

Holbox (p. 38)

Lasa

Los Angeles

What
Modern Filipino-American restaurant in LA

Who
Chase Valencia, general manager/co-owner & Chad Valencia, chef/co-owner

When
Lunch Tuesday to Sunday, dinner Wednesday to Sunday

Address
727 North Broadway #120, Los Angeles, CA 90012

+1 213 400 8610

lasa-la.com

Bookings
Resy.com

Price guide

What they say
"We are a Filipino-American restaurant, and our entire team has direct immigrant roots. One of our goals is to grow a sense of community, creativity, and artistry. Our menu is based on the seasons and we only purchase from reputable purveyors to provide the best quality food and good practices. Most of our staff meals are made from leftover cuts and vegetables to reduce food waste. We work in partnership with Britt Browne of Finca Tierra to compost any remaining produce."

Signature dishes
Crispy duck *arroz caldo* (confit duck leg with brown rice porridge made with a ginger and leek broth, pea tendrils tossed in calamansi juice, and crispy garlic); beef *kilawin* (raw meat marinated in fish sauce, vinegar, and spices, dusted with scallion powder and served with taro chips); *kinilaw* (rockfish cured in sugar, palm, coconut, native vinegars, and spices, with coconut cream vinaigrette, fermented chili paste, kohlrabi slices, scallions, and crispy shallots).

What others say
"The [Valencia] brothers, L.A.-bred Filipino-Americans, are simultaneously showcasing their heritage and embracing the bountiful produce of California."

-Andy Wang, *Food & Wine* magazine

What we say
Lasa began as an experimental pop-up, and that sense of ever-evolving creativity fuels this inventive take on Filipino cuisine through a Californian lens. Unique ingredients awaken the senses and make eating at Lasa a true delight.

n/naka

Los Angeles

What
Modern kaiseki restaurant

Who
Niki Nakayama, chef/owner

When
Dinner Wednesday to Saturday

Address
3455 Overland Avenue, Los Angeles, CA 90034

+1 310 836 6252

n-naka.com

Bookings
Resy.com

Price guide

What they say
"We believe kaiseki's philosophy of gratitude for ingredients and the environment naturally extends to our guests, so we take great care to ensure the dishes we serve represent that philosophy. We grow our own produce in Chef Nakayama's organic garden and source our seafood locally and sustainably with fish caught within a few hours of the restaurant's location in West LA as often as possible. In addition, we have eliminated bluefin tuna from the menu and we heavily focus on California wines. Our dinners are thirteen courses, with red meat in only one or two of these, and we also offer a thirteen-course vegetarian menu. Since we know exactly what we are going to serve, our food (and associated product) waste is relatively low. We don't use single-use plastics or a delivery service."

What others say
"Niki Nakayama's individualistic kaiseki meals stir up a wondrous, wordless sort of emotional resonance. Dishes marry Japanese and Californian cuisines, a direct reflection of Nakayama's heritage and her Los Angeles upbringing. The progression of dishes segues through a breadth of cooking techniques and presentations."

-Bill Addison, *Eater*

What we say
Chef Nakayama's commitment to seasonal and local ingredients highlights Southern California within the context of a traditional and extraordinary Japanese kaiseki experience.

Native

Los Angeles

What
A restaurant aiming to connect people at the dinner table

Who
Nyesha J Arrington, executive chef

When
Dinner Tuesday to Sunday

Address
620 Santa Monica Boulevard, Santa Monica, Los Angeles, CA 90404

+1 310 429 2664

eatnative.la

Bookings
Resy.com

Price guide

What they say
"We combine techniques and flavors from around the world and present them through the lens of Los Angeles. Every Wednesday and Saturday we head to the local farmers' market for inspiration.We are simply stewards of the land celebrating the growers, ranchers, and artisans that make our menu truly special. We never waste and are always challenging ourselves to create new dishes out of bi-product. We are also very passionate about mentorship; we do cooking demonstrations at local schools and help with local gardens."

Signature dishes
Braised rabbit with turmeric spatzle and collard greens; Kombu scented potatoes with green arugula butter and toasted nori; mushroom spaghetti with local *burrata* and fresh star snap peas.

What others say
"A place where flavors from a dozen culinary traditions collide on a plate, tied together with exquisitely seasonal produce from the nearby Santa Monica farmers' market, a list of funky natural wines and music that seems drawn from a KJLH playlist circa 1983 ... [Arrington] is a chef whose food tastes like L.A."

-Jonathon Gold, *Los Angeles Times*

What we say
Nyesha Arrington's "native" Angeleno cuisine is culled from the diverse culinary cultures of the her own background and the city at large prepared with ingredients from the Santa Monica farmers' market. Kimchi, pastrami, artisan grain porridge, and French lentils all appear on the menu in a harmonious and inviting mix.

Providence

Los Angeles

What
A fine dining menu focused on sustainable seafood from the Pacific

Who
Michael Cimarusti, chef/owner & Donato Poto & Cristina Echiverri, co-owners

When
Dinner daily, lunch Friday

Address
5955 Melrose Ave,
Los Angeles, CA, 90038

+1 323 460 4170

providencela.com

Bookings
Phone, OpenTable.com

Price guide

What they say
"Dock to Dish Los Angeles, our wholesale fish business (housed and operated via our sustainable seafood shop, Cape Seafood), sources the finest, most responsibly harvested, local, and traceable seafood. We know our fishermen, pay them fairly, and distribute their catch immediately. We source produce at local farmers' markets, and we grow herbs and flowers on our rooftop, using water from the kitchen. Vegetable scraps are used for our cocktail program, otherwise we compost and offer scraps to local farmers for feed. Gender equality and cultural diversity are important to us and that is reflected in our staff."

Signature dishes
Live Santa Barbara spot prawns roasted in sea salt and carved table side; Santa Barbara rockfish with turnips from the garden and giant clam; Santa Barbara box crab with soy milk and black truffle.

What others say
"[Cimarusti's] commitment to local flavors - not just yellowtail, rockfish and sea urchin but also Asian notes that find their way into his dishes as naturally as the expected European ones - and the flow of his menus (geoduck and oyster with Vietnamese basil, local squid with the Japanese pepper paste *yuzu kosho*, abalone with sunchoke, rockfish with cranberry beans) reflect Los Angeles not just as a great port city but also as part of a specific ecosystem, a unique intersection of land and sea."

-Jonathan Gold, *Los Angeles Times*

What we say
Providence is top rated while offering a revolutionary approach to sourcing seafood in a fine dining setting.

Providence (p. 42)

Rustic Canyon

Los Angeles

What
Acclaimed neighborhood restaurant, focusing on hyper-seasonality

Who
Josh Loeb, Zoe Nathan & Colby Goff, partners & Jeremy Fox, chef/partner

When
Dinner, daily

Address
1119 Wilshire Boulevard, Santa Monica, Los Angeles, CA 90401

+1 310 393 7050

rusticcanyonrestaurant.com

Bookings
Website, Resy.com, walk-ins

Price guide

What they say
"Our focus is on ingredients and simplicity - we want to represent and maintain the integrity of the product and have each dish tell a story. In addition to using local and seasonal produce, and sustainable meat and seafood, we use honey from a farm in Malibu and beans from Rancho Gordo in Napa. We also partner with Upward Bound House to help local homeless families, and we work with Alex's Lemonade to raise money for childhood cancer research."

Signature dishes
Roasted chicken with carrot purée, vinaigrette, roasted chicken drippings, fried carrot tops, pecans, and chili; *Pozole verde* (mussels with mussel broth and purée of green chilies, coriander, and garlic); Thao's white yams with garlic butter, aïoli, celery, pickled onion, and benne seed za'atar.

What others say
"Chef Jeremy Fox made his name with super-seasonal vegetables at Ubuntu in Napa, but at this Santa Monica wine bar, he's making an even bigger name for himself by joining them with the lesser-loved parts of animals."

-Emily Hart, *bon appétit*

What we say
Rustic Canyon represents the epitome of Southern Californian dining. At once refined and inviting, this is comfort food at its finest. Simple ingredients - such as carrots and potatoes - are used in unique, interesting ways to elevate dishes to a new level. Conscious of the need for the culinary world to reduce its carbon footprint, Rustic Canyon uses every product in its entirety so as to avoid waste. This means drying, preserving, and fermenting.

Sqirl

Los Angeles

What
A preserves brand that blossomed into a breakfast & lunch café in tune with the market

Who
Jessica Koslow, chef/owner

When
Breakfast & lunch, daily

Address
720 North Virgil Ave, no. 4, Los Angeles, CA 90029

+1 323 284 8147

sqirlla.com

Bookings
Walk-ins

Price guide

What they say
"Sqirl is passionate about making unique food for everyday eating using farmers' market ingredients and techniques gleaned from refined dining. We work directly with farmers and ranchers to source our ingredients. For example, we'll get fifty flats of Ollalieberries per week delivered from Murray Family Farms just for jam. We source sustainable protein such as tuna from American tuna and sturgeon from Passamore Ranch. We use local grain milled by Grist and Toll. We are very keen on rotational legumes like chickpeas and lentils that place nitrogen back in the soil. We also work with the Tehachapi Grain Project, Edible School Yard, SEED, René Redzepi's MAD board, Brigaid for school lunches, Direct Relief and other organizations."

Signature dishes
Sorrel rice bowl with organic Californian brown rice, house-preserved Meyer lemons, lacto-fermented hot sauce, sorrel pesto, French feta, dill, and an organic free-range egg; brioche toast with house-made ricotta and seasonal jam; free-range Marin Sun organic chicken with rotational bok choy, dehydrated citrus and root vegetables, grated carrots, and black garlic vinaigrette.

What others say
"For breakfast food, it's downright revolutionary."

-Mark Bittman, *The New York Times Magazine*

What we say
What started with seasonal jam is now so much more. The utterly original and carefully composed all-day fare served at Sqirl has made the casual and hip shop a must-visit destination.

Cala

San Francisco

What
Mexican seafood restaurant in the heart of San Francisco

Who
Gabriela Cámara, chef

When
Dinner, daily

Address
149 Fell Street,
San Francisco, CA 94102

+1 415 660 7701

calarestaurant.com

Bookings
OpenTable.com

Price guide

What they say
"At Cala, we are passionate about well-being as it applies to our employees, the animals and ingredients we serve, our local Bay Area community, and the guests that we have the pleasure to serve. We also offer an inclusive, caring work environment for employees with conviction histories, many of whom do not have prior restaurant work experience."

Signature dishes
Trout tostadas with chipotle, avocado, and fried leeks; sweet potato with bone marrow *salsa negra*; rockfish *a la talla*.

What others say
"It's clear Cámara examined every element, particularly the food. And it shows. The menu at Cala blazes a new path for Mexican food - not only in the Bay Area, but in the United States."

The San Francisco Chronicle

What we say
A renowned chef-restaurateur in her native Mexico City, Gabriela Cámara made her stateside debut with Cala, an airy, casually sophisticated restaurant that has transformed how the city sees Mexican food. Housed in a former garage, Cala is a haven for seafood-centric dining fans: one of its popular dishes is rockfish a la talla, a showstopper featuring a butterflied fish covered with red and green salsas. The food's stripped-down elegance may be best personified by the blackened whole sweet potato with bone marrow salsa negra, an unassuming but ruthlessly addictive pairing. Service is warm and attentive, adding to the general feeling of good fortune and celebration that pervades the restaurant.

Little Gem

San Francisco

What
A modern California restaurant for the way we live & eat today

Who
Eric Lilavois & Dave Cruz, founders

When
Lunch & dinner, daily, weekend brunch

Address
400 Grove Street, San Francisco, CA 94102

+1 415 914 0501

littlegem.restaurant

Bookings
Website

Price guide

What they say
"We care deeply about the source of our food. How it's grown. Who grows it. And what's in season. All of our produce is naturally raised and free of additives, preservatives, harmful chemicals, and modification. All of our cooking is also free of gluten, dairy, and refined sugar. We wanted a restaurant where everyone could enjoy a delicious, wholesome meal, regardless of their dietary restrictions. Collectively, our criteria has led us to be recognized as a modern restaurant that is redefining what it means to eat well."

Signature dishes
King of Hayes (Ōra King salmon, sweet corn succotash, fava beans and leaves, piquillo peppers, red onions, and parsley vinaigrette); bibimbap with seasonal vegetables; macro bowl with California brown rice, vegetables, avocado, and a boiled egg.

What others say
"All of Little Gem's dishes are crafted with an artful touch ... For a quick, laid-back, and healthy bite to eat, Little Gem doesn't disappoint."

-Jenna Scatena, *Condé Nast Traveler*

What we say
Natural, seasonal food free of gluten, dairy, and refined sugar is at the heart of Little Gem, a bright and airy restaurant in San Francisco's Hayes Valley neighborhood. There's no fake meat or ersatz dairy here; instead, there are vibrant flavors and artfully-plated dishes. Little Gem knows its salads, but it also excels with heartier fare like a beef short rib and kale bowl and a rich, delightfully clever cauliflower cassoulet.

DOSA

San Francisco

What
A modern Indian restaurant specializing in South Indian flavors using local ingredients

Who
Anjan Mitra, owner & Arun Gupta, executive chef

When
Dinner, daily, weekend brunch

Address
1700 Fillmore Street, San Francisco, CA 94115, plus other locations - see website

+1 415 441 3672

dosasf.com

Bookings
Yelpreservations.com

Price guide

What they say
"We are passionate about cooking regional Indian cuisine and staying true to the flavors and spices, while using all the great produce that Northern California has to offer. We source halal meats and highly rated chicken, and do our best to only use sustainable and recommended fish. All of our lamb and goat comes from local California purveyors. South Indian cuisine is by definition very vegetable and grain-heavy, so we are using a lot of grains. We do not sell beef in either of our two restaurants. Much of our menu is vegetarian and even vegan-friendly."

Signature dishes
Smoked Arctic char with peach moilee; Philipkutty chicken curry; Brokaw avocado *chaat*.

What we say
With two San Francisco locations and one in Oakland, Dosa has put its stamp on regional Southern Indian cooking in the Bay Area. While Dosa's crispy namesake crêpes are well represented on its menu (you can order them stuffed with fillings like spiced potato masala and habanero chutney), the restaurant also excels at street food fare like *vada pav* (a sort of mashed-potato slider) and avocado chaat, a savory snack with grapefruit, coconut, and habanero chili. There are also richly spiced curries and an impressive spice-driven cocktail list. Many of Dosa's ingredients are organic and come from local farmers' markets, and its stylish, high-ceilinged Fillmore Street location features solar panels on its roof.

Foreign Cinema

San Francisco

What
A restaurant celebrating the bounty of Northern California under a courtyard movie screen

Who
Gayle Pirie & John Clark, co-owners

When
Dinner, daily, weekend brunch

Address
2534 Mission Street, San Francisco, CA 94110

+1 415 648 7600

foreigncinema.com

Bookings
Phone, OpenTable.com

Price guide

What they say
"At Foreign Cinema, our passion lies in creating a heartfelt and captivating experience for our guests, taking them away from the stresses of everyday life. We are deeply committed to our community and believe in demonstrating a spirit of generosity to all who enter our environment. As a team, we strive to make diners feel special, to be nurtured and nourished, by good food, carefully sourced and conceived, with good wine and goodwill to all who join us. We support a system of trust and sustainability."

Signature dishes
Full selection of oysters on the half shell with imperial and royal seasonal fruits de mer; plancha of Monterey calamari with Oaxacan mole; beef carpaccio.

What we say
Since 1999, Foreign Cinema has elevated the concept of dinner and a movie to spectacular effect, becoming one of San Francisco's most popular restaurants, as well as one of its most original. At the Mission restaurant, you can either eat in the dining room near the fireplace or the amber lit courtyard, where films are projected onto a wall. The menu is daily changing, with Mediterranean accents. To begin, you might order brandade with house pickles and toast, or goat cheese baked in lavender. Foreign Cinema's brunch is also renowned; like dinner, be sure to book early - and often.

Nopalito

San Francisco

What
A Mexican restaurant in San Francisco

Who
Gonzalo Guzman, chef

When
Lunch & dinner, daily

Address
306 Broderick Street, San Francisco, CA 94117, plus other locations - see website

+1 415 437 0303

nopalitosf.com

Bookings
Walk-ins

Price guide

What they say
"Masa [maize] is the heart and soul of Nopalito: we make it from scratch everyday and it is in almost every dish we prepare, from our tortillas to our chips to some of our sauces. Without masa or tortillas there would be no Nopalito. I am most passionate about cooking and serving food that represents my people, and being able to create a dish that does justice to its history and heritage."

Signature dishes
House-made tortillas; mole; *ensalada de lechuga con* smoked jalapeño vinaigrette.

What we say
One of San Francisco's most beloved and authentic Mexican restaurants, Nopalito marries traditional cookery with local, organic ingredients, and sustainable practices. Homemade masa flour underpins much of chef Gonzalo Guzman's menu, from the tortilla chips to the luscious tacos. Sustainably sourced meats are braised, marinated, and seared to glorious effect in dishes like *birria de res* (grass-fed beef stewed in ancho chile) and marinated skirt steak with cactus and chorizo. Moles are also at the heart of Nopalito; to Guzman, the rich, complex sauces tell a story of history, community, and family.

Nopalito's behind-the-scenes practices, from composting to repurposing kitchen grease into biofuel, are as sustainable as its food. Its two locations are usually attended by lines, a testament to both the quality of its cooking and its place in its community.

Octavia

San Francisco

What
An elevated neighborhood restaurant offering local, seasonal cuisine

Who
Melissa Perello, executive chef/owner

When
Dinner, daily

Address
1701 Octavia Street, San Francisco, CA 94109

+1 415 408 7507

octavia-sf.com

Bookings
Phone, OpenTable.com

Price guide

What they say
"We are inspired by local, seasonal ingredients, and use them to create elevated yet approachable cuisine."

Signature dishes
Sweet onion soup with wild morels, English peas, crème fraîche, mint, and lemon *agrumato*; Monterey calamari with house *guanciale*, grilled Armenian cucumber, nectarine, and miso; "deviled egg", soft-boiled with Fresno chili relish, marash pepper, and spice.

What others say
"Octavia is not a place that emanates ego. Rather, it exudes intentionality."

Eater San Francisco

What we say
Chef Melissa Perello's follow-up to her beloved restaurant Frances, Octavia is a clean-scrubbed beacon of simple but elegant Californian cooking located in San Francisco's lower Pacific Heights neighborhood. Housed in an airy space suffused with natural light, the restaurant serves simple, understated food elevated through gorgeous execution and technique. This approach is encapsulated by Octavia's signature dish, the "deviled egg", a soft-boiled local farm egg garnished with fresno chili relish, marash pepper, and spice, a combination that layers heat, brine, and yolk richness. Duck liver mousse is paired with charred medjool dates and pickled cipollini onion; king salmon comes anointed with preserved lemon aïoli and is accompanied by favas, new potatoes, and roasted artichokes.

Pastry Chef Sarah Bonar's desserts are also not to be missed: her chocolate soufflé tart is a decadent delight, while toasted angel food cake pairs local strawberries with matcha ice cream and Meyer lemon curd. Right up to the last bite, Octavia is seasonal California magic personified.

Nightbird

San Francisco

What
An intimate tasting menu restaurant in the heart of Hayes Valley

Who
Kim Alter, chef/owner & Ron Boyd, manager/owner

When
Dinner Tuesday to Saturday

Address
330 Gough Street,
San Francisco, CA 94102

+1 415 829 7565

nightbirdrestaurant.com

Bookings
Phone, website, walk-ins, OpenTable.com

Price guide

What they say
"Cooking for the community that I have been part of for twenty years is where my passion lies: it's in talking with farmers every day and handpicking what my cooks and I will serve every night, and it's in talking with guests about what boat the fish came off of. It's very personal to me and I have dedicated my life to it."

Signature dishes
Soft-boiled quail egg with fried leeks and brown butter hollandaise; confit chicken leg with turnip purée, burnt kaffir lime, chicken jus and farro chip; aerated cheesecake with pistachio dacquoise, rhubarb purée and *brunoise*.

What others say
"[Kim Alter] cuts a shy profile, but Nightbird is in many ways the boldest of projects: a very worthy restaurant that doesn't try to call attention to itself."

–Josh Sens, *San Francisco Magazine*

What we say
Nightbird is the rarest of birds: a sophisticated, grown-up restaurant that doesn't take itself too seriously. It is very much a reflection of its chef-owner, Kim Alter: her quiet confidence and lack of pretension pervade her restaurant's elegant, understated atmosphere and cooking. Alter's five-course tasting menu changes every two weeks. You might find oysters paired with tomatoes and seaweed, or a pistachio dacquoise topped with aerated cheesecake. What doesn't change is Nightbird's warm, gracious service and effortless class. It is a restaurant that's as in tune with the seasons as it is the desires of its customers.

Nightbird (p. 52)

NOON All Day

San Francisco

What
Your neighborhood kitchen, serving tasty, nourishing food all day long

Who
Kerry Glancy, director & Sher Rogat & Margherita Sagan, owners

When
Breakfast & lunch, Monday to Friday, weekend brunch

Address
690 Indiana Street,
San Francisco, CA 94107

+1 415 619 3240

noonallday.com

Bookings
Walk-ins

Price guide
●●○○○

What they say
"We love hospitality and welcoming everyone in to our 'home'. We want NOON All Day to be a respite, a place where people can take a deep breath, let us take care of you, and recharge your batteries."

Signature dishes
"Holy Molé" danish with fontina, house-made molé, and an egg; Moroccan spiced socca chickpea pancakes; the "Big Salad" with feta, mixed seeds, chickpeas, market vegetables, and sweet and spicy greens.

What others say
"The people behind Dogpatch staple Piccino have done the neighborhood another solid with NOON All Day, a counter-service restaurant and café for Piccino favorites and exciting new pastries like kimchi-stuffed or taro-coconut dusted danishes."

Eater San Francisco

What we say
The second restaurant from the owners of Piccino, a redoubtable stalwart of San Francisco's Dogpatch neighborhood, NOON All Day is a counter service spot dedicated to the fine art of easygoing seasonal eating. The breakfast menu is headlined by a retinue of creative sweet and savory pastries like an apple scone spiked with Chinese five-spice powder. At lunch, you'll find inventive bowls and plates ranging from a kale and yuba noodle salad to savory chickpea pancakes with yogurt, roasted brassicas, and herb jam. The space itself is bright, clean, and modern, though its most arresting detail is the contents of its pastry display case.

Onsen

San Francisco

What
Offering a unique dining & bathing experience

Who
Sunny Simmons & Caroline Smith, owners

When
Dinner Wednesday to Sunday

Address
466 Eddy Street,
San Francisco, CA 94109

+1 415 441 4987

onsensf.com

Bookings
Phone, Resy.com

Price guide

What they say
"We strive to create an environment that feels like you have both come home and been whisked away to a secret oasis. We love to offer our guests the opportunity to receive a unique treatment in the bathhouse and then sit down for a meal that is intentional and enriching."

Signature dishes
Mushroom dumplings in *katsuoboshi* broth; house-made pickles; McFarland Springs trout poke with smoked soy, crispy rice, *shiso verde*, and pickled kohlrabi.

What others say
"From start to finish, every dish is fully realized. My initial desire to go there may have been motivated by curiosity, but by the third visit I was there because of the integrity and passion displayed in the food. It was the best kind of a happy ending."

-Michael Bauer, *San Francisco Chronicle*

What we say
A restaurant, tea house, and Japanese-style bathhouse, Onsen is one of the most unique dining experiences in San Francisco. You have the option to soak and steam before or after a meal, but you can also go simply to enjoy Onsen's intimate dining room.

Chef George Meza Onsen's menu is on the lighter side; there's no fried food, but there is plenty of sustainable seafood and seasonal produce. An array of small bites are a good way to begin a meal, while larger plates like mushroom dumplings in a *katsuoboshi* broth are simultaneously hearty and delicate. Carefully sourced beverages accompany the food, as does an air of complete and utter relaxation.

The Perennial

San Francisco

What
A restaurant dedicated to reversing climate change through food & drink

Who
Anthony Myint & Karen Leibowitz, restaurateurs

When
Dinner Tuesday to Saturday

Address
59 Ninth St, San Francisco, CA 94103

+1 415 500 7788

theperennialsf.com

Bookings
Phone, website, OpenTable.com

Price guide

What they say
"The Perennial celebrates regenerative agriculture - that is, food raised with the climate in mind. We source our ingredients from farmers and ranchers who are working to draw down carbon dioxide, build healthy soil, and create a deliciously sustainable future."

Signature dishes
Heirloom carrots with black rice, pea greens, and toasted chili oil; beef tartare and grasses; bread baked with kernza.

What others say
"The Apocalypse Burger is one of Mr. Myint's many memorable, darkly funny creations, and a look at how a chef's politics might shape the food on his plate in unexpected ways."

The New York Times

What we say
When husband-and-wife restaurateurs Karen Leibowitz and Anthony Myint opened The Perennial in 2016, they set out to run an environmentally friendly restaurant with a minimal carbon footprint. They've since proven it can be done, with delicious results. The San Francisco restaurant's seasonal menu embodies Myint and Leibowitz's goal of shifting the plate's focus away from animal proteins and towards vegetables and other fresh produce. What beef the restaurant does serve is sourced from Stemple Creek Ranch, whose cattle management practices promote carbon sequestration. Seafood comes from similarly sustainable sources, while some vegetables are grown in the restaurant's own aquaponic greenhouse. The beautifully plated food is paired with wine and batch cocktails, and served in an exquisitely simple dining room accented with reclaimed lumber. Not only does sustainable eating taste good, it looks good, too.

Robin

San Francisco

What
San Francisco-style omakase sushi

Who
Adam Tortosa, chef/owner

When
Dinner, daily

Address
620 Gough Street, San Francisco, CA 94102

+1 415 548 2429

robinsanfrancisco.com

Bookings
Website, Resy.com

Price guide

What they say
"We're passionate about making our guests happy by serving sushi with a Californian ethos in a fun, high-energy space. While many high-end sushi restaurants take pride in sourcing from Japan, we look to our local oceans and farms as much as possible."

Signature dishes
Mount Lassen steelhead trout with candied kumquat; Pacific albacore with walnut miso and wasabi *furikake;* Santa Barbara *uni* with *shiro dashi* emulsified yolk.

What we say
San Francisco has plenty of sushi bars, but none of them are quite like Robin, a sexy, lively omakase-only spot where chef and owner Adam Tortosa makes sushi that swims easily between Northern California and Japan. Tortosa's concept - sushi with a Californian ethos - is manifested in both the provenance of his ingredients and the way he uses them: you might find tomato confit on top of New Zealand salmon, or candied kumquat paired with Mount Lassen steelhead trout. Tortosa's flavor and textural combinations are as improbable as they are thrilling - Robin is probably the only sushi restaurant that uses house-made potato chips in its repertoire - and make each course an invigorating surprise. A well-curated list of beer and sake rounds out Robin's menu, while plush caramel-colored leather chairs make it that much easier to linger over the restaurant's sophisticated yet unpretentious pleasures.

Sorrel

San Francisco

What
A restaurant offering California-inspired cuisine with authentic & vibrant Italian influences

Who
Alex Hong, executive chef

When
Dinner Tuesday to Friday

Address
3228 Sacramento Street, San Francisco, CA 94117

+1 303 931 2870

sorrelrestaurant.com

Bookings
Website, Resy.com

Price guide

What they say
"Our menu highlights what we can buy and forage from our local farmers' markets and our rooftop gardens. We hope your experience is refreshingly unique and beautifully delivered, lending itself to an unforgettable meal with loved ones, friends, or acquaintances. We believe in only working with superior, fresh, organic, and local ingredients that Bay Area farmers' markets have to offer. We work with the seasonal harvest in an effort to showcase each perfectly in-season ingredient."

Signature dishes
Sourdough focaccia with cultured butter, sorrel, green garlic, and bagna *càuda*; *cappellacci* with English pea, ricotta, and mint; dry-aged duck for two with Hakurei turnip, spring onion, and Balaton cherry.

What we say
Perched in San Francisco's Presidio Heights neighborhood, Sorrel, as its name implies, takes inspiration from the natural bounty of Northern California. Chef Alex Hong cooks food that wears both its seasonal and Italian influences proudly: in the late spring, you'll find wild ramps accompanying pastas like *bigoli alla carbonara* and *scorza di fagioli*, while English peas accompany *cappellacci* with ricotta and mint. There's a short list of meat and fish, including a bright kampachi crudo and a Wagyu *zabuton* with parsnips and *maitake* mushrooms. The restaurant, which started its life as a successful pop-up, is whitewashed and airy, both intimate enough for a date and relaxed enough for groups of friends out to enjoy the San Francisco good life.

Waterbar

San Francisco

What
Widely regarded as San Francisco's foremost seafood restaurant

Who
Pat Kuleto & Mark Franz, co-owners

When
Lunch & dinner, daily, weekend brunch

Address
399 Embarcadero, San Francisco, CA 94105

+1 415 284 9922

waterbarsf.com

Bookings
OpenTable.com

Price guide

What they say
"We are passionate about providing sustainable seafood offerings for our guests, using local and organic sourcing wherever possible, and staying market-fresh throughout each season. We receive a lot of fish from Half Moon Bay and oysters from Tomales Bay. We procure proteins from the Bay Area, and use as much local farm produce as we can from Nicasio, Half Moon Bay, and Sonoma, along with dairy and cheese. We also have our own rooftop honey."

Signature dishes
Gulf of Mexico whole red snapper with Hong Kong XO sauce, miso baby turnips, and snap peas; roasted shellfish platter with poblano chile cream; pink grouper with fried green tomato, sweet potato hash, and avocado gazpacho.

What we say
Perched on the Embarcadero, overlooking the Bay Bridge, Waterbar boasts some of the best panoramic views in San Francisco, along with some of the best sustainable seafood. In the restaurant's main dining room you'll find dramatic floor-to-ceiling aquariums and a menu that kicks off with an impressive selection of raw oysters and platters of iced shellfish and caviar. Shared bites include creamy *uni* on toast with fava pesto, prosciutto, and pickled chili, while entrées like pan-roasted pink grouper with sweet potato hash, fried green tomato, avocado gazpacho, and bacon are both hearty and refined. You can also dine at the restaurant's oyster bar or on its terraces, where the bay breeze provides a perfect accompaniment to a meal.

Gather

Alameda

What
A showcase for organic farm fare, craft cocktails & local wines

Who
Eric Fenster, owner & Anthony Lee, executive chef

When
Dinner, daily, lunch Monday to Friday, weekend brunch

Address
2200 Oxford Street, Berkeley, Alameda, CA 94704

+1 510 809 0400

gatherrestaurant.com

Bookings
Website, Reserve.com, phone

Price guide

What they say
"Gather is a values-based concept that exists to serve and give back to the community, honor and support local, sustainable producers, serve thoughtful, clean dishes and drinks, and build a familial team environment. We work with tremendously talented farmers, ranchers, and artisan food producers who utilize cutting-edge sustainable production methods. In addition, all our spices, flours, oils, vinegars, and legumes are organic."

Signature dishes
English pea dumplings with snap peas, young carrots, house farmer's cheese, chocolate, and mint; spicy tomato pizza with olives, capers, cashew purée, and chili oil; Marin Sun Farms thirty-six-ounce grass-fed bone-in ribeye for two with béarnaise, duck fat fingerlings, grilled gem hearts, slow-cooked alliums, and *boquerones* dressing.

What others say
"Gather has established itself as the go-to place for righteous vegetarians and unrepentant carnivores who can forgive one another their culinary dogmas and trespasses."

-Derk Richardson, *Oakland Magazine*

What we say
Tucked into a downtown Berkeley building that's reputed to be the most environmentally friendly in the East Bay, Gather has been synonymous with organic dining since it opened in 2009. The restaurant's seasonal creative Californian cooking is equally accommodating of meat-eaters and herbivores, with delicious options for both. The spacious, glass-enclosed restaurant is also known for its dynamic cocktail program, some of the proceeds of which are donated to various charitable organizations.

Cultura

Monterey

What
Cultura is a modern Oaxacan restaurant inspired by our travels

Who
John Cox & Michelle Estigoy, chefs & Sarah Kabat, owner

When
Dinner, daily, weekend brunch

Address
Dolores Street, between 5th and 6th, Carmel-by-the-Sea, Monterey, CA 93923

+1 831 250 7005

culturacarmel.com

Bookings
Yelpreservations.com

Price guide

What they say
"We are passionate about the foods and culture of Oaxaca, Mexico, created with locally sourced ingredients. It's an incredible honor to share the flavors of our travels with guests each night and, in turn, do our own small part in giving back to the Oaxacan community. We source our seafood and produce from Monterey farms and forage herbs and blossoms from the trails surrounding Carmel. Our Mezcal is sourced exclusively from small family operations in Oaxaca. We also highlight alternative proteins like grasshoppers and utilize entire animals for meat."

Signature dishes
Smoked pork cheek mole with orange and sesame grasshoppers; toasted grasshoppers with chile *piquin*; local rockfish ceviche with chile *manzana* and avocado.

What others say
"Even though Cultura is casual, a fine dining quality infuses every aspect of the restaurant. One of the exceptional dishes on my visit was a whole steelhead trout presented as if it were swimming, on a pad of cilantro rice garnished with wedges of lime. It was one of the best preparations of fish I've seen."

-Michael Bauer, *San Francisco Chronicle*

What we say
Cultura is a refined yet welcoming destination inspired as much by Chef Michelle Estigoy's Mexican grandmother as by the incredible produce and suppliers of the Carmel Valley. The chefs have honed traditional Oaxacan specialities while showcasing the bounty of their own region, from wild seaweeds to foraged herbs.

Pizzaiolo

Alameda

What
A neighborhood restaurant serving 100 percent organic, local pizza, pasta & salads

Who
Courtney Rockwell-Gehrett, chef

When
Breakfast & dinner, Monday to Saturday

Address
5008 Telegraph Avenue, Oakland, Alameda, CA 94601

+1 510 652 4888

pizzaiolooakland.com

Bookings
Walk-ins, phone, website

Price guide

What they say
"We believe in treating the plants and animals that we source and serve with the utmost respect. We buy whole animals from ranchers that we know and trust, and buy organic flour milled in Oakland by people who bring their children to the restaurant for dinner. We change the menu daily to reflect the offerings of these remarkable local food purveyors in their freshest, most beautiful form. We also believe in creating absolutely delicious food - the chef has to taste every salad, pasta, and salsa verde, every time."

Signature dishes
Buttermilk fried chicken with sweet corn succotash, Jimmy Nardello peppers, and chili oil; spaghetti with Hog Island Manila clams, house-made sausage, hot peppers, and parsley; wood-fired pizza with Monterey bay squid, cherry tomatoes, and aïoli.

What we say
Pizzaiolo is committed to providing dedicated service and making the customer feel at home. This kind of care extends to the way in which they treat their food. Produce is 100 percent organic and grown within 150 miles of the restaurant, with ninety percent bought directly from small local farmers and foragers. The menu revolves around what these suppliers have in stock, ensuring guests are given a unique dining experience every time. And Pizzaiolo gives back to the community, too - a monthly Sunday supper sees all proceeds donated to a local Oakland non-profit organisation.

Chez Panisse

Alameda

What
A restaurant & café serving locally sourced, organic food with a daily changing menu

Who
Alice Waters, owner/founder

When
Lunch & dinner, Monday to Saturday

Address
1517 Shattuck Avenue, Berkeley, Alameda, CA 94709

+1 510 548 5525

chezpanisse.com

Bookings
Phone

Price guide

What they say
"At Chez Panisse we celebrate each year with a re-statement of our commitment to good food, community, and sustainability. We are passionate about supporting purveyors who take care of the environment; we support one Sonoma farm almost entirely, and buy from approximately eighty-five other California farmers throughout the year. We see farming, foraging, cooking, and table service as an unbroken sequence, and the meal as a centerpiece of the human experience. Our purveyors are committed to healthful products and practices that are as pure and natural as possible, without synthetic additives or pollutants, and without the unnecessary complexities of packaging and marketing."

What others say
"No other restaurant has better ingredients or treats them with more respect."

–Michael Bauer, *San Francisco Chronicle*

What we say
The grand dame of the sustainable food movement, Chez Panisse, has, since its founding in 1971, become synonymous with the kind of local, farm-to-table eating that has inspired countless restaurants around the world. Alice Waters' Berkeley establishment is both a restaurant and café: the former is prix fixe and reservations only, while the latter, which opened in 1980, offers more moderately priced à la carte lunch and dinner menus. The selections change daily: in summer, you might find a roasted eggplant and rocket salad or sweetcorn soup with fried stuffed squash blossoms at the restaurant. Regardless of when you visit, you'll find attentive service on both floors, and a wine list as thoughtfully sourced as the food on your plate.

Cosecha

Alameda

What
Fresh Californian Mexican food prepared from scratch in Downtown Oakland

Who
Dominica Rice-Cisneros, chef/owner

When
Lunch & dinner, Monday to Friday, brunch Saturday, dinner Sunday

Address
907 Washington Street, Oakland, Alameda, CA 94607

+1 510 452 5900

Bookings
Walk-ins

Price guide

What they say
"Those who find their way to our location in Old Oakland experience the communion of California and Mexico and will find comfort in our home-style offerings. We prepare everything from scratch every day, including handmade tortillas, pastries, and complex traditional entrees, as well as seasonal salads and soups. We strive to provide high quality, affordable meals that can be eaten inside or on the go. We serve California wines, beers, and ingredients that use an abundance of high quality, local products."

Signature dishes
Cosecha salad; grilled corn on the cob; toasted almond mole with red chili.

What others say
"It's a harmonic combination of Mexican and Californian cuisine, located within the historic Swan's Market in Old Oakland. Tacos with tortillas from scratch, salads, soup, and traditional entrees like braised pork in chile guajillo are on offer from chef/owner Dominica Cisneros-Rice (who also happens to be a Chez Panisse alum). Place your order, grab a number and a seat in the communal dining area, and prepare for flavorful, fresh Mexican food."

-Ellen Fort, *Eater*

What we say
Fresh, flavorsome food isn't the only thing you can expect from Cosecha. This Oakland-based restaurant also sources sustainable seafood from the Monterey Fish Market and produce from organic, California farms. They have spent the last three years trying to inform locals of the need for a sustainable food industry. Guests are encouraged to dine in and use real glasses, silverware and plates, eliminating takeout waste in the process.

Ramen Shop

Oakland

What
Serving local & sustainable Northern California ramen inspired by Japanese techniques

Who
Rayneil De Guzman, Jerry Jaksich & Sam White, owners

When
Dinner, daily, weekend lunch

Address
5812 College Ave Oakland, CA 94618

+1 510 640 5034

ramenshop.com

Bookings
Walk-ins

Price guide

What they say
"We work directly with farmers to hear what they have in peak season. All the produce is sourced from local and sustainable farms. It's more about having great relationships with farmers than trying to stick to a label. Our pork comes from Llano Seco. They manage organic, pasture-raised pigs on the oldest land grant in California. This is the best pork in California, if not the United States!"

Signature dishes
Tempura-fried local anchovies and heirloom tomatoes with yuzu kosho mayonnaise, potatoes, Jimmy Nardello peppers, lemon cucumbers, fermented green garlic, and shungiku; and tomatillo miso ramen with ground pork belly, shoyu egg, butter corn, blistered shishito peppers, purple cabbage, and cilantro.

What others say
"The noodles have a distinct, slightly firm texture you won't find anywhere else, the broths are as well crafted as ever, and the pristine ingredients continue to channel the owners' time at Chez Panisse."

-Michael Bauer, *The San Francisco Chronicle*

What we say
This cosy Oakland restaurant has a community made up of farmers, brewers, local industry professionals, and winemakers. The people making great local products are the celebrities here, with Ramen Shop championing local fare in every dish. To reduce their environmental impact, the menu features several vegetarian dishes, including one of the most popular – the Veggie Meyer lemon shoyu ramen with maitake and king oyster mushrooms, baby carrots, bok choy, Tokyo turnips and frilly mustard greens. 100 percent vegetarian, this juicy dish is loved by both meat-eaters and vegetarians alike.

こだわり
つけ麺

Fish

Marin

What
A socially conscious establishment that's about more than just food

Who
Bill Foss & Kenny Belov, owners & Doug Bernstein, chef

When
Lunch & dinner, daily

Address
350 Harbor Drive, Sausalito, Marin, CA 94965

+1 415 331 3474

331fish.com

Bookings
Walk-ins

Price guide

What they say
"Knowing our ingredients, knowing who grew the produce, and knowing who caught the fish is important to us. We get excited for certain seasons to arrive and change the menu accordingly. That, to us, is what keeps food interesting and special, by honoring the producer and respecting the seasons. What we provide is pure and simple food, with an emphasis on quality and sourcing. We value our products, our vendors, our customers, the seasons and our food."

Signature dishes
Tuscan white bean and tuna salad.

What we say
There's usually a line trailing from the front door of Fish, a Sausalito restaurant synonymous with sustainable seafood. Located right on the water, it's the kind of charmingly barebones place where you order at the counter and then find a seat at a picnic table. The food here is simple, allowing the exceptionally fresh seafood to speak for itself: the Tuscan white bean and tuna salad uses poached albacore tuna and locally grown butter beans, and the "Peacemaker" sandwich tucks cornmeal-crusted oysters, sliced ham, shredded lettuce, and mayo into a soft roll. Fish's owners have taken extra steps towards sustainability, buying direct from local fishermen, incorporating invasive species into their dishes and using fish that are lower on the food chain. The restaurant even lands fish on its dock. It doesn't get more local - not to mention delicious - than that.

Montrio Bistro

Monterey

What
A green-certified full-service restaurant that opened its doors in Monterey in 1995

Who
Tony Baker, chef/partner

When
Dinner, daily

Address
414 Calle Principal, Monterey, CA 93940

+1 831 648 8880

montrio.com

Bookings
Website

Price guide

What they say
"We buy a lot of our products locally from two markets; even some of our dairy comes from within twenty miles. Food waste is composted, but we first use a lot of trimmings for stocks and sauces. We insist delivery trucks shut off their engines while stopped at our business. Lots of little things all of the time can add up to a great thing. Our staff are our family; we have so much tenure in our restaurant that everyone knows each other like we know our own family. That creates a level of service and warmth that is hard to ignore."

Signature dishes
House-made lamb *merguez* with pickled cauliflower and feta purée; Ōra King salmon with citrus risotto, baked tomato, and *nduja*; forty-eight-hour bacon with bacon-almond butter, pickled-apple salad, and local honey.

What we say
A Green Restaurant Association green-certified restaurant, Montrio Bistro has a been a Monterey mainstay since 1995, drawing both locals and visitors with expansive hospitality and hearty food.

Chef Tony Baker's Euro-American menu draws heavily from surrounding farms and the waters around Monterey. There are Dungeness crab cakes and smoked wild salmon, and seared scallops served alongside carrot quinoa with raisins, cucumber, and coconut. Entrées skew carnivorous: there's a surfeit of red meat, along with lamb and chicken.

Montrio's dining room reflects its comfort-driven approach to food: the high-ceilinged space is plush and festive, encouraging you to linger a little longer.

Taco María

Orange County

What
Innovative food packed with flavor

Who
Carlos Salgado, executive chef/proprietor

When
Lunch & dinner, Tuesday to Saturday, brunch Sunday

Address
3313 Hyland Avenue, Costa Mesa, Orange County, CA 92626

+1 714 538 8444

tacomaria.com

Bookings
Email reserve@tacomaria.com

Price guide

What they say
"Our menu is based on our relationships with the good people vending at the Santa Monica farmers' market. Our menus are specifically centered on the maize corn we use for tortillas, masa, etc. We source organic landrace maize from small producers in Mexico in collaboration with our partner Masienda. We were the - first and remain - one of the largest end-users of maize heirlooms, which helps to support small artisan farmers in Mexico. We believe we should leave the land better than we found it, and this extends to our philanthropic mission as well. We allocate a percentage of profits to organizations aligned with our ethics (e.g., Planned Parenthood, ACLU, and local initiatives). We have also established new parent leave, health benefits, election day holidays, religious holiday accommodations, and education reimbursements to support our staff in their personal, professional, and civic lives."

Signature dishes
"Flamin' Hot Fried Corn and Sunchoke Things."

What others say
"By regarding tortillas with a seriousness familiar to any fanatical French baker, by using perfect seasonal produce and by treating regional Mexican dishes with both imagination and respect, Salgado has propelled California-Mexican cooking into the jet stream of abstracted modernist cuisine."

-Jonathan Gold, *Los Angeles Times*

What we say
Simultaneously rooted in tradition and upending it, Taco María offers exceptional modern California Mexican cuisine that has earned many accolades, including Los Angeles Times' Restaurant of the Year for 2018.

Grange

Sacramento

What
A locally driven restaurant with the finest ingredients

Who
Dane Blom, executive chef & Jason Hardin, front of house

When
Breakfast, lunch & dinner, daily

Address
926 J Street, Sacramento, CA 95814

+1 916 492 4450

grangesacramento.com

Bookings
Phone, OpenTable.com

Price guide

What they say
"We try to source the most sustainable products that we can. Taking care of our resources is important to our team as we want to pass on our philosophies about running a sustainable business."

Signature dishes
Alaskan halibut with cornbread purée, bacon, frisée, clams, basil, and pickled chilis; tomahawk ribeye for two with potato gratin, grilled asparagus, bone marrow, and E1 sauces; lamb loin with falafel, chickpeas, grilled onion, garlic yogurt, mint, and olive relish.

What others say
"Grange now rates as one of Sacramento's finest eateries."

-Carla Meyer, *The Sacramento Bee*

What we say
A leader in Sacramento's farm-to-fork movement, Grange serves big-hearted New American fare that speaks eloquently and inventively of California's Central Valley. Although Executive Chef Dane Blom's menus change with the seasons, creativity is a constant. Cherry *mostarda* gives grilled quail a sweet, yet tart, bump, while ahi tuna crudo is teamed ingeniously with pickled green peaches; even a side of grilled asparagus comes toting a saffron sabayon. At brunch, you might find smoked pork belly in a hash of asparagus, snap peas, and spring alliums. Regardless of what's on the menu, you will find it matched by expertly mixed seasonal cocktails. Located in the Citizen Hotel, Grange is open morning through night. It is an elegant, lively place to indulge in the region's delectable terroir any time of day.

Mulvaney's

Sacramento

What
A restaurant celebrating California's farmers & their bounty

Who
Bobbin Mulvaney, co-owner & Patrick Mulvaney, chef/co-owner

When
Lunch & dinner, Tuesday to Friday, dinner Saturday

Address
1215 19th Street, Sacramento, CA 95811

+1 916 441 6022

mulvaneysbl.com

Bookings
Phone, website, OpenTable.com

Price guide

What they say
"We are passionate about celebrating our community around the table, along with the food, the history, and the future. Our menu, written daily, is based on what our friends the farmers bring in; the twelve-month growing season means there is always something new just around the corner. For us an important part of a healthy lifestyle is sourcing the best food we can find and treating it simply and with respect."

Signature dishes
Bintje potato gnocchi with morels and fava beans; smoked salmon and Irish brown bread; Aldon Farms lettuces with purple daikon and Tokyo turnip.

What we say
Even in Sacramento, the so-called farm-to-fork capital of America, Mulvaney's stands out for its commitment to sustainability - or what owners Bobbin and Patrick Mulvaney call its "green promise". From the honey harvested on the restaurant's roof to the anaerobic composter that disposes of ninety-nine percent of the kitchen's waste, Mulvaney's is as much a steward of the land as it is a place to eat an exceptional meal. The frequently changing menu is a showcase for area farmers. Dinner may begin with a plate of heirloom tomatoes and creamy hand-pulled mozzarella, or a pairing of peaches and prosciutto, and then progress to a hearty Niman Ranch ribeye with panzanella or succulent roast chicken with grilled vegetable moussaka. Located in an 1893 firehouse, Mulvaney's is a place that indeed keeps its promises, particularly to the cause of good eating.

Bird Dog

Santa Clara

What
A multicultural pile-up of sorts celebrating the cuisine of the modern-day Peninsula

Who
Robbie Wilson, chef/owner

When
Dinner, daily, lunch Tuesday to Friday

Address
420 Ramona Street, Palo Alto, Santa Clara, CA 94301

+1 650 656 8180

birddogpa.com

Bookings
Phone, Resy.com

Price guide

What they say
"We love simply connecting with our guests, whether it's via flavors, hospitality, aesthetic, attitude, or all of the above. Hopefully, when you leave Bird Dog you feel as if you know us on a personal level, as if you enjoyed your time meeting someone at a friend's dinner party."

Signature dishes
Wood-grilled avocado with ponzu, kelp, and wasabi; fried chicken thighs with green curry and smoked *uni* emulsion; buri *crude* with horseradish, citron, and dashi.

What others say
"Not only is [Wilson's avocado] the Platonic ideal of avocado; it's also a convincing encapsulation of what good can come when California cuisine is reduced to its essence, and then taught how to fly."

-Rebecca Marx & Josh Sens, *San Francisco Magazine*

What we say
When Bird Dog opened in Palo Alto, it shook up the local dining scene with its stylish design, and thoroughly modern take on California cooking.

Raw, sustainable seafood is a highlight of Chef Robbie Wilson's menu: wild *buri* is anointed with a dashi vinegar made from the fish's bones, while *kampachi* is teamed with coconut, banana, cashew, and puffed rice. Though Wilson knows meat - his fried chicken thighs, soaked in green curry instead of buttermilk, are a must-have - it's his wood-grilled avocado, teamed with Marin kelp, fresh wasabi, and ponzu, that has become one of Bird Dog's most celebrated dishes.

Between its exceptional food, welcoming service and well-curated drinks list, Bird Dog is worth sniffing out again and again.

The Bear and Star

Santa Barbara

What
Extreme farm-to-table restaurant featuring refined ranch cuisine

Who
Eli & Ashley Parker, owners & John Cox, chef/partner

When
Breakfast, lunch & dinner, daily

Address
2860 Grand Ave, Los Olivos, CA 93441

+1 805 686 1359

thebearandstar.com

Bookings
OpenTable.com

Price guide

What they say
"We have an 800-acre ranch where we raise Wagyu beef, chicken, quail, and lamb to supply 100 percent of our menu. We raise our Wagyu beef on open pastures during the spring (on green grass) and then finish them on a diet of spent grains and grape pomace (from our brewery and winery). We have an organic farm and orchard and we forage items such as acorns, wild watercress, and mushrooms when available. We observe the Monterey Aquarium Seafood Watch list and have also re-purposed old wine barrels and commercial grape picking bins into raised beds and aquaponics systems for catfish."

Signature dishes
Smoked Wagyu meatloaf with pickled mustard seeds, tomato glaze, and garden vegetables; charcoal-grilled fava beans with soft-poached quail eggs; wild foraged herbs and greens with house-made strawberry vinegar and cold-pressed olive oil.

What we say
The Bear and Star is redefining the concept of farm-to-table, while offering guests a luxurious experience of ranch-style cuisine. While delicious dishes are reason enough to visit this restaurant, the sustainably minded vision behind it is another. "We are actively pursuing Air Not Water, a technology we developed to replace the pre-rinse used in all commercial kitchens with a mix of high-pressure air and water for clearing plates", Chef John Cox explains. "This promises to save millions of gallons of water each year in California alone."

The Land & Water Company

San Diego

What
An evolving philosophy of responsibly sourced food from the land & water

Who
Robert A. Ruiz, chef/owner

When
Dinner, daily

Address
2978 Carlsbad Boulevard, #110 Carlsbad, San Diego, CA 92008

+1 760 729 5263

landandwaterco.com

Bookings
Website

Price guide

What they say
"We source produce from local organic farmers, Cannon Family Farms and our on site restaurant garden. Our seafood is strictly traceable and sustainable, using only local sources. We work closely with the National Oceanic and Atmospheric Administration (NOAA), Scripps institute of Oceanography, UCSD's Center for Marine Biodiversity and Conservation, and the Highly Migratory Species Lab at NOAA's Southwestern Fisheries Science Center. We compost our waste, which has led to the development of city-wide organic waste composting program. We re-use water for blanching vegetables, washing rice, and bar ice, and we do not use heating or air-conditioning. We have volunteered with the Ocean Discovery Institute and local high schools and organizations supporting, for example, victims of domestic violence."

Signature dishes
"No waste" beets with brown butter thyme vinaigrette, crème fraîche, and spiced vegetable ash; *tsukemono* house-pickled vegetables; miso-glazed kama seasonal fish collar.

What others say
"Rob Ruiz is single-handedly making the seafood we consume in the United States more sustainable."

-Todd Reubold, *Ensia*

What we say
The Land & Water Company's location north of San Diego, perched on the Pacific coast, is central to Chef Robert Ruiz's approach. It is a refined restaurant that sources only local and sustainable seafood to create artful Japanese sushi and sashimi, as well as a range of New American dishes inspired by the restaurant's own heirloom garden and nearby farms.

Dad's Luncheonette

San Mateo

What
A historic train caboose on Highway 1, showcasing the best farms in the area

Who
Scott Clark, chef/co-owner & Alexis Liu, co-owner

When
Lunch & dinner, Thursday to Sunday

Address
225 Cabrillo Highway South, Half Moon Bay, San Mateo, CA 94019

+1 650 560 9832

dadsluncheonette.com

Bookings
Phone, walk-ins

Price guide

What they say
"We strive to provide a unique dining experience that is accessible to all. We started with something classically American and humble – a hamburger on sliced white bread – and elevated the ingredients to break the misconception that eating well needs to be fancy and/or expensive. We are a very casual roadside stand on Highway 1, and this context informs our menu. Eating while on the road is often a drag and an excuse to eat poorly, but we strive to highlight the amazing, fresh food that comes out of the area."

Signature dishes
Hamburger sandwich with white cheddar cheese, red oak lettuce, homemade pickled red onions, and a free-range local egg; weekly soup; herb salad with herbs, root vegetables, and edible flowers.

What others say
"Their version of a classic roadside stand speaks with a distinct California accent ... But this is not food that puts on airs. If anything, it puts ideas in your head."

–Rebecca Flint Marx, *The New York Times*

What we say
A train caboose parked next to a highway might not seem the most likely location for one of Northern California's best dining experiences, but Dad's packs plenty of surprises into its tiny confines. Owned by Scott Clark, a former chef de cuisine at San Francisco's Saison, and his partner Alexis Liu, Dad's is an update on the roadside stand. On sunny days, eager patrons form a line from Dad's fifteen-seat patio for a taste of California's good life.

Backyard

Sonoma

What
A restaurant that draws its inspiration from the amazing bounty of Sonoma County

Who
Daniel A. Kedan & Marianna Gardenhire, chefs/owners

When
Lunch & dinner, daily, weekend brunch

Address
6566 Front Street, Forestville, Sonoma, CA 95436

+1 707 820 8445

backyardforestville.com

Bookings
Phone, website, Yelpreservations.com

Price guide

What they say
"We draw our inspiration from Sonoma County, with all of its amazing orchards, farms, ranchers, foragers, and fishermen. Every fruit, vegetable, and animal is grown, raised or line-caught locally with the most ethical sustainability practices. We also grow our own produce at our farm, Bee Run Hollow. Our restaurant has a very casual atmosphere, with a focus on classic technique and craft. We always strive to support all dietary needs. Our menu highlights this by offering a wide range of dishes: there are always vegan and gluten-free items to allow for every guest to have a memorable experience."

Signature dishes
Fried chicken; pickle plate; charcuterie board.

What we say
Tiny Forestville has become a favorite destination for in-the-know diners thanks to the charms of Backyard, the friendly, affordable, and deeply flavorful restaurant run by the husband-and-wife team of Daniel A. Kedan and Marianna Gardenhire.

The couple's menu hews closely to the seasonal, local, and sustainable, with many ingredients coming from their own farm. One of Backyard's year-round calling cards is its buttermilk fried chicken. Depending on when you visit, you might also find wild line-caught vermillion rock cod with stewed carrots, braised radishes, and almond pesto, or, at lunch, a robust bacon and kimchi grilled cheese or equally hearty meat-free mushroom Reuben.

Desserts, like the chocolate *budino* with salted caramel and sweet cream, are also not to be missed, while the back patio - befitting the restaurant's name - is one of the nicest in Sonoma County.

The Drawing Board

Sonoma

What
A feel-good food kitchen with an apothecary-inspired craft cocktail bar

Who
Rosie Wiggins, owner

When
Dinner Tuesday to Sunday, weekend brunch

Address
190 Kentucky Street, Petaluma, Sonoma, CA 94952

+1 707 774 6689

tdbpetaluma.com

Bookings
OpenTable.com

Price guide
●●●  

What they say
"At The Drawing Board we are passionate about the health of our patrons and the planet. We believe that good food should come from the earth, be grown nearby, prepared simply, and served with love. The Drawing Board strives to be a place where the community feel engaged, not only with the restaurant but also with each other."

Signature dishes
Kimchi pancakes with Kewpie mayo; spring baby vegetable *crudité* with miso-tahini paste; *burrata* with asparagus, sea vegetables, and tamari vinaigrette.

What others say
"The downtown space is clean, open and airy, with sunlight flowing in through the huge windows in the afternoon and evening. Suspended garden boxes and antique lighting fixtures hang from heavy beams to help the Drawing Board retain a sense of warmth and community."

-Houston Porter, *The Argus-Courier*

What we say
Nutrition may be the foundation of The Drawing Board, but the restaurant's vibrant flavors and warm service are the building blocks of its success. The downtown Petaluma restaurant is serious about locality: the vast majority of its ingredients come from surrounding Sonoma County, right down to the foraged botanicals used in its cocktails. You may find coastal sea vegetables in a dish of asparagus and burrata, or dried Douglas Fir tips dusting the gravlax. Owner Rosie Wiggins opened the restaurant with the mission to make customers feel good. Between her open, airy dining room and nuanced, beautiful food, her mission has certainly been accomplished - and then some.

Camino

Sonoma

What
An Oakland restaurant with a daily changing menu cooked in a giant fireplace & wood oven

Who
Russell Moore, chef/co-owner & Allison Hopelain, front of house/co-owner

When
Dinner Wednesday to Sunday

Address
3917 Grand Avenue, Oakland, Sonoma, CA 94610

+1 510 547 5035

caminorestaurant.com

Bookings
Phone, website, OpenTable.com

Price guide

What they say
"We're passionate about being part of a community of farmers and craftspeople, creating a restaurant culture that reflects our values, and making memorable and delicious food."

Signature dishes
A bowl of English peas; wood oven-roasted whole local rockfish with farro and herb salad; rhubarb-buckwheat tart with grilled fig leaf ice cream.

What others say
"What's important but is impossible to describe is the strength and utter brilliance of [Moore's] flavor combinations and the downright simplicity of it all. Moore has a palate that cannot be stopped; everything tastes as if it were created to go with everything seasoning it."

-Mark Bittman, *The New York Times*

What we say
A wood-burning hearth and communal tables dominate Camino, giving the Oakland restaurant the look of a medieval banquet hall. But Chef Russell Moore's cooking is a thoroughly modern interpretation of seasonal Californian cooking, combining simple preparations and local ingredients to create bold, true flavors.

Moore, a Chez Panisse alum, keeps his constantly changing menu short and sweet: dinner may start with a bowl of English peas and then progress to a whole oven-roasted rockfish or juicy grilled pork loin and slow-cooked pork shoulder served with lovage, fava beans, and Bintje potatoes. Desserts, like a Tunisian orange cake with dates and yogurt, are not to be missed.

The emphasis on sustainable ingredients extends to the bar, where the cocktails are made with traceable, non-GMO spirits procured through small distributors. Just like the food, they go down easily.

Glen Ellen Star

Sonoma

What
A farmhouse restaurant specializing in wood-fired cooking with Californian sensibilities

Who
Ari and Erinn Weiswasser, chef/co-owners

When
Dinner, daily

Address
13648 Arnold Drive, Glen Ellen, Sonoma, CA 95442

+1 707 343 1384

glenellenstar.com

Bookings
Reserve.com, email reservations@glenellenstar.com

Price guide

What they say
"Seasonal ingredients and guest interactions are our passions; we source fifty percent of the product for our vegetable-driven menu from our own biodynamic gardens and the Marin Farmers' Market."

Signature dishes
Housemade rigatoni with artichokes, morels, peas, hen egg, and green garlic butter; wood-roasted padron peppers and *shabazi*; *fattoush* salad with our garden's lettuces, house-made pita chips, pickled ramps, black olives, watermelon radish, and a sumac-buttermilk vinaigrette.

What others say
"The country charm of this quaint cottage belies the level of culinary chops that will impress even a hardened city slicker."

Michelin Guide

What we say
A wood-fired oven is the engine behind many of the lusty, refreshingly simple dishes at the Glen Ellen Star, the tiny restaurant that Chef Ari Weiswasser and his wife Erinn Weiswasser run in the equally tiny Sonoma town that bears the restaurant's name.

A vet of Thomas Keller's French Laundry, Weiswasser has created a seasonal menu that sings of Sonoma: dinner might begin with wood-roasted vegetables or a spring pea soup with ricotta gnudi. Succulent chicken cooked under a brick signature, while a chorus of blistered pizzas tempts year-round.

Handline

Sonoma

What
A coastal Californian restaurant in a breezy modern building featuring sustainably sourced seafood

Who
Natalie Goble, chef/owner

When
Lunch & dinner, daily

Address
935 Gravenstein Highway South, Sebastopol, Sonoma, CA 95472

+1 707 827 3744

handline.com

Bookings
Email manager@handline.com

Price guide

What they say
"At Handline we are most passionate about sourcing seasonal and sustainably grown and harvested ingredients from Sonoma County. We have our own two-acre farm as well as many relationships with local farmers and foragers, and work with local seafood companies to bring in the freshest, most sustainable seafood the California coast has to offer.

"We believe that eating with the seasons from local farms and ranches brings with it added nutritional benefit. If our food travels a shorter distance to get to us, it retains more nutritional value. It is also healthier for the planet."

Signature dishes
"The La Sirena": poached Monterey squid with snap peas, scallion, and mint on a freshly milled corn tostada; local king salmon sandwich with dill mayo, butter lettuce, pickled radish, and wholegrain mustard; smoked trout and clam chowder with local mushrooms, potatoes, cream, and thyme.

What we say
Housed in a revamped fast-food restaurant, Handline takes regional, sustainable Californian cuisine for an invigorating fast-casual spin.

The restaurant's menu is a vibrant merger of local ingredients with state culinary traditions: fresh oysters, milled corn tacos heaped with seasonal produce and sustainably caught seafood, and a roster of juicy hamburgers that look south to Los Angeles. The food is accompanied by an impressive selection of wine and craft beer, along with a laid-back ambience. Everything is ordered at the counter, a twist that nods to California's fast-food heritage while offering a tantalizing vision of its future.

Lowell's

Sonoma

What
A slightly off-kilter community hub offering seasonal, organic & locally sourced food & wine

Who
Lowell Sheldon, owner & Joseph Zobel, chef

When
Breakfast, lunch, & dinner, Monday to Friday, weekend brunch & dinner

Address
7385 Healdsburg Avenue, Sebastopol, Sonoma, CA 95472

+1 707 829 1077

lowellssebastopol.com

Bookings
Phone, Yelpreservations.com

Price guide

What they say
"We are passionate about local sourcing and the relationships that come with it, and our regularly changing menu reflects our connection with seasonality and the creativity it inspires. We are here in service to our community, bringing together food, wine, and the people we love in a comfortable and inclusive setting. We are honored that the restaurant has become such a communal hub. Our regulars are our lifeline."

Signature dishes
Antipasti platter; seasonal pizza; macro bowl with wholegrain rice, heirloom beans, organic vegetables, and homemade kimchi or sauerkraut.

What we say
"From the Garden" is a section on Lowell's menu, but it could also describe the laid-back Sebastopol restaurant as a whole. Owner Lowell Sheldon is passionate about sourcing from the surrounding Sonoma County countryside - including from his restaurant's very own Two Belly Acre farm.

Lowell's Italian-inspired, vegetable-centric menu is the result of collaborations with sustainable and local fisheries, foragers, farmers, winemakers, and small-scale cattle ranchers. Thin-crust pizzas with seasonal toppings and house-made pasta are menu mainstays, as is the macro bowl, a wholesome riot of wholegrain rice, beans, and fresh, marinated, and fermented vegetables. Although the restaurant serves minimal meat, it emphasizes creative, nose-to-tail preparations; its pork sausage shows up in several dishes. The beverage selection is packed with organic and biodynamic wine, beer, and cider. And, as befits a community hub, the dining room is usually packed with regulars.

SHED

Sonoma

What
A market, café & community space celebrating good farming, good cooking & good eating

Who
Cindy Daniel & Doug Lipton, founders/owners & Perry Hoffman, chef

When
Breakfast & lunch, Tuesday to Sunday, dinner Wednesday to Monday

Address
25 North Street, Healdsburg, Sonoma, CA 95448

+1 707 431 7433

healdsburgshed.com

Bookings
OpenTable.com

Price guide

What they say
"SHED Café and Larder sources locally and sustainably-caught seafood and sustainably-raised trout. Much of our produce is sourced from farms located within ten miles as well as our own sixteen-acre HomeFarm, where we grow an array of fruits and vegetables, olives, grapes, flowers and herbs, and tend chickens and bees."

Signature dishes
Roasted strawberries with lovage, purslane, wild peas, and pennyroyal lychee; wild king salmon Nicoise with new potatoes, fermented green garlic, crimson little gems, and olive aïoli; braised Valley Ford rabbit with summer squash, charred wild onions, apricots, za'atar, preserved lemon, and flowering thyme.

What others say
"The Shed celebrates its location in a way that no other place duplicates. It feels like the most authentic and beautifully conceived restaurant in Sonoma County right now."

The San Francisco Chronicle

What we say
Part market, coffee bar, home goods shop, events space and café, SHED is a multifaceted foodie mecca that celebrates Sonoma County's extra-ordinary natural resources. At the café, Chef Perry Hoffman's frequently changing menus employ the best of local agriculture - including SHED's own biodynamic farm - in generous, endlessly creative ways: Hoffman might tweak a wild king salmon with fermented green garlic, team Mendocino urchin with satsuma, wood sorrel, and kumquat, or pull a Swiss chard and bottarga pizza from the wood oven. SHED also mills its own flour and makes fermented products, some of which are available to buy as delectable mementos of Sonoma's terroir.

Reem's California

Sonoma

What
An Arab street corner bakery that connects people through the warmth of bread & hospitality

Who
Reem Assil, owner

When
Breakfast, lunch & dinner, Tuesday to Friday, weekend brunch

Address
3301 E. 12th Street, suite 133, Oakland, Sonoma, CA 94601

+1 510 852 9390

reemscalifornia.com

Bookings
Phone, walk-ins

Price guide

What they say
"We believe the best experience of hospitality is to have your bread freshly baked for you. It's a lost art. In the spirit of Arab street corner bakeries and the communities that surround them, we create this experience in the United States though Reem's."

Signature dishes
Za'atar *man'oushe* (freshly-baked flatbread); *muhammara* (roasted pepper-walnut spread; *musakhan* (whole chicken baked with sumac and onions).

What others say
"At a moment when touchstones of Middle Eastern cuisine like tahini and pomegranate molasses appear on menus all over the country, Reem's offers an opportunity to see those flavors, often attributed to Israel, through a wider lens, one inclusive of the Arab perspective."

Food & Wine magazine

What we say
If bread is the staff of life, then *man'oushe*, a flatbread baked on a domed griddle, is the staff of Reem's California, Reem Assil's community-minded Arab bakery and café in Oakland's Fruitvale neighborhood. The sunny, lively space started its life as a farmers' market stand built around the stretchy flatbread that Assil baked to order; at the bakery, the *man'oushe* comes with toppings like za'atar, a spice mix, and *akkawi*, a brined cheese. A roster of meze and traditional Arab pastries, both sweet and savory, round out the daytime menu, while breakfast features a voluptuous *shakshuka*, a thick tomato-pepper stew topped with an egg. Reem's menu is brief, but its flavors are generous; the same could be said of the spirit of hospitality that pervades the café.

SingleThread

Sonoma

What
A farm-driven restaurant & inn that offers guests a unique & authentic taste of Sonoma County

Who
Kyle Connaughton, chef

When
Dinner, daily, weekend lunch

Address
131 North Street, Healdsburg, Sonoma, CA 95448

+1 707 723 4646

singlethreadfarms.com

Bookings
Exploretock.com

Price guide

What they say
"Our five-acre farm drives our restaurant and its eleven-course menu each day. The produce from the farm, as well as the rhythms of each moment within the season are the inspiration for each day and the menu we create for our guests."

Signature dishes
Black cod "*fukkura-san*"; Duclair duck with grilled broccoli, sunchoke, and pickled garlic; Sonoma grains.

What others say
"Every evening, Kyle's *prix fixe* opens with what he calls 'a snapshot of Sonoma County'. A composition of small bites made from ingredients at their often short-lived peak, it's meant to mirror what's transpiring at that very moment in nearby farms, fisheries, and fields."

–Josh Sens, *AFAR*

What we say
Precision, elegance, and extreme seasonality lie at the heart of SingleThread, a Sonoma County restaurant, inn, and farm that set a new bar for fine dining when it opened in downtown Healdsburg in 2016.

A collaboration between Chef Kyle Connaughton and his farmer wife, Katina, the restaurant serves a tasting menu fully customized to each guest's dietary preferences. Its dizzying array of dishes showcase ingredients hailing from SingleThread's own five-acre farm and the surrounding region, as well as Kyle's expertise in clay pot cooking. His black cod *fukkura-san*, featuring the buttery fish and twelve to fourteen vegetables from the farm, perfectly encapsulates both.

Though the experience is impossibly refined, the service is warm, making each meal at SingleThread feel like as much a celebration of hospitality as place.

87

Hawaii

Merriman's

Hawaii County

What
Driven by a long-standing commitment to Hawaiian regional cuisine

Who
Peter Merriman, chef/ restaurateur

When
Lunch & dinner, daily

Address
65-1227 Opelo Road, Waimea, Hawaii, HI 96743, plus other locations - see website

+1 808 885 6822

merrimanshawaii.com

Bookings
Resy.com, OpenTable.com

Price guide

What they say
"A pioneer in the farm-to-table concept, we serve only the freshest products, at least ninety percent of which are locally grown or caught using sustainable methods."

Signature dishes
Kālua pig and sweet onion quesadilla; ahi with Asian slaw and wasabi dipping sauce.

What others say
"When it comes to farm-to-table restaurants in Hawaii, all roads lead to Peter Merriman. He's like the Alice Waters of the islands, forging connections between farmers and diners since he started his first restaurant in 1988."

-Russ Parsons, *Los Angeles Times*

What we say
Widely known as the pioneer of the Hawaiian regional cuisine movement, Chef Peter Merriman has been instrumental in the growth of Hawaii's local agriculture. The Waimea flagship of his namesake restaurant is now one of five Merriman's locations, and sources some ninety percent of its ingredients locally.

At Merriman's, Hawaiian regional cuisine means dishes like a kālua pig and sweet onion quesadilla, set aflame with kimchi, and extremely fresh and sustainably caught ahi, *kampachi*, and mahi mahi that are paired with vegetables, crusted with macadamia nuts, or, in the case of lobster and dayboat scallops, show up in a pot pie spiked with vermouth. A signature Caesar salad with fried green tomato croutons headlines the so-called "Dirt Farm Salads" section.

Merriman's is a white-tablecloth restaurant, but its warm service - and generous cocktails - create a pleasantly relaxed atmosphere that embodies laid-back Hawaiian hospitality.

Kahumana Organic Farm and Café

Honolulu

What
A nonprofit-based holistic community modeling wholeness, wellness, sustainability & inclusivity

Who
Robert Zuckerman, manager

When
Lunch & dinner, Tuesday to Saturday

Address
86-660 Lualualei Homestead Road, Waianae, Honolulu, HI 96792

+1 808 696 8844

kahumana.org

Bookings
Phone, walk-ins, email rjzman7@gmail.com

Price guide

What they say
"We are passionate about providing super healthy, diverse, and well-balanced meals for our community members and customers and serving them through our café. We are located directly on an organic farm with a year-round growing capacity, so truly farm-to-table. The restaurant and farm are programs of a nonprofit, 501(c)3 organization founded as an intentional community in 1974, with the purpose of people coming from diverse spiritual and cultural backgrounds living and working in community to create a place for healing. The organization has a long history of serving the local community through its social service programs."

Signature dishes
Organic wholewheat linguine with house-made macadamia nut pesto; coconut vegetable dal curry with fresh turmeric-seasoned brown rice; Cajun-seared ahi with sautéed farm vegetables, mashed Okinawan purple sweet potato, and mango-dragon fruit salsa.

What we say
Social service and simple farm-to-table fare are the calling cards of the Kahumana Organic Farm and Café, a rustic spot on the west coast of O'ahu. The café was founded to nourish both customers and the local community, providing job training to those in need. Kahumana's organic, biodynamic farm provides many of the ingredients for the café's menu, which is stocked with salads, soups, and vegetable-driven entrées like stir-fries and curries. Meat, seafood, and beverages are also locally sourced, and the farm's own herbs star in its Kahumana Cooler, a blend of herbs and dried organic hibiscus as invigorating as the café's stunning views.

Town

Honolulu

What
A neighborhood spot with the motto: local first, organic whenever possible & with aloha always

Who
Ed Kenney, chef/owner

When
Lunch & dinner, Monday to Friday, dinner Saturday

Address
3435 Waialae Ave, Honolulu, HI 96816

+1 808 735 5900

townkaimuki.com

Bookings
Phone, OpenTable.com

Price guide

What they say
"In a market that is driven by the visitor industry, we instead chose to create a neighborhood restaurant for a local clientele. Over the past thirteen years, Town has become 'home base' for a vast circle of regulars. The power that food has to bring people together, to connect them to the earth, and to create memories is what fuels us to do what we do every day. Restaurants, more than any other business, address the social aspects of the sustainability equation by providing a place for people to reconnect to each other and to the food they eat. Food is an agent for positive change."

Signature dishes
Aku tartare; gnocchi with seasonal vegetables; 2 Lady Farmers pork.

What we say
Opened in Honolulu in 2005, Town was the first restaurant of Chef Edward Kenney's powerhouse Town Hospitality Group, and also a beachhead of Hawaii's farm-to-fork and regional cuisine movements. Town's constantly changing menu is thick with local meat and produce, as well as sustainable seafood - like Kenney's other three restaurants, it is Seafood Watch-certified. Depending on which ingredients are available, pork from 2 Lady Farmers might be served with polenta, escarole, and pickled mushrooms, and the catch of the day with sprouted green lentils and Tokyo turnips.

'Ulu Ocean Grill

Kailua-Kona

What
An elegant restaurant serving hyper-local farm & ocean-to-table island cuisine

Who
Four Seasons Resort Hualalai

When
Breakfast & dinner, daily

Address
72-100 Ka'upulehu Drive, Kailua-Kona, HI 96740

+ 1 808 325 8000

fourseasons.com

Bookings
Phone, website, OpenTable.com

Price guide

What they say
"One of the signature restaurants at the Four Seasons Resort, we exemplify the resort-wide culinary philosophy of providing hyper-local, seasonal, and fresh food. Ninety-five percent of our ingredients are from the state of Hawaii, while seventy-five percent are from Hawaii Island. Hawaii Island is bountiful in natural resources, with hundreds of farms, ranches, fishermen, and culinary artisans right at our fingertips. At 'Ulu, we strive to showcase the island's unique and natural flavors through surprising and refined preparations."

Signature dishes
Ahi "Loco Moco" with ahi tartare, quail egg, and *kabayaki* gravy; oven-roasted whole local snapper; Polynesian coconut curry with broccolini, heirloom tomatoes, and rice noodles; ahi poke with *ogo*, Maui onions, white *shoyu*, and sesame oil.

What we say
The 'Ulu Ocean Grill takes full advantage of Hawaii's natural resources, from its romantic al fresco views of the Pacific to the ingredients in its refined, innovative dishes.

The seafood-heavy menu is a showcase for local fishermen and aquaculture, including the Resort's own Pūnāwai Lake, where its organic oysters are cultivated. Many of the herbs used in their dishes (including the Hawaiian chili pepper used in the house-made hot sauce) are grown in the restaurant's garden. If you order any of 'Ulu's pristine sushi and sashimi, chances are you'll be eating fish that was pulled from the ocean only hours earlier. 'Ulu's extensive wine list features boutique wines that further enhance a surpassingly elegant but laid-back dining experience.

91

Oregon

Bamboo Sushi

Portland

What
Certified-sustainable sushi

Who
Kristofor Lofgren, founder

When
Lunch & dinner, daily

Address
404 Southwest 12th Ave, Portland, OR 97205, plus other locations - see website

+1 503 444 7455

bamboosushi.com

Bookings
OpenTable.com

Price guide

What they say
"Driven by a deep commitment to environmental and social change, we set out to make an impact in this world. We combine the values and guidelines of multiple international organizations to ensure every plate we serve reflects our deep dedication to sustainability. As we grow, we seek to inspire change ... change in the way people eat, the way restaurants do business, and the way we treat our environment."

Signature dishes
Ora king salmon yakumi with lightly-dressed nigiri; MSC albacore; kimono roll with layered Alaskan salmon and flavors of sage and apple.

What we say
You won't find bluefin tuna at Bamboo Sushi. That's because they really put their money where their mouth is and eschew industry staples that don't pass muster with certifying organizations for healthier ocean ecology.

Bamboo was one of the first restaurants of its kind to enact firm policies for sustainability in their field. Now, they're thinking even bigger than what's on the plate. They're becoming a model for how a big company can leave a small footprint by finding creative ways to offset emissions. In 2017, they became carbon neutral. This is sushi you can feel really good about eating.

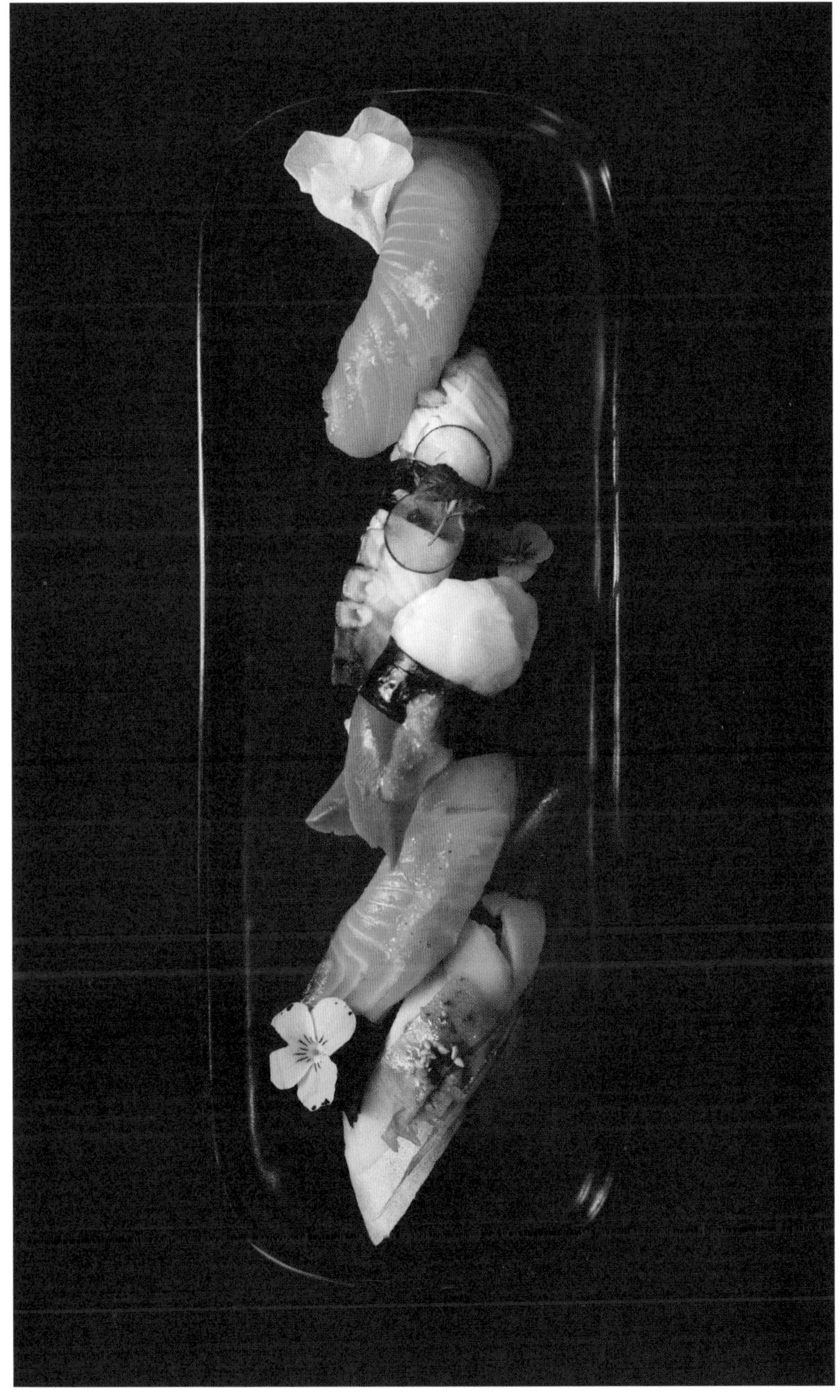

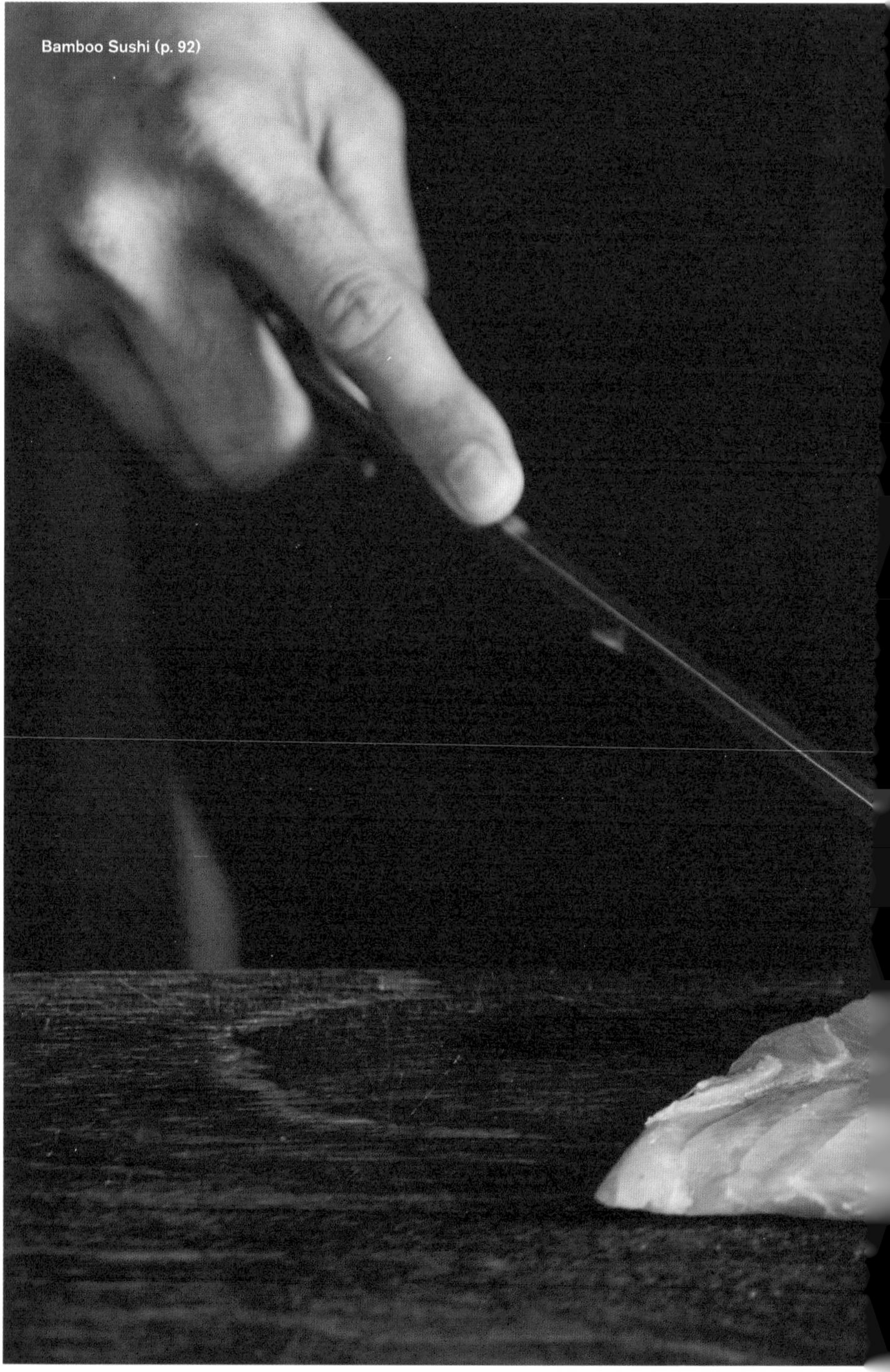

Bamboo Sushi (p. 92)

Ava Gene's

Portland

What
Roman-inspired menu emphasizing the best produce & meats from local farmers and ranchers

Who
Joshua McFadden, chef/owner & Luke Dirks, owner

When
Dinner, daily

Address
3377 Southeast Division Street, Portland, OR 97202

+1 971 229 0571

avagenes.com

Bookings
Phone, walk-ins, Resy.com

Price guide

What they say
"Roman-inspired menu highlights the best produce and meats raised by local farmers and ranchers in the Pacific Northwest. We believe that eating seasonal foods is not only the most ethical and sustainable choice, it is also the best-tasting choice."

Signature dishes
Spring cavatelli with foraged mushrooms and local brassicas; pasta made with house-milled grain.

What others say
"I used to judge a chef by the way he or she roasted a chicken. But now that farm-to-table is the standard, it's more about what they can do with a carrot. At the trattoria-inspired Ava Gene's ... green-thumb cuisine becomes masterful."

-Andrew Knowlton, *bon appétit*

What we say
Ava Gene's brings all the pieces together with excellence food, professional service, and a sustainable kitchen approach. It speaks loudly that the menu always features a bio of one of the restaurant's producers and puts their farming partners right by their side.

Farm Spirit

Portland

What
Plant-based chef's counter serving Northwest Cuisine in Portland, Oregon

Who
Aaron Adams, owner

When
Dinner Wednesday to Saturday

Address
1414 Southeast Morrison Street, Portland, OR 97214

farmspiritpdx.com

Bookings
Website

Price guide

What they say
"At Farm Spirit, our biggest passion is connecting eaters to the foods of Cascadia and the story of where their food comes from. As our name implies, we hope people will come away with as much passion, love, and respect for our farmers and foragers as we have."

Signature dishes
Early morel with Abenaki hominy and romesco; Adirondack red potato with wild watercress purée and sorrel juice; local strawberries with a sunflower milk yogurt, spruce, strawberry gel sheet, and elderflowers.

What others say
"Big-name chef and restaurateur John Gorham recently described vegan counter Farm Spirit as 'one of the only places in Portland worthy of a Michelin Star'."

-Michelle DeVona, *Eater Portland*

What we say
People step into Farm Spirit because it's one of Portland's most celebrated restaurants, and they are often unaware that the menu is free of any animal products whatsoever. Farm Spirit makes an effort to support their larger community. To them, being sustainable is not only in the details of their ingredient choices, but they remunerate all people on their staff fairly. They are also involved in fun community events and are working on new projects to watch out for in the near future.

Lovely's Fifty Fifty

Portland

What
Seasonally inspired, naturally leavened pizza & organic ice cream

Who
Sarah Minnick, chef/owner, & Jane Minnick, owner

When
Dinner Tuesday to Sunday

Address
4039 North Mississippi Avenue, Suite 101 Portland OR 97227

+1 503 281 4060

lovelysfiftyfifty.com

Bookings
Walk-ins

Price guide

What they say
"We are passionate about seasonal produce from Oregon farmers, fermentation, and organic, naturally-leavened, and wholegrain baking. We have a very low-meat menu. I buy cured meats from a processor that is innovating larger scale production by certifying different levels of animal care, so I can choose to spend more money to help them achieve their goals."

Signature dishes
Ayers Creek Farm polenta; pizza with shell peas, spring onions, spinach, and dill yogurt; fresh chamomile ice cream with walnut toffee.

What we say
Lovely's Fifty Fifty sits on a street in North Portland where not many tourists end up. This spot for locals encapsulates all the very best of Pacific Northwest cuisine in the disguise of a pizza and ice cream joint. Most nights, you'll find Chef Sarah Minnick at a station between her wood-fired oven and the small counter where she hand-stretches the dough.

Sarah is self-taught, and has fostered close relationships with local farmers and producers. She buys 100 percent of the vegetables, cheese, and meat used in her pizzas from them. Lovely's sets the bar for sourcing locally. She puts away hundreds of pounds of tomatoes each summer by drying and canning them for the pizza. And then in late winter, she supports her main farmer by purchasing what he calls "farm-foraged" produce - little shoots, starts, and cover crops that might not interest other chefs.

Nostrana

Portland

What
Seasonally influenced Italian dishes including popular thin-crust pizzas in a grandiose dining room

Who
Cathy Whims, chef/owner

When
Lunch Monday to Friday, dinner, daily

Address
1401 Southeast Morrison Street, suite 101. Portland, OR 97214

+1 503 234 2427

nostrana.com

Bookings
OpenTable.com

Price guide

What they say
"Nostrana celebrates the Pacific Northwest with inventive regional Italian cuisine, built on simplicity and fresh, local ingredients. The restaurant's hearth makes cooking with fire a central theme. Chef Cathy Whims has many close, personal relationships with farmers in the region, and these ingredients shine in her deft use of them."

Signature dishes
Potato gnocchi with Marcella's tomato butter sauce; Nostrana's wood-fired pizzas.

What others say
"There's a reason this warm, gracious Southeast Portland restaurant has a wall filled with accolades, including a half-dozen James Beard Award nominations and *The Oregonian*'s 2006 Restaurant of the Year. Here, chef Cathy Whims and her team serve fine-tuned salads, beautifully blistered Neapolitan pizzas, juicy wood-charred steaks and faithful Italian pastas inspired by Whims' mentor, the late Italian cookbook author Marcella Hazan."

-Michael Russell, *The Oregonian*

What we say
Nostrana is the kind of place that doesn't boast about sustainability for marketing purposes. Chef Cathy Whims has been living by these principles for many years. She sources ninety percent of their produce from local farmers, and eighty percent of their proteins from local suppliers. They have long been active with slow food, and we think it's especially cool that once a year, they invite all of their farmers to join them for dinner at Nostrana to break bread together.

Stacked Sandwich Shop

Portland

What
A counter service sandwich shop using local & sustainable ingredients

Who
Gabriel Pascuzzi, chef

When
Dinner, daily, lunch Monday to Friday & weekend brunch

Address
1643 Southeast 3rd Ave, Portland, OR 97214

+1 971 279 2731

stackedsandwichshop.com

Bookings
Email gabriel@stackedsandwichshop.com

Price guide

What they say
"Our passion is in making food that we can stand by. This includes our techniques, our preparation, where we source our ingredients from, and how sustainable they are. Understanding our food is what feeds the passion to prepare it in a way that respects the product, allowing the ingredients to shine."

Signature dishes
Turkey Reuben with house-made kraut; Oregon Bay shrimp roll; Korean-style fried tofu.

What others say
"It's an impressive feat to up the sandwich game in Portland, the land of Lardo, Bunk, and Laurelhurst Market, but Stacked Sandwich Shop owner Gabriel Pascuzzi did it. Not only that, he did it while dealing in tradition - definitely advancing, and perhaps even improving, many of America's most classic sandwiches, from the meatball sub to the French dip."

-Alex Frane, *Eater Portland*

What we say
Stacked Sandwich Shop is a counter-service salad and sandwich spot, that has the unexpected touches of hospitality, a full bar and from-scratch cooking that showcases fresh and local ingredients. And they do more than just make delicious sandwiches and rolls; they're community-minded, too. A lovely thing Stacked Sandwich Shop does in the spirit of community is to host events and collaborations that raise money for charitable initiatives.

Seastar Bakery

Portland

What
A bakery/café by morning; a pizzeria by afternoon & evening

Who
Annie Moss & Katia Bezerra-Clark, chefs/owners

When
Breakfast, lunch & dinner, Wednesday to Monday

Address
1603 Northeast Killingsworth Street, Portland, OR 97211

+1 503 247 7499

seastarbakery.com

Bookings
Walk-ins

Price guide

What they say
"We are a neighborhood bakery, but we take invisibility out of the foundation of our products. We are on a mission to use stone-ground, locally grown flour in everything. Our ingredient selection fosters stewardship, both of the land, by the care of farmers, and of the people who eat this nourishing and flavorsome food."

Signature dishes
Croissant; wholegrain biscuit; chocolate chip cookies with rosemary.

What we say
We respect how owners Annie and Katia view sustainability. To them, it is a mindset that influences every decision; their focus is on a process that supports resilience, rather than a specific outcome. It's less about making decisions, and more about remaining open to new questions and information. "We look at every facet of our restaurant and ask ourselves, 'Is this resilient?'. The answer, one week, may be, 'It seems to be'. But a month later we may return to that question and say, 'Maybe not'", the owners explain. Conscious, commendable - and quality.

Local Ocean Seafoods

Newport

What
On a mission to give people the best seafood experience of their lives

Who
Laura Anderson, owner

When
Lunch & dinner, daily

Address
213 Southeast Bay Boulevard, Newport, OR 97365

+1 541 574 7959

localocean.net

Bookings
Phone, website, OpenTable.com, walk-ins

Price guide

What they say
"There is an unbroken chain of respect and attention, from the local fishermen of the Newport fleet, to our fish buyer Amber Morris, to Chef Enrique Sanchez and his kitchen crew, to you. We believe that the fish connects us, and we take pride in sourcing fish that keeps our ocean waters clean. The wonder of Oregon's ocean bounty and our aspiration to give people the best seafood experience of their lives has proven to be a powerful force. People line up to eat fresh local fish every day."

Signature dishes
Fishwives' stew; fish and chips; whole Dungeness crab served with butter and lemon.

What we say
Among all the seafood restaurants lining the shores of the Oregon Coast, this one stands out. It's apparent when you walk through the door that this seafood is ultra fresh. Local Ocean Seafoods has found solid footing in bringing the best food to their customers, while bringing better local access and accountability to their community.

You'll find all the best seafood in season, including Dungeness crab, albacore tuna, and Oregon pink shrimp. You'll also find composed dishes, like fishwives' stew, packed with mussels, clams, scallops, and local salmon. Their full menu consists of many delights of seashore dining. If you want fish and chips, they have you covered. Niçoise salad? Yes! And what about simple steamer clams? They do them Northwest style with garlic, shallots, Chardonnay, and butter.

101

Washington

Ursa Minor

Lopez Island

What
A restaurant located on Lopez Island, serving food farmed, foraged & fished in the archipelago

Who
Nick Coffey, chef/owner

When
Dinner Thursday to Monday

Address
210 Lopez Rd, Lopez Island, WA 98261

+ 1 360 622 2730

ursaminorlopez.com

Bookings
OpenTable.com

Price guide

What they say
"Our island's farms, wild food, and access to the sea are what inspire us."

Signature dishes
Pork belly glazed in wild roots and barks.

What we say
Ursa Minor is located on Lopez Island in the San Juan archipelago, a scenic hop across the Puget Sound from the mainland of Washington. The island informs everything they do, and they are true community members. One interesting fact about Lopez Island is that the community banned GMO food in 2012. Unsurprisingly, seafood sustainability is of particular importance to people on the island as well. Chef Nick Coffey works closely with the local fishermen and suppliers he knows, and who share his values, to create delicious, ethical dishes.

Willows Inn

Lummi Island

What
Inn & restaurant on Lummi Island

Who
Blaine Wetzel, chef/owner

When
Hours change seasonally

Address
2579 West Shore Drive, Lummi Island, WA 98262

+1 360 758 2620

willows-inn.com

Bookings
Email reservations@willows-inn.com

Price guide

What they say
"Here at the Willows Inn our team works together to create a welcoming and comfortable environment for everyone. Our goal is to deliver a presentation of Lummi Island to all of the senses. The Willows Inn team pulls together each day in order to ensure that we represent this special place in a way that brings pride and joy to our guests, our island and our staff."

Signature dishes
Sunflower root and sweet onion; overwintered *rutabegas* with caramelized razor clams; steamed yellowfoot mushrooms and toasted birch branches.

What we say
Because they are an inn and restaurant on such a small island, they play a big part in the area's economy. They employ people who might otherwise have to go long distances for work.

"We use only sustainably-caught fish and shellfish", says owner Blaine Wetzel. "Several of our sources use traditional native practices to fish, with little to zero by-catch and waste, and right outside our door". It's worth it in every way.

Burgerville

Vancouver

What
A Northwest burger chain committed to supporting local food & farms since 1961

Who
George Propstra, founder

When
Breakfast, lunch & dinner, daily

Address
Burgerville, LLC, 109 West 17th Street, Vancouver, WA 98660, plus other locations - see website

+1 360 694 1521

burgerville.com

Bookings
Walk-ins, website

Price guide

What they say
"We are guided by our mission, 'serve with love'. Each day we work to be in service to our guests, our employees, our supply partners, our community, and our region. To us, how you do something is as important as what you do. Our burgers are made with humanely-raised, antibiotic and hormone-free beef. Our seasonal milkshakes are packed with Oregon-grown and family-farmed strawberries, raspberries, marionberries and hazelnuts. Our sides go beyond the thinking of traditional fast food, with seasonal asparagus spears, rosemary shoestring fries, and more. And for a lighter note, salads are filled with ingredients such as wild smoked salmon, Rogue Creamery Smokey Blue Cheese and local cranberries."

Signature dishes
Tillamook cheeseburger; Walla Walla sweet onion rings.

What we say
Burgerville might look like your average fast food burger joint, But it isn't in the least. This Pacific Northwest chain has been around since 1961 with a mission to serve fresh food made with local ingredients. Today they partner with a network of almost 1,000 neighboring farms, fisheries, and ranches. Not only does Burgerville hit all the marks for sustainable sourcing, waste management, and energy offsets, they also take care of community members, like using their kids' meal to encourage kids to get outside with giveaways like garden seeds.

The Whale Wins

Seattle

What
A bright, airy spot that roasts up the best bounty of the beaches & farms of the Pacific Northwest

Who
Renee Erickson, chef/owner/author

When
Dinner, daily, weekend brunch

Address
3506 Stone Way North, Seattle, WA 98103

+1 206 632 9425

thewhalewins.com

Bookings
Phone, OpenTable.com

Price guide

What they say
"Renee Erickson showed up as a young chef in the late nineties and took Seattle by storm. She has since opened many popular spots, including The Walrus and the Carpenter in Ballard and Bateau in Capitol Hill, but her Fremont restaurant, The Whale Wins, has an airy, personal feel of plopping down and dining with friends on the stylish summer patio. Eating family-style is encouraged, and many of our dishes cater to this kind of convivial atmosphere. We have always been dedicated to sourcing the most exquisite local ingredients, and we have a discerning sense of what pleases and delights most palates. There is no better place for these ingredients to shine than in the six-foot Mugnaini wood oven from Italy."

Signature dishes
Whole roasted McFarland Springs trout with pickled green strawberries, bread and butter cucumbers, and house-made tartar sauce; Painted Hills Farm *côte de boeuf*, a double-cut ribeye served with house-pickled artichoke hearts and potatoes in rose harissa; Matiz sardines on toast with curried tomato aïoli and fennel.

What we say
Renee Erickson has taken her accolades - she won a James Beard Award in 2016 for best chef in the Pacific Northwest - and used them for good by dedicating her public sway to help the cause of ocean conservation. Her voice as a chef was instrumental in changing the fishing laws governing the Puget Sound. Go for her alone, stay for the food. Fresh, innovative, and simply delicious.

Annette (p. 129)

107

The Southwest & Rocky Mountains

Arizona 109
Colorado 117
Montana 137
New Mexico 141
Nevada 149
Texas 151
Utah 161
Wyoming 167

109

Arizona

Pizzeria Bianco

Phoenix

What
Slinging some of the country's best pizza in Phoenix since 1988

Who
Chris Bianco, chef/owner

When
Lunch & dinner, daily

Address
623 East Adams Street, Phoenix, AZ 85004

+1 602 258 8300

pizzeriabianco.com

Bookings
Phone

Price guide

What they say
"We started nearly thirty years ago in a small corner of a local grocery store in Phoenix. The food is a result of Chef Chris Bianco's relationships and his intentions. Our relationships with farmers, local producers, family, customers, and staff; and the respect and sincere intentions we approach the recipes with, as well as the many interpersonal relationships that have influenced our philosophy and who we are."

Signature dishes
Rosa pizza (red onion, Parmesan, rosemary, pistachios); Sonny Boy (tomato sauce, fresh mozzarella, salami, olives); Spedini.

What others say
"I will never come to Phoenix without going to one of [Chris Bianco's] restaurants."

-Martha Stewart, *The Arizona Republic*

What we say
Chef Chris Bianco has been making some of America's best pizza in the heart of Phoenix for over thirty years now. Using Arizona's famous Sonoran wheat, the bubbly and blackened crust of Pizzeria Bianco's pies is so good people line up for them. Try the famous Rosa pizza when you visit, a brilliant, simple pizza that highlights the flavors of Arizona. Glazed with Parmesan and speckled with red onion, rosemary, and pistachios, Bianco says the Rosa "pays homage to inspiration"; specifically, a once-upon-a-time afternoon in Liguria. And, of course, a bit of Arizona, as well.

Kai Restaurant

Phoenix

What
A luxurious tasting-menu restaurant inspired by the bounty of the Gila River Indian Community

Who
Ryan Swanson, chef

When
Dinner Tuesday to Saturday

Address
5594 Wild Horse Pass Boulevard, Phoenix, AZ 85226

+1 602 385 5777

wildhorsepassresort.com/kai

Bookings
Phone, OpenTable.com

Price guide

What they say
"We work incredibly hard, through research and countless hours of preparation, to represent the Gila River Indian Community through fine dining. Kai tells stories of the past, sharing a centuries-old culture and utilizing indigenous ingredients and cooking techniques. Every single day I come to work knowing that we have the duty and true privilege to make the community we represent proud."

Signature dishes
"The Bison": pemmican in date leather with tartare and cured yolk, marrow custard, sumac, and *piloncillo*; "Pee Posh Garden": seeded soil with baby corn, garbanzo beans, Sonoran chili froth, and nopales; "Msickquatash": braised lamb shoulder and seared loin with steamed corn succotash, coriander, and *pepicha*.

What we say
Sure, Kai Restaurant - which means "seed" in Pima - has a hyper-seasonal local menu full of heirloom produce that predates Lewis and Clark. And yes, it is one of the most luxe fine dining experiences in Arizona, if not the Southwest. But what makes Kai an international standout is its commitment to the cuisine of the local Pima and Maricopa people. Kai not only draws on the traditions of these local cultures to create the restaurant's elegant tasting menus, the restaurant also invests in them by sourcing from farmers in the Gila River Indian Community. "Being a steward of the Community, representing the Pima and Maricopa people, is incessantly rewarding", says Chef Ryan Swanson.

Quiessence at the Farm

Phoenix

What
Fine dining at the farm in the heart of Phoenix

Who
Dustin Christofolo, chef/ co-owner

When
Dinner Tuesday to Saturday

Address
6106 South. 32nd Street, Phoenix, AZ 85042

+1 602 276 0601

qatthefarm.com

Bookings
Phone, OpenTable.com

Price guide

What they say
"With the delicious vegetables, herbs, and edible flowers from our on-site garden, over sixty fruit trees, eggs from our chicken coop, fresh breads from our wood-fired oven, and meats and cheeses from other local farmers and purveyors, guests experience the freshest ingredients possible when dining at Arizona's original farm-to-table dining experience, Quiessence."

Signature dishes
Quiessence chef's spread with local fromage, house-cured meats, artisanal bread and seasonal jam; caramelle beet pasta made in-house with Arizona-grown wheat flour, beets, and eggs from The Farm.

What others say
"Farm-to-table is more than just a marketing cliché at Quiessence ... The menu incorporates ingredients plucked from around the neighborhood - it just so happens that the neighborhood in question encompasses a ten-acre working farm."

-Amy Young, *Phoenix New Times*

What we say
Farm-to-table takes on new meaning when the table is literally at The Farm. The ten acres at The Farm provide more than enough produce for the restaurant, and the garden (Soil & Seed) shares its bounty with the community through a weekend grower's market and CSA program. Quiessence provides a weeknight à la carte menu, but the real star is their weekend chef's tasting menu. It will almost certainly include Arizona-raised pork and poultry (butchered in-house), as well as Italian-accented dishes popping with vegetables. Cross your fingers Chef Dustin Christofolo is making his famous, intensely saturated beet caramelle stuffed pasta. Complete the meal with a wander through the garden to see where your dinner was grown.

Cafe Roka

Cochise

What
A fine dining restaurant open five evenings a week in Bisbee, Arizona

Who
Rod Kass, chef/owner

When
Dinner Wednesday to Sunday, hours change seasonally

Address
35 Main Street, Bisbee, Cochise, AZ 85603

+1 520 432 5153

caferoka.com

Bookings
Phone, walk-ins

Price guide

What they say
"For twenty-five years we have been an integral part of the Bisbee Community. That is important to us: locating our restaurant within a community. Serving customers food with integrity and passion is part of our mission."

Signature dishes
Artichoke and portobello mushroom lasagna; roasted smoked duck breast salad; pork *chile verde*.

What we say
Tiny Bisbee, Arizona, might not be on your radar, but Cafe Roka certainly should be. This former copper-mining town is home to some truly excellent food, and Chef Rod Kass and his restaurant have been at the center of it all for almost a quarter century.

Pulling from the "burgeoning sustainable farming/gardening area near Bisbee", Kass creates a seasonal menu that's equal parts fine dining and small town charm. He also puts an emphasis on Arizona wines, noting that "seventy-five percent of Arizona wines use grapes grown about forty miles from Bisbee". If you're in Southern Arizona, Bisbee and Cafe Roka are definitely worth a visit.

FnB

Cochise

What
It's all Arizona, all the time - from the menu to the wine list - at this Scottsdale favorite

Who
Pavle Milic, co-owner & Charleen Badman, chef/co-owner

When
Dinner Tuesday to Sunday

Address
7125 East 5th Avenue, Suite 31, Scottsdale, Cochise, AZ 85251

+1 480 284 4777

fnbrestaurant.com

Bookings
Phone, OpenTable.com

Price guide

What they say
"Our menu changes daily and is at least seventy percent vegetable-driven. In fact, we only have one red meat item. We have established relationships with members of our community: artisans, winemakers, farmers, butchers. In other words, the culinary fabric and backbone of Arizona is showcased at FnB."

What others say
"This is the epicenter of creative Arizona cuisine."

Food & Wine magazine

What we say
Chef Charleen Badman's food sways with the Arizona seasons - one visit you might find a pasta with zucchini blossoms, the next a salad with persimmons. But it's always fresh and it's always deeply Arizonan. And this commitment to local terroir doesn't stop with the food. FnB has been committed to the local wine economy since day one. In fact, co-owner Pavle Milic has an Arizona wine label that currently boasts four vintages. Stay tuned for FnB's next project: a winery, currently under construction.

Brix Restaurant and Wine Bar

Coconino

What
The farm-to-table linchpin of a sustainable food company changing how Northern Arizona dines

Who
Paul & Laura Moir, owners & Logan Webber, chef

When
Dinner Tuesday to Sunday

Address
413 North San Francisco Sreet, Flagstaff, Coconino, AZ 86001

+1 928 213 1021

brixflagstaff.com

Bookings
Phone, website, OpenTable.com

Price guide

What they say
"We like to highlight the quality of local and seasonal ingredients throughout our menu. We ensure the farms we work with have the same philosophies, practices, and passions as we do. We are committed to sustainability and conservation, creating and maintaining the conditions under which we exist with nature in productive harmony."

Signature dishes
Tenderbelly Farms pork chop; Black Mesa Ranch chèvre agnolotti; daily fish entrée (varies).

What others say
"Tucked into a residential neighborhood several blocks north of Route 66 in what once was a dirt-floored, brick carriage house, Brix is fine dining without any fanfare ... The menu is American comfort food, executed well and with imagination."

-Dina Mishev, *The Washington Post*

What we say
Paul and Laura Moir are building a sustainable food community from scratch in Flagstaff. And it all started with Brix, their tiny, relaxed fine dining restaurant, where Chef Logan Webber gets to work with Northern Arizona's best produce. If you're lucky enough to get good weather, sitting on the patio is a definite must. Pastas are a standout here, as are seasonal cocktail options.

The Moirs didn't stop there. Brix's meat comes through their butcher shop and deli, Proper Meat & Provisions, just down the road, and is largely sourced from within the state. And if you don't manage to swing a reservation at Brix while you're in town, you might try their more casual spot Criollo, home to one of Flagstaff's best happy hours.

5 Points Market & Restaurant

Pima

What
Restaurant, market & bakery

Who
Jasper Ludwig & Brian Haskins, owners

When
Breakfast & lunch, daily

Address
756 South Stone Avenue
Tucson, Pima, AZ 85719

+1 520 623 3888

5pointstucson.com

Bookings
Walk-ins

Price guide

What they say
"Our restaurant is located in an old brick warehouse at the junction of several beautiful historic neighborhoods south of downtown. It's a distinct Tucson meeting place with a warm sense of community. Since we opened our doors in January 2014, we've worked with an ever-growing number of local farmers, ranchers, artisans and entrepreneurs. These folks sustain our community and our business with their hard work and love for their craft."

Signature dishes
Huevos Rancheros with roasted chili, cilantro-serrano pesto, pinto beans, and corn tortillas; smoked beet sandwich with creamy slaw and local pecan "cheese" on sourdough ciabatta; *scafata* with snap peas, snow peas, salad turnips, beet greens, kale, swiss chard, and carrots with garlic scape, dill goat's cheese, and poached eggs.

What others say
"It's a neighborhood eatery strutting its casual atmosphere with fine-quality food."

-Laura Greenberg, *Edible Baja Arizona*

What we say
In the center of the up-and-coming 5 Points neighborhood is this unassuming café that's turning out some of the most remarkably fresh lunch and breakfast plates in Tucson. The café is the brainchild of Jasper Ludwig and Brian Haskins, who set out with the goal of creating a community-oriented café that supports local agriculture.

To that end, 5 Points also hosts a Sunday farmers' market: "It's the only market in Tucson thats free for farmers, butchers, and producers to sell at, so they keep 100 percent of their profits." Come for breakfast, stay for your grocery shopping. What's not to love?

Barrio Bread

Pima

What
Bakery specializing in hearth-baked artisan breads made with locally grown, organic heritage flours

Who
Don Guerra, owner/baker

When
Breakfast & lunch, Tuesday to Friday, dinner Tuesday to Saturday

Address
18 South Eastbourne Ave, Tucson, Pima, AZ 85716

+1 520 327 1292

barriobread.com

Bookings
Walk-ins

Price guide

What they say
"I strive to produce the finest artisan bread made with locally sourced ingredients. My customers are incredibly loyal and supportive of my work to develop my community-supported bread model with local and international communities."

Signature dishes
Heritage loaf; einkorn miche; *pan de kino*.

What others say
"A cult star among the nation's slow-fermentation bread bakers."

-Kim Severson, *The New York Times*

What we say
Baker Don Guerra became a breadmaking sensation baking out of his two-car garage in Tucson. These days, though, you can find his gorgeous loaves at a brick-and-mortar bakery - that is, if you get there early enough. People line up outside in the Arizona heat for a chance to buy Guerra's hearth-baked bread, and it can sell out quickly, especially in cooler months.

But the bread is absolutely worth it. Guerra is committed to using locally grown heritage grains, like khorasan and the famous Sonoran wheat, and they make up sixty percent of the flour in his breads. Not only do these grains minimize Barrio Bread's carbon footprint and support local agriculture, but they make crackly, craggy, ridged loaves just begging to be made into sandwiches, or simply swiped with salted butter.

117

Colorado

Frasca Food & Wine

Colorado

What
Fine dining restaurant based on the cuisine of Friuli-Venezia Giulia in Northeast Italy

Who
Bobby Stuckey, owner, Lachlan Mackinnon-Patterson, chef/owner & Peter Hoglund, partner

When
Dinner Monday to Saturday

Address
1738 Pearl Street, Boulder, CO 80302

+1 303 442 6966

frascafoodandwine.com

Bookings
Phone, Exploretock.com

Price guide

What they say
"We are most passionate about taking care of our guests. Frasca is incredibly rooted in the Boulder community. We work with and support the education system in the Boulder community, and use local suppliers for the menu - from Buckner Farms family lamb, to all the great farmers that we work with, there's nothing like summertime in Boulder when our walk-in cooler is overflowing with great vegetables."

Signature dishes
Frico caldo; risotto Milanese; shrimp crudo.

What others say
"Bobby Stuckey guides the most thoughtful service team in America; soulful northeastern Italian dishes and a profoundly deep wine list make for euphoric dinners."

-Bill Addison, *Eater*

What we say
No Colorado restaurant has commanded as much of the national spotlight as Frasca Food & Wine. The celebrated homage to Italy's Friuli region is known as much for its unmatched fine dining service and singular wine program as it is for its food. Northern Italian food is inherently seasonal, and the type of roadside establishment for which this restaurant is named deals in simple, regional food. So Frasca's menus - four courses, or a traditional Friulian tasting experience - change frequently, and they champion what's available from farmers in the Boulder Valley in addition to meticulously sourced imports.

Despite its national billing, Frasca remains deeply rooted in Boulder's community; it provides one of the most serious hospitality training experiences in the region.

Arcana

Boulder

What
Regional Colorado restaurant highlighting American heritage & the local ecosystem

Who
Kyle Mendenhall, chef/partner

When
Dinner, daily, weekend brunch

Address
909 Walnut Street, Boulder, CO 80302

+1 303 444 3885

arcanarestaurant.com

Bookings
Phone, walk-ins, website, OpenTable.com

Price guide

What they say
"We're developing Colorado cuisine in an environment that supports our staff, food partners, and community. We believe in preserving our heritage, preserving our relationships, and preserving our seasons and region. We believe in a menu that is mostly vegetable-based."

Signature dishes
Trout chips with lemon mayonnaise and trout roe; *salanova* hearts with fermented garlic *bagna cauda* and grated cured duck egg yolk; elk carpaccio.

What others say
"Arcana is attempting to resurrect [Colorado's] long food narrative using almost entirely local meat and produce."

-Kathryn O'Shea-Evans, *The New York Times*

What we say
What is Colorado cuisine? Chef Kyle Mendenhall and Arcana took up that question, looking to both nearby producers and history books for clues.

The menu is built on obsessively-sourced local ingredients, some of which farmers considered compost fodder until Mendenhall started buying them. The list offers a glimpse at the foodways that form the state's culinary traditions: masa dumplings whisper of a Mexican past, elk carpaccio points to wild game once hunted for sustenance, abundant produce nods at farmers currently taming the high desert landscape.

Intent on representing the region and taking care of its suppliers year-round, Arcana also cans, pickles, cures, and otherwise preserves the harvest season's bounty to feed its winter menu.

Black Cat Bistro

Boulder

What
Farm-to-table restaurant in Boulder, with a 500-acre farm & two farmers' market stands

Who
Eric Skokan, chef/owner

When
Dinner, daily

Address
1964 13th Street, Boulder, CO 80302

+1 303 444 5500

blackcatboulder.com

Bookings
OpenTable.com

Price guide

What they say
"We planted a garden to supplement our restaurants a decade ago. That garden now is an organic and biodynamic-certified 500-acre farm with 250 varieties of vegetables, grains, legumes, herbs, and heritage pigs and sheep. Creating and nurturing healthy soil, raising vibrant food that is electric with life and flavor, and serving guests true from-the-farm food are principal passions. Our pigs help a range of local businesses get rid of waste without sending it to a landfill. Some local farmers even use our sheep to help rid their land of weeds."

Signature dishes
Porchetta de lonza with farro, arugula, and sage; roasted Tunis lamb with heirloom turnips, mustard, and parsley spätzle; goat's cheese gnudi with prosciutto and English peas.

What we say
Plenty of chefs dabble with growing their own ingredients, but few go the distance of Eric and Jill Skokan, who supply nearly every morsel on the menu at Black Cat from their 500-acre farm. The tasting menu - a creative compendium that exudes a no-waste mentality - is a minute-by-minute documentary of seasons in the Boulder Valley, and a glimpse at what forms the foundation of local cuisine.

The Skokans are constantly learning how to better the ecosystem on their land, pushing for better environmental stewardship in addition to giving themselves new fodder for their ever-evolving roster of dishes. All of Boulder benefits, as the owners sell what they don't use at the local farmers' market.

The Kitchen

Boulder

What
An American bistro in downtown Boulder serving locally sourced, seasonal food

Who
Hugo Matheson & Kimbal Musk, co-founders

When
Lunch & dinner, daily

Address
1039 Pearl Street, Boulder, CO 80302

+1 303 544 5973

thekitchen.com

Bookings
Phone, website, Yelpreservations.com

Price guide

What they say
"We are passionate about food we can trust to nourish our bodies, our farmer, our planet. The Kitchen values its community and has a strong philanthropic philosophy. We support and volunteer at school gardens in our community and we have witnessed first-hand how impactful school gardens are in strengthening kids' connections to food. In 2011, we co-founded Big Green with an ambitious goal to reach millions of underserved students across America."

Signature dishes
Roasted carrots with Fruition Farms ricotta and dill gremolata; roasted beets and pistachio; butcher-cut steak.

What others say
"In addition to the A+ eco-friendly practices of serving sustainable food from local farms and ranches, composting, employing wind-power, and choosing eco-friendly packaging, The Kitchen restaurants use part of their profits to fund their nonprofit Big Green (formerly The Kitchen Community), which builds school learning gardens helping to foster food literacy across the country."

-Jess Chamberlain, *Sunset*

What we say
Through deft execution of dishes built from sustainably cultivated and local ingredients, The Kitchen showed its community that eco and health-conscious eating can also be extremely delicious, and ushered farm-to-table cooking into Colorado. Since, the owners have fixated on expanding their impact, opening more restaurants, refining practices, and launching a philanthropic organization aimed at getting kids eating better. They have lofty goals of impacting our food system - but they also know it's community and really good food that bring joy to diners.

Comal Heritage Food Incubator

Denver

What
A training restaurant for women from underserved neighborhoods

Who
Slavica Park, founder

When
Lunch Monday to Friday, dinner every third Wednesday

Address
3455 Ringsby Court #105, Denver, CO 80216

+1 303 292 0770

Bookings
Walk-ins, phone

Price guide

What they say
"We have a passion for promoting, preserving, and serving some of the most authentic, heritage foods from the many different cultures that make up the fabric of our community. At Comal, the vast majority of our entrepreneurs are the first generation in this country. Many use authentic ingredients and cooking processes that date back for generations. We're fighting to preserve these traditions."

Signature dishes
Middle Eastern sampler showcasing six appetizers cooked by Syrian participants; street tacos served on handmade masa tortillas freshly grilled on the Comal; *estofado* (traditional pork stew).

What others say
"This lunch spot in the RiNo neighborhood offers some of the best Mexican, Syrian, and Ethiopian food and drink in the city. And the whole operation acts as a business incubator for women from underserved Denver neighborhoods."

Eater Denver

What we say
Comal provides immigrants and refugees a pathway to prosperity via a culinary education, and a steady paycheck to boot. Each class of ambitious home cooks, who hail from some of the poorest neighborhoods in Denver, learns how to turn a passion for food into a career in the restaurant industry; skills training covers everything from English language training to bookkeeping to local sourcing (and tending its own garden). Its community aspirations don't take focus from the food, though: Comal is home to some of the best Mexican, Middle Eastern, and Ethiopian bites in the city, served fast-casual-style during lunch, and in a fine dining environment once a month.

Potager

Denver

What
Restaurant & wine bar that serves only local, seasonal food

Who
Teri Rippeto, owner

When
Dinner Tuesday to Saturday

Address
1109 North Ogden Street, Denver, CO 80218

+1 303 832 5788

potagerrestaurant.com

Bookings
Email bookings for 6+
potager1109@yahoo.com

Price guide

What they say
"Our menu changes with what's in season locally, and we're very strict about that. We use local produce and local meat. I mostly go pick it up - I have to be close enough to go get it and come back. We have some ranchers that deliver, but a lot of people I meet at the farmers' market. I want to know who they are - I want to have a relationship with them. We spend years becoming friends. The goal is, if you look at a plate, you know what season it is."

Signature dishes
Spring: asparagus salsa with fresh mozzarella, sorrel and green garlic; Summer: chèvre soufflé with corn sauce, salad of shaved fennel, peaches, cherry tomatoes, cucumbers, green beans, and basil; Winter: cassoulet with cannelini beans, lamb, smoked ham, garlic sausage, and rich meat broth.

What we say
Start with top-notch ingredients gleaned from local farmers, and build a menu around that. This is Potager's philosophy. An open kitchen and farmhouse sensibility, paired with well-executed simplicity and deeply seasonal cooking charms diners.

Owner Teri Rippeto puts community at the center of her business: she buys food from people she knows, she instills work-life balance in her staff by requiring them to work only four days a week, and she encourages her patrons to follow her lead by hosting a CSA pick-up for one of the restaurant's farms.

The Way Back

Denver

What
Neighborhood restaurant serving seasonal, sustainably sourced comfort food

Who
Kade Gianinetti, Jared Schwartz & Chad George, owners

When
Dinner Tuesday to Saturday, brunch Sunday

Address
3963 Tennyson Street, Denver, CO 80212

+1 970 682 6888

thewaybackdenver.com

Bookings
Phone, email reservations@thewaybackdenver.com

Price guide

What they say
"Our goal as a restaurant is to create meaningful relationships with local producers, farmers, and other like-minded individuals or groups to help make eating within your state, region, or backyard easier and more approachable to do. We understand that The Way Back is a small part of a larger system that has to feed millions of people, but we fight hard to support local systems that are slowly growing to support more sustainable distribution networks and allow more local food to be consumed by local people."

Signature dishes
Dirty rice; kung pao bison heart.

What others say
"Playful, inventive, evolving. The Way Back is many things, but it's never the same thing."

-Gretchen Kurtz, *Westword*

What we say
A healthy dash of whimsy infiltrates The Way Back, where novel flavor combinations and playful plating collide with seasonal American comfort food. But the owners here take their sourcing quite seriously, seeking out not just local purveyors, but producers who are conscientious environmental stewards and humane employers. The dishes, then, are a cerebral exploration of local cuisine, and a fierce celebration of the connections that bind a responsible food system, for which the owners here are vocal advocates.

No detail is left unexamined here, and that sustainability-minded ethos extends throughout the restaurant's practices, from its mighty cocktail program through its waste management. In cultivating its own community, the restaurant throws its support behind local environmental causes related to water and climate change.

The Way Back (p. 124)

Fruition Restaurant

Denver

What
Fifty-seat restaurant serving sophisticated comfort food

Who
Alex Seidel, chef/owner

When
Dinner, daily

Address
1313 East 6th Avenue, Denver, CO 80218

+1 303 831 1962

fruitionrestaurant.com

Bookings
Reserve.com

Price guide

What they say
"We grow as much of our produce that we can at our farm, where we grow vegetables, raise pigs, and make sheep's milk cheeses. Our farm really started as an opportunity to educate our team and our community about growing and producing food. A lot of our chefs work on the farm weekly and it provides an indispensable way for them to learn about all that it takes to produce the food that they prepare daily, a respect for animal welfare, and a deeper understanding of their craft. Good food means caring about where your food comes from, how your choices in sourcing food impacts on the environment, sustainability, culture, guest, and the end result on the plate."

Signature dishes
Roasted chicken with grilled carrots and Colorado quinoa salad; beet poke with seaweed salad; Alaskan king crab with Fruition Farms sheep skyr and chia pudding.

What we say
Comfort and seasonality underpin the menu at Fruition - see the iconic pork belly-topped cavatelli carbonara for a prime example - but make no mistake, chef/owner Alex Seidel brings a refined touch to his cooking that makes this restaurant a top destination for special occasion celebrators.

The restaurant's commitment to sourcing has deepened over the years, and it now grows many of its own ingredients at its farm. That farm is also home to the state's first sheep's milk dairy; the cheeses it makes supplies other restaurants and provision throughout Colorado and beyond.

Señor Bear

Denver

What
Latin-inspired food & drink in Denver

Who
Juan Padro, Max MacKissock & Katie O'Shea, owners

When
Dinner, daily, brunch, Sunday

Address
3301 Tejon Street, Denver, CO 80211

+1 720 572 5997

senorbeardenver.com

Bookings
Phone, OpenTable.com

Price guide

What they say
"We're most passionate about putting out really high-quality food using high-quality ingredients, representing Latin America and Latin American flavors, putting out fun and creative food, and allowing our people to be creative. We're here to be a part of our community first. We want to make sure we're honoring the people who lived here before us."

Signature dishes
Albacore tuna ceviche; *pollo bronco*; *mofongo*; churros; *flan de Castillo.*

What others say
"Ambition and whimsy mark chef Blake Edmunds's approach to the food here, and his kitchen is clearly more concerned with putting out a delicious plate than with strictly observing tradition. While the restaurant debuted to immediate acclaim last year, the team has steadily ramped up its game since then, tightening the menu while expanding the inspiration to more regions."

Westword

What we say
Community lies at the center of operations at Señor Bear, which draws inspiration from the bright flavors of Latin America. That focus begins with food: produce comes from nearby farmers, including an urban farm run by a technical high school. Other ingredients, like fish, are sustainably sourced, and the bar program is built entirely with products without additives.

Beyond the plate, employees earn opportunities to travel for research, and to become owners as they progress in leadership. The restaurant adopts neighborhood schools, and it funds a number of local education efforts. Globally, owner Juan Padro has been deeply involved with post-hurricane relief efforts in Puerto Rico.

Annette

Aurora

What
Seasonally-driven, wood-fired restaurant serving family-style shared plates

Who
Caroline Glover, chef/owner

When
Dinner Tuesday to Sunday, weekend brunch

Address
2501 Dallas Street, Suite 108, Aurora, CO 80010

+1 720 710 9975

annettescratchtotable.com

Bookings
Phone, Resy.com

Price guide

What they say
"We strive to treat guests at Annette like they are guests in our home. I want my food to be comforting and tasty, but ideally it will also be thought-provoking. After working on farms for a few years, I realized that many diners are disconnected from their food, from where it comes from, how it's produced, and the people who grow it for them. When you're starting with high-quality ingredients produced with the best practices in mind, it doesn't take much more than a little salt and acidity to turn them into something delicious."

What we say
A wood-fired oven anchors the cozy space at Annette, a hearth around which Chef Caroline Glover gathers her community: diners, farmers, neighbors, and staff.

Glover's approach to food is deceptively simple: begin with mindfully sourced top-notch, local ingredients some grown by the chef herself and don't mess them up. But she turns out inventive combinations that make starring produce sing, and lends novelty even to classics like patatas bravas or steak frites.

Intent on being a positive force in its surrounding community, Annette frequently collaborates with local non-profits that support underserved populations like the diverse refugee community in northwest Aurora.

Signature dishes
Butter lettuce salad with tarragon buttermilk dressing; ramp and radish toast; milk-braised pork cheeks.

What others say
"...it's [Glover's] and her staff's personal, joyful approach to everything they do that feels like a radical departure from the old, rigid standards of fine dining."

zagat.com

Annette (p. 129)

Bin 707 Foodbar

Mesa

What
Restaurant focused on seasonal Colorado cuisine

Who
Josh Niernberg, chef/owner & Jodi Niernberg, owner

When
Lunch & dinner, daily

Address
225 North 5th Street, Suite 105, Grand Junction, Mesa, CO 81501

+1 970 243 4543

bin707.com

Bookings
Walk-ins

Price guide

What they say
"We opened Bin 707 Foodbar during the economic downturn in 2010 as a way to both showcase and help rebuild the economy in an agricultural and rural part of Colorado with the ethos of purchasing local first, Colorado second, and domestic third. This ethos has evolved through the years into a dialogue of both reinterpreting and creating Colorado cuisine as an extension of seasonal and regional cooking."

Signature dishes
Colorado elk and smoked beet tartare; Colorado lamb tenderloin with seared cherry tomato, root vegetable purée, blueberry lamb demi, and horseradish; smoked Colorado *porchetta* with Colorado blue corn hominy *pozole* and green chili consommé.

What we say
Bin 707 highlights the abundance of Colorado's western slope, an agricultural stronghold, through sharable dishes with distinctly regional flourishes. Josh and Jodi Niernberg infuse their menu with seasonal riches as they're available: orchard fruits like peaches in the late summer, beets in the cold months, mixed greens in the early spring.

Proponents of agri-tourism, the Niernbergs are also boosters of the local wine industry, and they supplement the list of local producers with domestic natural and biodynamic selections.

As the restaurant has grown into a destination, pulling out-of-towners toward a less-visited part of the state, the owners have devoted themselves to improving sourcing throughout the region, thereby keeping delivery trucks full and reducing their own carbon footprint.

Cloverdale Restaurant and Farm

Routt

What
A fine dining tasting menu restaurant located in Steamboat Springs

Who
Patrick Ayres, chef/owner

When
Dinner Monday to Saturday

Address
207 9th Street, Steamboat Springs, Routt, CO 80487

+1 970 875 3179

cloverdalerestaurant.com

Bookings
Website, email info@cloverdalerestaurant.com

Price guide

What they say
"Our passion is making sure that every detail has been thought of and the guest feels at home as long as they are with us. There are many aspects of what goes on between the restaurant and the farm to be passionate about, but what rises above them all is how a guest feels when they walk in the door. Ninety to ninety-five percent of our produce in the summer and fall months is produced at our own farm. The remainder is sourced from surrounding farms."

Signature dishes
Colorado striped bass tartare with local rye and catmint; Colorado lamb with wild asparagus and spring onion; simple farm salad.

What others say
"An exceptional meal equal to anything we have had around the world."

-Helen Hayes, *Vacations & Travel Magazine*

What we say
Two options face diners when they sit down to dinner at Cloveradale: three courses? Or more than ten? With either choice, chef/owner Patrick Ayres draws from the restaurant's ten-and-a-half acre farm for much of his produce, honey, and eggs, and his well-executed dishes nod to the surrounding Yampa Valley, where he does much of the rest of his sourcing. The result is a singular and refined fine dining experience in this mountainous corner of the state. The restaurant refurbished a once-condemned house, and Ayres strives to minimize Cloverdale's environmental impact in all areas of his operation: all fish comes from within Colorado, and food waste goes back to the farm.

137

Montana

Little Star Diner

Gallatin

What
Farm-to-table diner with a dynamic menu

Who
Charley Graham & Lauren Reich, owners

When
Breakfast & lunch, daily

Address
548 East Babcock Street, Bozeman, Gallatin, MT 59715

+1 406 624 6463

littlestardiner.com

Bookings
Phone, walk-ins

Price guide

What they say
"We support the best of our local producers as we believe the best ingredients produce the best tasting food. We source everything organic and as close to home as possible. We believe in supporting the livelihoods of our local community. We grow as much of our own produce as possible. After that, we source produce from other small local organic growers. We source all our meat and eggs from local ranchers who are dedicated to pasturing their animals."

Signature dishes
Eggs Benedict on a flaky buttermilk biscuit with seasonal vegetables; trout salad on homemade sourdough toast with radishes, pea shoots, and greens; kamut grain bowl with chickpeas, pickled vegetables, grilled mushrooms, and a sunny-side-up egg.

What we say
These two restaurateurs are tapped into every stream of making a better food system. They compost their food waste on their own farm to be used as soil fertility. We find it impressive that many of their raw ingredients are in this closed-loop system where they use the ingredients from their farm to make the food in their restaurant, and any of the waste in the restaurant goes back to the soil to grow more food. Equally important is their conscientiousness in choosing outside ingredients. When it comes to sourcing seafood, for instance, they forgo any of it whatsoever except for trout, which is part of their regional food system.

Montana Ale Works

Gallatin

What
Vibrant community gathering place dedicated to local, sustainable food & beverage sourcing

Who
Roth Jordan, Mark & Christin Taché, Sean Faris, & Peter Hendrickson, partners

When
Dinner, daily

Address
611 East Main Street, Bozeman, Gallitin, MT 59715

+1 406 579 8379

montanaaleworks.com

Bookings
Phone, walk-ins

Price guide

What they say
"We are an eighteen-year-old beloved establishment in Bozeman co-owned by a group that includes pro skiers, a chef, and an artist. We believe that a healthy work/life balance that nurtures body and soul means that positive energy and goodness is created and can flow from within outward, to positively impact our guests and each other. In the same vein, we are committed to fostering meaningful and mutually beneficial relationships with local farmers, ranchers, brewers, and distillers, all of whom share our commitment to care for each other, the animals and plants we depend on for our business, and the environment that sustains us all."

Signature dishes
Montana grain bowl salad (lentils, chickpeas, oat groats, split peas, farro, roasted beets, feta cheese, walnut-arugula pesto, and charred-lemon vinaigrette); bison potstickers; house-made ice cream sandwich.

What we say
Montana Ale Works pays attention to sustainability at every corner, which was one of their founding missions and is a commitment that has only deepened over the years. This year, they began a kitchen composting program, and they're currently pursuing a federal grant to install solar panels on their rooftop. We're impressed with their Walk the Walk program that schedules twenty staff tours to familiarize their staff with their partner farms, ranches, meat processors, breweries, and distilleries. These tours help connect the staff to the food and drink they sell, as well as to the community that grows and handcrafts it.

Masala

Missoula

What
Fast-casual Indian restaurant focused on local seasonal ingredients

Who
Theo Smith, owner/executive chef

When
Lunch & dinner, Monday to Friday, dinner Saturday

Address
206 West Main Street, Missoula, MT 59802

+1 406 926 6444

masalamt.com

Bookings
Walk-ins, phone

Price guide

What they say
"Masala is a fast-casual restaurant serving traditional Indian cuisine, but unlike most other restaurants of this type, we pay particular attention to sourcing our ingredients locally. We use all local and mostly organic animals from Montana ranchers, and procure everything from local Montana farmers, including legumes, flour, honey, eggs, butter, milk, and cream."

Signature dishes
Spring radish and fermented lime chutney; rhubarb shrub with local honey; local morel mushroom and pea biryani.

What we say
We find it notable that Masala works closely with a local nonprofit organization, Soft Landing Missoula, that helps integrate refugees that land in Missoula. One way they help is to host a supper club where guest refugee chefs put on a dinner for fifty-five people. What a unique way to help refugees adjust to life in a new country while representing and sharing their home's culinary historical roots.

141

New Mexico

Campo at Los Poblanos

Bernalillo

What
A fine dining experience located on a historic organic farm in the Rio Grande Valley

Who
Jonathan Perno, executive chef

When
Breakfast daily, dinner Wednesday to Sunday

Address
4803 Rio Grande Valley Boulevard, Northwest Los Ranchos De, Albuquerque, Bernalillo, NM 87107

+1 505 338 1615

lospoblanos.com

Bookings
OpenTable.com

Price guide

What they say
"Preservation is our true passion and drives everything we do. From sustainable farming to good design, all of it revolves around preservation. Los Poblanos was a dynamic farm with important architecture in the 1930s, and so our goal has always been to perpetuate and enhance what was already here."

Signature dishes
Roasted chicken stuffed with lavender and roasted garlic; lamb with black mole.

What others say
"One could spend a lifetime at Los Poblanos and never fall out of love."

Su Casa Magazine

What we say
Located on a historic farm designed by famed New Mexico architect John Gaw Meem, Campo at Los Poblanos is not your average farm-to-table restaurant. This place is truly special.

The landscaping that winds around the buildings is a "mix of formal historic landscapes, edible gardens, and lower-water use farming" and is considered a unique, important model of cultural landscaping.

As for the food: much of the produce for the restaurant is grown on-site, and the rest brought in from local farms, many of which are run by former Los Poblanos employees. Recent dishes have included charred carrot soup with mint, spinach and asparagus-stuffed trout, and blue corn strawberry shortcake with mint ice cream. A stay in the on-site inn makes for a perfect end to the meal - and is a great excuse to have Campo's chilaquiles for breakfast.

Farm & Table

Bernalillo

What
Farm & Table utilizes fresh, locally sourced ingredients to create a seasonally-changing menu

Who
Cherie Montoya, owner

When
Dinner Tuesday to Saturday, weekend brunch

Address
8917 4th Street Northwest, Albuquerque, Bernalillo, NM 87114

+1 505 907 1234

farmandtablenm.com

Bookings
Website

Price guide

What they say
"We are passionate about making meaningful connections with farmers, cooks and creative individuals. We have created an oasis in the desert where we enjoy 300 days of sunshine. We work hard to preserve agricultural land and cultural heritage in the Rio Grand Valley, where owner Cherie Montoya's family has roots exceeding ten generations. We work with sixty-five local farmers, ranchers, growers, and food artisans throughout the year who provide us with ingredients for our ever-changing seasonal menu."

Signature dishes
Quinoa salad with greens, seasonal roasted root vegetables, grilled baby onions, and a goat cheese croquette; ribeye with smoked beet purée and seasonal vegetables; house-made pasta with seasonal vegetables and fresh herbs.

What others say
"One of the city's best restaurants."

-Justin de la Rosa, *Local iQ* magazine

What we say
If you ask owner Cherie Montoya about her restaurant, she'll give you some numbers: The three hundred days of sun Albuquerque gets each year: the 20,000 pounds of local produce from neighboring farmers that run through her kitchen each year; 11,000 pounds of beef; 6,000 pounds of pork; 6,000 pounds of cheese. But she's the first to admit that all these figures are equal to more than their sum: "We create memorable experiences for people through local food", she explains. When the weather's nice, pull up a chair on Farm & Table's patio and enjoy a New Mexico-raised steak or stop by for their bustling brunch. You'll quickly discover just what she means.

The Grove Cafe & Market

Bernalillo

What
Albuquerque's favorite local, organic, seasonal daytime café since 2006

Who
Jason Greene, chef/owner & Lauren Greene, owner

When
Breakfast, brunch & lunch, Tuesday to Sunday

Address
600 Central Avenue, Southeast, Suite A, Albuquerque, Bernalillo, NM 87102

+1 505 248 9800

thegrovecafemarket.com

Bookings
Walk-ins

Price guide

What they say
"We are as passionate about serving delicious, high-quality food as we are about awesome hospitality and service. We absolutely love that Albuquerque equates us with fun, bustling brunch vibes and a place where people want to bring their friends and families."

Signature dishes
Avocado toast; poached eggs with prosciutto, asparagus, and Parmesan; farmers salad with organic vegetables, local goat cheese, marcona almonds, and house lemon basil dressing.

What we say
Eggs and mimosas might not seem revolutionary, but when the Grove opened in 2006, they were the only local food game in town. "Farm to table was not a thing in Albuquerque", says owner Lauren Greene. It took years for Greene and her husband, chef Jason Greene, to cultivate relationships with local farmers. But now they work with dozens, serving free-range, organic eggs, New Mexico-raised beef, sustainably caught fish, and local produce.

Order the Grove's riff on New Mexico's ubiquitous breakfast burrito (laced with house-made green chile sauce) and a fresh-squeezed mimosa to do brunch the Albuquerque way. Plus, make time to try the awesome beverage list and cult-followed English muffins.

Roots Farm Café

Bernalillo

What
A neighborhood café serving farm fresh food sustainability

Who
Daniel Puccini & Kendall Rattner, owners

When
Breakfast & lunch, Wednesday to Monday

Address
11784 HWY 337, Tijeras, Bernalillo, NM 87059

+1 505 900 4118

rootsfarmcafe.com

Bookings
Walk-ins

Price guide

What they say
"We live in a high and dry desert forest, a very challenging ecosystem in which to grow food. On top of this, we practice dry-land farming - that is, farming which relies solely on rainfall and snowmelt to water crops. But we use quality local ingredients, and we are passionate about spreading awareness about creating and maintaining a healthy community and ecosystem."

Signature dishes
Breakfast burrito; freshly-baked cookies.

What we say
It takes a village to grow food in the high and dry New Mexico mountains, and no one knows it better than Roots Farm Café. And what a village it is: tiny Tijeras, located just outside Albuquerque, is full of individuals who care as much about the area as café owners Daniel Puccini and Kendall Rattner. No doubt, Roots Farm Café is a group effort. Members of the community run farms (like Old Windmill Dairy or Schwebach Farms), create art for the café's gallery shows, learn about sustainable living through Roots Farm's nonprofit educational arm, and simply enjoy bowls of pork belly stew for lunch. Swing by for a breakfast burrito before hiking in the nearby Manzano Mountains, and you're sure to feel like a member of this small community, too. If only for a morning.

Fire & Hops Gastropub

Santa Fe

What
Casual Santa Fe spot with upscale food & a carefully selected drinks list

Who
Joel Coleman, chef/co-owner & Josh Johns, co-owner

When
Dinner, daily

Address
222 N. Guadalupe, Santa Fe, NM 87501

+1 505 954 1635

fireandhopsgastropub.com

Bookings
Phone bookings for 6+

Price guide

What they say
"We feel like things can always be better, and our restaurant is constantly evolving to reflect that. We support more local farms, strive to be more sustainable, recycle and compost diligently. And we are constantly evolving and finding ways to be better for ourselves, our customers and the community."

Signature dishes
Local arugula salad with Green Tractor farm radish, local spring onions, shaved asparagus, and spicy honey lemon vinaigrette; grilled shepherds lamb kefta with bulgar wheat salad, cucumber, red onion, tahini vinaigrette, and preserved lemon purée; miso ramen with Kyzer Farm pork, Freshies Farm mushrooms, cabbage, organic egg, and green onion.

What we say
Lots of people dream about the restaurant they'd open with their best friend, but Joel Coleman and Josh Johns actually went ahead and did it. Fire & Hops, therefore, is incredibly comfortable, yet serves dishes that would be recognized in much fancier establishments. And, of course, there's a killer drinks list. Coleman and Johns are constantly looking for sustainable measures to take. They recycle cooking oil and compost; they're part of a local water usage reduction initiative; they volunteer in local schools and hire graduates from the local culinary academy. After all, Fire & Hops is all about "local, seasonal ingredients, and being sustainable as possible", says Coleman.

The Compound Restaurant

Santa Fe

What
Nationally ranked contemporary American restaurant in the historic arts district

Who
Mark Kiffin, chef/owner

When
Lunch Monday to Saturday, dinner, daily

Address
653 Canyon Road, Santa Fe, NM 87501

+1 505 982 4353

compoundrestaurant.com

Bookings
Phone, OpenTable.com

Price guide

What they say
"This restaurant has been a cornerstone of the Santa Fe community since the day we opened back in 1966. I always say I am just the caretaker of this place. Someday I will be gone, but this place will go on and on because the community demands it."

Signature dishes
Spring pea soup; cockle clam risotto; beef tenderloin with cepès and foie gras hollandaise.

What we say
This historic Santa Fe restaurant has been in business since 1966, but current owner, Chef Mark Kiffin, has been in the kitchen since 2018. Under Kiffin, the French menu was updated to feature lighter seasonal fare. Think of it as New Mexico's answer to the California-fresh ethos, with a touch of European influence. Kiffin and his team serve local beef and lamb, mushrooms from Taos, and as much produce from the Santa Fe farmers' market as they can. "Sourcing organic, chemical-free, and humanely raised produce and animals is the only way to cook", he says. But, perhaps, the most important aspect of their work is maintaining and evolving this cherished Santa Fe institution.

Vinaigrette

Santa Fe

What
Salads are the star at this vegetable-centric Santa Fe restaurant

Who
Erin Wade, chef/owner

When
Lunch & dinner, Monday to Saturday

Address
709 Don Cubero Alley, Santa Fe, NM 87505

+1 505 820 9205

vinaigretteonline.com

Bookings
Website, OpenTable.com, phone

Price guide

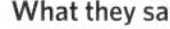

What they say
"We call it 'food for thriving.' But thriving means the entire experience counts - so we are equally passionate about our farms and sourcing of ingredients, our environmental impact, and the energy and design of our spaces. I live on the farm that grows a lot of our produce so I am always thinking of ways we can be a more efficient, self-sustaining loop."

Signature dishes
La Pepita salad with kale, avocado, spicy roasted pepitas, cotija, pulled herb-roasted chicken, and lemon-cumin citronette; Vinny Paillard salad with arugula, chopped avocado, tomatoes, pecorino, grilled lemon-herb chicken, and a hot vinaigrette made with piñons, jalapeños, and lemon; kale stem fritters with sriracha aïoli.

What we say
Hundreds of pounds a week, from April to November. That's how much arugula Vinaigrette's farm in Nambe, New Mexico grows to supply the restaurant's in-season salad needs. Why salads? "Our menu flips traditional meat-veg ratios on their head, moving salads and greens to the center of the plate and meats to the side", says chef/owner Erin Wade. "This represents a profound but achievable shift". In addition to growing most of their own vegetables, Vinaigrette runs a compost program, uses eco-friendly cleaners and regionally raised proteins, and raises money for local charitable nonprofits. They also happen to make a pretty mean salad, and have expanded to locations in Albuquerque and Austin.

149

Nevada

Esther's Kitchen

Las Vegas

What
Seasonal Italian soul food in the arts district of Las Vegas

Who
James Trees chef/owner

When
Lunch & dinner, daily

Address
1130 S. Casino Center Boulevard. Las Vegas, NV 89104

+1 702 570 7864

estherslv.com

Bookings
OpenTable.com

Price guide

What they say
"We specialize in fresh, handmade pastas and seasonal ingredients procured from nearby farmers, including local produce and grains. Localism is literally seen in our dishes - we source our tabelware from a studio down the street. We also source our flour from Central Milling in Utah, and our seafood from co-ops and sustainable fishermen. We butcher one or two pigs a week to produce multiple dishes on the menu. We use every part of the animal and never purchase bones for stock or extra random pieces. Though it is not a large part of our menu, all of our beef is grass-fed from Flannery Farms in Northern California. Through an outreach program we work with local farms and schools to educate our community about seasonality and cooking vegetables to make them appealing to kids. We also throw our own food festival every year to highlight great independent restaurants in Las Vegas."

Signature dishes
Cacio e pepe with Tellicherry peppercorns and Locatelli Pecorino Romano; white asparagus with garlic *panna* and cauliflower; hamachi crudo with pickled Murray Farm cherries, fennel, pistachio, and basil.

What we say
Thanks to Esther's Kitchen, Las Vegas now has superb Italian cuisine made with locally sourced ingredients. This conscious eatery works with local community farms and schools to educate about seasonal produce and how to cook vegetables. Don't miss the exceptional handmade pasta, complemented simple, perfectly-executed sides.

Liberty Food & Wine Exchange

Washoe

What
An artisan eatery located in downtown Reno that serves locally sourced American cuisine

Who
Mark Estee, chef/owner

When
Lunch & dinner, daily, weekend brunch

Address
100 North Sierra Street, Reno, Washoe, NV 89501

+1 775 336 1091

libertyfoodandwine.com

Bookings
Website, phone

Price guide

What they say
"We are a community-driven business that aims to create a culture of learning, caring, and respect among our team members, guests, and suppliers. This is also demonstrated in what we cook and serve. We use seasonal and local ingredients whenever possible, we give scraps and old bread to farmers for compost, and we prefer wild, sustainable fish and local products. We provide biodegradable straws, cutlery and containers upon request. We also live by a whole-animal philosophy and make great use of the DROPP program (Distributors of Regional and Organic Produce and Products), an online platform where local Reno-area farmers post their bounty for chefs to immediately purchase."

Signature dishes
Pork platter (allows full use of the animal from the offal, the cured, the stuffed, the classic, and the creative); "DROPP" salad (comprised from the Great Basin Food Co-Op DROPP program); arepas with daily chef's choice topping.

What we say
Liberty Food & Wine Exchange is more than simply an approachable restaurant featuring locally sourced, classic American fare; it is a mission-driven market offering a range of butchered meats and specialty foods showcasing the best of Western Nevada. Perfect cuisine for the health-conscious consumer.

151

Texas

Dai Due Butcher Shop & Supper Club

Austin

What
A hyper-Texas restaurant featuring seasonal produce, meats & wild game

Who
Jesse Griffiths & Tamara Mayfield, owners & Janie Ramirez, executive chef

When
Lunch Tuesday to Friday, dinner Tuesday to Sunday, weekend brunch

Address
2406 Manor Road, Suite A, Austin, TX 78722

+1 512 524 0688

daidue.com

Bookings
Phone, OpenTable.com

Price guide

What they say
"Serving from-scratch, unprocessed, clean food to our community, taking care of our staff and treating them like family, and providing genuine hospitality to our guests - these are things we truly care about."

Signature dishes
Grilled giant beef rib with caraway-paprika honey, pickled carrots, whey-fermented cabbage, green onions, and dill; wild boar confit with bone broth, salsa macha, fermented greens, red onion, pickled ash hominy, and coriander; spring vegetable salad with radish, cucumber, snow peas, beets, coal-roasted squash, and basil vinaigrette.

What others say
"Griffiths has created a place and a cuisine that are uniquely Texan - almost every ingredient, from olive oil to meat to wine, comes from within 200 miles - without any Lone Star State clichés."

-Andrew Knowlton, *bon appétit*

What we say
When Dai Due says local, they mean it. Take their wine list, for example - all Texas wines that use only Texas grapes. Or their commitment to serving wild boar, an invasive species in Texas. Even the furniture is made by local craftsmen. And as for vegetables? If they're not in season, they're not on the menu. Thanks to an in-house butcher program and an open-fire cooking rig, the meat options - especially the wild boar - truly shine at Dai Due. But don't overlook the vegetarian options: a seasonal mezze board full of pickled vegetables, spiced purées, and grilled flatbreads is a knockout.

Barley Swine

Austin

What
An Austin original serving farm-to-table meals since 2010

Who
Bryce Gilmore, owner/chef

When
Dinner Tuesday to Saturday

Address
6555 Burnet Road, Suite 400, Austin, TX 78757

+1 512 394 8150

barleyswine.com

Bookings
Resy.com

Price guide

What they say
"We source locally and support the farmers and ranchers of central Texas, offering guests a snapshot of the taste of place (Austin, that is). Our shared plate and tasting menu options are truly seasonal and always changing based on the ingredient availability and the aspirations of the kitchen."

What others say
"When you go to Barley Swine, you know that you'll be getting creative dishes that utilize farm-fresh ingredients, along with cocktails from one of the most enjoyable beverage programs in town, but you never know exactly how Bryce Gilmore's team is going to transform the region's bounty."

-Matthew Odam, *Austin American-Statesman*

Signature dishes
Shiitake dumplings with scrambled egg and summer squash; fried pig skin slaw with red cabbage, avocado and sesame; quail with spicy sausage, carrot, and pecan.

What we say
True seasonality can be tricky, especially in a place like Texas, where the summers are harsh and dry. But Austin native Bryce Gilmore achieves just that at his flagship restaurant Barley Swine, where his team produces an elegant tasting menu and à la carte shared plates in rhythm with the seasons.

Gilmore draws on the food traditions of central Texas as well as its ingredients, and the result is a cuisine that is centered in place. Recent dishes include goat shoulder with sweet potatoes and boiled peanuts, and fried zucchini pickles with green onion goat cheese. And don't skip the seasonal cocktail menu; the bar takes as much care with ingredients as the kitchen does.

Eden East

Austin

What
A dreamy outdoor restaurant in the middle of a five-acre farm in East Austin

Who
Sonya Cote, chef/owner

When
Dinner Thursday to Saturday, brunch Wednesday & Saturday

Address
755 Springdale Road, Austin, TX 78702

+1 512 428 6500

edeneastaustin.com

Bookings
Website, OpenTable.com

Price guide

What they say
"We often hear that we are a unique experience for Texas. Located minutes from the Texas state capitol on an organic farm oasis, people feel as though they have left the city and wandered into the country. We are passionate about sustainability, local food, supporting local businesses and preserving green spaces in our rapidly growing city."

Signature dishes
Chilled avocado cucumber soup with pickled Chioggia beets, edible blossoms, and *sal de gusano*; smoked duck confit with molasses and date *gastrique*, pickled cabbage, and cilantro flower tostada; chicken-fried quail with baby blue Caesar salad and fermented chili sauce.

What we say
When the farmers who had run Springdale Farm for decades decided to retire, Chef Sonya Cote picked up their shovel. She now farms the five acres of urban farm in rapidly gentrifying East Austin, and serves the harvest at her on-site restaurant, Eden East.

Situated under twinkling lights strung between heritage trees, the dining area of Eden East seems like it's miles (and years!) away from the hustle of modern-day Austin. Behind the scenes, though, Cote and her team are working hard to reduce the restaurant's waste (they've almost achieved zero waste through composting and recycling initiatives), contribute to their community, and preserve the farmland they've worked so hard to farm.

Rancho Loma

Coleman

What
A rural destination restaurant drawing diners from all over Texas & beyond

Who
Laurie Williamson, chef/owner

When
Dinner Friday & Saturday

Address
2969 County Road 422, Talpa, Coleman, TX 76882

+1 325 636 4556

rancholoma.com

Bookings
Website

Price guide

What they say
"When we built the restaurant in the midst of nowhere, in Texas, it was a leap of faith. If we build it, they will come - and come they have. After fifteen years we have a very loyal following that thinks nothing of driving an hour, two hours, or more to support what we deliver."

Signature dishes
Heirloom tomato salad with white balsamic granita; spicy grilled quail; fresh house-made pasta.

What others say
"Two former commercial filmmakers managed to create a destination restaurant and inn in the middle of nowhere - with not a day of professional chef, restaurateur, or hotelier experience between them."

-Francesca Mari, *Saveur*

What we say
Surely, this is the dreamiest restaurant in Texas. Located in tiny Talpa - population 127 - Rancho Loma seats thirty souls twice a week for Laurie Williamson's homegrown, seasonal fare. Along with her husband Robert, Williamson opened the restaurant after their farm produced "an abundance of heirloom tomatoes we couldn't get rid of ... Remarkably, we could not find any restaurants interested in those organic tomatoes." So they started their own.

Grab a bottle of wine and drive three hours northwest of Austin. Then settle in for a Texan meal like you've never seen. Recent dishes include sustainably-caught barbecue shrimp, a tart made from local blackberries, and, of course, those famous tomatoes. After dinner, retire to one of the ranch's guest rooms for an evening of incomparable stargazing.

Café Momentum

Dallas

What
Internship program for at-risk youth that happens to serve amazing food

Who
Chad Houser, founder/CEO/chef

When
Dinner Thursday to Saturday

Address
1510 Pacific Avenue, Dallas, TX 75201

+1 214 303 1234

cafemomentum.org

Bookings
Phone, OpenTable.com

Price guide

What they say
"We provide a transformative experience through a twelve-month paid post-release internship program for young men and women coming out of juvenile facilities. They rotate through all aspects of the restaurant, focusing on life and social skills, coaching and development. We employ a case management staff, providing an ecosystem of support around our interns to help them achieve their greatest potential."

Signature dishes
Smoked fried chicken; octopus *tiradito*.

What others say
"In short, Café Momentum is an organization that provides mentorship, support, culinary, job, and life-skill training to at-risk youth and former juvenile offenders in the Dallas area. ... The goal of Café Momentum is to break the cycle of crime and help these young people reach their full potential."

-@foodbitch, *Dallas Observer*

What we say
Smoked fried chicken, served with a side of helping young people. Café Momentum is the brainchild of Chad Houser, a chef whose mission is to "take kids out of jail and teach them to play with knives and fire". The restaurant's twelve-month internship program trains and supports formerly incarcerated Dallas youth, with the goal of helping them achieve their full potential as culinary professionals.

And if that were all they did, that would be plenty. But Café Momentum also happens to serve up amazing seasonal specials sourced from local farms, including urban farms within Dallas. The wine list is excellent and reasonably priced, and, yeah, the smoked fried chicken is as good as it sounds.

Gemma

Dallas

What
California, France & Italy combine for a seasonal restaurant that's all Dallas

Who
Allison Yoder, owner & Stephen Rogers, chef/owner

When
Dinner Tuesday to Sunday

Address
2323 North Henderson Avenue, Suite 109, Dallas, TX 75206

+1 214 370 9426

gemmadallas.com

Bookings
Phone, website, OpenTable.com

Price guide

What they say
"At Gemma we provide a warm, inviting environment, where the products are sourced from reputable sources. The food is real, the people are real, and staff are warm and authentic."

Signature dishes
Baby bok choy salad with spring peas, fennel, mint, toasted cashews, and rhubarb vinaigrette; bucatini with porcini mushrooms, garlic confit, and parsley pesto; rabbit pappardelle with chard, pancetta, thyme, and Pernod.

What others say
"The cooking at Gemma is sharp and focused; the execution splendid ... We have a gem in Gemma."

-Eve Hill-Agnus, *D Magazine*

What we say
Light, bright and seasonal are words that are, perhaps, not commonly associated with Dallas restaurants, but they perfectly describe the food and atmosphere at Gemma. Allison Yoder and Stephen Rogers bring a California sensibility to Rogers' hometown, thanks to years spent working in Napa Valley restaurants.

With Gemma, the duo have conjured a deceptively simple menu of locally sourced dishes. The house-made pastas are not to be missed, nor are the (rightfully famous) fried Castelvetrano olives with Texas pecans. Grab a seat at the bar, trust us.

Coltivare

Houston

What
Italian cuisine with a Gulf Coast perspective, dictated by Houston's seasons & a backyard garden

Who
Ryan Pera, chef/owner

When
Dinner Wednesday to Monday

Address
3320 White Oak Drive, Houston TX 77007

+1 713 637 4095

agricolehospitality.com

Bookings
Walk-ins

Price guide

What they say
"First, we prioritize making the food taste great. But just as important is where the food comes from, how it was grown and the method with which it was cooked. The 3,000-square-foot garden at Coltivare does more than just supplement our menu. It connects our employees and guests to the ingredients on their plate."

Signature dishes
Agnolotti with golden beets, spring vegetables, and herbs; *'nduja* bruschetta with wildflower honey and arugula; Mesquite grilled lamb with lamb pancetta.

What others say
"Season after season, chef Ryan Pera's rustic Italian spot delivers well-edited dishes with a vivid sense of Gulf Coast place - thanks to sourcing from regional farms and a verdant backyard garden."

-Alison Cook, *Houston Chronicle*

What we say
Houston, Texas is where the produce of coastal Texas meets the bounty of the Gulf of Mexico. Nowhere is this intersection better utilized than at Colitvare, where Chef Ryan Pera takes an Italian sensibility to Texan ingredients. The restaurant boasts a 3,000 square foot garden, and 100 percent of what's grown there is used in the restaurant. This proximity to fresh produce means you can't really go wrong on the seasonal menu, although the pastas in particular stand out. And do save room for the ever-changing selection of gelatos and *sorbettos*.

Restaurant Mixtli

San Antonio

What
One boxcar, twelve seats, a different region of Mexico every forty-five days

Who
Diego Galicia & Rico Torres, chefs/owners

When
Dinner Monday to Saturday

Address
5251 McCullough Avenue, San Antonio, TX 78212

+1 210 338 0746

restaurantmixtli.com

Bookings
Exploretock.com

Price guide

What they say
"Mixtli started as a restaurant and has become a cultural destination due to the passionate work we do to rescue and bring back old Mexican recipes, dishes, and ingredients."

Signature dishes
Pipian mole with chayotes, purslane, and an ash made of roasted grasshopers garnished with chickpeas and micro-cilantro; deep-fried beef sweetbreads with coffee mayonnaise; alderwood-smoked honey and yogurt ice cream with whey snow and white grape syrup.

What others say
"Perhaps as much a theatrical experience as a meal, each seat in this polished up boxcar takes you on a journey through Mexico."

Texas Monthly

What we say
Inside a tiny boxcar in San Antonio's Olmos Park neighborhood are twelve seats where you can eat some of the best Mexican food out there. Every forty-five days, Chef Diego Galicia and Chef Rico Torres debut a new menu that focuses on a different aspect of Mexican cuisine: sometimes a region, sometimes an era. Always, always deeply researched and brilliantly executed. Their mission is to celebrate, revive, and evolve old Mexican recipes. And through their efforts, they've created a community of staff members and Mexican food aficionados. So buy a ticket to dinner - meals are pre-paid - and ride this boxcar wherever Galicia and Torres want it to go.

Restaurant Gwendolyn

San Antonio

What
Hyper-local fine dining restaurant that looks to the past to cook for the future

Who
Michael Sohocki, chef/owner

When
Dinner Tuesday to Saturday

Address
152 East Pecan Street, Suite 100, San Antonio, TX 78205

+1 210 222 1849

restaurantgwendolyn.com

Bookings
Phone, website or OpenTable.com

Price guide

What they say
"Restaurant Gwendolyn is the only restaurant in [San Antonio] that uses strictly 100 percent local perishable ingredients. We buy directly from farmers and ranchers within 150 miles of our location, and create dining experiences that change every day. Buying strictly local ingredients cultivates a food production system that is a reflection of our land, and keeps our money with our people."

Signature dishes
House-made camembert and roquefort-style cheeses; house-made charcuterie resulting from a whole animal philosophy.

What others say
"No perishable ingredient [from] more than a horseback ride away, no tool with a plug and no white trucks: the fishbowl kitchen and gem of a dining room provide a quintessential experience."

Texas Monthly

What we say
1850: that's the cutoff year. If it came after 1850, it has no place in Chef Michael Sohocki's kitchen. That means no electrical kitchen gadgets, no deliveries from big corporate restaurant suppliers. Animals - pork, beef, lamb - come in whole, and every bit gets used. Kitchen scraps are fed to the restaurant's flock of chickens and ducks, whose eggs, in turn, are transformed into luscious pastries. With no set menu and no dictated menu items, Sohocki encourages his chefs to get creative with the bounty of South Texas. Thus Gwendolyn's signature dishes are more like signature ingredients: the resulting dishes and the tasting menus they comprise change daily, often in delightful and surprising ways. "This", as Sohocki puts it, "is a thinker's restaurant".

The Inn at Dos Brisas

Washington

What
Restaurant with forty-two acres of USDA certified organic gardens

Who
Doug Bosch, owner & Zachary Ladwig, chef

When
Lunch & dinner, daily

Address
10000 Champion Drive, Washington, TX 77880

+1 979 277 7750

dosbrisas.com

Bookings
Phone, website, OpenTable.com

Price guide

What they say
"I like to joke that there are 365 seasons at The Inn at Dos Brisas. We are most passionate about the ingredients located 100 yards from our back door. We have a tremendous opportunity to cook with an ever-changing larder of ingredients from our own gardens and pastures."

Signature dishes
Poached araucuna chicken egg with legumes and ember-roasted chicken broth; golden bantam corn *caramelle* with steamed royal red shrimp and flowering cilantro; Freedom Ranger chicken roasted on a bed of hay with asparagus, liver mousseline, and sauce velour.

What we say
Forty-two acres in Washington County, Texas, provide just about everything the Restaurant at the Inn at Dos Brisas needs. This vegetable-focused fine dining restaurant is situated in the middle of a luxury resort, but that's not about to stop Chef Zachary Ladwig and his team from getting their hands dirty. "Any item that makes its way to the plate is surely raised here or sourced from a responsible artisan within sixty miles of our ranch", he says.

Settle in for a five-course meal inspired by the resort's USDA-certified organic gardens, all served with that famous, warm Texas hospitality. You can just make a reservation for dinner, although spending the night on the property is well worth it.

161

Utah

Hell's Backbone Grill

Garfield

What
Restaurant, now in its nineteenth season, serving a farm-based cuisine of the Four Corners region

Who
Jen Castle & Blake Spalding, chefs/owners

When
Hours change seasonally

Address
20 North Highway 12, Boulder, Garfield, UT 84716

+1 435 335 7464

hellsbackbonegrill.com

Bookings
Website

Price guide

What they say
"We see Hell's Backbone Grill as the warm, welcoming hearth for those venturing into the incredible wilderness that surrounds us. Since we are located in one of the nation's most remote areas, sourcing ingredients is a point of both necessity and ethics. Our farm provides our vegetables and fruit, and much of our craft cocktail menu features Utah-made spirits. Even local gardeners stop by to drop off freshly picked herbs they know we need."

Signature dishes
Orange brandy cream grilled leg of lamb with lemony mashed potatoes; pumpkin-piñón enchiladas with habanero sweet corn cream Sauce; locally-raised, grass-fed and finished steaks.

What we say
Most of the food from the menu at Hell's Backbone Grill is raised on their nearby six-acre farm: chickens lay the eggs that form the foundation of many breakfast items, and seasonal vegetables, fruits, herbs, and flowers make their way into a rotating roster of dishes rooted in a fanciful amalgam of historical Mormon pioneer, western range cowboy, mixed in with traditional flavors of the Southwest. What's not grown there hails from nearby: grass-fed beef, for instance, comes from down the road. Some of this is by necessity. Hell's Backbone is located on the edge of the Grand Staircase Escalante National Monument, in one of the most remote towns in the United States. But owners Jen Castle and Blake Spalding are deeply committed to environmental stewardship, too: all food waste from the restaurant goes back to the farm.

The Copper Onion

Salt Lake City

What
American restaurant with a farm-to-table approach to sourcing

Who
Ryan Lowder, chef/owner

When
Lunch & dinner, daily, weekend brunch

Address
111 East Broadway, Salt Lake City, UT 84111

+1 801 355 3282

thecopperonion.com

Bookings
Website

Price guide

What they say
"We're passionate about being able to showcase the items that we are able to procure locally, and the consistency of our execution. We tend to call ourselves an American restaurant - which gives us the option of saying we do whatever we want to do. We're a very high-volume restaurant. We work directly with a couple of farmers with our specific needs for what we want to be able to get."

Signature dishes
"The Copper Onion burger" on a house-made bun with red wine caramelized onions and duck fat aïoli; *saag paneer* with rotating market greens, cheese, and fried coconut rice balls; bone marrow.

What others say
"[The] Copper Onion leads the way on food trends in Salt Lake City. Owner Ryan Lowder's bone marrow makes even the most timid eater want to lick their fingers while his ricotta dumplings have food critics writing rave reviews."

-Becky Rosenthal, *The Guardian*

What we say
Nearby ranches, farms, and the Salt Lake City farmers' market inspired Ryan Lowder to open The Copper Onion, and local artisans and purveyors - plus sustainability-minded producers like Niman Ranch - feature prominently on the menu. The board reflects the restaurant's mountainous roots, with hearty fare like rabbit, local trout, and a variety of house-made pastas (breads and ice creams are also made on-site), balanced by seasonal produce good enough to star. Local beers comprise a notable portion of the beverage list, too.

Laziz Kitchen

Salt Lake City

What
Restaurant serving modern Lebanese food

Who
Moudi Sbeity, chef/owner & Derek Kitchen, owner

When
Lunch & dinner, Tuesday to Sunday

Address
912 South Jefferson Street, Salt Lake City, UT 84101

+1 801-441 1228

lazizkitchen.com

Bookings
OpenTable.com

Price guide

What they say
"I wanted to bring my [Lebanese] culture and my food and the way I understand it to Salt Lake City. We exclusively hired refugees when we opened. A majority of our cooks are still refugees. We bring them in, teach them to operate in a US environment, and teach them the English skills they need. We've created a very safe and accepting space for our staff. When you walk into the place, you feel the love and acceptance for everyone here."

Signature dishes
Shakshouka; man'ousheh; kafta burger.

What others say
"At Laziz, [refugees] gain valuable work experience for their lives in a new world and also gain something perhaps more valuable - a circle of support and sense of community."

-Mary Brown Malouf, *Salt Lake Magazine*

What we say
Laziz owners Moudi Sbeity and Derek Kitchen have long fought to create accepting spaces within their community - the couple was a plaintiff in the suit that brought marriage equality to Utah - so in their restaurant, they've created an accepting community hub. Laziz gives back to the LGBTQ community and trains refugees in its kitchen, giving them the tools and support they need to succeed in a homogenous city. Community commitment here extends to sourcing: Lebanese dishes are built with locally-supplied ingredients and imports with altruistic aims - an olive supplier, for instance, who works with small-town producers in Lebanon and gives a percentage of sales to support families on the West Bank.

Pago

Salt Lake City

What
Intimate restaurant serving seasonal New-American cuisine

Who
Scott Evans, sommelier/owner, & Phelix Gardner, chef

When
Dinner, daily, weekend brunch

Address
878 900 East, Salt Lake City, UT 84102

+1 801 532 0777

pagoslc.com

Bookings
Phone, OpenTable.com, walk-ins

Price guide

What they say
"Pago features local products year-round from Utah trout and lamb to eggs, flour, honey, and vegetables. For five years we had our own small farm plot and grew heirloom vegetables for Pago. After I moved last year, we are still buying vegetables from my old property and it is being farmed today. The source of ingredients is what inspires us to develop new dishes and build compelling beverage programs."

Signature dishes
Pan-seared organic chicken with local carrot-almond butter, pickled ramps, fiddlehead ferns and spring vegetables; Morgan Valley Lamb sausage with poached Clifford Farm eggs, split pea falafel, lacinato kale, red-veined sorrel, mint, and cucumber yogurt sauce; lamb sugo with mint, house-made ricotta cavatelli, green olive, and pecorino.

What others say
"Evans built relationships with many tiny local growers, showcasing their produce and changing the menu with the seasons, at the same time emphasizing wine exploration by offering a broad selection of wines by the glass. Now everyone's doing it."

Salt Lake Magazine

What we say
Through a then-groundbreaking seasonal menu built around locally procured ingredients, Pago gave Salt Lake City its first glimpse of what farm-to-table cooking could look like; it's still a leader in the space.

Relationships with local farmers drive the ingredients and the menus here, which are long on vegetable options and sustainably raised meats. The sustainability ethos extends throughout: the restaurant sources natural wines applying the same standards it applies to its food, and the space is built from sustainable materials.

Table X

Salt Lake City

What
Innovative, chef-driven restaurant rooted in seasonality

Who
Mike Blocher, Nick Fahs & David Barboza, chefs

When
Dinner Wednesday to Sunday

Address
1457 East 3350 South, Salt Lake City, UT 84106

+1 385 528 3712

tablexrestaurant.com

Bookings
OpenTable.com

Price guide

What they say
"Our cuisine evolves. We align our menus with the seasons because we know eating in season provides excellent food. Our techniques are bedrocked in classical training, but also driven by an insatiable curiosity of to-be-discovered possibilities. Just out the door, we've outfitted the restaurant with an extensive culinary garden. We're interested in using ingredients at their peak - directly out of the earth. The Table X garden reminds us, daily, to cook within the present season."

What others say
"This adventurous eatery, housed in a renovated warehouse once used for candling eggs and fermenting cheese, is proof that Salt Lake City has come into its own. Three young chefs - Mike Blocher, Nick Fahs and David Barboza - have created a playground where they take the best the season has to offer and do cartwheels with it."

The Salt Lake Tribune

What we say
The three chefs behind restaurant Table X have been best friends since culinary school, and their cerebral camaraderie in the kitchen coalesces into the stunning plates for which their restaurant is known. The guys start with high-quality ingredients harvested, raised, milled, or foraged nearby, and turn out an ever-changing roster of novel and innovative dishes that both highlight those items and elevate them. Table X's commitment to locality extends to working the earth via a kitchen garden, and the chefs are creative about their food waste, too, returning scraps to the earth.

Communal

Provo

What
Elevated farm-to-table restaurant in Provo

Who
Joseph McRae, chef/owner

When
Lunch & dinner, Tuesday to Saturday

Address
102 North University Avenue, Provo, UT 84601

+1 801 373 8000

communalrestaurant.com

Bookings
Phone, website

Price guide

What they say
"Whose responsibility is it to bring food and farm to Utah Valley? That's our responsibility. There are lots of opportunities to work with farmers, and that's what we did. We're Utah, and we're not trying to be anywhere else - we're trying to do the best we can with local products. We want to create a dining experience for people who don't always have an opportunity to eat this way. We like giving people the opportunity to have a nicer meal."

Signature dishes
Short rib; local trout; butterscotch pudding.

What we say
Before Communal arrived in Provo, the town was short on refined dining experiences. And so the restaurant is focused primarily on delighting its audience, with food that's precise but not precious - dishes are tied together by a note of homey familiarity and focus on good ingredients over complicated technique.

The restaurant lures special occasion diners alongside large groups who feast at its communal table, and operates as a hub for neighbors (and travelers) seeking an elevated meal. Community doesn't stop with patrons here, though: owners Joseph McRae and Colton Soelberg built relationships with surrounding farmers, and the haul from those producers fuels not only the menu at Communal, but at the other restaurants in this burgeoning restaurant group, as well.

167

Wyoming

Persephone Bakery

Teton

What
French bakery & café serving breakfast & lunch

Who
Kevin & Ali Cohane, owners

When
Breakfast & lunch, daily

Address
145 East Broadway, Jackson, Teton, WY 83001

+1 307 200 6708

persephonebakery.com

Bookings
Email
ali@persephonebakery.com

Price guide

What they say
"We live as we bake and we bake as we live: with heart, hard work, and creativity. We want to find the best of everything we offer, from the incredible direct-trade coffee of Intelligentsia to local and sustainable dairy, produce, and meat for our food, to the small-scale, artisan-designed kitchen and home products for our retail, and, of course, to the wonderful people of our town who make the experience more than a transaction."

What others say
"Persephone Bakery turns out lovely fare from honest ingredients, like a winter grain bowl and squash and ricotta toast using their own fresh-baked breads, in a charming, wood-floored space with cafe tables and mismatched china."

–Alex Postman, *Condé Nast Traveler*

Signature dishes
Croque-madame; everything seeded avocado bowl; Belgian Liège waffle.

What we say
Persephone Bakery puts locality at the center of its mission, and strives to be very much of Jackson Hole: the café menu is built from local produce, eggs, dairy, and meat plus the bakery's own house-baked breads; its food waste goes back to a local farm; its owners mentor local women in both baking and entrepreneurship.

Its vegetable-forward and health-conscious approach to dishes, pantry items, and baked goods proves that mountain-oriented cooking doesn't always have to center around game meats and heavy fare – and that thoughtful, well-executed food doesn't only come from high-dollar fine dining restaurants.

Rendezvous Bistro

Teton

What
Fine dining French-American bistro

Who
Gavin Fine, owner

When
Dinner, daily

Address
380 South US Highway 89, Jackson, Teton, WY 83001

+1 307 739 1100

rendezvousbistro.net

Bookings
Phone

Price guide

What they say
"We are passionate about providing excellent food at affordable prices, all paired with fantastic service. We are proud to support the farmers and ranchers that call the Rocky Mountains home. We source produce from the surrounding area whenever possible."

Signature dishes
Duck confit with braised red cabbage, herbed spaetzle, lardons, and orange gastrique; *moules frites* with wild Maine mussels, garlic-herb butter, and house fries; veal Marsala with roasted fingerling potatoes, sautéed greens, and crimini mushrooms.

What we say
Gavin Fine and Roger Freedman may now preside over a raft of Jackson Hole's best restaurants, but their story starts with Rendezvous Bistro, a French-American bistro with refined service that continues to anchor dining here. The kitchen turns to local purveyors for inspiration in giving the French-American food here a Jackson twist, highlighting nearby huckleberries and morels or working with a local vertical farm to procure local greens even in winter, and it sustainably sources its seafood, much of which goes into its famed raw bar. Fine has also become a pillar for his philosophy of enlightened hospitality, a community-centric approach to service that underpins all of his restaurants.

What others say
"If there's one name to know in the Jackson Hole culinary community, it's Gavin Fine. The Tetons' answer to Danny Meyer, Fine reigns over his seven-restaurant fine dining empire ... and the flagship Rendezvous Bistro, which he opened 15 years ago at the ripe old age of 25."

–Brandon Perlman, *Town & Country*

Catalpa (p. 228)

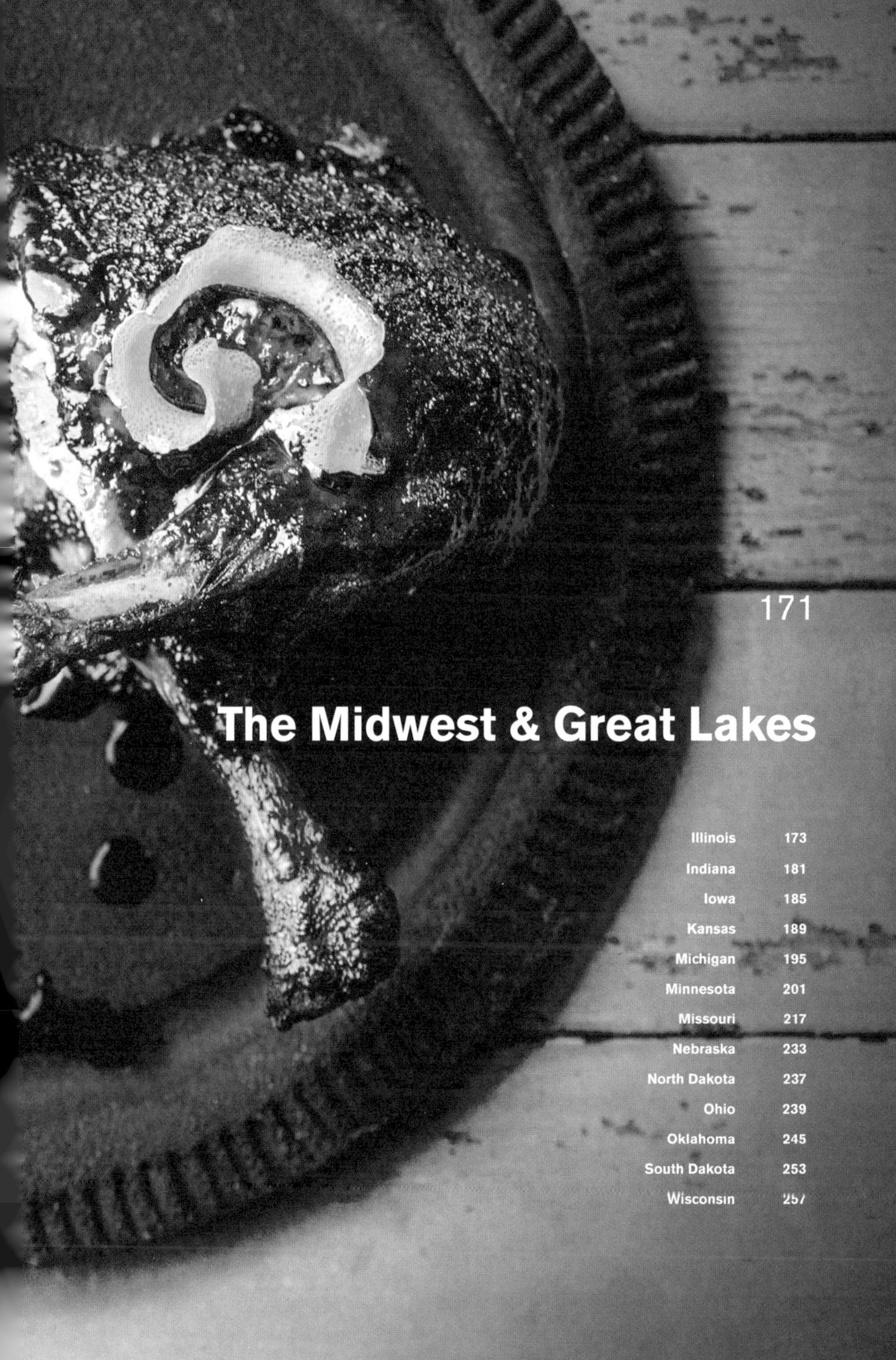

The Midwest & Great Lakes

Illinois	173
Indiana	181
Iowa	185
Kansas	189
Michigan	195
Minnesota	201
Missouri	217
Nebraska	233
North Dakota	237
Ohio	239
Oklahoma	245
South Dakota	253
Wisconsin	257

173

Illinois

Baker Miller

Chicago

What
A neighborhood café & stone mill bakery featuring breakfast & lunch foods

Who
Dave Miller, chef & Megan Miller, pastry chef

When
Breakfast & lunch, daily

Address
4610 North Western Avenue, Chicago, IL 60625

+1 773 654 3610

bakermillerchicago.com

Bookings
Walk-ins

Price guide

What they say
"We're passionate about sharing love. For us that means treating people well, sourcing ingredients we believe in and constantly learning new skills. We try to build balanced dishes and incorporate 'health food' concepts into indulgent dishes."

Signature dishes
Smashed avocado on sunflower seed toast with salsa verde, a poached egg, and watermelon radishes; heirloom grain oatmeal topped with cultured cream, cinnamon sugar, and pecans; chocolate peanut butter buckeye pies.

What others say
"Chicago's Baker Miller is changing the way we think about grains, one customer at a time."

-Julia Kramer, *bon appétit*

What we say
A meal at Baker Miller is inherently indulgent, as you tuck into a bowl of grits or oatmeal, peruse the jam bar with a pile of toast, and finish with a pecan jammer cookie. It's no wonder they are two-time semifinalists for James Beard Foundation awards. Dave and Megan Miller combine comfort food with sustainability at their bakery cafés, on their grain-focused menu and in their business practices. As founding members of the artisan grain collaborative, they work with grain farmers, chefs, millers, and others to ensure higher quality grain in the Midwest. In their cafés, they serve ethically sourced coffee and support their community by teaching free classes to underprivileged youths. Their employees enjoy a strong work-life balance and living wages. This all makes a trip to Baker Miller good for the heart and the soul.

Blackbird

Chicago

What
One Off Hospitality's critically acclaimed flagship concept & home base for Paul Kahan

Who
Paul Kahan, chef/partner & Ryan Pfeiffer, chef de cuisine

When
Lunch & dinner, Monday to Friday

Address
619 West Randolph Street, Chicago, IL 60661

+1 312 715 0708

blackbirdrestaurant.com

Bookings
OpenTable.com

Price guide

What they say
"Since we opened twenty years ago, the foundation of Blackbird has been rooted in sustainability, from mindful sourcing to the philosophy behind the enrichment of the staff, and teaching them to use what they've learned in our kitchen to make our industry better as a whole. We strive for constant growth and continue to educate those that follow in our footsteps to do the same."

Signature dishes
Tempura asparagus with dill pickle, sweet fish sauce, and sorrel; roasted Amish chicken with brioche, morels, romaine, and clam cuisson; farm egg *chaud froid* with lavender.

What others say
"Virtually every chef I met credited Paul Kahan with leading the war for independents in a city long known for the extremes of high-end places."

-Regina Schrambling, *The New York Times*

What we say
A meal at Blackbird is a must for any serious food lover. Some of the most talented chefs in the country learned ingredient-based cooking and an appreciation for farmers from chef/partner Paul Kahan, who co-founded Chicago's Pilot Light, a food-based educational non-profit helping kids make healthier food choices. Chef de Cuisine Ryan Pfeiffer continues Kahan's mission with inspired, soulful seasonal American cooking, a positive kitchen atmosphere, and composting and food waste reduction programs that speak to the team's respect for ingredients.

City Mouse

Chicago

What
All-day restaurant with a focus on fun, delicious, locally-sourced food

Who
Jason Vincent, Ben Lustbader & Patrick Sheerin, chefs

When
Breakfast, lunch & dinner, daily

Address
311 North Morgan St., Chicago, IL 60607

+1 312 764 1908

citymousechicago.com

Bookings
Website, walk-ins

Price guide

What they say
"We focus on taking care of the guest. We want to make sure we are making choices that are the right ones for all people. Environmental impact is part of our thought process in sourcing, and we also compost and work with farmers whenever possible. We want to be part of the solution, not contributing to the problem. Whenever and wherever possible we try and source seasonally - we let the 'first chair' ingredients stand out and then try and source the same quality for the background players."

Signature dishes
Klug Farm asparagus with egg yolk jam, salad of sliced kumquats, fried shallots, chiles, and tangerine oil; sandwich with hash browns, egg, cheese, grape jelly, and sausage; fried artichokes with pork ragu and Italian breadcrumbs.

What others say
"Everything's delicious and every plate's a party."

-Steve Reddicliffe, *The New York Times*

What we say
When you hear Executive Chef Patrick Sheerin talk adoringly about his asparagus, you can tell immediately that he is in love with local, seasonal produce. Sheerin prepares each ingredient with care and complexity, but keeps the dishes simple enough so that the flavor of each ingredient shines through. He thinks about food the way a conductor approaches music, making sure the central ingredients - whether from his rooftop garden or a local farm - are the star. The result is plates that echo his mantra for the food to be vibrant, and have some soul at the same time.

Frontera Grill

Chicago

What
The beautiful food of Mexico expressed with Midwestern ingredients

Who
Rick Bayless, chef

When
Lunch Tuesday to Friday, dinner Tuesday to Saturday, brunch Saturday

Address
445 North Clark Street, Chicago, IL 60654

+1 312 334 3691

rickbayless.com

Bookings
Reserve.com, walk-ins

Price guide

What they say
"Great tasting food and beverages promotes a sense of well-being at our guests' tables, is a catalyst for conversation and culture, and leaves a lasting, positive impression. Our food and drink reflects our deep knowledge of Mexico's cuisine and its ingredients, as well as a healthy, natural and cultural environment. We nurture our communities through our generosity and care. Education is our fuel, and we are always educating ourselves about ways to make Frontera Grill better. And financial health is our stability - without it, we cannot accomplish our mission."

Signature dishes
Twenty-hour-smoked beef brisket with Oaxacan black mole, *queso añejo* mashed potatoes, and local, seasonal vegetables; shrimp and scallop ceviche verde with pink shrimp, bay scallops, avocado, cucumber, jícama, serrano, and knob onions.

What others say
"Eating at Frontera was an awakening."

-Bill Addison, *Eater*

What we say
People know Rick Bayless for creating carefully prepared Mexican food that helped change the perception of that cuisine in America. This is true. Also true: Bayless is also a community leader who runs the Frontera Farmer Foundation, which has given millions of dollars to local family farms, among other initiatives, including a culinary training program for Chicago's unemployed, low-income population. His food reflects his ethos, featuring humanely raised beef, complex mole sauces, and produce as local as Bayless' backyard garden. Make sure to try some of the wines offered from Mexico's Valle de Guadalupe; a dollar from select bottles sold funds culinary scholarships for Mexican-American students.

Honey Butter Fried Chicken

Chicago

What
Fried chicken restaurant

Who
Christine Cikowski & Joshua Kulp, partners/chefs

When
Lunch & dinner, Tuesday to Sunday, weekend brunch

Address
3361 North Elston Avenue, Chicago, IL 60618

+1 773 478 4000

honeybutter.com

Bookings
Walk-ins

Price guide

What they say
"We are passionate about our food and our staff - the cornerstones of any successful restaurant! We are proud of our food, we use wholesome ingredients that are grown/raised in a responsible, sustainable way from area farmers. Our commitment to the health and happiness of our team is shown in our great wages and benefits, including PTO, health insurance, paid sick leave, paid parental leave, and gain sharing."

Signature dishes
Fried chicken with honey butter; seasonal dumpcake with in-season strawberries and sweet corn whipped cream; Camchi fried chicken sandwich with fried chicken strips, fermented local in-season vegetables, and spicy mayo on a buttery bun.

What others say
"Honey Butter Fried Chicken has been making swathes of Chicagoans feel like kids again when they dip their birds in that addictive honey butter."

-Daniel Gerzina, *Eater*

What we say
If your expectations for a counter-service fried chicken spot aren't very high, then you've never been to Honey Butter Fried Chicken. The line that regularly snakes out the door should be your first clue that this is no ordinary chicken.

Christine Cikowski and Josh Kulp, who have become leaders in fair and sustainable restaurant staffing, source local, cage-free chickens, fry them, season them with spices, and serve them with corn muffins and soft pats of honey butter to slather over everything. Vegetables for sides like kale slaw come from local farms, and everything is plain delicious.

Lula Cafe

Chicago

What
Since 1999, creatively seasonal cuisine in a cool place filled with art, good people & love

Who
Jason Hammel, chef/owner

When
Breakfast, lunch & dinner, Wednesday to Monday

Address
2537 North Kedzie Boulevard, Chicago, IL 60647

+1 773 489 9554

lulacafe.com

Bookings
Website

Price guide

What they say
"We are most passionate about creating connections between people through food. Between our chefs, our guests, our farmers, between us and our neighborhood. We believe that creating delicious, real, thoughtful, clean, and fair food can build community and empathy between many people."

Signature dishes
Farro *campanelle* with nettle pesto and ricotta; the classic 1999 turkey sandwich (turkey from Local Foods, tomatoes from MightyVine, lettuces from Werp Farms, bread from Publican Quality Bread); chickpea sweet potato tagine with green harissa, fennel, pickled golden raisins, and grilled bread.

What we say
Chicago's farm-to-table movement exists because of Jason Hammel. For two decades, Lula Cafe has been the epicenter of Chicago's farm-driven restaurant scene, and it remains a favorite restaurant for chefs to dine, especially those who have followed in Hammel's footsteps.

As one of the co-founders of Pilot Light, a local organization devoted to teaching Chicago children how delicious farm food can be, Hammel is still educating the next generation. He was among the first chefs to host farm dinners, and continues to do so, offering a different three-course vegetable-focused menu every Monday night. In addition to buying from farmers, he employs an on-staff gardener and grows herbs and greens on the outdoor patio, rooftop garden, and in the four-season grow room. All of that passion can be found in every plate at this funky, energetic restaurant.

North Pond

Chicago

What
Seasonal American fine dining restaurant set amid the natural beauty of Chicago's Lincoln Park

Who
Bruce Sherman, chef/partner

When
Brunch & dinner, hours change seasonally

Address
2610 North Cannon Drive, Chicago, IL 60614

+1 773 477 5845

northpondrestaurant.com

Bookings
Phone, OpenTable.com

Price guide

What they say
"At North Pond, we strive to successfully express the seasons through our delicious and modern interpretations of the produce, proteins, and products appropriate to their time of year."

Signature dishes
Soft-boiled hen's egg with green and purple asparagus, Grayson cheese, jam-filled waffle, red and green strawberries; roasted and candied Chioggia gold and red beets with cured sardines, smoked caviar, watercress, crème fraîche, and pretzel; prosciutto-wrapped rabbit saddle with nasturtium-apricot chorizo *verde*, sweet peas, Hakurei turnips, flax cracker, and blossoms.

What others say
"Chef Bruce Sherman isn't shy about his principles, and it's hard to eat here and conclude that he's wrong: the quality of his ingredients is evident, and the cooking is enjoyably adventurous."

–Nicholas Day, *Chicago Reader*

What we say
Tucked in Chicago's Lincoln Park, North Pond is an oasis where you can enjoy some of the best food in the city in a beautiful arts and crafts style school dining room overlooking a pond surrounded by wildflowers. Chef Bruce Sherman makes sure the food is as spectacular as the setting, having worked with local farmers and purveyors to create dishes that reflect the season.

Sherman is a leader in the Midwest's sustainable food movement, and works to compost and otherwise reduce and eliminate waste. He also founded Solidarity Soup, a chef-based initiative designed to show solidarity with the immigrants who form the backbone of the restaurant industry and the fabric of the community.

Smyth

Chicago

What
Offering inventive fine dining with hyper-local produce in a relaxed atmosphere

Who
John Shields, executive chef & Karen Shields, executive pastry chef

When
Dinner Tuesday to Saturday

Address
177 North Ada Street #101, Chicago, IL 60607

+1 773 913 3773

smythandtheloyalist.com

Bookings
Phone, website

Price guide

What they say
"The thing that really drives us is a real understanding of the products we use - not only the function and use of products, but understanding who is actually producing them, where the products are coming from, and fully understanding the work that goes into them. Because things are here today and gone tomorrow, it forces us to preserve and react quickly and logically, which translates into very fresh, nuanced, and - on the surface - simple dishes."

Signature dishes
Green asparagus with fermented white asparagus juice; rhubarb marinated in flowers with salted strawberries; dessert of egg yolk soaked in salted licorice with frozen yogurt and meringue.

What others say
"The cooking is unconventional and innovative, but by no means is it experimental. Instead, it delivers constant satisfaction alongside a few wow-inducing surprises."

Michelin Guide

What we say
Smyth has a restaurant partner, but at least an equal part of the restaurant is The Farm, a twenty-acre family-run farm located an hour away. Chefs and owners John and Karen Shields partner with the farmers to source most of their produce, herbs, and flowers. Ingredients from The Farm are highlighted on the menu in the varying steps of the growing and ripening process, making eating at Smyth an elegant meditation on the quickly changing moments in the growing season, executed by chefs with nuanced skill. This fine dining restaurant boasts a relaxed feel, where mid-century modern meets Japanese influence with Midwestern hospitality.

Uncommon Ground

Chicago

What
A local, organic, sustainable, farm-to-table restaurant with a certified-organic rooftop farm

Who
Helen & Michael Cameron, owners

When
Brunch, lunch & dinner, daily

Address
3800 North Clark Street, Chicago, IL 60613, plus other locations - see website

+1 773 929 3680

uncommonground.com

Bookings
Website

Price guide

What they say
"We are passionate about sourcing food locally, knowing our farmers, growing our own organic produce and brewing our own certified-organic beer."

Signature dishes
Seasonal greens and grains salad with asparagus, snap peas, roast spring onions, quinoa, arugula, pea shoots, and lemon-herb vinaigrette; seared sustainable Creole-spiced crusted salmon with root vegetable hash and rémoulade; grass-fed skirt steak frites with black garlic butter, Parmesan-herb frites, and lemon-pepper aïoli.

What others say
"The Wrigleyville eatery is a perfect spot for diners who appreciate organic and locally sourced food."

-Carly Boers, *Chicago* magazine

What we say
When you are eating at Uncommon Ground, the greens, vegetables, and herbs were likely sourced directly above your head, on the restaurant's rooftop farm. Named the 2012 and 2013 Greenest Restaurant in the World by the Green Restaurant Association, Uncommon Ground established America's first certified-organic rooftop farm, which provides ingredients for dishes like vegan chilaquiles and cauliflower risotto, perfect for a dinner washed down with a beer from Greenstar Brewing, the restaurant's brewery (the first certified-organic brewery in the state). The farm is the heart of the restaurant's mission to nurture nature and nourish the community.

In addition to growing their own organic produce on the rooftop farm, owner Helen Cameron also educates the community through the annual urban-agriculture program all summer long at the rooftop farm.

Vie

Cook

What
Seasonal menu showcasing ingredients from Midwest farms

Who
Paul Virant, chef/owner

When
Dinner Tuesday to Saturday

Address
4471 Lawn Avenue, Western Springs, Cook, IL 60558

+1 708 246 2082

vierestaurant.com

Bookings
Phone, OpenTable.com

Price guide

What they say
"I want to exceed people's expectations when they come in and I want my staff to feel excited about coming to work and doing what we do best."

Signature dishes
Seared Great Lakes whitefish with White Earth wild rice, grilled ramps, garlicky spinach, pickled ramp rémoulade, and za'atar; foraged morel mushroom and garlic mustard omelet with Red Barn Dairy cupola and preserved tomato jam; spicy lamb sausage with a steamed bun, roasted ramps, cress, cumin yogurt, and crispy quinoa.

What others say
"Virant comes up with some interesting and creative combinations; he's particularly touted for his innovative pickling, canning and aigre-doux techniques, which are seamlessly (and often surprisingly) incorporated into dishes that, at their root, are familiar. A great supporter of local and sustainable produce, Virant fashions fleeting delights on his ever-changing menu."

Gayot

What we say
Vie executive chef/owner Paul Virant is known for his pickling and preserving, but that's just one component of the sustainability program at this gem of a restaurant, where their farmers are part of the restaurant family. Their belief in operating in a way that is good for their suppliers, customers, and community is clear on every plate. The menu features locally sourced and foraged ingredients that are carefully prepared, seasoned with spices from around the world and, in Chef de Cuisine Dan Compton's words, follows the mission of food that is "simple, embracing of the fleeting seasons, and bolstered by our constant preservation endeavors".

181

Indiana

Bluebeard

Marion

What
Contemporary American cuisine featuring the best local produce & meat our farms have to offer

Who
Eddie Battista & Charles McIntosh, owners

When
Lunch Monday to Friday, dinner, daily

Address
653 Virginia Avenue, Indianapolis, Marion, IN 46203

+1 317 605 0250

bluebeardindy.com

Bookings
Walk-ins

Price guide

What they say
"We are passionate about creating micro-economies through supporting local farmers. Our menu changes twice a day, every day and is completely dependent on what is seasonally and locally available to us. We wholeheartedly support our local community and love to love Indy."

What others say
"Somehow, Bluebeard has managed to make the trendiest of foods taste like home – like comfort food before comfort food was cool."

-Julia Spalding, *Indianapolis Monthly*

Signature dishes
Crab with Marcona almonds, arugula, gremolata, lemon aïoli, fried shallots, and Orgeat lemon vinaigrette on semolina toast; beet tartare with pistachio, rosemary, gremolata, shallot, egg yolk, beef fat vinaigrette, and parsnip chips; lamb lollies with burnt onion hummus, chard, *baba ganoush*, and burnt chili yogurt.

What we say
When the team at Bluebeard says they love Indianapolis, they aren't kidding. They show their affection in several ways, among them, providing compost to their farmers and hosting a vote with the staff about which local charity they want to donate to each week. But for diners, the love also comes across in Abbi Merriss' Italian-meets-Indy menu, which changes twice a day, every day, as she takes locally sourced ingredients and transforms them into dishes that comfort the spirit as they explore new depths of flavor.

Cafe Patachou

Marion

What
Long described as "a student union for adults", Cafe Patachou® is an award-winning cafe

Who
Martha Hoover, founder

When
Breakfast & lunch, daily

Address
4901 North Pennsylvania Street, Indianapolis, Marion, IN 46205, plus other locations - see website

+1 317 202 0765

patachouinc.com

Bookings
Website

Price guide

What they say
"We are passionate about local sourcing, use of premium, wholesome ingredients and cooking from scratch, sustainability and commitment to the community."

Signature dishes
Made-to-order omelettes made with Indiana farm-fresh eggs; salads; soups.

What others say
"A pioneering force for restaurants that doubles as vehicles for social change."

Fortune

What we say
Founded by Martha Hoover in 1989, Patachou Inc. is an independently owned, female-led company operating a collection of vibrant restaurants. Hoover's restaurants give the Indianapolis community delicious food – think fried chicken at Crispy Bird, Champagne and steak tartare at Petite Chou, a killer omelet at Cafe Patachou – with a mission.

Her restaurants source sustainably farmed and humanely raised proteins (local when possible), compost food waste, use biodegradable packaging, have a no-straws policy, and recycle all bottles, cans, cardboard, and plastics. As well, Hoover founded The Patachou Foundation, with a mission to feed food-insecure school children in Indianapolis. She brings that mission to her staff, conducting continued education with her team about food sourcing and sustainability, plus providing farm trips, culinary trips to other cities, and other training opportunities.

FARMbloomington

Monroe

What
Farm-to-table restaurant by Chef Daniel Orr

Who
Daniel Orr, chef/owner

When
Lunch & dinner, Tuesday to Sunday; breakfast Tuesday to Friday

Address
108 East Kirkwood Avenue, Bloomington, Monroe, IN 47408

+1812 390 2223

farm-bloomington.com

Bookings
Email farmsamantha@gmail.com

Price guide

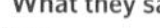

What they say
"We are passionate about locally sourced food with global flavors. We create seasonally inspired dinner menus and daily specials that change with the availability of local ingredients and the bounty of both Southern Indiana and the world. We care deeply about the environment and from day one have used biodegradable straws, to-go containers, and to-go utensils. We also recycle all of our spent oil."

Signature dishes
"Lugar burger" using Buffalo Nickel Ranch bison with a chili-espresso rub, local cheeses and Mariah smokehouse bacon; wood-stone oven bacon and egg brunch pizza with Good Life Farms baby spinach, Rhodes Family eggs, Mariah peppered bacon, smoked gouda, and house red sauce; sweet potato *vichyssoise* topped with Capriole Farms goat cheese and home-grown chives.

What we say
At FARMbloomington, chef and owner Daniel Orr brings the influences of cuisines around the world to Bloomington, and at the same time, puts the town on the map as home to one of the best destination restaurants in the United States. Orr and his team grow much of the produce used at the restaurant using compost from the kitchen, and partner with local famers to provide the rest. Orr's book, *The Wellness Lifestyle*, encompasses the restaurant's values. Here, you'll sample everything from house-made mini corn dogs to Valencian paella, getting tastes here and there from Orr's experiences as a chef in the Caribbean and New York City. But most of all, you'll enjoy the best of what Midwestern farm-to-table dining can be.

185

Iowa

Harbinger Restaurant

Des Moines

What
Vegetable-focused, Iowa-artisan aligned small plate & tasting menu restaurant

Who
Joe Tripp, chef/owner & Jason Simon, owner

When
Dinner Tuesday to Sunday

Address
2724 Ingersoll Avenue, Des Moines, IA 50312

+1 515 244 1314

harbingerdsm.com

Bookings
Phone, Resy.com or email harbingerdsm@gmail.com

Price guide

What they say
"Harbinger is all about Iowa, the wonderful place we call home. We strive to support local, not just with our food, but with the soap we use in our bathrooms, the candles burning in the dining room, and the art upon our walls. Iowa-based artisans give our space its character. A Des Moines company made our bar of barnwood reclaimed from one of our favorite farms - after it was paved over by the state for a new road. Its presence continuously reminds us of the importance of supporting and strengthening our Iowa community."

Signature dishes
Smoked sablé *banh xeo*, a reimagined Vietnamese crêpe made with local dark rye flour, smoked sablefish, capers, and cultured cream; crispy pig face, a breaded torchon of pork with house-preserved last-summer tomatoes, with Chinese mustard, blistered cabbage and preserved mouse melons; asparagus *chawanmushi*: custard of asparagus broth and egg with roast asparagus, fresh asparagus, morel mushrooms, yuzu vinaigrette, and brioche *furikake*.

What others say
Semifinalist: Best Chef - Midwest.

James Beard Foundation

What we say
An artful spot. Iowa's best bar-program is here, and they turn the pits of stone fruits into unique bitters. Acclaimed Chef Joe Tripp translates his love of southeast Asia through his own heritage and memory, serving it all in local artists' handmade ceramics, in a dining room likewise abundant in local makers' ambitious projects.

HoQ

Des Moines

What
Farm-to-table restaurant where over ninety percent of ingredients come from within thirty miles

Who
Suman Hoque, chef & Cynthia Hoque, restaurateur

When
Brunch, lunch & dinner, Monday to Saturday

Address
303 East 5th Street, Des Moines, IA 50309

+1 515 244 1213

hoqtable.com

Bookings
Phone, email hoqrestaurant@gmail.com

Price guide

What they say
"Over ninety percent of our ingredients come from small surrounding farms, typically within about thirty miles. We are the first and only true farm-to-table restaurant in Des Moines. We focus on grass-pasture animals for meat, dairy, and eggs, and reduce food waste by buying whole animals and butchering ourselves. We use locally grown, freshly ground wholewheat flour.

"We are also well known for our vegetarian and vegan options, though what we are most passionate about is sourcing high quality delicious food from local suppliers to make unique dishes reflecting our love of our world and Iowa!"

Signature dishes
Grass-fed Iowa steak; Iowa bison burgers, vegetarian potato and kohlrabi cakes.

What others say
"He does a tremendous job with his highly stylish restaurant that offers a farm-to-table concept with quality, freshness and an eye for detail."

-Carl Wertzberger, *Des Moines Register*

What we say
The ratio of hogs to people in Iowa is seven to one - please know if you eat ham or bacon in America, there's a good chance it comes from Iowa. Iowa also raises one out of every five of America's eggs, and is the country's main corn producer. With all that farm power, it's surprising that farm-to-table restaurants in Iowa are rarer than hens' teeth. That's why, if you want to taste the unmediated products of some of the most productive farmland on earth, you must go to HoQ - they're the leading farm restaurant in the kingdom of the farm.

Le Jardin

Des Moines

What
Des Moines bistro sourcing from local farms & gardens

Who
Tag Grandgeorge, chef/owner

When
Dinner Thursday to Saturday, weekend brunch

Address
2815 Beaver Avenue, Suite 101, Des Moines, IA 50310

+1 515 255 5787

lejardindsm.com

Bookings
Phone

Price guide

What they say
"Le Jardin's food philosophy is that we try to be absolutely fresh, with inspiration and ideas and an approach that is grounded in proper and basic French technique. We feature a new menu every eight to ten weeks and a nightly dinner feature. Le Jardin's rustic French cuisine adheres to an organic operational model allowing Chef Grandgeorge to participate in the planning, planting, cultivating, growing, and harvesting cycles of independent, organic, and local community farms.

"Our cuisine manifesto is hinged on local, seasonal, and sustainable ingredients. The pantry is stocked with ingredients from the gardens of friends, family, local farmers, and regional producers, bringing the abundance of the field to our table. We source products locally and seasonally. We also purchase whole animals to maximize utilization. We enjoy gardening and we often use the abundance of our garden in the restaurant."

Signature dishes
Smoked garden tomato sauce with spaetzle, shrimp, and sausage; harissa chicken with angel hair pasta, asparagus, tomatoes, dill butter, and lemon oil; steak tips in garlic sauce with roasted potatoes and chipotle mayonnaise.

What we say
A sweet, modern spot with an art gallery feel where the "shows" change every eight weeks. Although, instead of displaying paintings, Le Jardin features Chef Tag Grandgeorge's work with ingredients from local farms, including Berkwood Farms pork, Rooster Ridge Farm eggs, Holdeman Poultry, farmers' market vegetables, and local brewers including Peace Tree and Madhouse.

Trellis Cafe

Des Moines

What
Trellis highlights a monthly changing menu focused on Iowa's seasonal ingredients

Who
Lisa Mills LaValle, chef

When
Tuesday to Sunday, hours change seasonally

Address
909 Robert D. Ray Drive, Des Moines, IA 50309

+1 515 323 6288

trelliscafedsm.com

Bookings
Walk-ins, phone

Price guide

What they say
"Locally sourced meats, cheeses, eggs, and vegetables contribute to the monthly changing menu. The priority is to serve healthy, respectfully cultivated foods, carefully and creatively prepared, for taste and beauty. My goal is for customers and staff to enjoy all aspects of the dining experience."

Signature dishes
Wild rice salad with fresh local summer vegetables, creamy miso dressing, and nasturtium sprouts; local sweet corn and hominy soup with cumin broth; fresh asparagus pasta with saffron cream sauce and lemon basil sprouts.

What others say
"Lisa Lavalle opened the spectacular Trellis garden café, in the Des Moines Botanical Garden, the best designed café in many years. My favorite place for soup is Trellis. Lisa Lavalle specializes in vegetable stocks of complexity, and her café offers two soup lunch specials."

-Jim Duncan, *Cityview*

What we say
The mission of the Greater Des Moines Botanical Gardens is to advance and promote gardening in Iowa, and what better way than to have an elegant plant-forward restaurant serving the Botanical Gardens visitors their lunches? The dining room is chic and modern, with all-white surfaces and simple modern tabletops, and Chef Lisa LaValle changes the menu twelve times a year, on the first of the month, to reflect the best of the seasons.

Brazen Open Kitchen

Dubuque

What
Brazen is an open, from scratch kitchen creating honest food sourced locally

Who
Kevin Scharpf, chef/owner

When
Dinner Tuesday to Saturday, brunch Sunday

Address
955 Washington Street, Suite 101, Dubuque, IA 52001

+1 563 587 8899

brazenopenkitchen.com

Bookings
OpenTable.com, email razenopenkitchen@gmail.com

Price guide

What they say
"Brazen is the very heart and soul of chef and owner Kevin Scharpf, who cares about technique and taking the time to do it right, but cares more about being a genuine person. We strive to shine for our guests. Brazen is honest."

Signature dishes
Spring gnocchi with fresh herbs, olive oil, kale, roasted garlic, lemon, and pine nuts; salmon with asparagus velouté, dill buttermilk, spring pea, mushroom, asparagus, and baby greens; and vegan miso ramen with miso broth, alkaline noodle, nori, mushrooms, carrot, cabbage, and radish.

What we say
The Tri-State region of Illinois, Iowa and Wisconsin is Mississippi River bluff country, where soaring cliffs box in the wide river. Dubuque, only the tenth biggest city in Iowa, is nonetheless the capital of this particularly pretty bit of America which holds five colleges and a number of seminaries. Brazen is the sort of restaurant you'll only find in a collegial, healthy, pretty town like Dubuque - they have their own garden ten miles from the restaurant, and a prep cook who doubles as the garden manager. They have no freezer, and get everything fresh in daily. It's not hard to imagine that life in this river town was similar when Mark Twain was chugging up and down the river - the garden produce, the way everyone knows each other. Except Mark Twain probably never saw a microgreen, and Brazen not only has plenty, they helped their microgreen grower start her business.

189

Kansas

Merchants Pub & Plate

Douglas

What
A proud Midwestern gastropub trying for an impact beyond the table

Who
T.K., chef/co-owner & Emily Peterson, co-owner

When
Lunch & dinner daily, brunch Sunday

Address
746 Massachusetts Street, Lawrence, Douglas, KS 66044

+1 785 843 4111

merchantsonmass.com

Bookings
Phone, website

Price guide

What they say
"Here in the heartland of Kansas we promote the idea of 'come as you are'. This isn't a dress code; it's our philosophy for all we do. We are here to make folks feel comfortable. For us, it all starts with the menu, that's where we work with our neighbors to bring the best of what's available locally to the table, showcase the specialties of our region, support our local economy, and host guests for a great meal. Our menu speaks volumes: it features an old-timey map of Kansas with pinpoints of our local suppliers and what they supply - twenty-six and counting. On that menu, you'll see we've reimagined familiar dishes through our lens of seasonal, local, flexible and fun. We believe it all adds up to our community, and our community is why we do what we do."

Signature dishes
Bison burger with blueberry barbecue sauce; crispy chicken with creamed greens, yam fries, and tomato-Peppadew jam; kale Caesar salad with candied garlic, Manchego, focaccia crouton, and anchovy vinaigrette.

What we say
Lawrence, Kansas, is home to the University of Kansas, and Merchants is where this college town's smart-set go; for the thirty draft beers, for the locally pasture-raised lamb and eggs, and, above all, for the true spirit of Kansas, where being smart and close to the farm go hand-in-hand.

Story

Johnson

What
Upscale, chic & modern fine dining restaurant in Kansas City

Who
Carl Thorne-Thomsen, chef/owner

When
Dinner Wednesday to Sunday

Address
3931 W. 69th Terrace, Prairie Village, Johnson, KS 66208

+1 913 236 9955

storykc.com

Bookings
Website, OpenTable.com

Price guide

What they say
"The name 'story' is meant to signify that I'm a chef inspired and motivated by ingredients. I try to source ingredients carefully. Inevitably, the more time I spend looking for and learning about ingredients, the more I wind up knowing about them - where they are grown, pastured, fished, etc. Frequently my imagination goes to work on those details and produces a landscape or seascape, people at work in it - a 'story' of sorts. In addition, I grew up with gardens: my mother had one; my grandmother had one. In spring, summer, and fall we ate food that came out of the gardens. I didn't think about it much then, but later in life I realized that eating that way made me feel healthy and consequently good about myself. It is a feeling I would like our guests to have after dining at Story."

Signature dishes
Ceviche of fluke with apple, tomatillo, and lime; Alaskan halibut with asparagus, capers, and fingerling potatoes; braised beef short ribs with gnocchi, bacon, green beans, and onion rings.

What we say
Story is like a modern art museum in which you can eat the artworks, some of which just happen to be local turnips, radishes, tomatoes, eggplant, squash, and corn. A must-visit for conscious, unique dining.

Public

Wichita

What
Serving local food & beer in the heart of Wichita, Kansas's Old Town district

Who
Travis Russell chef/owner, Brooke Russell & Drew Thompson owners/operators

When
Lunch & dinner, Tuesday to Sunday, brunch Sunday

Address
129 North Rock Island Road, Wichita, KS 67202

+1 316 263 4044

publicoldtown.com

Bookings
Website

Price guide

What they say
"We named our restaurant 'Public' because our number one priority was to be community driven and all-inclusive here in Wichita. Our goal is to create dishes inspired by seasonal and local ingredients for the masses. It's been rewarding to help local farmers grow their businesses while they help us elevate the quality of food we are serving. We work with over thirty local purveyors to source the finest products in our region."

Signature dishes
Shrimp and grits with shrimp from Sunflower Shrimp Company, organic yellow corn grits, Yoder Meats andouille sausage poached in Wichita Brewing Company WuShock Wheat and pea sprouts from KanGrow Hydro Farm; Serenity Smash Steak Burger with Creekstone Farms steak patties, Alma Creamery aged cheddar, Serenity Farms green tomato relish, lettuce, grilled onions, and secret sauce; farm fresh carbonara with house-made smoked garlic fettuccine and duck ham.

What we say
Smack-dab in central Kansas on a bend in the Arkansas river, Wichita is the biggest city in Kanas, and a place where folks know the value of a dollar - which is why everything at locally minded Public is priced about what you'd pay at a mindless big-box restaurant. But you'll never find bright farm-fresh eggs like Public has at a chain, so it all works out very well for the people of Wichita, who get top quality at a price they feel good about.

Elderslie Farm

Sedgwick

What
A rural Kansas farm-to-table restaurant, blackberry farm & goat creamery

Who
Katharine Elder, chef/ co-owner

When
Dinner Thursday to Saturday, breakfast & lunch seasonally

Address
3501 East 101st Street North, Valley Center, Sedgwick, KS 67147

+1 316 305 2984

eldersliefarm.com

Bookings
OpenTable.com

Price guide

What they say
"We are dedicated to this place in Kansas, nestled in one of the many turns of Chisolm Creek. We have a diverse team from the kitchen squad to the goat milking crew, to the gardener, blackberry farmer, and all of those in between, including Chef Katharine's children who seem to pop up everywhere. As a small family-run business we delight in bringing life and joy to this place and sharing what we hope is an authentic experience with all our guests. We believe that true sustainability begins with affection; affection for this land, for what it brings to us, and for one another."

Signature dishes
Summer beets with Elderslie chèvre, four types of beets (bull's blood, Chiogga candy stripe, white, yellow) in a lemon shallot vinaigrette, with toasted pistachio and pea shoots; herbed focaccia with young goat cheese, lemon zest, and green olive oil; goat agnolotti with beurre blanc and asparagus tips.

What we say
Kansas is a road-trip destination that will fill your heart - and belly. At Elderslie Farm, discover a rural Kansas blackberry farm and goat creamery run by a chef whose ambition is to share all she has with any traveler curious enough to get off the usual roads. A passion for local fare, bold flavors, and community is evident at this exciting venue, urging diners to return again and again.

195

Michigan

Salt of the Earth

Allegan

What
Honest food & friendly folks highlighting the best quality ingredients Michigan has to offer

Who
Mike Kenat, chef, & Matthew Campbell, general manager/sommelier

When
Dinner Wednesday to Sunday, brunch Sunday

Address
114 East Main Street, Fennville, Allegan, MI 49408

+1 269 561 7258

saltoftheearthfennville.com

Bookings
Phone, website, Yelpreservations.com

Price guide

What they say
"The phrase 'salt of the earth' is defined as basic, fundamental goodness. We thrive on giving the best experience to our patrons as well as building strong relations with our purveyors, our community, and our staff. We offer an authentic Midwest-American rustic food experience built from the foundation of fresh high-quality ingredients."

Signature dishes
Chilled asparagus with chargrilled asparagus, foraged ramp *gribiche*, and shaved radish; chèvre panna cotta with pickled beets, house-cultured yogurt, citrus, and micro arugula; wood-fire oven-roasted chicken with heirloom tomatoes, salsa verde, smoked peppers, and crispy polenta.

What others say
"The kitchen [views] every culinary element as important, no matter how basic."

-William R. Wood, *Michigan Live*

What we say
Driving past farms around Fennville, you quickly see how much Michigan produce is all around. At Salt of the Earth, Chef Mike Kenat is taking those ingredients, the community that produces them, and his own talent to create homey yet striking dishes he calls Midwestern rustic American. His philosophy is to source the best quality ingredients from the area, then work in tandem with the rest of the restaurant family to create a memorable, caring experience for guests, from the house-made bread and butter that starts the meal to the cheddar pierogies, *panzanella* from the restaurant garden, and locally farmed shrimp served with grits and smoked tomato sauce that follow. It's thoughtfully prepared food that comes from the heart of Western Michigan.

Granor Farm

Berrien

What
A certified-organic vegetable farm hosting dinners that feature our produce, eggs & grain

Who
Katie Burdett, farm manager & Abra Berens, chef

When
By reservation only

Address
3480 Warren Woods Road, Three Oaks, Berrien, MI 49128

granorfarm.com

Bookings
Website

Price guide

What they say
"We are the most passionate about connecting our customers with how our farm operates and how they can use what we grow in their own household. We write our menu based on what is showing best in the garden rows and then provide recipes for each dish served. We also believe in minimizing food waste on our farm. The tomatoes that aren't perfect enough to be sold at the farm stand can be preserved and converted into a delicious meal for our guests."

Signature dishes
Relish tray of raw and roasted vegetables, dips, spreads, and wood-baked rye cracker bread made with Granor Farm rye and baked in a wood oven with wood from the restaurant's trees; green salad with the greens, herbs, and edible flowers that are available each day; cheese course of hand-selected cheeses from Michigan creameries paired with house-made bread and preserves.

What others say
"Abra Berens is a strong young voice in the region's chef advocacy community on issues such as fair treatment of farm and food industry workers and reduction of food waste."

GoodFood.org

What we say
Abra Berens is quick to note that the opportunity to eat well is a privilege not enjoyed by many. Berens, who is both a chef and a farmer, is deeply immersed in cooking and advocacy, focusing on helping solve that problem, while educating her guests about how simple and delicious great food can be.

Avalon Breads

Detroit

What
A socially responsible bakery, serving freshly baked goods made with 100 percent organic flour

Who
Jackie Victor, co-founder/CEO

When
Breakfast & lunch, daily

Address
422 West Willis, Detroit, MI 48201

+1 313 832 0008

avalonbreads.net

Bookings
Walk-ins

Price guide

What they say
"We are most passionate about serving our community by providing a warm and welcoming atmosphere and supporting individuals and organizations that create a just, vibrant Detroit."

Signature dishes
"Gardenworks sandwich" with avocado, locally sourced sunflower sprouts, and roasted red bell peppers on our "Motown Multigrain" bread; Motown Multigrain bread, naturally leavened and packed with grains and seeds; best-selling sea salt chocolate chip cookies.

What others say
"Avalon has an incredible selection of crusty baguettes and mouthwatering sourdough (made using organic yeast cultures)."

USA Today

What we say
A true pioneer in Detroit's baking community, Avalon International Breads is a socially responsible bakery, serving freshly baked breads and sweets made with 100 percent organic flour since it opened in 1997. Co-founder Jackie Victor calls the bakery a gathering place for the community, and says they aspire to make every person who walks through the door feel welcome. You can't help but feel good after digging into one of their sourdough breads, hearty sandwiches and soups or famous sea salt chocolate chip cookies.

Those positive vibes carry through to Avalon's work helping other independent local businesses develop a customer base and establish themselves. On top of this, they support countless Detroit area organizations, and have a diverse staff trained to further their goal to feed Detroit's heart and soul.

Lady of the House

Detroit

What
Modern American menu with an emphasis on freshness & creativity

Who
Kate Williams, chef/owner

When
Dinner Wednesday to Sunday, weekend brunch

Address
1426 Bagley Avenue, Detroit, MI 48216

+1 313 818 0218

ladyofthehousedetroit.com

Bookings
Reserve.com

Price guide

What they say
"The goal of our hospitality team is to provide an unforgettable dinner party every night and make each visit a unique experience for travelers far and near, or neighbors across the street. We have visited, and in some cases worked alongside, every one of our artisans, and believe wholeheartedly in their commitment to their land, their people, the environment, and the quality inherent in their work."

What others say
"Williams pursues a style of hospitality ... that recognized the power that comes from feeding visitors, from teaching them about the place they're in by handing them something delicious they've never had back at home."

–Pete Wells, *The New York Times*

Signature dishes
Steak tartare with charred leeks, oyster aïoli, and rye sourdough; carrot steak with hollandaise and pesto; potato donuts with chamomile, dried yogurt, and sugared thyme.

What we say
When Kate Williams created Lady of the House, her intention was to have a restaurant that felt like a dinner party. And, as you sit at your table, nibbling on Irish rarebit crackers and sipping tea from her grandmother's china, you can't help but be charmed by Lady of the House, where Williams combines her love of local produce with culinary influences from as far away as Copenhagen and as close by as the cookies she and her father baked together when she was a kid. This is a deeply personal restaurant, where Williams nurtures her farm partners, employees, guests, and community.

Grove

Kent

What
Farm-to-table cuisine, creatively prepared & sustainably sourced

Who
Jeremy Paquin, chef

When
Dinner, daily, brunch Sunday

Address
919 Cherry Street, Southeast, Grand Rapids, Kent, MI 49506

+1 616 454 1000

groverestaurant.com

Bookings
Phone, OpenTable.com, walk-ins

Price guide

What they say
"At Grove, we are extremely passionate about the relationships we develop with area farmers and local purveyors. This gives us the ability to showcase what West Michigan has to offer, and creates a strong connection between the source of the food on the table and the guests sitting in the seats. These connections, along with the seasonality of the food, really allows us to engage our creativity when it comes to developing a unique experience for the guests in our community."

What others say
"Restaurant of the Year"

Grand Rapids Magazine

Signature dishes
Morel *mafaldine* with nettle-infused house-made pasta, Parmesan brodo, pickled and smoked mushrooms, truffle powder, local greens, and local garlic crumbs; confit duck leg with carrot soubise, asparagus *socca*, pickled mustard seeds, smoked peaches, charred asparagus, and lavender honey; steelhead crudo with citrus, fiddlehead ferns, asparagus, lime and beet tuille.

What we say
One of the stalwarts of Grand Rapids' sustainable restaurant scene, Grove ties its success and future to the community, striving to add value to the neighborhood in which they do business. They are a big part of the local food movement, as demonstrated on Chef Jeremy Paquin's menu of healthy, farm-to-plate dishes, with fish sourced from the Great Lakes, fruits and vegetables from local gardens and specialty ingredients foraged from the area. The restaurant staff further gives back with park clean-ups and tree planting, and using their time and resources to support people in need.

Luna

Kent

What
Higher-end, authentic Mexican restaurant

Who
Mario A. Cascante, owner

When
Lunch & dinner, Monday to Saturday

Address
64 Ionia Avenue Southwest, Suite 100, Grand Rapids, Kent, MI 49503

+1 616 288 6340

lunagr.com

Bookings
Walk-ins, phone, email hello@lunagr.com

Price guide

What they say
"Food is a bridge that unites. Sharing a meal at a table can bring everyone together, and we hope to provide such a forum. Luna is the love child of Latin American and West Michigan cultures, best mixed beneath a shared light. We love this food, we love this place, and we're excited to add another dimension to an already vibrant city."

Signature dishes
Ceviche with wild-caught white fish, red onion, cilantro, lime, jalapeño, and tostada; organic quinoa salad with black beans, bell peppers, red onions, feta, spicy chipotle vinaigrette, and Mud Lake Farm greens; *elotes* with corn on the cob, chili, lime aïoli, butter, *cotija*, and cilantro.

What we say
Ecology is central to the ethos at Luna, where Mario Cascante believes that any sustainable entity should view itself as a part of a vibrant living community, and makes the ingredients from his modern Mexican menu, staff, dining space, and customers part of an ongoing Midwestern narrative. Cascante calls them simple, heartfelt, intense flavors that reflect our lived experiences; we call the house-made salsa flight, tart, punchy *aguachile* and mussels cooked with jalapeños, chorizo, achiote, and coriander the best way to combine Mexico and Michigan.

What others say
"Whether you order the salsa flight or the pork tacos ... you can be sure every bit of the dish is organic, homemade, and grown from within West Michigan."

-Lauren Matison, *Travel + Leisure*

Zingerman's Roadhouse

Washtenaw

What
Specializing in traditional American regional food & drink

Who
Ari Weinzweig & Paul Saginaw, co-owners

When
Breakfast, lunch & dinner, daily

Address
2501 Jackson Avenue, Ann Arbor, Washtenaw, MI 48103

+1 734 663 3663

zingermansroadhouse.com

Bookings
Phone, website

Price guide

What they say
"We are passionate about sharing stories of great, sometimes little-known American dishes with a great service experience from a committed, well-informed, passionate staff."

Signature dishes
Eastern North Carolina pulled pork made with heirloom pasture-raised pork served with an Eastern North Carolina apple cider vinegar sauce; macaroni and cheese made with artisan *maccheroni* from Tuscany, house-made béchamel, and Vermont Cheddar; potlikker fish stew served over Anson Mills organic heirloom grits.

What others say
"When you source and cook like this, it is hard to not produce great food, and it is really hard to go wrong eating here."

-Larry Olmsted, *USA Today*

What we say
Ari Weinzweig and Paul Saginaw turned the small college town of Ann Arbor, Michigan, into a foodie destination with their original Zingerman's Deli. Zingerman's Roadhouse continues that mission, offering classic American comfort food created with love from sustainably sourced ingredients. The Zingerman's businesses broaden their mission to serve the community by giving back with programs like Food Gatherers, an independent nonprofit food rescue program and food bank they founded and continue to support, and by putting a zero-waste ethos at the heart of their guiding principles. They serve their employees with an inclusive, no-drama work initiative and several leadership programs, following their mission that staff and guests feel they are making a good environmental choice when they shop, eat, and work at Zingerman's businesses.

201

Minnesota

Alma

Minneapolis

What
Minneapolis icon combining a boutique hotel, fine dining restaurant & casual café

Who
Alex Roberts, chef/owner

When
Breakfast, lunch & dinner, daily

Address
528 University Avenue Southeast, Minneapolis, MN 55414

+1 612 379 4909

almampls.com

Bookings
OpenTable.com

Price guide

What they say
"At Alma we strive to create simplicity, elevated. We do this by providing distinct, quality-driven dining experiences, for both celebratory and everyday meals. We do this by bringing genuine care and integrity to all things food and hospitality. We aim to have this same thread of genuine care run through all relationships staff, guest, vendor, and greater community."

Signature dishes
Duck breast and carnitas with Swiss chard, masa fritter, cumin *mojo*, and black bean purée; crispy soft-cooked egg with arugula, smoked mushrooms, fontina fondue; house rigatoni with pepperoncini braised lamb, pecorino, and garlic breadcrumbs.

What we say
Since opening in 1999, Alma has set the standard in Minneapolis, for both sensitivity and sustainability. Today, the restaurant has grown into a little complex near the Mississippi River. Up top are seven boutique hotel rooms stocked with house-made organic soaps, below is an all-day café offering delicate croissants, farm-driven cocktails (an autumn squash daiquiri sounds mad but is madly delicious), and lunches built around items like their legendary tomato soup, and then on that same ground floor is a prix fixe exceptionally fine restaurant. All of it runs on an engine of close relationships with farms and the surrounding community, oiled by graciousness and intentional kindness.

The Bachelor Farmer

Minneapolis

What
The Bachelor Farmer is a restaurant in the capital of America's North, Minneapolis

Who
Andrew & Eric Dayton, co-owners

When
Dinner, daily

Address
50 North 2nd Avenue, Minneapolis, MN 55401

+1 612 206 3920

thebachelorfarmer.com

Bookings
Phone, website, walk-ins

Price guide

What they say
"The Bachelor Farmer is rooted in a strong sense of place; the North. We set out to represent our hometown of Minneapolis and the surrounding region through food, design, and hospitality when many were looking to the coasts. Our part of the country has something important to contribute to the national conversation and we've done our very best to help discover that distinct Northern voice. In design, this means we use local furniture companies, artists, and design. In the kitchen, it means ingredients available locally and seasonally. A northern orientation also means a strong tradition of preservation: things like garlic scapes and strawberries, fleeting in the summer months, are preserved for use in the dead of winter to top dishes when summer seems furthest away."

Signature dishes
Red Wattle pork chops; smoked rainbow trout rillettes with watercress, herring roe, a duck egg, crème fraîche, pickled cucumber, and dill; salad with Salanova lettuces, aged goat's milk cheese, cider vinegar, and walnuts.

What others say
"In countless ways, our Restaurant of the Year more than exceeds the sum of its parts. The Bachelor Farmer has managed to capture the zeitgeist of modern-day Minneapolis."

-Rick Nelson, *StarTribune*

What we say
Bachelor Farmer has done more than any restaurant in America to define Northern Cuisine. (Most briefly, imagine Southern Cuisine, then imagine the opposite.) Apples, potatoes, and Scandinavian and native Northern pine-forest elements flow through every plate, making locals see their culture with fresh, appreciative eyes.

Birchwood Cafe

Minneapolis

What
A neighborhood Minneapolis gem, Birchwood is about fostering community & inspiring gratitude

Who
Tracy Singleton, owner; Marshall Paulsen, chef

When
Breakfast, lunch, & dinner, daily

Address
3311 East 25th Street, Minneapolis, MN 55406

+1 612 722 4474

birchwoodcafe.com

Bookings
Website

Price guide

What they say
"'Innumerable measures bring us this food, we should know how it comes to us.' This is our mantra. We are passionate about connecting people to where real food comes from and how our food choices do matter and can make a difference when we choose to support a local sustainable food system."

Signature dishes
Savory spring Parmesan and millet waffle with asparagus, house-made rhubarb-jalapeño marmalade, radish butter, a Locally Laid egg, Fischer Family Farms lardons, sunflower seeds, powdered sugar, and local maple syrup; "Mushrooms and Sweet Peas": a blend of foraged and cultivated mushrooms with snap peas, foraged ramps, organic butter, and lemon; tahini tomato chicken with fingerlings, ramps, mixed herbs, bibb lettuce, hemp seed buttermilk vinaigrette and garden "doodads" (edible flowers and herbs).

What we say
As close to their many farms as a tree is to its forest, the Birchwood seems to have become inextricable from the many farms that supply it, so much so that they now work with eight seasons, to reflect farmers' reality. There's not just summer, but also "scorch", when the heat makes tomatoes sugary and lettuce bolt. Not just autumn but also "dusk", when growing stops, but vegetables remain in their fields. Meanwhile, Birchwood's different community justice initiatives make it a crossroads. They say of forests that you can't see them for the trees, but Birchwood lets you see both the forest and the trees, the farms and the community, in one sustained gaze.

Common Roots Cafe

Minneapolis

What
Minneapolis cafe focused on locally sourced & organic ingredients

Who
Danny Schwartzman, owner

When
Breakfast, lunch & dinner, daily

Address
2558 Lyndale Avenue South, Minneapolis, MN 55405

+1 612 871 2360

commonrootscafe.com

Bookings
Walk-ins

Price guide

What they say
"We opened our restaurant in 2007 as an expression of our values in action. From the beginning, the idea was to create a socially responsible business that actively and continually supported local farmers, put environmental stewardship in the forefront of every decision, created a fair and supportive workplace for our staff, and intentionally built a community gathering place in a location that serves as the cross section for diverse and growing neighborhoods. Also, we track all the sourcing and report by dollars spent."

Signature dishes
Bagels made in-house daily made using local and organic ingredients; wild rice burger; organic cauliflower seasoned with a light curry spice, roasted, and served with a local yogurt tahini sauce.

What we say
The founder of the national "Hate Has No Business Here" movement, Common Roots, has made a name for itself as an intentional business leading the way nationally in diverse realms of ethical behavior, including fair wages for staff, local sourcing, supporting small organic farms, supporting immigrant communities and immigrant community farms - we could go on. Most significantly, Common Roots is a place to go when you want a delicious grass-fed latté and a beautiful caramel roll, and you want to be sure that your money is doing the most good it could possibly do.

Corner Table

Minneapolis

What
A neighborhood based, seasonally-driven casual fine dining restaurant in South Minneapolis

Who
Nick Rancone, owner & Thomas Boemer, chef/owner

When
Dinner Monday to Saturday

Address
4537 Nicollet Avenue, Minneapolis, MN 55419

+1 612 823 0011

cornertablerestaurant.com

Bookings
Phone, OpenTable.com, email events@twistdavisgroup.com

Price guide

What they say
"At Corner Table we strive to be intimate, and detail focused. We designed and built most every element within this restaurant ourselves, and that translates into a guest feeling taken care of from every angle, without pretense or fuss. The menu is inventive but relies on what grows best around us when it is at its peak. We just want the resource to shine. We source all of our proteins within 200 miles, most within fifty. If it isn't in season locally, it isn't on our menu."

Signature dishes
Morel mushrooms with spruce tips, pine nuts, and house-made creme fraiche; Lake Superior lake trout with house-cured ham, fava bean ragout, and pea shoots; Wild Acres Duck breast with local maple sap-glazed radishes and turnips, sorghum, miners lettuce, and parsnips.

What we say
The flagship of a Twin Cities team which also runs Revival, a cult fried-chicken spot, and In Bloom, a new hearth-cooking vegetable destination, Corner Table is one of those restaurants where chefs bring other out-of-town chefs to show what is locally possible - and where foragers bring their best foragings to get the showiest showcase. The house *omakase*, called "Feed the sh*t out of me", is legendary. So is the local wild pastured foie gras. The center of a certain tasty Minneapolis food world.

Spoonriver

Minneapolis

What
Brenda Langton's vision to provide wholesome, sustainable food in a setting of elegant simplicity

Who
Brenda Langton, chef/owner

When
Lunch & dinner, Tuesday to Sunday

Address
750 South 2nd Street, Minneapolis MN 55401

+1 612 436 2236

spoonriver.com

Bookings
Phone

Price guide

What they say
"I have been serving delicious, sustainable cuisine for over forty years, utilizing the freshest, most sustainable, local products possible. I have always dealt with a coterie of small, local purveyors and suppliers; I created The Mill City Farmers' Market out of this approach, as well as Spoonriver. My life's work has been to create a serene space to offer beautiful, sustainable, organic cuisine."

Signature dishes
"Spirit of White Earth": braised fall vegetables, with local duck confit, Minnesota wild rice, sage, and dried cherries; "Okisuki": fresh salmon in savory Japanese ginger broth with rice noodles, vegetables, and poached egg; Vietnamese sautéed shrimp and lemongrass salad of noodles with farm vegetables, and aromatic fresh herbs.

What we say
Rare are the chefs with a forty year career, and rarer still are those who have made such a mark on their community, but since she founded Cafe Kardamena in 1978, Spoonriver's chef/owner Brenda Langton has transformed the Twin Cities dining scene. First, she supported so many local farmers that those farmers grew, and needed more customers. To help them, she founded Minneapolis' boutique farmers' market, Mill City, creating a citywide destination. She was named a senior fellow at the University of Minnesota's Bakken Center for Spirituality and Healing for her wealth of nutrition and food system knowledge. Spoonriver is Chef Langton's saffron-bright jewel of a restaurant, but it's also a landmark of her accomplishment.

French Meadow Cafe & Bluestem Bar

Minneapolis

What
An organic farm-to-table café & bakery from one of the foremothers of organics

Who
Lynn Gordon, founder/owner

When
Breakfast, lunch & dinner, daily

Address
2610 Lyndale Avenue South, Minneapolis, MN 55408, plus other locations - see website

+1 612 870 7855

frenchmeadowcafe.com

Bookings
Walk-ins, phone, OpenTable.com

Price guide

What they say
"French Meadow Bakery & Cafe aims to provide people with food that is pure, wholesome, and crafted with integrity. In this era of greenwashing, French Meadow remains passionate about walking the walk and staying true to the same strict organic and environmental standards that we began with. Since our opening we have sourced our produce from truly organic, and mostly local, farms who practice biodynamics. All meats are local, hormone-free, humane, and grass-fed from farmers we know and trust. We never sacrifice quality, and have total respect for our guests by working hard each and every day to provide an environment where everyone comes away feeling healthy, indulged, and satisfied."

Signature dishes
"Earth Wings": roasted cauliflower "wings" in sesame barbecue sauce with organic celery and coriander-soy dressing; hand-rolled butternut squash ravioli with squash from Dragsmith Farms; almond-encrusted walleye with garlic potatoes and organic broccolli rabe.

What we say
Is there an Alice Waters of American baking? If so it might well be Minneapolis' Lynn Gordon, who, as a health-minded macrobiotic cook in 1985, had her neighborhood cafe and yeast-free bakery certified as the country's first organic bakery. Later, she was instrumental in the United States' legal fight to allow hemp seeds in food, and founded the People's Organic quick-serve chain. Many of Gordon's relationships with farmers predate any American notion of a farm-to-table movement. But more importantly, her food is made with care and passion - and is always delicious.

French Meadow Cafe & Bluestem Bar (p. 206)

Tiny Diner

Minneapolis

What
A Minneapolis neighborhood institution with gigantic planet-healing ambitions

Who
Kim Bartmann, instigator

When
Breakfast, lunch & dinner, daily

Address
1024 East 38th Street, Minneapolis, MN 55407

+1 612 767 3322

tinydiner.com

Bookings
Walk-ins, phone

Price guide

What they say
"The Tiny Diner was created using a 'whole-system design' framework. The restaurant showcases bio-intensive urban farming methods and efficient water use strategies through its edible gardens and complex rainwater catchments systems. With a solar paneled patio roof, the Diner offsets a good portion of its energy usage. Tiny Diner sports rooftop honey bees and grows on-site annual crops in our garden beds to foster pollinator habitat and soil fertility. Permaculture classes and other growing classes are offered for free (or for materials costs) year-round. Oh, and good food, beer, and wine! Specials are inspired by different American cities and their hometown diners. What can we say? This Tiny Diner does a lot, because we're passionate about food and where it comes from."

What others say
"The grass-fed burger, meaty and juicy, is solid, craveable, everything you want in your corner diner. The beet terrine is prettily composed, fresh, light, just right in every way ... Onion rings are light as balloons and some of the best in the Twin Cities."

-Dara Moskowitz Grumdahl, *Mpls Saint Paul*

Signature dishes
Peterson Farms Limousin beef burgers; macrobiotic and ultra-seasonal macro bowl.

What we say
Not many American flapjack-and-burger diners have their own urban vegetable farm, but Tiny Diner does – as well as rooftop bees, house-made cucumber mint soda, and a pretty flower garden with a woven-vine house in the middle for kids to play in once they've finished their breakfast. It's a place where the oldest American urban traditions meet the most forward-looking urban, environmentally sustainable vision.

TINY DINER

TINY
DINER

Angry Trout Cafe

Cook

What
Small town waterfront café in Grand Marais, Minnesota, specializing in fresh fish from Lake Superior

Who
Barb LaVigne & George Wilkes, owners

When
Lunch & dinner, daily

Address
416 West Highway 61, Grand Marais, Cook, MN, 55604

+1 218 387 1265

angrytroutcafe.com

Bookings
Walk-ins

Price guide

What they say
"Open since 1998, the Angry Trout Cafe is a small indoor and outdoor restaurant cobbled together from an old commercial fishing shanty clinging to the edge of Grand Marais Harbor on Lake Superior forty-five miles from Canadian Border by road; twenty miles as the raven flies. From this beautiful setting we offer a menu based on the bounty of Lake Superior and the surrounding region, locally-grown produce, hand-harvested wild rice, and our specialty, fresh Lake Superior fish."

Signature dishes
Fresh fish from Lake Superior, grilled with a simple basting sauce of olive oil, lime, salt, pepper, and tarragon; hand-harvested natural lake wild rice from northern Minnesota, with shiitake mushrooms, dried cranberries, peas, and toasted hazelnuts; and maple syrup soda: nothin' but carbonated water and local maple syrup.

What we say
Find a lakeside table at Angry Trout, up on the northern reaches of Lake Superior. Ask for a Voyageur beer, made in town, and watch the loons. Soon someone in a locally sewn, organic cotton apron will bring you trout or herring caught by the family running the little fishing boat that you can see right there. Your fish comes, with some veggies from a neighbor - maybe rutabaga from Rutabaga Ridge? It's delicious fish, pure and clean, on a plate from nearby Cooter Pottery. Don't forget the pie - it's made from local North Shore berries. That's what Barb and George have been doing at Angry Trout since 1998, when they made an American treasure.

ninetwentyfive

Hennepin

What
Chef Lenny Russo's relentlessly regional cuisine

Who
Lenny Russo, chef

When
Breakfast, lunch & dinner, daily

Address
925 Lake Street East, Wayzata, Hennepin, MN 55391

+1 952 777 7900

ninetwentyfive.com

Bookings
Phone, website, OpenTable.com

Price guide

What they say
"Everything we do is driven by the quality, wholesomeness and location of our ingredients. We source the vast majority of our ingredients from small family farms and artisans located within a 200-mile radius of the restaurant, and supplement those ingredients with produce from our own garden and with locally foraged wild edibles. Our heritage breed livestock is pasture raised and comes from farms that employ humane and chemical-free practices. Our fish is primarily sourced from sustainable Native American fisheries and is strictly local and freshwater in keeping with our regional cuisine focus."

Signature dishes
Sheep's milk ricotta agnolotti with spring onions, pine nuts, and shell pea mint sauce; lake trout with cucumber salad, house-fermented yogurt sauce and Lake Cisco caviar; bison tenderloin with juniper, pumpkin seed pistou, spinach, and blackberry *glacé de viande*.

What we say
Chef Lenny Russo ran Heartland, a legendary Saint Paul restaurant, for many years, legendary because he sourced everything within 200 miles, and reinvented much familiar European cuisine using only ingredients from the region of Minnesota, Wisconsin, and Iowa. Heartland closed, and in 2018 he opened a new restaurant inside a boutique hotel, Wayzata's Hotel Landing. This new ninetwentyfive focuses on local freshwater fish, offering fennel-cured whitefish and Lake Superior trout with Lake Superior ciscoe roe. It carries the Heartland legacy forward, into new, watery territory.

Heirloom

Ramsey

What
Modern farmhouse cuisine in a comfy neighborhood setting in Saint Paul

Who
Wyatt Evans, chef/owner

When
Dinner, daily

Address
2186 Marshall Avenue, Saint Paul, Ramsey, MN 55104

+1 651 493 7267

heirloomstpaul.com

Bookings
Walk ins, phone, website, Exploretock.com

Price guide

What they say
"At Heirloom I'm trying to create a new language around Midwestern cuisine by taking part in training and coaching the next generation of cooks, interacting with our amazing guests and working with our communities of farmers, ranchers, foragers, and growers. We adhere to seasonality of product as a guiding principal of our menu and use that seasonality as inspiration for developing new dishes. We also have a small garden of our own that we utilize extensively, from flowers on tables to garnishes and vegetables that adorn the food."

Signature dishes
Carrot cavatelli with goat butter, dill, cocoa Cardona cheese, and smoked carrot crumble; pan-roasted walleye with Hmong vegetables and yellow curry; roast chicken with baked potato purée, seasonal vegetables, and poultry juices.

What we say
One of the best restaurants in the Twin Cities, Heirloom's chef and owner Wyatt Evans is sensitively attuned to the best of local farms, and the dishes he creates skate a remarkable line between unpretentious rusticity and elevated elegance.

Tongue in Cheek

Ramsey

What
Unpretentious neighborhood restaurant committed to the most sustainable, good local meats

Who
Leonard Anderson, chef/owner

When
Lunch & dinner, Tuesday to Sunday

Address
989 Payne Avenue Saint Paul, Ramsey, MN 55130

+1 651 888 6148

tongueincheek.biz

Bookings
Website, Eveve.com

Price guide

What they say
"We believe living a good life tastes better. Ethically raised livestock, sustainably caught seafood, creative vegan options, and locally sourced produce from small farmers are the strategies we use to get the best food in front of our customers. The happier the animals are while being raised and cared for, the better they taste. You can come get great service and food while wearing jeans and a T-shirt, and not feel out of place. At the same time, you can come get the same thing all dressed up and still not feel out of place."

Signature dishes
"Bacon & Egg": a sous-vide egg yolk breaded and fried to create a custard-like texture with bacon powder, a spicy hot fluid gel, avocado purée, and sea salt; "vegasm" a weekly changing vegan entrée sourced from what's in season at local farms.

What we say
The very definition of a neighborhood hero, Tongue in Cheek supports a different community or neighborhood group every week, offers a vegan tasting menu for those not seeking their famous local small-farm pork, and is a pillar of the East-side Saint Paul good life.

New Scenic Cafe

Saint Louis

What
An artisan dining experience along the scenic North Shore of Lake Superior

Who
Scott Graden, chef/owner

When
Lunch & dinner, daily

Address
5461 North Shore Drive, Duluth, Saint Louis, MN 55804

+1 218 525 6274

newsceniccafe.com

Bookings
Phone, walk-ins

Price guide

What they say
"Since opening in 1999, I have sought to introduce the North Shore of Lake Superior community to new cooking styles and cuisine. Today, I try to keep three core ideas in mind: simplicity, honesty, and awareness. Simplicity; ingredients should not be overly altered. This demands that each ingredient is of exceptional quality. Honesty; no tricks, no gimmicks, no hidden surprises, just sincerely genuine good food. Awareness; conceive, prepare, and present your food with mindfulness. Lately, beer has become a particularly exciting area to showcase fantastic local Minnesota products. We currently have beers and ciders from twelve Minnesota breweries. The best part is they're not just on our menu because they're from Minnesota, they're on our menu because they are truly great products."

Signature dishes
Caramelized carrot with béarnaise, garlic, thyme, butter, maldon salt, sour, and bitter greens; goat cheese cake with white peach, rosé, and elderflowers.

What we say
The narrow strip of highway that heads out of Duluth and threads between the Sawtooth Mountains and Lake Superior is the summertime path of armies of tourists, all of whom seem to stop to find out what Scott Graden is cooking up where pine trees and gray wolves define the Northern forest. Graden cooks with local lake herring from one of the few remaining commercial boats that work Lake Superior's waters, and does beautiful work with local maple syrup and north country blueberries.

Northern Waters Smokehaus

Saint Louis

What
Deli filled with smoked fish, handcrafted smoked meats, salumi, sandwiches & sausage

Who
Eric Goerdt, owner & Mary Tennis, general manager

When
Lunch & dinner, daily

Address
DeWitt-Seitz Marketplace, 394 Lake Avenue South, Suite 106, Duluth, Saint Louis, MN 55802

+1 218 724 7307

nwsmokehaus.com

Bookings
Walk-ins

Price guide

What they say
"We believe that food is delightful. We believe that food is powerful. Food connects community. Food engages visitors. Food comforts the uneasy. Food facilitates celebration. Food provides a trade. Food showcases skill. Food highlights tradition. Food provides room for endless innovation and creativity. We serve high-quality, creative food, focusing on fish and pork. We work with several local fishermen to source our Lake Superior lake trout, herring, and whitefish. We buy all of our pork from local producers. We have been purchasing happy pigs, bison, beef, and poultry from Midwestern producers since we started in 1998. Some of our hero suppliers include Steve Dahl, our herring fisherman, and Dave Rogotzke, our salmon fisherman."

Signature dishes
Sitka sushi sandwich: supple house-smoked sustainably-raised Atlantic gravlax with pickled ginger, shredded cabbage, cucumber, cilantro, wasabi mayo, and sriracha; *Banh Faux Mi*: house-smoked Minnesota Berkshire ham with country-style liver pâté, pickled vegetables, cilantro, hoisin, sriracha, and butter.

What others say
"You gotta go to Northern Waters. You just gotta."

-Mecca Bos, *City Pages*

What we say
Wood-smoked freshwater fish was once a staple on Lake Superior, one of the largest fresh water lakes in the world. The tradition is little carried on today, except at Northern Waters Smokehaus, where owners Eric and Lynn Goerdt, having met and married in Sitka, Alaska, founded their new fish and pork smoking operation, in 1998. Their little sandwich shop all but single-handedly carries these northern freshwater traditions forward, and is a regional treasure.

217

Missouri

Black Dirt

Kansas City

What
Kansas City farm-to-table, nose-to-tail, & vegetable-heavy to citywide acclaim

Who
Jonathan Justus, executive chef/co-owner

When
Lunch & dinner, daily

Address
5070 Main Street,
Kansas City, MO 64112

+1 816 214 5947

BlackdirtKC.com

Bookings
Phone, website

Price guide

What they say
"Respect is my first principle. It is very important that we respect our farmers, respect the produce and proteins that they bring us, respect the life that their animals have given, and respect each other in the restaurant family, our clients, and by our respectful actions ensure the earth's viability. If all is given respect, everything else will follow."

Signature dishes
Missouri Caesar: brûléed romaine, local dairy cow's milk cheese, cornmeal crusted Heartland catfish, and traditional dressing with anchovy replaced by house-cured Missouri trout; crispy Keifheiver Farm pigtail pieces with mung beans, garlic, jalapeño, coriander, and barbecue vinaigrette of chilies and coriander from our farm; grilled Campo Lindo Farms chicken with pan-roasted sunchokes, Shatto Dairy aged cheddar, wild arugula, and Hammons Missouri black walnut oil.

What we say
Globally, you'd be hard pressed to find a more passionate chef than Jonathan Justus, or one less interested in shortcuts. He makes his own soda with living whey and a secondary natural fermentation. He makes his own Missouri-terroir vermouth. He and his wife Camille Eklof worked without a salary for a decade establishing their internationally acclaimed restaurant Justus Drugstore, and Black Dirt does for the rich land where the Missouri and Kaw rivers meet what chefs like Alex Atala or René Rezepi have done for their own home territories. An American treasure.

Bluestem Restaurant

Kansas City

What
One of the finest restaurants between the coasts, a James Beard Award-winner for Best Chef Midwest

Who
Colby Garrelts & Megan Garrelts, chefs/owners

When
Dinner Tuesday to Saturday

Address
900 Westport Road, Kansas City, MO 64111

+1 816 561 1101

bluestemkc.com

Bookings
OpenTable.com, walk-ins

Price guide

What they say
"Bluestem has always been dedicated to celebrating Kansas City with local meat and dairy, farmer produce, breweries, distilleries, and locally crafted cheeses. Kansas City has a very tight knit community of chefs, beverage and hospitality professionals which makes it the perfect environment for collaborative efforts for events, dinners, and community outreach. We love our big, small town! We also grow some of our own produce on our family farm, and on good years our menu is filled with homegrown herbs, flowers, tomatoes, and summer squashes."

Signature dishes
Spring pea soup of freshly shelled peas puréed and poured over local sheep's cheese, served with pink peppercorns and farmer greens; in fall: glazed pork belly with white beans, turnips, glazed chard, and a touch of smoke from chilies.

What we say
Named for the all-American prairie grass, Bluestem and it's casual sister restaurant, Rye, hold an outsize place in the culinary life of Missouri. Many of the best local chefs have come up through the Garrelts' kitchens, where they showcase the best of all that comes from local farms. Bluestem is the standard-bearer of fine food in Kansas City. The restaurant was nominated in 2015, 2016, and 2017 as a James Beard Semifinalist for Outstanding Restaurant; Colby Garrelts won in 2013 for Best Chef Midwest.

Novel

Kansas City

What
Kansas City contemporary American food using sustainable, local ingredients

Who
Ryan Brazeal, chef & Jessica Armstrong, pastry chef

When
Dinner Tuesday to Saturday

Address
1927 McGee Street, Kansas City, MO 64108

+1 816 221 0785

novelkc.com

Bookings
Yelpreservations.com

Price guide

What they say
"We are committed to providing an exceptional regional experience to define and create unique Midwestern cuisine and hospitality based around the food and camaraderie that has always been a staple of Kansas City dining. We use seasonal produce, we buy from local farmers, and we source responsibly raised meat."

Signature dishes
Soft-poached farm egg breaded in rice pearls with beef oxtail stew, chilis, tamarind and salad; tagliatelle with white bolognese; raspberry chiffon cake with caramelized white chocolate mousse, violet marshmallows, and lemon brown butter ice cream.

What others say
"The ethos of experimentation, digression and creativity operate at full throttle."

-Steve Paul, *Kansas City Star*

What we say
Novel isn't named for the long work of prose but for newness, as in novelty. To that end, Ryan Brazeal and Jessica Armstrong try to add whimsy, beauty, and surprise to each dish they present. That's why the spring pea soup conceals wasabi tapioca pearls, and the local farm pork belly is presented as pork toast, breaded and fried. If local farms are as old as anything, can the food from them be brand new? Novel says yes.

The Farmhouse

Kansas City

What
A small Kansas City farm-to-table restaurant working with three dozen local farms

Who
Michael Foust, chef/owner

When
Breakfast & lunch, daily, dinner Wednesday to Friday

Address
300 Delaware Street, Kansas City, MO 64105

+1 816 569 6032

eatatthefarmhouse.com

Bookings
Phone, walk-ins, Exploretock.com

Price guide

What they say
"I am most passionate about connecting our friends family and community to our farms and farmers. We work with around forty local and regional farmers, depending on the time of year, to source our produce, dairy, animals, and grains."

Signature dishes
Breakfast blood sausage with a sunny-side-up quail egg, pickled mustard greens and a sorghum and local Norton wine reduction on grilled bread; crispy pork tongue with wild garlic, goats milk grits, roasted baby turnips, and morel sauce; rabbit stew with baby root vegetables, field onions, potatoes, and spring herbs.

What we say
Red velvet pancakes for breakfast, smoked turkey sandwiches at lunch, stuffed chicken – these are the staple dishes of American workaday life. But just because they're staples doesn't mean they have to be made from the lowest-cost ingredients, with the lowest care. At Farmhouse, chef and owner Michael Foust works with local farmers to make a stuffed chicken using local rhubarb from one farm and local goat's cheese from another, and serves it with leek and potato hash, and spinach from yet more local farms. He does it because that's how you sustain a community: by supporting farmers, who in turn have enough money in their pockets to support him. The staples of workaday American life all used to be sourced this way, and at the Farmhouse they are again.

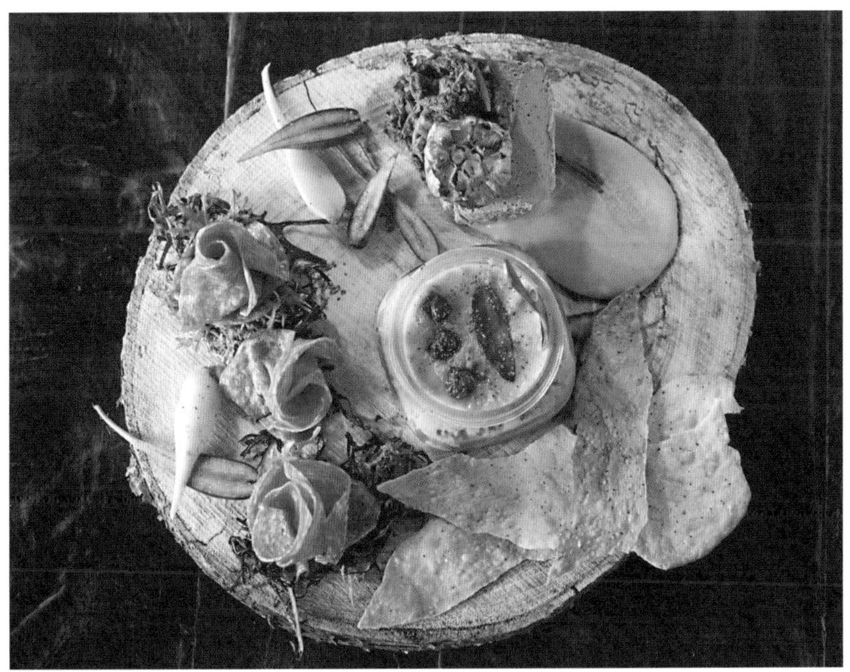

Webster House

Kansas City

What
A Romanesque historical Kansas City landmark transformed into a dining destination

Who
Shirley Bush Helzberg, owner & Brandon Winn, chef

When
Lunch, daily, dinner Wednesday to Saturday

Address
1644 Wyandotte Street, Kansas City, MO 64108

+1 816 221 4713

websterhousekc.com

Bookings
Phone, OpenTable.com

Price guide

What they say
"Buying from the person that saved the seed, put the seed in the ground, cared for the plant, toiled to make sure it was something they were proud of and delivered it to our door with a story attached, that's the core of Webster House. We aim to source thoughtfully in order to deliver not only a delicious meal but the story behind the diner's experience. We believe wholeheartedly that it is our responsibility to take every measure within our power to provide our guests with wholesome products and support local agriculture. The only way to do this is by thoughtful procurement and foresight."

Signature dishes
Skuna Bay salmon with Himalayan red rice, house-fermented black garlic and local spinach; soft-shell crab with house-made XO sauce, a purée of miso and local root vegetables, and grilled scallions; vegan creme brûlée using house-made tofu from non-GMO soybeans, pickled pecans, maple syrup, and cardamom-dusted charred berries.

What we say
Webster House is justly famed for its gorgeous building and truly breathtaking cityscape views. Once inside, it's delightful to find a pretty place, that could easily coast on its looks, taking food seriously, sourcing locally, curing and pickling on site, and bringing much more to destination dining than a pretty face.

Farmhaus

St. Louis

What
A beloved chef-driven restaurant where most of the daily menu comes from the bi-state area

Who
Kevin Willmann, chef/owner

When
Dinner Tuesday to Saturday

Address
3257 Ivanhoe Avenue St. Louis, MO 63139

+1 314 647 3800

farmhausrestaurant.com

Bookings
Phone

Price guide

What they say
"We're nearly 100 percent sourcing produce locally at this point, and have been building relationships with the best small production farms in our area for over a decade. We grow on-site as well, and have discovered many sustainable treats to share. All of this is comes together so we can provide an outstanding experience for our guests, through excellent service and the highest quality and seasonality in our cuisine."

Signature dishes
Marcoot Jersey Creamery alpine custard with English peas, house-made coppa ham, and frico; Ozark Forest mushrooms salad; Crop Circle farms spicy greens with Missouri pecans, house bacon, and Baetje goat's cheese.

What we say
St. Louis is known by outsiders for the Gateway Arch, but insiders know it as the capital of the rich farmland of Missouri and southern Illinois, as well as a Mississippi River town with a close connection to the downstream Gulf. Farmhaus is where you can taste what St. Louis insiders know about where they live, and what is altogether unique about it. It's no surprise this humble restaurant is so widely acclaimed.

Sidney Street Café

St. Louis

What
St. Louis' fine-cooking standard-bearer is also a rustic neighborhood destination

Who
Kevin Nashan, chef/owner

When
Dinner Tuesday to Saturday

Address
2000 Sidney Street, St. Louis, MO 63104

+1 314 413 9095

sidneystreetcafestl.com

Bookings
Phone, email sidneystreet@sbcglobal.net

Price guide

What they say
"We're a family-owned restaurant that has been supporting local farmers and other producers for fifteen years. We have 100 yards of raised garden beds right here in the middle of the city."

Signature dishes
Morel-stuffed *scarpinocc* pasta with pickled ramps, hazelnuts, and black vinegar emulsion; rabbit porchetta with creamy polenta, rhubarb compote, charred scallions, and mustard jus; roasted scallops with grilled asparagus, ragout of spring vegetables, shaved lardo, and bone marrow jus.

What we say
At first glance, Kevin Nashan's Sidney Street Café doesn't look all that local, as it has achieved so much local fame for Nashan's treatment of ocean ingredients such as sea urchin and octopus. (This goes double for his popular Peacemaker Lobster & Crab Co., just down the street.) However, look more carefully and you'll see all the ways Nashan uses local farms and local ingredients to glorify the world's best ingredients - how else are you ever going to get to try a Missouri sunchoke purée with sea urchin bisque?

Vicia

St. Louis

What
Vegetable-forward, farmer-driven restaurant celebrating the daily bounty of the midwest

Who
Michael Gallina, chef/partner & Tara Gallina, partner

When
Lunch Monday to Friday, dinner Tuesday to Saturday

Address
4260 Forest Park Avenue, St. Louis, MO 63108

+ 1 314 553 9239

viciarestaurant.com

Bookings
Website, phone, walk-ins

Price guide

What they say
"At a minimum, eighty percent of the ingredients we serve are grown and produced locally. We have an edible garden surrounding our restaurant where we grow fruits, herbs, and flowers that are featured in our dishes and seasonal cocktails. We partner with several local farms that grow a unique mix of vegetables exclusively for the restaurant, and we also purchase their imperfect, bolted, or unwanted harvests as a commitment to supporting the entire farming operation."

Signature dishes
Purple top turnip tacos with crushed beans, pork charcuterie crumble, charred vegetable molé, pickles and vegetable scrap hot sauce; grain salad with local wheat berries, marinated seasonal vegetables, whipped goat's cheese, and radish or turnip-top pesto; goose-egg dessert with ice cream from the yolks of local goose eggs, preserved strawberries, poached rhubarb, and a crunchy meringue made with the goose-egg whites.

What we say
Owners Michael and Tara Gallina first began winning national attention working at Dan Barber's renowned Blue Hill at Stone Barns and have since become something of the Blue Hill of the Mississippi River Valley. Do ask about their inventiveness turning food waste into gold – it's astonishing.

Winslow's Home

St. Louis

What
Serving breakfast, lunch & dinner with fresh produce from our five-acre working farm in Augusta, Missouri

Who
Ann Sheehan Lipton, owner, Cassy Vires, chef & Josh Renbarger, front of house manager

When
Breakfast, lunch, & dinner, Tuesday to Saturday, breakfast & lunch, Sunday

Address
7213 Delmar Boulevard, St. Louis, MO 63130

+1 314 725 7559

winslowshome.com

Bookings
Website

Price guide

What they say
"Produce is supplied from our working farm in Augusta, and we seek to use our farm to create quintessential mid-American meals that remind our guests of home. We do this sustainably, growing fruits, vegetables, and flowers, including several unusual heirlooms. It costs a bit more and can take a bit longer, but we believe it's worth the time. Here at Winslow's Home, you order at the counter, lingering over the house-made pastries as you do, and then your meals are made to order with what we've grown, sometimes supplemented by other products we've sourced locally. Seated in a century-old building, you are surrounded by books, kitchenwares, and assorted tools for living. Since we don't offer Wi-Fi, maybe it's a good time to catch up with your companion? We try to create community and strengthen bonds here every way we can, through great food simply prepared, through conversation, passion, excellence, and with new ideas."

Signature dishes
Market greens salad with seasonal vegetables, lightly dressed in a honey-thyme vinaigrette; egg salad with pastured eggs, pickled onions, and sprouts; beef brisket stacked on house-made rye bun with Brie and horseradish mayo; chocolate chip cookies of locally grown and milled flour, with Guittard chocolate.

What we say
A farm-to-table restaurant that doubles as a general store that carries groceries, dry goods, and kitchen items. Winslow's Home is the perfect day trip when you want to experience the earth-connected values of a real, working Missouri farm, and also want all-day-braised brisket.

Sardella

St. Louis

What
Inspired by Italy, using the best Missouri & Midwest ingredients

Who
Gerard Craft, chef/owner, & Ashley Shelton, chef

When
Dinner, daily, weekend brunch

Address
7734 Forsyth Boulevard, Clayton, St. Louis, MO 63105

+1 314 814 6180

sardellastl.com

Bookings
OpenTable.com

Price guide

What they say
"We love to research old-world Italian recipes and bring them to life using seasonal and local ingredients. For instance, all of our flours come from the Midwest, but we have been working a lot with a new flour mill to create pasta recipes that more closely reflect the flavor of our area. We also use this mill for local heirloom corns and grains. Bohlen Family Farms - these guys are the best. They raise all sorts of heirloom produce and vegetables for us, including heirloom corn for grits and chicories from seeds I brought back from Italy."

Signature dishes
Potato *culurgiones* with fiddlehead ferns, buttermilk, asparagus, and mint; *burrata* with pickled green tomato salsa verde, candied sunflower seeds, and fry bread; and roasted chicken with house-made *fregola*, artichoke, roasted fennel, and radish.

What others say
Winner: Gerald Craft, Best New Chef award.

Food & Wine magazine

What we say
The most farm-forward restaurant from Gerard Craft, arguably St. Louis' top chef, who also leads Brasserie by Niche, Taste, Pastaria, Cinder House, and Porano Pasta. Sardella is where heirloom Italian chicories grown in Missouri might be wilted and served beside Missouri-grown and milled heirloom polenta and local Berkshire pork to create a plate that would be familiar to anyone who lived a whole life in Milan - and wanted a taste of the fertile world of the American Midwest.

Green Dirt Farm Creamery

Platte

What
This small sheep's milk dairy & farm has a café & ice cream shop

Who
Sarah Hoffmann, owner

When
Lunch Sunday & Tuesday to Thursday; lunch & dinner Friday & Saturday

Address
1099 Welt Street, Weston, Platte, MO 64098

+1 816 386 2156

greendirtfarm.com

Bookings
Walk-ins

Price guide

What they say
"Our core business is not the café, but rather our artisan small batch cheese, made on our grass-based sheep dairy nearby. Our café is a way for customers to take part in what we are doing and enjoy our cheese. We believe that healthy soil grows yummy grass, which nourishes our ewes and produces fantastic milk. That rich milk, in turn, creates wonderful cheeses and yogurts that nurture our customers, ourselves, and our community."

Signature dishes
Cheese and charcuterie board with Green Dirt cheeses, local jam, and local cured and smoked meats; "Ruby Don't go Bacon My Heart": sandwich with Green Dirt "Ruby" cheese and Dragonfly Preserves Strawberry Jam; "Raspberry Tuffet" ice cream made in-house with Green Dirt "Tuffet" cheese and Dragonfly Preserves Co. raspberry preserves.

What others say
Winner, Best in Class award.

World Cheese Championships 2018

What we say
Single-farm, grass-pasture cheesemaking operations are still a rarity in the United States, and rarer still is the chance to eat the single-farm cheese in a rural farming town like Weston, Missouri. Owner Sarah Hoffman raises the ewes, makes the cheese, and provides that rare, special chance.

Catalpa

Saline

What
A fine dining restaurant in the village of Arrow Rock, located on the bank of the Missouri River

Who
Liz Huff Kennon, chef/owner

When
Dinner Friday & Saturday

Address
510 High Street, Arrow Rock, Saline, MO 65320

+1 660 837 3324

catalparestaurant.com

Bookings
Facebook, phone, website

Price guide

What they say
"We are passionate about making memories for our customers. We love interacting with our customers, and the kitchen door doubles as the entrance to the restaurant so that customers are forced to walk literally two feet away from the cooking area. That way, we have the opportunity to greet everyone that comes in and they get to see what goes on in the kitchen. We don't believe in making our food look perfect, and avoid symmetry and even numbers. We also use natural garnishes, usually fresh herbs or zest. Simple is so much more appetizing."

Signature dishes
Sea scallops, sustainably raised, with a lemon saffron cream sauce and garlic crostini; herb-roasted half-duckling, with a cherry sauce, sautéed bacon, lemon, and garlic beet greens and smashed potatoes; fresh wild salmon steak with peach balsamic glaze, and salt-grilled white and green asparagus.

What we say
Could you fit the whole fifty-six-person village of Arrow Rock, Missouri in Chef Liz Huff Kennon's teensy restaurant? Yes, you might. Maybe you should, for backyard chicken eggs and to learn some things about true Midwestern culture and friendliness, as well as true farm-raised Midwestern food. Diners can rest assured they're in good hands when opening the doors to Catalpa – and will leave feeling full, satisfied and just a little sad it's over.

Catalpa (p. 228)

Harvest

Rogersville

What
Fine cooking on a nearly 100-year-old Missouri family farm

Who
Craig von Foerster, chef/owner

When
Dinner Thursday to Saturday, Sunday brunch

Address
8011 Highway AD, Rogersville, MO 65742

+1 417 830 3656

harvestmo.com

Bookings
Website, phone

Price guide

What they say
"We're hyper-seasonal and micro-local, focused on what we can raise and do well here on our family farm. Harvest is not just about me or the chef, it's about all of us. The hands that plant, fret and harvest, allow us to do what we love in the kitchen. My wife, Tamara, The Farmer's Daughter, grows produce, berries, and herbs for all of us. We source most the rest of what we need from local farms. We say we're rooted in the country, not too far from the city that's the heart of the Ozarks - Springfield, Missouri."

Signature dishes
Farm Road 168 Fordhook Swiss chard and fresh ricotta ravioli with grilled fennel-lemon cream; Farm Road 168 heirloom lettuce salad; J.B. Farms Wagyu beef with braised oxtail, harvest smoked bacon potato purée, grilled asparagus, red wine syrup, and bone marrow butter.

What we say
In an orchard within Sunshine Valley Farm in Rogersville, Missouri, Harvest is a true farm-based fine restaurant, with its own farm, Farm Road 168. Chef Craig Von Foerster works hand in hand with his wife, the farmer and gardener Tamara Pursley-Von Foerster, to create a menu that's truly hyper-local and precisely seasonal, based on what can be harvested that day on their nearly 100-year-old family farm.

233

Nebraska

The Grey Plume

Douglas

What
Relies on its locavore menu & eco-friendly practices

Who
Clayton Chapman, chef/owner

When
Dinner Monday to Saturday

Address
220 South 31st Avenue
Suite 3101, Omaha,
Douglas, NE 68131

+1 402 763 4447

thegreyplume.com

Bookings
Phone, website, OpenTable.com

Price guide

What they say
"We seek to inspire and elevate the way Omaha thinks about food through culinary excellence, the promotion of local foods and growers, and a commitment to community. We are devoted to creating innovative cuisine on the forefront of modern culinary art, while also maintaining traditional culinary roots in showcasing the food source and practicing a no-waste attitude in every aspect of the restaurant's operation. We believe that the life cycle of food begins even before the seed, and should always end with an emotional connection."

Signature dishes
House-butchered Heartland Ranch's elk; Blue Valley whole roasted steelhead trout; house-cured charcuterie board.

What we say
The best restaurant in the history of Nebraska? Likely yes, Chef Clayton Chapman created the most surprising of all things, a laid-back, elegant, unexpected peer to nationally regarded restaurants like Manresa, but on the Iowa Nebraska border. This is seasonally-driven, contemporary cuisine from locally-grown produce and livestock at its best.

Stirnella Bar & Kitchen

Douglas

What
A refined gastropub sourcing local food to create globally inspired dishes

Who
Matt Moser, chef/owner

When
Lunch & dinner, daily

Address
3814 Farnam Street, Omaha,
Douglas, NE 68131-3114

+1 402 932 0444

stirnella.com

Bookings
Website

Price guide

What they say
"Our goal is to give every guest the best possible experience. We love utilizing local seasonal ingredients that showcase what the Midwest has to offer. We use all local beef, chicken, and pork. Produce depends on the season and what is available. We work with five local organic gardeners that have gardens in the city and source as much local produce and protein as possible. Plum Creek Farms does an amazing job with supplying us with all of our chicken. Jon's Naturals sources amazing quality pork that our guests truly enjoy. We are honored and blessed to have such a support system in the Omaha community. We also have a private event space available for use."

Signature dishes
Burrata with grilled local peasant bread, sous vide local squash, and house-made apple butter; risotto with roasted beet purée, Parmesan cheese, truffles, celery root purée, and bruléed teleggio cheese; tagliatelle bolognese with roasted tomato, local Wagyu beef sauce, onion marmalade and house-made whipped ricotta.

What we say
A cozy gastropub where locavores head for an extensive selection of local beers, and then feast upon all-American comfort foods like deviled eggs, Caesar salads, pot roast and what many locals call Omaha's best burger – The Blackstone Burger. Don't miss it.

Prairie Plate Restaurant

Lancaster

What
A rural restaurant where guests enjoy a seasonal menu based on regional products

Who
Renee Cornett, chef & Jerry Cornett, farm manager

When
Hours change seasonally

Address
10405 Branched Oak Road, Waverly, Lancaster, NE 68462

+1 402 786 2239

prairieplaterestaurant.com

Bookings
Phone, walk-ins, email info@prairieplaterestaurant.com

Price guide
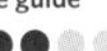

What they say
"Over eighty-five percent of the produce we serve comes from our colocated certified organic farm and more than ninety percent of our food expenditures go to local producers. We select seed varieties for flavor and prepare dishes with a respect for those ingredients. As a produce farm, vegetables are always front and center. The restaurant moves through the seasons with the farm and local producers and we highlight the incredible flavors of ingredients grown with care. Our farm and kitchen are designed to maximize the flavor of each ingredient."

Signature dishes
Bison meatloaf with sweet corn spoonbread and wilted fresh spinach; baby-shiitake Stroganoff with house-made pasta and wilted spinach; pork chop with rhubarb sauce, barley and sweet potato pilaf, and roasted asparagus.

What we say
Prairie Plate has got to be one of the most unique restaurants in the country. It was opened in farm-town rural Nebraska by Renee and Jerry, both former Navy helicopter pilots who dreamed of a straight-from-the-farm spot to showcase the cool things they grow on their forty-acre vegetable farm. Either Renee or Jerry tend to stop by each table, often offering extra produce to the dinner guests - it's a farmers' market visit along with dinner. Most American farm dinners are pop-up affairs of a single night, with tables set up in a field, but Prairie Plate is a dedicated farm dinner every growing season, spring through frost.

237

North Dakota

Pirogue Grille

Burleigh

What
Bismarck, North Dakota's most elegant restaurant

Who
Stuart & Cheryl Tracy, chef/proprietors

When
Dinner Tuesday to Saturday

Address
121 North 4th Street, Bismarck, Burleigh, ND 58501

+1 701 223 3770

piroguegrille.com

Bookings
Phone, walk-ins

Price guide

What they say
"At Pirogue Grille, our top priority is creating memories for our clients. We do this with sustainability in mind. Making our own stocks using vegetable scraps, fabricating our own seafood and steaks, all reduces waste. Our menu uses wild-caught freshwater walleye from Canada and wild-caught Alaskan king salmon from a second generation fishing boat. We grow our own rhubarb and chokecherries and, since North Dakota leads the nation in honey, bison, and sunflowers, we use locally raised versions of all in abundance. Of our twelve entrees, only four are centered on red meat. Our regional approach seemed new in North Dakota when we opened thirteen years ago, and we still try to help local producers. We are proud to say that our staff is well cared for by all of us. We feed them a meal each day and genuinely treat each other as we would like to be treated."

Signature dishes
House-made venison sausage with grilled onion relish; grilled Berkshire pork chop with rhubarb and thyme chutney; chokecherry and chocolate praline ice cream.

What we say
The capital city of North Dakota isn't too big, with fewer than 80,000 residents, and has an awfully long winter, but that may be part of what makes it so close-knit. It feels like every birthday and anniversary in the city is celebrated at Pirogue, where the bison and chokecherries are local, and the smiles very real.

Souris River Brewing

Ward

What
North Dakota brewery & restaurant serving locally sourced beer & food

Who
Aaron Thompson, founder

When
Lunch & dinner, daily

Address
32 3rd Street Northeast, Minot, Ward, ND 58703

+1 701 837 1884

sourisriverbrewing.com

Bookings
Walk-ins

Price guide

What they say
"As the first microbrewery in Minot, North Dakota, we use the most locally sourced and freshest ingredients available to create our quality beers and food. Sourcing our food and grains from our neighbors maintains our local economy and serves a true North Dakota brewing and culinary experience. Supplies must carry a First District Health certificate for us to use their items. We are a gathering place for all kinds of events and live music, as well as sponsoring our local minor league baseball team and local Roller Derby team. We contribute to numerous local charities and love to give back to our neighbors and friends."

Signature dishes
Beef burger; flank steak tacos; balsamic-marinated tri-tip steak.

What we say
Beer's main ingredient is barley, and the United States' leading barley producer is North Dakota, yet it is not easy to find a North Dakota-made beer! It is even rarer to find a North Dakota microbrewer that runs a pub where they hand-butcher North Dakota beef for a true Northern Plains beef-and-beer experience, but that's what they are doing at Souris River Brewing in Minot, fifty-odd miles south of the Canadian border, and in the middle of the barley fields that fill the world's beer mugs. Get the beer cheese sliders, put them beside a Souris River Brewing Bakken Brown ale, and you'll come to know a few important and delightful things about the real heart of American beer.

239

Ohio

Red Feather

Cincinnati

What
A contemporary American farm-to-table restaurant

Who
Brad Bernstein, chef/owner

When
Dinner, daily, Sunday brunch

Address
3200 Madison Road, Cincinnati, OH 45209

+1 513 407 3631

redfeatherkitchen.com

Bookings
Phone, website, OpenTable.com

Price guide

What they say
"We are a scratch kitchen that sources the best seasonal produce. We use our craftsmanship to make complete vegetarian and vegan dishes to the guest's preference. We purchase locally and use all our trim to make stocks, pickles, jams, and charcuterie. We pride ourselves on our relationships with local farmers and producers. Sourcing in season and locally ensures that we have the best ingredients at their peak, and understanding the process from which animal or ingredient is made allows us to stand behind the quality and practice."

Signature dishes
Double bone pork chop with red wine caramel, pearl onion, marble potato, and cremini mushrooms; roast chicken with biscuit spoon bread, asparagus, honey crema, and vermouth glacé; whipped house-made ricotta, grilled bread, truffle, and honey.

What others say
"While Crowe and Bernstein's allegiance to pedigreed comfort food is apparent, their real strength is subtly merging big and bold with delicate and nuanced."

Cincinnati Magazine

What we say
You can get carried away while snacking on fried chicken skins with hot honey and house-made ranch dressing or digging into a homey plate of roast chicken with spoonbread, but the ethos behind those dishes is always there as the team at Red Feather champions slow food while dazzling guests with indulgent plates of American food. Unafraid of hard work, they embrace their suppliers, guests, and employees, making sure all are treated with care and appreciation.

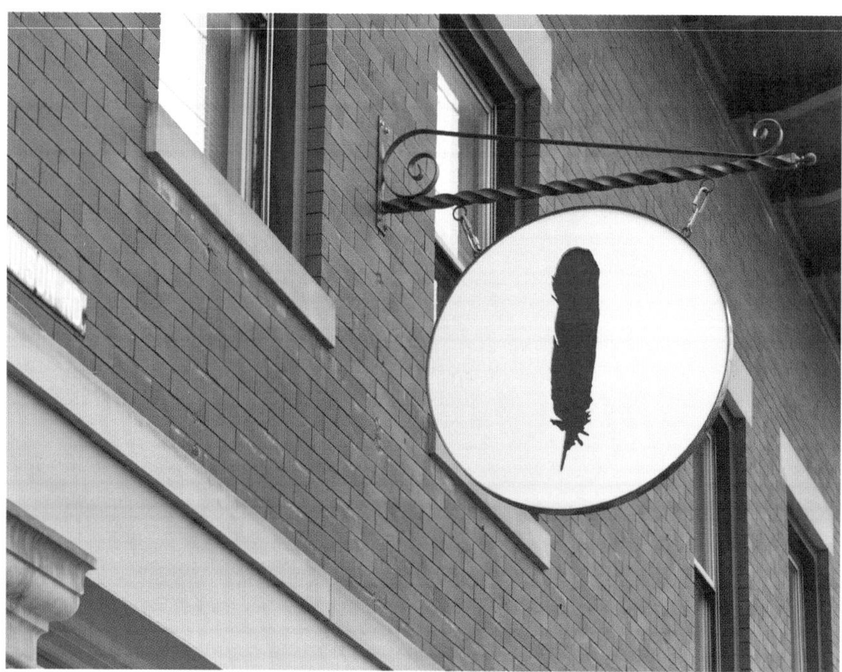

The Table

Columbus

What
Globally inspired & locally sourced small business

Who
Sangeeta Lakhani, chef/owner

When
Dinner Tuesday to Sunday, weekend brunch

Address
21 East 5th Avenue #101, Columbus, OH 43201

+1 614 291 4555

thetablecolumbus.com

Bookings
Phone, OpenTable.com

Price guide

What they say
"'Fork responsibly' is not just our motto, but the foundation of The Table. We are farm-to-table, kitchen-to-bar, and fork-to-mouth. Even our tables and chairs, the mismatched china, and 200-year-old barn wood have been repurposed. We are passionate in what we bring to The Table, and the community around us."

Signature dishes
Seasonal squash ribbons with seasonal pesto, mushrooms, pickled onions, local cheese, and peppers or tomatoes (depending on the season); sweetbread piccata, sous vide and fried, with lemon parsley aïoli and fried capers; spicy South Indian jackfruit curry with cauliflower and coconut milk purée, seasonal greens, cucumber, and mint raita.

What others say
"Embracing an elegant rusticity, The Table is French by nature, Columbus by nurture and modern-day Brooklyn in spirit. "

-G.A. Benton, *Columbus Alive*

What we say
The Table offers Columbus food inspired by global flavors with a menu that evolves with the seasons and availability of products, so that every part of the animal and product in season gets its moment in the sun. Chef/owner Sangeeta Lakhani considers herself part of the local food rebellion, noting that the suppliers who share her passion and conscious approach to craft are heroes. That passion is clear in the kitchen, where Indian-spiced scrambled eggs share space with star anise braised short ribs and vegan desserts. The kids' menu gets the same care and attention, making this the perfect spot to seed the next generation of food rebels.

the
TABLE

The Greenhouse Tavern

Cleveland

What
Ohio's first certified green restaurant focused on a fresh & local menu

Who
Jonathon Sawyer, chef/owner

When
Lunch & dinner, daily, weekend brunch

Address
2038 East 4th Street, Cleveland, OH 44115

+1 216 443 0511

thegreenhousetavern.com

Bookings
Phone, website, OpenTable.com

Price guide

What they say
"We are so passionate about the people that walk through our door. We got into this business because we love hospitality. Being able to share that hospitality with the people who work at The Greenhouse Tavern and the people who dine at the tavern is a gift I receive everyday."

Signature dishes
Barbecue pig's head with raw veggie salad, brioche, and lettuce cups; grilled Ohio lamb burger with stinky cheese fondue, champagne shallot mignonette, and tangy yogurt; vegan *tonkotsu* ramen with local Cleveland tofu, ramps, and shrooms.

What others say
"[Chef Sawyer] said relationships with local farmers become all the more important in winter, for securing ingredients like grains (in particular, farro, an Ohio specialty), shelled beans and legumes."

-Dan Saltzstein, *The New York Times*

What we say
The Greenhouse Tavern features food with integrity, from the house-made vinegars and pickles Jonathon Sawyer is famous for, to the roasted pig's head entrée that is a result of the whole pigs he sources, to the lamb burger he says he had to add to the menu to support a local lamb farmer's sustainable practices. Sawyer kick-started the city's commercial recycling program when he opened the restaurant, and says he does his best to minimize his environmental impact and support local, small, independent farmers and organizations. He does it all plate by plate, in a restaurant that also happens to be a rip-roaring good time.

245

Oklahoma

Ludivine

Oklahoma City

What
Oklahoma City farm-to-table fine dining with an artsy, lively bar scene

Who
Russ Johnson, chef/owner

When
Dinner Monday to Saturday, brunch Sunday

Address
805 North Hudson Avenue, Oklahoma City, OK 73102

+1 405 778 6800

ludivineokc.com

Bookings
Website

Price guide

What they say
"I'm passionate about true scratch cooking, classical technique, and proper execution without shortcuts, but with meticulous attention to detail. I'm passionate about being the leading restaurant destination in Oklahoma for people who take food seriously. I'm passionate about outstanding guest service and delivering to the guest an overall experience that they won't find elsewhere in the state. I'm passionate about creating an aesthetic and ambience that is at once cozy and sophisticated, and totally free of pretense."

What others say
"Their cooking showcases Oklahoma sourcing at its best ... It's a celebration of Oklahoma like none we've ever tasted."

-Karen Shimizu, *Saveur*

Signature dishes
Rabbit and goat's cheese agnolotti with pea shoots, radishes, and morels; Oklahoma Wagyu bavette steak with smoked garlic pecorino grits, roasted Brussels sprouts, charred cherry tomatoes, and chimichurri; bittersweet chocolate torchon with English Stilton, roasted grapes, candied pine nuts and Banyuls syrup.

What we say
Since 2010, when Russ Johnson opened Ludivine, he has made it the center of the fun part of the farm-to-table world in Oklahoma City. The bar (which has a separate entrance and longer hours) is known for drinks made with amusingly tweaked ingredients, like acidified local honey. The dining room is where Oklahoma Berkshire lardo and seared pound cake with preserved, native sand plums star. Don't miss a chance at trying Johnson's take on American native rarities like chickweed, lamb's quarter, dock, sumac, sand plums, and redbuds.

The Pritchard

Oklahoma City

What
Neighborhood restaurant offering contemporary tapas-style food

Who
Shelby Sieg, executive chef

When
Dinner Tuesday to Sunday, brunch Sunday

Address
1749 NW 16th Street, Oklahoma City, OK 73106

+1 405 601 4067

pritchardokc.com

Bookings
OpenTable.com

Price guide

What they say
"We source the best ingredients possible, we don't over garnish, or use a lot of heavy sauces. I believe cooking is all about balance. My approach to cooking is very hands-off. I do what is necessary to develop as much flavor as possible while letting the ingredients shine. We rotate plates through the menu every few weeks to make sure that we are using the best produce currently in season and we work with a local farmer at Prairie Earth Gardens to source many ingredients as well as several other small farms. We have a large variety of vegan and vegetarian options, and this is a big accomplishment for a restaurant operating in the heart of cattle country where steakhouses reign supreme!"

Signature dishes
Beet risotto with nasturtium pesto and crispy chickpeas; basted scallops with a blistered tomato vinaigrette and charred cauliflower; house-made strawberry shortcake with lemon *cremeux*, and lemon verbena fluid gel.

What we say
A chic woman-owned neighborhood restaurant and wine bar offering a full menu of small plates, cheeses, and charcuterie sourced as locally as they can get it, the Pritchard is full of surprises. For instance, their charred Brussels sprouts are an object of local obsession, and if they're serving Lovera's cheese, from Krebs, Oklahoma, don't miss your chance to try some. The Pritchard is a place to see the surprising side of high plains cattle country most Americans never see.

Mary Eddy's Kitchen x Lounge

Oklahoma City

What
Oklahoma City's former Model T factory, now a museum hotel with a terrific restaurant

Who
Jason Campbell, chef

When
Breakfast, lunch & dinner, daily

Address
900 West Main Street, Oklahoma City, OK 73106

+1 405 982 6960

maryeddysokc.com

Bookings
Phone, OpenTable.com, walk-ins

Price guide

What they say
"At Mary Eddy's, we're most passionate about providing the guest with an experience that they cannot get anywhere else in Oklahoma City. We source as local and regional as we can. We source our cheese locally from Lovera's creamery here in Oklahoma, we get most of our produce from different local farms here in OKC, we try to use Oklahoma beef when available, and we source our chicken from organic, free-range Crystal Lake Farms in Arkansas. Our motto is: Simple ingredients, let them shine, and then have fun and be yourself."

Signature dishes
Creekstone prime New York strip steak with potato purée, local charred snap peas, ramp Béarnaise made with fresh ramps, and last year's pickled ramps; Gulf shrimp lettuce wraps with local shishito peppers, made with one-month house-fermented black garlic and sambal vinaigrette; grilled octopus and crispy barbecue pork belly with creamless sweetcorn purée, charred okra, and frilly mustard greens.

What we say
You'd think it would be easy for Okies to get a local burger in Oklahoma City. After all, cattle trading is a leading OKC business, and the state has some 55,000 cattle farms and ranches raising 4.5 million head of cattle a year. In fact, it is not easy for Okies to get a local burger. That's why it's so important they can now seek out that burger at the hip and fun Mary Eddy's, the rare farm-oriented restaurant in a farm-powerhouse state.

Juniper

Tulsa

What
Tulsa, Oklahoma, farm-to-table, creative & modern cuisine

Who
Justin Thompson, chef

When
Lunch & dinner, daily

Address
324 East 3rd Street, Tulsa, OK 74120

+1 918 794 1090

junipertulsa.com

Bookings
OpenTable.com

Price guide

What they say
"At Juniper, we're passionate about creating fresh, new, seasonal dishes and specials from what's best at the farmers' markets. Since opening in 2011, Justin and the team have created more than 2,000 different tasty and creative dishes that made it onto our special menus. We believe in utilizing local farms and seasonal produce – including but not limited to 413 Farm, Symbiotic Aquaponic, Farrell Family Bread, 7K Family Farms, Tulsa Beef, Bodean Seafood, and Lomah Dairy – and creating dishes that support local while pairing perfectly with our fast-moving, often windswept, dramatic Oklahoma seasons."

Signature dishes
Farmers' market garden salad; grilled beef tenderloin of a ten-ounce fillet, with chimichurri butter, sautéed haricot verts, lardons, and cumin purple potato mash; spring risotto with seasonal vegetables, goat's cheese, and onion ash.

What we say
The Tulsa metropolitan area hosts about a million people who live in the windy state of Oklahoma, where the license-plate slogan is the blushingly modest "Oklahoma is OK". (There remains something to that Oklahoma cowboy myth – Oklahoma is the country's second most productive beef state, after neighboring Texas.) When Tulsa's creative class has a birthday to celebrate, they gravitate towards Juniper, a farm-connected spot mostly famous for being classy, lovely, and an oasis of pretty in a big windy world. Enjoy the modern cuisine and be sure to try one of the cocktails – we recommend the Pimm's cup for an instant refresher.

St. Mark's Chop Room

Nichols Hills

What
Neighborhood steakhouse serving single-ranch pastured beef

Who
Jonathon Stranger, chef/owner

When
Dinner Tuesday to Saturday

Address
6462 Avondale Drive, Nichols Hills, OK 73116

+1 405 848 6200

stmarkschoproom.com

Bookings
Phone

Price guide

What they say
"At St. Mark's Chop Room, all of our beef comes from Ironhorse Ranch in Macomb, Oklahoma, on the Little River bottom, where the Wagyu cattle live on green pastures with lots of trees for shelter. The Davis family started in the 1980s, raising what was at the time an unknown breed, and in a way that was different but they believed was right. Now they really have some of the best beef you will ever have. When Chef Jonathan Stranger was chatting with Ted from Ironhorse, the idea of a unique little steakhouse came up. Could Ted cover our need? He said yes, and our quaint little neighborhood hangout came to be. All of our produce comes from the OSU-OKC farmers' market and we are also fortunate to work with people like Scissortail Farms to get the best baby romaine for the house Caesar salad. It's a simple concept that just warms us and we love bringing that to our guests."

Signature dishes
Wagyu ribeye with "secret" compound butter and fresh herbs; Wagyu bacon with blue cheese, eggplant, and truffle syrup; farmers' market salad.

What we say
A single-ranch, family-farm, grass-fed American Wagyu steakhouse on the outskirts of Oklahoma City? This is where a modern cowboy would eat if he had a sense of duty that called him to care for the land (and great taste).

253

South Dakota

M.B. Haskett Delicatessen

Minnehaha

What
A community deli located in historic downtown Sioux Falls

Who
Michael Haskett, chef/owner

When
Breakfast, lunch, & dinner, daily

Address
324 South Phillips Avenue, Sioux Falls, Minnehaha, SD 57104

+1 605 367 1100

mbhaskett.com

Bookings
Phone, walk-ins

Price guide

What they say
"Using seasonal, local produce is important to us because it not only provides premium quality, but supports producers in our very community. Our commitment to local isn't just about our food, but extends to our paper products, bakery items, coffee, and anything else we can source from small, local, and community businesses."

Signature dishes
Poached eggs and toast: eggs from nearby Berrybrook Organics farm with multigrain toast from a local bakery; bison tavern sandwich (regional specialty made with "loose meat", served on a bun, and offered with house-made hot sauce); nightly "comfort-pub" dinner menu.

What we say
Even though South Dakota feeds us all, producing much of America's wheat, beef, and corn, restaurants that use local ingredients in the Mount Rushmore state are few and far between. That's why M.B. Haskett Delicatessen has so many fans, who come for the minimally processed, simple, early local breakfast, pop back in for a maple-dressed beet salad at lunch, and plan their evenings around pub fare like a "purple plate special" built around the produce of the day. The restaurant that serves as the heart of a farming community lives large in the American imagination, but barely exists in reality anymore - except in Sioux Falls at M.B. Haskett.

GERMAIN

Parker's Bistro

Minnehaha

What
Sioux Falls' finest restaurant, focused on local, seasonal fare

Who
Stacy Newcomb, owner

When
Dinner, daily

Address
210 South Main Avenue, Sioux Falls, Minnehaha, SD 57104

+1 605 275 7676

parkersbistro.net

Bookings
Phone, website, OpenTable.com, walk-ins

Price guide

What they say
"We are a chef-driven restaurant passionate about high-quality, great flavors, and unique ingredients in all of the food and drinks we serve, provided in a stimulating environment with great service. We partner with several local gardens to grow for our menu, as we use seasonal, local produce whenever possible. We have local pork, egg, chicken, dairy, and buffalo purveyors. Our beef is sourced regionally through small producers and our fish comes from all over the world through fish companies using sustainable practices. We treat our guests with respect and appreciation; they have chosen our restaurant and we strive to give them a great experience."

Signature dishes
Vegan lasagne made with house-made pasta, cashew cheese, and seasonal vegetables; halibut with asparagus and local ramps; braised duck breast with house-made mole sauce and duck confit tamale.

What others say
"At Parker's Bistro on Main Ave you'll find the most carefully crafted, modern dishes."

-Rachel Bires, *Matador Network*

What we say
Pheasant may have been the food of French kings, but those tasty birds are a contradictory phenomena in South Dakota. At once as common as sparrows because of all the cornfields, and also nearly invisible on local menus. Parker's Bistro is the rare place in "the Mount Rushmore state" that puts pheasant on the menu, sometimes with a pumpkin risotto and sage reduction, connecting the dots between the kingly local foods of the land and the people who live upon it.

257

Wisconsin

Forequarter

Madison

What
Small neighborhood restaurant focusing on ingredients from the upper Midwest

Who
Jonny Hunter & Melinda Trudeau, owners

When
Dinner Monday to Saturday, brunch Sunday

Address
708 1/4 East Johnson, Madison, WI 53703

+1 608 609 4717

forequartermadison.com

Bookings
Resy.com

Price guide

What they say
"We are passionate about ingredients and what the farmers and foragers from our community bring us to work with. We only use sustainably raised animals and fish products from local producers. If we do bring in seafood for a special event we will only work with sustainable United States fisheries. All the meat we use in the restaurant is from small family farms near us - we work with a network of over thirty farms all from the surrounding area."

Signature dishes
Asparagus with sauce *gribiche*, breadcrumbs, and spicy salami; shaved rare beef heart with juniper tarragon aïoli; pan-seared whitefish fillet with salt-baked celeriac, *katsou* dashi, and preserved lemon salsa verde.

What we say
If you are wondering how a tiny fine dining restaurant thrives in the college town of Madison, Wisconscin, it's the work of a group called the Underground Food Collective - helmed by the fearless Chef Jonny Hunter. Hunter and his team source ingredients from all around the area and use them to create beautiful, flavorsome food. The collective supports employees as much as farmers, maintaining a positive work environment led by several women in management. The results are incredibly creative; delicious plates of food, often every bit, from *salumi* to fish sauce, made in-house.

L'Etoile

Madison

What
New American, farm-to-table fine dining

Who
Tory Miller, executive chef/ proprietor

When
Dinner Tuesday to Saturday

Address
1 South Pinckney Street, Madison, WI 53703

+1 608 251 0500

letoile-restaurant.com

Bookings
Phone, website, OpenTable.com

Price guide

What they say
"We're passionate about supporting our local farmers and producers. We've been a farm-to-table establishment since the beginning, when Chef Odessa Piper first opened our doors in 1976, and have only grown and expanded that ethos since Chef Tory Miller took the helm in 2005. Our menu changes a few times a week, based on what our farmers have available and what the sometimes unpredictable Wisconsin weather allows to grow."

Signature dishes
Murphy's Farm cottage cheese with Blue Valley Gardens asparagus, toasted pepitas, and Driftless Organics pumpkin seed oil; Cape Cod Spanish mackerel with spring garlic, little gem lettuce, and wild grape buds; Blue Valley Gardens duck with Dreamfarm goat's cheese, wild oyster mushrooms, bacon, and fava shoots.

What others say
"L'Etoile is the Chez Panisse of the Midwest, and it's wonderful."

-Bill Addison, *Eater*

What we say
L'Etoile has been a Madison institution supporting farms for years, and Chef Tory Miller continues to push the bar forward with inventive, creative food that reminds you of the power of Midwestern ingredients. He works closely with local farmers to showcase the best area products and reduces waste by shifting ingredients among his four restaurants while recycling and working closely with UW / Madison's seed-breeder program to bring back heirloom vegetables to help further and revitalize produce biodiversity. Miller's best dishes showcase the terroir of the land and season. It's no surprise L'Etoile was a James Beard Foundation Outstanding Restaurant semi-finalist.

Braise

Milwaukee

What
A farm-to-table restaurant with a culinary school & a mission to reconnect people with their food

Who
David Swanson, chef/owner & Matt Plummer, chef

When
Dinner Tuesday to Saturday

Address
1101 South 2nd Street, Milwaukee, WI 53204

+1 414 212 8843

braiselocalfood.com

Bookings
Phone, Yelpreservations.com

Price guide

What they say
"I believe passion emanates from the relationships we've developed with farmers, staff, and guests. Knowing how something is produced or raised gives one context in how to prepare and respect that ingredient."

Signature dishes
Dirty chai beets: coffee-roasted beets with chai reduction, crème fraîche and toasted walnuts; lamb schnitzel with barley spaetzle, wilted spinach, black pepper Parmesan broth, and sunflower pesto; steamed pork buns with chive vinaigrette and crushed spicy peanuts.

What others say
"You might think eating seasonally and locally in Wisconsin in winter could be a grim affair. But dinners at Braise dazzled with their variety and flavors. These plates are among the most interesting being served in Milwaukee."

Milwaukee Journal Sentinel

What we say
At Braise, you'll find thoughtfully prepared dishes that exemplify chef/owner David Swanson's food philosophy: food that is simple, straightforward, and seasonal. It's also locally sourced and foraged, and delicious. Swanson and Chef de Cuisine Matt Plummer source produce from two hundred local farms, and developed a local distribution system to bring those items efficiently to the restaurant through their Restaurant Supported Agriculture model, the first in the country. They also grow 500 pounds of herbs annually on their rooftop garden, which is pollinated by their rooftop beehive that also yields honey products for the menu. The garden reduces their carbon footprint and is also an outdoor classroom for students in their hands-on cooking classes, offered to the public, and residents of nearby Hope House, a transitional housing program.

Driftless Café

Vernon

What
Farm-driven cafe offering lunch & dinner

Who
Luke Zahm, chef/owner

When
Lunch & dinner, Tuesday to Saturday

Address
118 W Court Street, Viroqua, Vernon, WI 54665

+1 608 637 7778

driftlesscafe.com

Bookings
Resy.com

Price guide

What they say
"Good energy equals good food. Surrounded by over two hundred certified organic farms in Vernon County alone, The Driftless Café utilizes the vast bounty and passion of the local farming community. We purchased the café in 2013 with the idea that we could create a restaurant that was about more than just food - we wanted to showcase the amazing farmers and food artisans that call this place home."

Signature dishes
Dan Badtke oyster mushrooms and local chicken of the woods mushrooms with Brovo Amaro and house-made *pané rustica*, Birdsong Ridge mustard greens, and organic Meyer lemon oil; River Root farm greens with Lake Michigan smoked lake trout, Scenic Valley strawberries, Montrachet goat cheese, red onion, and rhubarb balsamic vinaigrette.

What others say
"A reverent homage to the land through inventive farm-to-table menus and masterful flavors ... The café is a magnet for locals and visitors alike who appreciate rustic cuisine and sustainable ingredients grown nearby. Chef Zahm's menu is all heart, strained through a nouvelle cuisine-farmboy aesthetic."

-Bill Addison, *Eater*

What we say
Tucked in the tiny town of Viroqua, Driftless Café is a Midwestern gem. Chef Luke Zahm, who owns the restaurant with his wife, Ruthie, works closely with nearby farms; the restaurant is amid the highest concentration of organic farms in the country. As such, dinner menus are finalized just hours before the meal is served. Experience farm-to-table eating at this outstanding eatery.

Ardent

Milwaukee

What
An intimate twenty-three seat tasting menu-only restaurant

Who
Justin Carlisle, chef/owner

When
Dinner Wednesday to Saturday

Address
1751 North Farwell Avenue, Milwaukee, WI, 53202

+1 414 897 7022

ardentmke.com

Bookings
Tock.com

Price guide

What they say
"Wisconsin is very special to us. We wanted to showcase it naturally, in a simple yet complex way. We source beef and other products from our family farm, hire a part-time gardener to grow and forage greens for the restaurant, and support our staff with mentoring and other opportunities."

Signature dishes
Beef tartare made from animals from Chef Carlisle's family's farm, topped with devil egg mousse and whipped bone marrow; bread, butter, and cheese made from a single milking of cows from a local dairy farm.

What others say
"Ardent serves some of the most progressive food in the Midwest."

-Anthony Todd, *Tasting Table*

What we say
Milwaukee shook off its reputation for prime rib and fish fry dinners when Justin Carlisle opened Ardent in a former coffee shop space now home to some of the most exciting food in the Midwest. Here, Carlisle and his team offer tasting menus featuring Wisconsin produce, cheese and meat, some from Carlisle's fathers cattle farm, attracting chefs from around the world to join them for one of the restaurant's guest chef dinners. Guests at one of the tables or the kitchen bar can watch cooks preparing showcase ingredients like asparagus and celery root in several iterations-raw, pickled, roasted, even unexpectedly made into dessert. The opportunity to chat with Carlisle and the other cooks about the food as they prepare it for you makes the kitchen bar at Ardent the hottest seat in town.

610 Magnolia (p. 312)

265

The Southeast

Alabama	267
Arkansas	273
District of Columbia	281
Florida	295
Georgia	301
Kentucky	311
Louisiana	321
Maryland	329
Mississippi	333
North Carolina	339
South Carolina	355
Tennessee	361
Virginia	373
West Virginia	379

267

Alabama

Chez Fonfon

Birmingham

What
Cozy, casual French bistro

Who
Frank Stitt, chef/owner & Pardis Stitt, owner

When
Lunch & dinner, Tuesday to Saturday

Address
2007 11th Avenue South
Birmingham, AL 35205

+1 205 939 3221

fonfonbham.com

Bookings
Walk-ins

Price guide

What they say
"We are passionate about cooking with regional heritage ingredients and use seasonal Alabama produce in our kitchen. We also grow our own produce and raise chickens for eggs at our nearby farm, forty-five minutes away. Sustainability is very important to us. We admire purveyors who are implementing sustainable practices, such as Joyce Farm, which has adopted regenerative agriculture as standard practice. Finally, it's the attention to detail that matters to us when creating a dish. We pride ourselves in perfecting the little things."

Signature dishes
Poulet Rouge with spring onions, sweet peas, wilted lettuces, and tarragon; and country pâté of pork, ham, foie gras, pistachios; chocolate *pot de crème*.

What others say
"Chart a course for Chez Fonfon, and be sure to leave plenty of room for dessert. We'll save you a seat."

-Caroline Rogers, *Southern Living*

What we say
Bistro fare may be considered "petite cuisine", but the classics feel grand in this intimate space, the youngest of the Stitts' four restaurants. Meals here are fit for one, but it's not uncommon to see tables share the love. The food and vibe will place you in Nice, Lyon, or Paris, but Fonfon works with local ingredients as much as possible, often sourcing from their nearby farm where they raise hens for egg production and grow select produce. Joyce Farm is a favorite collaborator, purveyor of poultry, beef, and game that has adopted regenerative agriculture as standard practice.

Highlands Bar & Grill

Birmingham

What
Gracious service & regional ingredients treated to French technique

Who
Frank Stitt, chef/owner & Pardis Stitt, owner

When
Dinner Tuesday to Saturday

Address
2011 Eleventh Avenue South,
Birmingham, AL 35205

+1 205 939 1400

highlandsbarandgrill.com

Bookings
Phone, website, OpenTable.com

Price guide

What they say
"Sustainability is very important to us. We use seasonal Alabama and regional produce and source locally as much as possible. We also grow our own produce and raise chickens for their eggs at our nearby farm, forty-five minutes away. And we support local initiatives such as Jones Valley Teaching Farm and Pepper Place Farmers Market."

Signature dishes
Manchester Farms quail with Joyce Farms chicken livers, and a peach salad of mint, bulb onions, and Banyuls vinegar; Faroe Island salmon with chanterelle, morel, and porcini mushrooms, and brown butter vinaigrette; pecan génoise coconut cake made with pastry cream, chantilly, and crème anglaise.

What others say
Winner: 2018 Restaurant of the Year.

James Beard Foundation

What we say
Beauty, aplomb, and skill define this dining room, where dinner can evolve like a performance. Attentive yet tonally apt service plays second only to the other starring role: Frank Stitt's masterful blend of French influenced, Southern-sourced food.

But the magic of Highlands isn't dependent on just one. Pardis Stitt's front-of-house leadership is perceptive and inviting. Goren Avery, affectionately known as Red Dog, has been on staff since day one - his show-stopping command of the table is joyous and caring. And pastry chef Dolester Miles, also present since opening day and renowned for her pecan-flecked coconut cake, consistently dazzles.

Post Office Pies

Birmingham

What
Hand-tossed, wood-fired pizza with neighborhood vibes

Who
John Anthony Hall, chef/owner

When
Lunch & dinner, daily

Address
209 41st Street South, Birmingham, AL 35222

+1 205 599 9900

postofficepies.com

Bookings
Walk-ins

Price guide

What they say
"Our guests, our neighborhood, and employees are first and foremost. Buying local is important for us and nearly all of our produce comes from the local farmers' market."

Signature dishes
Lady peas and roasted squash salad with sherry vinaigrette; Swine pie with tomato sauce, pecorino romano, house-made sausage, slab bacon, pepperoni, aged mozzarella, and basil.

What we say
Pizza has long been the go-to community dish and Hall shows up when asked. He contributes to local elementary school pizza parties and sponsors youth baseball teams from the Avondale area. He also partners with Kulture City, a Birmingham nonprofit that creates accessible environments to those with autism and other special needs.

Hall brings the exacting nature of his fine dining training-stints at Per Se, Gramercy Tavern, Momofuku Ssäm Bar, and with Bocuse d'Or-winner Lea Linster-to this Avondale eatery where he makes pizza with a focus on local and house-made ingredients. Pies may be the main feature here, but his salads are not to be missed. Driven by the season, he mixes local lettuces with fresh fruit or roasted veggies, sometimes marked with onion, goat cheese, and tangy vinaigrette. Jones Valley Teaching Farm and Habersham Farm are among his favorite suppliers.

Fisher's at Orange Beach Marina

Baldwin

What
A beautiful restaurant located in the heart of a world-class marina

Who
Johnny Fisher, owner & Bill Briand, chef

When
Lunch & dinner, daily

Address
27075 Marina Road, Orange Beach, Baldwin, AL 36561

+1 251 981 7305

fishersobm.com

Bookings
OpenTable.com

Price guide

What they say
"We have amazing food, but it goes to waste if it isn't served professionally with genuine Southern hospitality - that's why hospitality is so important to us. Locality is also an integral part of our mission. Not only are our local producers amazing, but the money stays in our community."

Signature dishes
Seared jumbo sea scallops with roasted cauliflower and ginger herb salad; marinated crab claws with *nuoc mam cham*, candied jalapeño, shaved red onion, herbs, and basil oil.

What others say
"The bounty of the Gulf, in its freshest and finest expression. Beachside restaurants across the South often (distressingly) serve fish flown in from elsewhere. This dock-chic treasure, though, offers the true local catch."

-Bill Addison, *Eater*

What we say
Get two experiences at this beach town restaurant - upstairs is fine dining, and it's more relaxed by the dock. Fisher's sources as much as they can locally, including food and supplies. The fresh catch is from the Gulf so they do their part to protect it, thus avoiding styrofoam, plastic straws and paper napkins. Favorite purveyors include Murder Point Oysters and Local Appetite Produce farmer Will Mastin, who supply ingredients for popular dishes such as the "Fisher Burger" - think double patties with smoked tomato jam, and pimento cheese. "We think it's the best burger in town", says Fisher's owner, Johnny Fisher.

Johnny's Restaurant

Jefferson

What
Southern ingredients with Greek influences

Who
Tim Hontzas, chef/owner

When
Lunch Sunday to Friday

Address
2902 18th Street South, Suite 200, Homewood, Jefferson, AL 35209

+1 205 802 2711

johnnyshomewood.com

Bookings
Walk-ins

Price guide

What they say
"I love to make people happy through food. It's always been my goal and it's what drives me. That's what I want to accomplish. I'm there every day, seventy-five hours per week. I love to talk to my customers and see their expressions."

Signature dishes
Greek pork and beef meatballs with mint, sumac, thyme, oregano, and house-cultured tzatziki; beef and pork meatloaf with chipotle barbecue sauce; skewered lamb, pork, and chicken marinated in garlic, bay leaves, oregano, lemon juice, árbol chilis, red wine vinegar, with lemon tahini butter.

What others say
Semifinalist: Best Chef - South.

James Beard Foundation

What we say
This meat-and-three is the masterful outcome of Hontzas' Greek heritage, southern upbringing, and fine dining training. The menu expands on recipes learned from his aunt and his grandfather Johnny (the restaurant's namesake) and, like his family members, Hontzas values quality products and teaching his young staff how to care for them.

Lee Cary, Hontzas' fishmonger, determines the restaurant's seafood based on his weekly catch. Maple syrup comes from Justin Hill of the Eastaboga Bee Company in Lincoln, Alabama. Produce comes from one farmer, Dwight Hamm, who works fifty acres in Cullman. "He doesn't use pesticides or irrigation. He depends on God and the rain", Hontzas says. "We lean on him hard in terms of him dictating our menu". No micro horseradish to be found here, but ample squash, turnips, watermelon, and baby vidalia.

Acre

Lee

What
Modern Southern food with sophisticated charm

Who
David Bancroft, chef/owner

When
Lunch Tuesday to Sunday; dinner Monday to Saturday

Address
210 East Glenn Avenue, Auburn, Lee, AL 36830

+1 334 246 3763

acreauburn.com

Bookings
Phone, OpenTable.com

Price guide

What they say
"Acre was built intentionally on one acre of land near downtown Auburn. The parking lot and building is wrapped in edible landscape, including: peaches, pears, plums, apples, figs, persimmons, blueberries, strawberries, guava, bay laurel, Meyer lemons, a corn field, a watermelon patch, and a vegetable and herb garden. We source from our area's local farmers and Auburn University's meat and fish laboratories. Our mission is to 'give where you live'."

Signature dishes
Harman Farms tomato salad with sweet corn dressing, fried okra, smoked bacon, lemon thyme, and Georgia olive oil; "butt-rubbed" ribeye steak with baked sweet potato, white cheddar gravy, Brussels sprout salad, and mustard vinaigrette; butcher's board featuring house-cured meats served with pickles.

What others say
"Best Farm-to-Table Restaurant-Alabama."

Travel & Leisure

What we say
So named for the plot of land that offers a bounty, Acre's philosophy stems from the people who raise, grow, and cultivate their food. They work with Harman Family Farm, known locally for their hydroponic tomato garden, and Alabama Gulf Coast oyster farmers, who Bancroft helped rebound from extended closures by co-founding the Alabama Oyster Social.

Seasonality and availability guide this menu, as does a celebratory sense of place. Find grilled oysters doused in hickory-smoked Conecuh sausage butter and simple salads speckled with fruit picked on-site. The "butt-rubbed" ribeye tips a hat to Bancroft's San Antonio, Texas, roots where he spent most of his life, but at the core, Acre shows the depth of the Blackbelt Region.

Southern National

Mobile

What
Local clubhouse with Southern hospitality & a global influence

Who
Duane Nutter, chef/owner, Reggie Washington, owner

When
Dinner Tuesday to Saturday, weekend brunch

Address
360 Dauphin Street, Mobile AL 36602

+1 251 308 2387

southernational.com

Bookings
Phone, walk-ins

Price guide

What they say
"It doesn't matter if you can prepare great food - if the service isn't up to par, you have nothing. We provide Southern hospitality and parallel it with Southern food with international influences."

Signature dishes
Mussels and collard greens with mushrooms and sliced, toasted baguette; honeysuckle vodka-cured salmon with horseradish beet cream, house pickles, and beet salad; grilled okra and shishito pepper coriander with whipped goat cheese, and teriyaki vinaigrette.

What we say
This duo landed in Mobile after years in Atlanta, but it didn't take long for them to make the Gulf city their own. They made all local hires, including Chef de Cuisine Tammy Dawson. As African American owners in fine dining, they're celebrated locally and nationally for the positive impact they bring to their community.

Washington's family owns Shore Acres Plant Farm, a four-generation horticulture farm thats supplies muscadines, blueberries, and kumquats in season. The restaurant sources most ingredients from Alabama and Louisiana, including DK Farms for micro greens, Diamond Ranch for ethically raised pork, Claude's Cornmeal who swings grits out of a tire shop, farm-raised shrimp and crawfish, and the restaurant's own herb and vegetable garden. Their grease removal vendor recycles the product into diesel, recyclables are sorted, they've eliminated plastic straws, and are reducing single-use plastics. Nutter's team rarely produces food waste. When Fresno peppers appear in a dish, for example, the stem is used to make a spicy oil that marinates fish.

273

Arkansas

The Hive

Bentonville

What
A full service, casual fine dining restaurant set inside Bentonville's 21c Museum Hotel

Who
Matthew McClure, executive chef

When
Breakfast, lunch & dinner, daily

Address
200 Northeast A Street, Bentonville, AR 72712

+1 479 286 6575

thehivebentonville.com

Bookings
Phone, OpenTable.com

Price guide

What they say
"I want to serve our guests a unique Arkansas culinary experience. This starts with ingredients that are grown locally. We celebrate the seasons by constantly utilizing locally grown food. Part of our mission is to celebrate vegetables of our region to help reduce protein production. We engage with the community by supporting local farmers and causes that matter to us, like fundraising for childhood hunger relief. To tell the story of food in Arkansas is to start with the economics of the state - it is historically a poor state where nothing was wasted. That translates to our kitchen. I want the Hive to reflect the current food in Arkansas, using locally grown food with preparations and spices inspired by [the area's] immigrant communities."

Signature dishes
Berkshire hog chop with Ralston rice; chicken liver mousse made from Northwest Arkansas poultry; shiitake mushroom hummus with local shiitakes.

What we say
The Hive brings the vast and diverse pantry of Northwest Arkansas to the plate through its dynamic, seasonal menu. Set inside the 21c Museum Hotel, The Hive "supports those producers that have a moral code", McClure says, using humanely raised pork, pasture-raised poultry and eggs, and organic produce. The Hive strives to reduce food waste, while also seeking out diversity in both ingredients and staff, and supporting the greater food community through fundraising work. "I want to showcase the best possible example of what Arkansas food is", McClure says.

The Preacher's Son

Bentonville

What
The Preacher's Son is an American rustic farm-to-table style restaurant

Who
Ropeswing Hospitality Group

When
Lunch & dinner, daily

Address
201 Northwest A Street, Bentonville, AR 72712

+1 479 445 6065

thepreachersson.com

Bookings
OpenTable.com

Price guide

What they say
"A preacher's son himself, Chef Matthew Cooper's passion for culinary art stems from its ability to bring people together. His style of cooking is rustic and traditional, keeping true to his roots in the South and the Pacific Northwest. His celiac condition has enabled him to passionately and creatively cook gluten-free food. His dedication to local community is evident in his commitment to using local ingredients, encouraging community building, and local cooperation."

Signature dishes
Grilled radicchio salad with vadouvan gorgonzola dolce dressing, pickled celery, and pine nut; elderberry-cured salmon over local fennel salad; Pacific halibut with ratatouille and *agrodolce*.

What others say
"The space's simple tables and banquettes serve to focus your attention on a trinity of details: the massive king post looming overhead. The vibrant glass-window installations by Fayetteville artist George Dombek. The gold-bricked bar, tucked into what was once the church's apse, aka the inset alcove where the altar once stood. It's an extraordinary space, one that evokes reverence and serenity while at the same time feeling downright luxurious."

-Bonnie Bauman, *Arkansas Life*

What we say
Each fall, Cooper participates in a low impact duck production to provide a limited quantity duck dish. Throughout the year, he partners with forty-four farms and seafood purveyors to ensure all protein is sourced sustainably. He's also mentoring staff, teaching students the fundamentals of farming, and providing local sustainable fertilizers to area farmers - all in an effort to support the Bentonville community.

Tusk & Trotter American Brasserie

Bentonville

What
A local, sustainable & farm-to-table restaurant

Who
Rob Nelson, chef/partner

When
Lunch, daily, dinner Tuesday to Sunday

Address
110 Southeast A Street, Bentonville, AR 72712

+1 479 268 4494

tuskandtrotter.com

Bookings
Phone, website

Price guide

What they say
"Our food philosophy is simple: fresh, regional, and sustainable. We use many farmers and ranchers throughout the year. We use our local farmers' market in the spring and summer. We buy from different foragers. We work to establish long-term, win-win relationships and promote them through local restaurants and chefs, helping to develop a sustainable source of supply. We have established a local food recovery program in partnership with food banks, purveyors, and culinary schools [and we are] working with various corporations to set up a statewide food recovery and food waste program."

Signature dishes
Charcuterie board; catfish "pastrami"; pig ear nachos with house-made sausage and bacon.

What we say
True to its name, Bentonville's Tusk & Trotter celebrates the entire animal - not just pork but bison, boar, venison, elk, and seafood - by presenting a range of cuts and cooking techniques across the menu. Beyond the meat, a third of the menu is focused on vegan and vegetarian dishes as well.

The kitchen, which practices zero food waste, uses ethically raised meats, and as many organic products as they can source. Meanwhile, Chef Rob Nelson reaches far beyond the dining room - he's an alumni of the James Beard Foundation's Chef's Boot Camp for Policy and Change. "With the great work being done every day at Tusk, it has allowed me to be more politically active in food policy", he says.

South On Main

Little Rock

What
Exploring the story of Southern culture through food, cocktails & music

Who
Matthew & Amy Bell, chefs/owners

When
Lunch Sunday to Friday, dinner, Saturday

Address
1304 Main Street, Little Rock, AR 72202

+1 501 244 9660

southonmain.com

Bookings
OpenTable.com

Price guide

What they say
"We are passionate about exploring Southern food through the lens of Arkansas with an emphasis on local and regional ingredients. We employ a root-to-leaf practice with vegetables and a nose-to-tail practice with all our local proteins. We work with food policy action to continue to educate ourselves in best practices. We are partnered with Urban Food Loop composting to insure waste we do produce are handled in a responsible way."

Signature dishes
Catfish *maque choux*: spring stew with corn, tasso ham, tomatoes, and fried okra; trout with soybeans and peanut romocco; grilled ribeye with spinach cream, JoJo potatoes, and homemade Worcestershire sauce.

What others say
"In Matt Bell's hands, [there are] dishes that impress by their simple ingredients coming together to form complex layers of flavour ... dessert was a fine ending to a wonderful meal that places South on Main firmly into the category of elite Little Rock restaurants."

Arkansas Times

What we say
In partnership with *Oxford American* magazine, this Little Rock gem, set in a live performance venue, keeps the emphasis on Arkansas products, while also showcasing live music regularly. Through personal relationships with vendors, the lively restaurant sources locally from farmers and co-ops to craft creative small and large plates with elevated Southern flavors.

Outside of their own community, the Bells are actively pursuing food policy legislation to reduce food waste and food insecurity.

The Root Cafe

Little Rock

What
Farm-to-table restaurant whose mission is building community through local food

Who
Corri & Jack Sundell, co-owners

When
Breakfast & lunch, Tuesday to Sunday, dinner Wednesday to Saturday

Address
1500 South Main Street, Little Rock, AR 72202

+1 501 414 0423

therootcafe.com

Bookings
Walk-ins

Price guide

What they say
"Local sourcing is at the core of everything we do. We buy from local farmers and producers to showcase the great food and drink available in Arkansas. Building community is the reason we do it, because it brings people together, benefits the environment and the local economy, and offers transparency that leads to stronger relationships. Our incredible staff is how we do it. We're dedicated to paying a living wage, fostering a culture of respect and inclusion, and making The Root Cafe a place where people love to come to work and have opportunities for personal growth and expression."

Signature dishes
Homemade drop biscuits and gravy with two eggs; "The Burger" with house garlic mayo, Dijon, grilled onions, dill pickle, and local spring mix; smoked shiitake mushrooms with cornbread, pickled purple hull pea relish, and braised local greens.

What others say
"Set in an old dairy bar, beside a vest-pocket garden plot, the restaurant leverages a back-to-the-land sensibility rooted in free love and home canning."

-John T. Edge, *Garden & Gun*

What we say
Local. Community. A meal at The Root Cafe delivers more than good food. Having expanded from a dairy barn café to a full-scale restaurant (with the use of shipping containers), it is now a community hub that also supports its hometown. Seventy-seven percent of The Root's ingredients are sourced from more than fifty area farms, making the dishes - many vegetarian, vegan, and gluten-free - thoughtful, intentional, and delicious.

Three Fold Noodles + Dumpling Co.

Little Rock

What
Making simple, healthy food using cooking methods rooted in Chinese tradition

Who
Lisa Zhang, chef/owner

When
Breakfast, lunch & dinner, Monday to Saturday

Address
611 South Main Street, Little Rock, AR 72201

+1 501 372 1739

eat3fold.com

Bookings
Walk-ins

Price guide

What they say
"As an immigrant, I've always had a passion for introducing the good side of Chinese cuisine to American society. I want to help people recognize the benefits of Chinese cuisine as healthy, fresh, simple, and sustainable.

"When we established this business, we tried making it a place that educated people about Chinese cuisine and that acted as a window into the Chinese culture. We don't exclusively hire Chinese cooks; rather, my goal has been to hire and teach Americans to cook dumplings. I'm happy to say that I've achieved this goal. We have Americans who can make perfect dumplings that, I think, would even rival some Chinese."

Signature dishes
Noodles; dumplings; steamed buns.

What we say
In her new location, a sparse, modern space in downtown Little Rock, chef/owner Lisa Zhang is bending the minds of Arkansas diners by offering "a mouthpiece for traditional Chinese cuisine". Dishes like *ban mian*, or tossed noodles, vegetarian dumplings, and *hongshao* beef noodle soup are challenging customers - but also bringing them back. The menu at Three Fold is dairy-free and a third of it consists of vegetarian or vegan dishes. And Zhang takes pride in cooking without MSG. "We put a lot of thought into our menu design, and not just so that we can please our customers' taste buds, but also to cultivate and educate them", she says.

281

District of Columbia

A Rake's Progress

Washington

What
Hyper-local, Mid-Atlantic fare in a majestic old church

Who
Spike Gjerde, chef/owner

When
Dinner, daily, weekend brunch

Address
1770 Euclid Street Northwest, Washington, DC 20009

+1 202 864 4190

thelinehotel.com

Bookings
Resy.com

Price guide
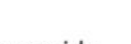

What they say
"We source from our local food system. Period. Down to using *verjus* instead of lemons, canola oil instead of olive oil, local spirits instead of imports, and locally grown and milled grains for bread and pastries. Every ingredient is used in its season, and we believe there are fifty-two seasons per year. Even our uniforms and place settings are made domestically. Our ceramics, placemats, and even our hearth are made in the mid-Atlantic."

Signature dishes
Baltimore canyon lobster toast with green goddess dressing, garlic chili crunch, and chervil on house-made spelt bread; bone broth with charred ramp tops and rabbit dumplings; stuffed whole porgy with crab fried rice, flowering broccoli, ramps, herbs, and sorghum soy.

What others say
"Because Gjerde and his team eschew products that can't be sourced within a certain geographic range (no lemons, limes, or black pepper, for instance), their food has acquired a certain Chesapeake terroir and their arsenal of ingredients has become extremely creative."

Saveur

What we say
James Beard award-winning chef Spike Gjerde is near-maniacal in his pursuit of Mid-Atlantic splendor, a trait on full display in this gem of an eatery tucked away on the second floor of the trendy Line hotel. Set in an old church, the space is a contemplative setting for ingredients like the heirloom Chesapeake fish pepper, which Gjerde rescued from near extinction when he asked farmers to start growing them for his fermented hot sauce, and Eastern oysters plucked from the nearby Chesapeake Bay.

Blue Duck Tavern

Washington

What
A contemporary neighborhood restaurant welcoming guests to gather & celebrate in good taste.

Who
Troy Knapp, executive chef

When
Breakfast & dinner, daily, lunch Monday to Friday, weekend brunch

Address
1201 24th Street Northwest, Washington, DC 20037

+1 202 419 6755

blueducktavern.com

Bookings
Website, phone

Price guide

What they say
"We provide experiences that nourish our guests and our staff and we also thoughtfully source local purveyors that are working to nourish the planet and not deplete our shared resources."

Signature dishes
Wood-oven roasted bone marrow with bourbon chili butter, pretzel crumble, and roasted garlic; hand-cut BDT fries; moulard duck breast with peach marmalade, brûlée stone fruit, and basil.

What others say
"Check out Blue Duck Tavern, where the spring fashions include sweet day-boat scallops arranged on a bright pea purée, shot through with lemon grass and punched up with pickled ramps."

-Tom Sietsema, *The Washington Post*

What we say
Blue Duck Tavern is home to Washington, D.C.'s first professional Molteni range. Additionally, the restaurant features an open staff pantry and kitchen and a menu which consists of the freshest ingredients available from local purveyors and artisans. Three quarters of the menu is cooked in a wood-burning oven - dishes are genuine, time-honored and traditional. Slow roasting in wood embers, braising, preserving and smoking techniques bring the true flavors of America's great, simple and wholesome foods to the Blue Duck Tavern.

The menu notes every farm where the main ingredient for the dish was raised before its journey to the table. Blue Duck Tavern also has anoutdoor garden with communal table as well as a private and semi-private chef's table. During the spring and summer seasons the chefs use the herbs planted in the outdoor garden for service.

Bresca

Washington

What
Seasonally driven menu with zero food waste & a rooftop garden

Who
Ryan Ratino, chef/owner

When
Dinner Tuesday to Sunday

Address
1906 14th Street Northwest
Washington, DC 20009

+1 202 518 7926

brescadc.com

Bookings
Resy.com

Price guide

What they say
"We are committed to zero food waste, so we accept imperfections in our produce and try to use all the parts of our animals and vegetables. For example, our animal fat gets completely repurposed and used, and we use no plastic anywhere in the restaurant to encourage and instill good environmental practices."

Signature dishes
Ramp linguine "carbonara" with wood-grilled *maitake* mushrooms, mint, fava beans, and pecorino; burrata and baby carrots with figs, blue basil, pistachio *duqqa*, and chamomile; barbecued lamb shoulder with black garlic, rhubarb molasses, bread and butter pickles, spring greens salad, lamb bacon lardons, and lamb fat sherry vinaigrette.

What others say
"If decadence were a crime, Ratino would get at least a few years."

The Washington Post

What we say
The cooking is inventive and whimsical at 14th Street's Bresca, whose name is Spanish for "honeycomb". Ratino has worked in wide-ranging kitchens from the Playboy Mansion to a Todd English property in Orlando to Virginia's elegant L'Auberge Provençale, and his menu is delightfully quirky as a result. The Asian-inflected scallop crudo bathed in duck dashi shares space with an Italian-accented yellowfin tuna and green garlic *tonnato*, while the foie gras cake pop for dessert may as well be from outer space. It's all built on a foundation of top-notch seasonal ingredients, often plucked straight from the rooftop garden.

Chaia

Washington

What
Plant-based tacos with a planet-saving mission

Who
Bettina Stern, co-owner

When
Lunch & dinner, daily

Address
3207 Grace Street Northwest, Washington DC 20007

+1 202 333 5222

chaiadc.com

Bookings
Walk-ins

Price guide

What they say
"Want to save the environment? Eat more plants. Our style of cooking focuses on what's freshest at the farmers' market and what's in season. We are not doing this because of a fad. This is about long-term shifts in the way people are eating – and how they will need to eat moving forward to save their bodies and the planet. We have been recognized as one of the industry's most innovative brands by offering our customers a little something extra to differentiate us from our competitors. Our heavy emphasis on employee training, high-quality ingredients, brand culture and a passion for giving back to the community combined with creativity, progressiveness and hard work means that we are leading the restaurant industry."

Signature dishes
Creamy kale and potato taco with pepper jack cheese, poblano crema, salsa verde, and pickled onions; roasted beet taco with ricotta *salata*, coriander-lime yogurt, and fresh jalapeño; chipotle sweet potato hash taco with feta, arugula, pumpkin seed salsa, and coriander.

What we say
Inspired by the flavors of Tulum, this pop-up turned bricks-and-mortar taqueria on the Georgetown waterfront is a vegetarian's dream. Corn tortillas are stuffed with all manner of electric-hued organic produce from local growers topped off with creamy embellishments such as lemon ricotta and goat cheese. But the top-notch fast-casual fare is underscored by a dramatic sustainability mission: everything in the shop is compostable, from the food to the plates, cups, and forks.

Centrolina

Washington

What
Stylish Italian osteria & market featuring urban produce

Who
Amy Brandwein, chef/owner

When
Lunch Monday to Friday, dinner daily, brunch Sunday

Address
974 Palmer Alley, Washington, DC 20001

+1 202 898 2426

centrolinadc.com

Bookings
Website, OpenTable.com

Price guide

What they say
"We work very hard to procure the best produce, fish and meat in the mid-Atlantic area to support our local farmers and artisans. Our menu changes every day which allows us the flexibility to work with the freshest food. We pride ourselves on diversity, starting from the top. Our senior management team is composed of women and we are devoted to driving a culture of equality, diversity, and respect."

Signature dishes
Artichokes four ways: creamed, roasted, shaved, and fried; spaghetti with scallops, calamari, morel mushrooms, basil, and olive oil; roasted whole Mediterranean sea bass with potato confit, tomato, olive, and basil.

What others say
"Amy Brandwein can cook for me anytime. I love her response to the seasons, sheathing spring's ramps, for instance, in a crackling tempura to be dipped in shiso aïoli. ... Then again, whatever she pulls from the wood-fired oven makes a good case for moving to the top of the list."

-Tom Sietsema, *The Washington Post*

What we say
Chef Amy Brandwein's much-loved Italian spot, tucked away in glitzy DC, hasn't skipped a beat since opening in 2015. Known for its meticulously crafted homemade pasta, this sleek, light-filled restaurant and market is inspired by seasonal produce from local farms, which determines the menu on any given day. Among those outfits is DC Urban Greens, a nonprofit grow operation located in DC's Ward 7. Centrolina is the group's only pro-profit client, and receives roughly fifty pounds of produce a week.

Cork Wine Bar & Market

Washington

What
Intimate wine bar & market with an emphasis on local & organic vintages

Who
Diane Gross & Khalid Pitts, co-owners

When
Lunch & dinner, Tuesday to Sunday, brunch Sunday

Address
1805 14th Street Northwest, Washington, DC 20009

+1 202 265 2675

corkdc.com

Bookings
OpenTable.com

Price guide

What they say
"We are passionate about offering an affordable, casually elegant experience that demystifies the world of wine. Our wine selection process for the restaurant and market is rigorous. We've curated a list by tasting everything and making sure each bottle is something we would personally enjoy drinking. The list focuses on traditionally-made estate wines that are organic and biodynamic - that means no intervention and the people growing the grapes are making the wine. The majority of our wine selection represents Old World wines."

Signature dishes
Avocado toast with grilled bread, pistachios, pistachio oil, and sea salt; duck confit with blackberry gastrique, sautéed nettles, and lambs quarter; roasted rainbow carrots glazed in local honey and topped with fennel pollen.

What others say
"While the upstairs dining area keeps pushing vintage pours picked by the wine-obsessed Gross, the casual downstairs bar has the flexibility to offer experimental wines (Canary Islands varietals, anyone?) and accommodate curious customers during the day."

-Tierney Plumb, *Eater Washington DC*

What we say
Spanning an upstairs dining area, a downstairs bar, and a tempting market, this 14th Street mainstay has been filling Washingtonians' wine glasses for over a decade. The outstanding wine list has always been the spot's main draw, chock-full of delicious organic and biodynamic wines across fifty pours by the glass and 250 bottles. Now, owners Diane Gross and Khalid Pitts are getting into the winemaking business themselves: beginning in 2018, Cork's produced-on-site rosé - made with Virginia-grown grapes - will be available on draft in the market and restaurant.

The Dabney

Washington

What
Elegant mid-Atlantic farmhouse fare over an open hearth

Who
Jeremiah Langhorne & Alex Zink, co-owners

When
Dinner Tuesday to Sunday

Address
122 Blagden Alley Northwest, Washington, DC 20001

+1 202 450 1015

thedabney.com

Bookings
Website, Resy.com

Price guide

What they say
"Influenced by Chef Jeremiah Langhorne's upbringing in Charlottesville, Virginia, our menu looks to showcase the mid-Atlantic region's diverse food culture from the finest farmers and purveyors."

Signature dishes
Fried Chesapeake sugar toads with spring lettuces, buttermilk dressing, and hot honey; crispy soft-shell crab with green garlic honey glaze, mustard greens, citrus mayo, and chili; charred bok choy with hush puppies, bacon, bread and butter cucumbers, smoked honey, and charred green garlic mayo.

What others say
"If Alice Waters asked for the Washington equivalent of Chez Panisse, I would send the mother of California cuisine to the locally rooted creation of Jeremiah Langhorne in Blagden Alley."

-Tom Sietsema, *The Washington Post*

What we say
The centerpiece of this dramatic dining room, lined with rustic exposed-brick walls, antique mirrors, and paintings of hunting dogs, is the massive wood-burning hearth. It's not just for show - nearly every dish on the menu relies upon it, from the ember-roasted mushrooms dabbed with velvety hollandaise to the crispy barbecue quails, their claws still attached. The menu changes daily to reflect what area producers have on offer, and features an eclectic variety of seafood from the Chesapeake Bay watershed, including by-catch, like the native puffer fish called sugar toads. It's all part of Jeremiah Langhorne's scheme to bring mid-Atlantic cuisine to the fore, and, fortunately for his diners, it's working.

Ellé

Washington

What
All-day café & bakery serving ambitious nighttime fare

Who
Nick Pimentel & Lizzy Evelyn, co-owners

When
Breakfast & lunch, daily, dinner Wednesday to Monday

Address
3221 Mount Pleasant Street Northwest, Washington, DC 20010

+1 202 652 0040

eatatelle.com

Bookings
Resy.com

Price guide

What they say
"Fermentation - food, alcohol, breads - is our passion. As an all-day restaurant, we work hard at incorporating the bakery, kitchen, and drinks into our program. We only source sustainable seafood and think outside of food. We use farm co-ops in the area to help source local ingredients. We source local and reclaimed woods from the area for our furniture and design as well."

Signature dishes
Kimchi toast with labneh on country sourdough bread; honey goat cheese cheesecake with over-ripened strawberries and rhubarb stems; hot duck and biscuits with fermented vegetable slaw and homemade hot sauce.

What others say
"This site for marvelous breads and pastries by day and enticing medium plates by night is the former Heller's Bakery, a vestige of which remains in the sign out front, now lit so that just the name of the new restaurant appears. (Clever use of leftovers, right?)"

-Tom Sietsema, *The Washington Post*

What we say
Keeping all the moving pieces of an all-day café in motion is no easy feat. At Ellé, a casual, red-bricked space in leafy Mount Pleasant, that means the in-house bakery program (which churns out everything from baguettes to doughnuts), the extensive drinks program (which spans coffee, wine, and cocktails), and, of course, the kitchen, which offers thoughtful plates from morning til night. Chef Brad Deboy's menu is veg-forward and draws on ingredients from local farm co-ops, and he saves all the scraps to be fermented into sauces and vinegars.

Espita

Washington

What
Mexican eatery with extensive sustainable mezcal menu

Who
Josh Phillips, partner

When
Dinner, daily, weekend brunch

Address
1250 9th Street Northwest, Washington, DC 20001

+1 202 621 9695

espitadc.com

Bookings
OpenTable.com

Price guide

What they say
"We are most passionate about our people, and the culture we are shining a light on. We take pride in giving our people the freedom to be creative, push boundaries, and show southern Mexican food and mezcal through the lens of our own personal experiences. Our creed is 'authentic, not traditional'. We take authentic techniques and flavors from our many visits to Mexico, and create dishes and drinks combined with our own personal experiences to create something that is authentic to us, true to the flavors of the culture we are presenting, but unique. We sell a lot of mezcal, a product that is in danger of becoming over-industrialized. Our company ethos, when it comes to agave spirits, is traditional, sustainable production. None of the bottles on our wall come from producers we don't know personally, or through another *mezcalero* that we respect."

Signature dishes
Tacos with roasted romanesco, *mole verde cruda* and smoked cashew crema; tostada with Wagyu beef crudo, radish, Fresno pepper, and beef tendon; octopus *aguachile* with black bean purée and squid ink tostada.

What we say
Wafer-thin tostadas made with half a dozen varietals of heirloom, non-GMO corn are packed with flavor at this handsome, graffiti-scrawled spot in DC's white-hot Shaw neighborhood. Fiery salsas are chock-full of complex flavored Oaxacan chili like *chilhuacle rojos* or *pasilla mixe*, sourced from small family businesses. And all microgreens, edible flowers, and salad greens come by way of urban farmers. But perhaps the most compelling story is told by Espita's finely-tuned mezcal menu, which features more than 130 traditional, sustainably-produced bottles.

Founding Farmers

Washington

What
Farmer-owned restaurant with locations across the DC area

Who
North Dakota Farmers Union, Dan Simons & Mike Vucerevich, co-owners

When
Breakfast, lunch, & dinner, daily

Address
1924 Pennsylvania Ave Northwest, Washington, DC 20006, plus other locations - see website

+1 202 822 8783

wearefoundingfarmers.com

Bookings
Farmersrestaurantgroup.com

Price guide

What they say
"We make every effort to embody the values of the farmers who partner with us. For us, that means paying attention to every detail, from the way we treat our team like family, to the way we choose our ingredients. We love cooking and creating from scratch - we've even launched our own micro-distillery, Founding Spirits, which produces spirits with grains from farmers we know; we use these spirits in all of our restaurants. Being environmentally conscious is at the forefront of what we do every day, alongside serving delicious, sustainably sourced food and drink."

Signature dishes
Founding Farmers Mid-Atlantic Scallops: perfectly caramelized scallops with sweet potato confit, quinoa salad, and creamy homemade parmesan grits.

What we say
This growing mini-empire, co-owned by the North Dakota Farmers Union, now spans seven locations and shows no sign of slowing down. The food is straightforward - think burgers, chicken pot pie, and crab cakes - but the overarching message is grand. With a modern farmhouse vibe and an emphasis on fresh ingredients and sustainable practices, the flagship eatery sets the tone with LEED and Green Restaurant Association certifications, plus a group-wide ban on plastic straws via their OurLastStraw.org movement. In 2012, the restaurant also partnered with George Washington University to build the school's working rooftop apiary, which currently houses twelve hives, and continues to offer the Founding Farmers Bees Fellowship to two research students.

Garrison

Washington

What
Vegetable-forward, seasonal food in an elegant setting

Who
Rob Weland, chef/owner

When
Dinner Tuesday to Sunday, brunch Sunday

Address
524 8th Street Southeast, Washington, DC 20003

+1 202 506 2445

garrisondc.com

Bookings
Phone, OpenTable.com, email info@garrisondc.com

Price guide

What they say
"We love being a place where neighbors, friends and special guests can come together to enjoy lovingly prepared seasonal offerings from Chesapeake Bay, Virginia, Maryland and Pennsylvania. We are a family-owned restaurant whose owners and staff live just blocks away. We source exclusively from local farms and co-ops. When summer is in full swing, you will find Rob working his three community garden plots, where he grows as many herbs, heirloom tomatoes, and other seasonal veggies as urban gardening permits!"

Signature dishes
House-made pancakes with local beets, figs, kitchen garden spring greens, and local goat cheese; house-rolled toasted farro *corzetti* pasta with spring peas, asparagus, morel mushrooms, and local pecorino; pan-seared Maryland soft-shell crabs with heirloom grits and grilled ramp and nettle salsa verde.

What others say
"Chef/owner Rob Weland spoils guests with hyper-seasonal, soul-warming fare that combines local ingredients in marvelous ways .... The minute you leave, you look forward to the next visit. Luckily, no invitation is needed."

Washingtonian magazine

What we say
At this wood-paneled Barracks Row restaurant, the menu relies exclusively on seasonal produce from area producers. A heavy hitter is One Acre Farm, which also runs a neighborhood CSA; at the close of drop-off days, the restaurant scoops up the farm's excess produce and transforms it into weekly menu specials. Chef Rob Weland also runs a mentoring program for his cooks and externs, training them to plan and grow their own kitchen gardens in the restaurant's plots.

Kaliwa

Washington

What
Authentic Southeast Asian flavors with local ingredients

Who
Cathal Armstrong, chef/co-owner & Meshelle Armstrong, co-owner

When
Lunch & dinner, daily

Address
751 Wharf Street Southwest, Washington, DC 20024

+1 202 516 4759

kaliwadc.com

Bookings
Walk-ins, phone, Exploretock.com

Price guide

What they say
"Every recipe showcased on our menu represents years of consultation with grandmasters and grandmothers, as well as immersive culinary and personal research. This is not pan-Asian or fusion food. Each region is represented in all its strength and beauty."

Signature dishes
Kalderetang cordero: braised lamb shoulder with vegetables and chili; *pak ruam*: plate of stir-fried greens; *nuer pad prik*: beef with green pepper.

What others say
"There's nothing quite like Kaliwa, where three popular cuisines are offered in what feels like a fun house ... I thought I hated slushies with booze until I tried the restaurant's frozen mai tai: icy, yes, but wicked and wonderful with rum. Even desserts show thought. Try the downy pandan cake with coconut cream icing and tell me otherwise."

-Tom Sietsema, *The Washington Post*

What we say
Co-owner and chef Cathal Armstrong hails from Ireland, but his love affair with Southeast Asian cuisine began twenty-five years ago at family gatherings with his Manila-born wife, Meshelle. Together, the seasoned restaurateurs have turned heads with Kaliwa, a meditation on the flavors and aromas of the Philippines, Korea, and Thailand. It's all built on a foundation of fresh and natural produce from small sustainable farms, which the Armstrongs have enlisted to grow region-specific ingredients special for them, like turmeric, Kaffir lime, and calamansi. Dry goods and spices like heirloom rice and artisan salts are imported directly from the appropriate region, while spice pastes and gravies are made in-house.

Kyirisan

Washington

What
Inventive Chinese-French cuisine

Who
Tim Ma, chef/owner

When
Dinner daily, weekend brunch

Address
1924 8th Street Northwest, Suite 140, Washington, DC 20001

+1 202 525 2383

kyirisandc.com

Bookings
Reserve.com

Price guide

What they say
"Chinese cuisine in America is generally not known for practicing local sourcing, but as a casual fine dining restaurant, we have that in our standards. We also believe that restaurants should be a temporary reprieve or escape from everything else going on outside of the walls. We want to welcome people to Kyirisan as if they are coming into our home."

Signature dishes
Seared scallops with coconut risotto and Thai basil ice cream; *mapo* tofu gnocchi; crème fraîche wings.

What others say
"The interior, refreshingly free of reclaimed wood but not sonic booms, has a unique point of view. It's all angles at Kyirisan, where brass triangles jut from the walls, the ceiling could pass for a giant children's chatterbox and even some of the plates are neither round nor square but somewhere in between. The engaging visuals extend to the clientele."

-Tom Sietsema, *The Washington Post*

What we say
French-trained Chef Tim Ma puts his Chinese heritage on display at this sleek Shaw hotspot, where cuisine-bending dishes like English pea tofu gnocchi spiked with white miso and lamb tartare splashed with Chinese chili oil open adventurous palates to new possibilities. You'll want to swing back here for brunch, too: the scallion waffle with chicken is not to be missed, nor are the delicate vanilla custard bao and donut holes glazed with red miso.

Seylou Bakery & Mill

Washington

What
Bakery specializing in freshly milled organic whole grain bread & pastries

Who
Jonathan Bethony & Jessica Azeez, co-owners

When
Breakfast & lunch, Wednesday to Sunday

Address
926 N Street Northwest, Suite A, Washington, DC 20001

+1 202 842 1122

seylou.com

Bookings
Walk-ins

Price guide

What they say
"We are in continual contact with our farmers in order to give and receive feedback. We see our fate as tied and our success mutual. We would be nothing without them."

Signature dishes
"Horse bread": wholegrain sourdough loaf of whole wheat, millet, sorghum, marfax beans, camelina seeds, and mustard seeds all from the same farm; millet baguette with fifteen percent wholegrain millet; millet chocolate chip cookie with sorghum syrup and dark chocolate.

What others say
"Seylou also offers a selection of wholegrain pastries, including quiches, tarts, scones and croissants so flaky they nearly disintegrate upon touch. A no-refined-sugar policy means treats are sweetened with additions like honey and maple sugar."

-Holley Simmons, *The Washington Post*

What we say
There isn't a lick of white flour to be found at Seylou, the one-hundred-percent wholegrain and vegetarian bakery in DC's hip Shaw neighborhood. Expect less common grains like millet, sorghum, and buckwheat, which impart wonderfully complex flavors and textures. The loosely formed whole grain rustic loaves as well as the pullman 100 percent Einkorn loaves are baked in a massive wood-fired oven, which traps steam from the loaves, making them even more aromatic and delicious. Several times a month, the wood ash is collected and distributed to the local fields on which the grains were grown - including those of organic, Amish, and Mennonite farms - helping to return health and vitality to the soil.

The Salt Line

Washington

What
Modern New England-style fish & ale house

Who
Kyle Bailey, chef/co-owner

When
Dinner, daily, weekend brunch

Address
79 Potomac Avenue Southeast, Washington, DC 20003

+1 202 506 2368

thesaltline.com

Bookings
Phone, website

Price guide

What they say
"We source from within 100 miles where possible. We also practice whole animal utilization and creative solutions to eliminate waste, like making our own hot sauce from the dehydrated waste product we get from peppers used elsewhere in the menu."

Signature dishes
Kanpachi crudo with English peas, mint, preserved lemon and *agrumato;* spring bucatini with ramp green pesto, middleneck clams, rabbit sausage, ricotta *salata,* and fennel pollen; monkfish saltimbocca with prosciutto, sage, royal trumpet mushrooms, roasted spring onions, and Marsala sauce.

What others say
"Chef Kyle Bailey's innovative takes that keep us most excited to return. Cacciatore is making a comeback, but nobody except for Bailey is trying to pull it off with eel - and it's a marvel."
-Ann Limpert, Anna Spiegel, Jessica Sidman, and Cynthia Hacinli, *Washingtonian* magazine

What we say
The District may be home to The Salt Line, but this attractive wood-and-tile spot in Southeast has a look that's New England by way of Brooklyn. Fish and shellfish are the name of the game here, all of them sustainable. Many arrive at the restaurant via Dock to Dish, a community-supported fishery program that uses the most traditional methods for harvesting wild seafood in the safest manner possible. To wit, you can feel good about slurping bivalves in one of the oyster bar's sea foam-green booths, or lapping up clam chowder on the waterfront patio.

Tail Up Goat

Washington

What
Mediterranean-inflected, bread-focused menu driven by local farms

Who
Jon Sybert, co-owner/chef

When
Dinner, daily

Address
1827 Adams Mill Road Northwest, Washington, DC 20009

+1 202 986 9600

tailupgoat.com

Bookings
Website, walk-ins

Price guide

What they say
"We never serve any seafood that is on any watch lists, and all of our seafood is sustainably caught. All of the meats we serve are raised with kindness and care, by people I know."

Signature dishes
Carrot ravioli with ramps, dill, and pistachio breadcrumbs; dry-aged pork loin with belly confit, rhubarb glaze, charred green tomatoes, and salsa verde; focaccia with burnt bread sauce, *stracciatella*, and basil.

What others say
"When food critics describe a dream restaurant, it's often a place like this Mediterranean-leaning spot - small and lovely, with a great bar; highly ambitious but not hugely expensive; service that's friendly and relaxed but also seamless and keenly knowledgeable."

-Ann Limpert, Anna Spiegel, Jessica Sidman and Cynthia Hacinli, *Washingtonian* magazine

What we say
Mediterranean-accented cuisine is the star of Tail Up Goat, but its name is derived from an old Caribbean phrase. How do you tell the difference between a goat and a sheep? Tail up - goat. Tail down - sheep. Goat may not always be on the menu, but the restaurant boasts an impressive whole-animal butchery program, showcased spectacularly in an unctuous dry-aged pork dish with a sweet-sour rhubarb glaze and charred green tomatoes. The cut of pork changes as the restaurant works its way through a whole hog, ensuring little goes to waste. Also of note: the in-house bread program. Nothing is wasted here, either: breadcrumbs features in several dishes, another effort to save scraps from the trash bin.

Timber Pizza

Washington

What
Wood-fired pizza spot

Who
Andrew Dana & Chris Brady, co-owners

When
Dinner Tuesday to Sunday, weekend breakfast

Address
809 Upshur Street Northwest, Washington, DC 20011

+1 202 853 9746

timberpizza.com

Bookings
Walk-ins

Price guide

What they say
"We are passionate about using our own produce. We have our own garden directly across the street from Timber, where we grow herbs, greens, and peppers for the restaurants."

Signature dishes
"The Taylor Pizza" with lamb, peas, mint, spicy almonds, and watercress; "The Julia Pizza" with sugar snap peas, watercress pesto, pea shoots, lemongrass dressing, and sesame seeds; "The Mina Salad" with local plums, greens, almonds, and peas.

What others say
"Quirky details endear me to this snug storefront in Petworth. Quick, name another pizzeria that hangs a swing for two in its front window or offers empanadas as appetizers. The crimped hot pockets, stuffed with juicy roast pork or corn and sweet peppers, are courtesy of chef Daniela Moreira, an Argentine native who shops the farmers market for her toppings."

-Tom Sietsema, *Washington Post*

What we say
Once but a roving food truck, Timber Pizza has settled into the bricks-and-mortar life with its snug thirty-six-seat digs, jam-packed with communal tables and a swing-for-two up front. All the produce here - spotlighted in pies like the Green Monster, vibrantly colored with pesto, kale, and shaved zucchini - comes from area farms, not to mention its own modest garden plots. But if you come for the farm-fresh veg, you'll stay for the crispy crusts, lightly scorched in the Neapolitan style in a copper pizza oven.

Toki Underground

Washington

What
Tiny ramen shop & izakaya

Who
Olivier Caillabet, creative director/general manager

When
Lunch & dinner, Monday to Saturday

Address
1234 H Street Northeast, Washington, DC 20002

+1 202 388 3086

tokiunderground.com

Bookings
Website, Reserve.com

Price guide

What they say
"We're a very busy restaurant and sell a lot of soup. The beauty of soup is that you can throw most scraps in! Consequently, we produce very little food waste and can reuse some of the flavoring agents - like kombu and shiitake mushrooms - in other delicious dishes."

Signature dishes
Tonkotsu soup with braised pork shoulder *chashu* and pickles; vegan ramen with charred onion and carrot soup, lemongrass, garlic, ginger, and pear with kombu and shiitake dashi; local asparagus with vegan, sesame-mirin-soy-rice vinegar dressing, and dill.

What others say
"Take the broth for this kitchen's Toki Classic bowl - it's hefty, porky, almost creamy, the result of a daylong simmer of pork bones, which is mixed with chicken stock and a dashi broth. The base soup alone is worth standing in line for, even without the chewy noodles and smart accessories like slow-poached egg, pickled ginger, and greens."

-Todd Kliman, Ann Limpert, Anna Spiegel, and Cynthia Hacinli, *Washingtonian* magazine

What we say
This pint-sized Atlas District hideaway first started slinging ramen way back in 2011, but lines of noodle-worshippers haven't stopped clamoring for one of its twenty-eight stools since the restaurant's opening. Toki Underground remains one of the DC area 's most reliable sources of deeply flavorful soup. Much of the produce comes from local producers and suppliers, often directly from farmers. Many herbs and vegetables are from the restaurant's very own organic garden, located on its rooftop.

Whaley's

Washington

What
Waterfront seafood palace & raw bar

Who
Nick & David Wiseman, owners & Daniel Perron, chef

When
Dinner, daily, weekend brunch

Address
301 Water Street #115, Washington, DC 20003

+1 202 484 8800

whaleysdc.com

Bookings
Website, OpenTable.com

Price guide

What they say
"We want to leave our rivers, streams, and oceans more bountiful for generations to come. In that spirit, we believe in full transparency in how we source our seafood. We work exclusively with purveyors that can trace the origin of every fish we use at Whaley's. We are a proud partner of Seafood Watch, a comprehensive rating system that assures highly responsible seafood choices. All of our seafood meets their strict sustainability criteria."

Signature dishes
Dayboat scallop crudo with wild spring onion, English cucumber, Sorrento lemon, and trout roe; tempura soft-shell crab with radish kimchi, baby farm greens, pickled ramps, and *furikake* seasoning; seafood risotto with vadouvan curry, coconut, Thai basil, and pickled Fresno chili.

What others say
"The seafood tower that four of us shared at Whaley's seems like a novel, one you can't put down, each page building on the momentum of the previous one and revealing a twist that says something compelling about the characters or maybe the author."

-Tim Carman, *The Washington Post*

What we say
With its sky-high ceilings and all-glass front wall, you might mistake Whaley's light-filled dining room for an aquarium. It's an appropriate comparison, considering the menu: seafood is the main event. The successful seasonal plates are aplenty, among them a big-eye tuna crudo awash in chili-spiked consommé and a delicately fried oyster po'boy. But a must-order is the famous seafood towers, piled high with local oysters, sweet clams, grilled squid, glowing lobes of uni, and poached mussels.

295

Florida

Gilbert's Social

Duval

What
Southern barbecue made for sharing

Who
Kenny Gilbert, chef/owner

When
Lunch & dinner, Tuesday to Saturday

Address
4021 Southside Boulevard, Suite 200, Jacksonville, Duval, FL 32216

+1 904 647 7936

gilbertssocial.co

Bookings
Website, OpenTable.com

Price guide

What they say
"I'm passionate about bringing the community together through my food. We created this restaurant to have a place where people felt comfortable and it didn't matter who you were. That's what Gilbert's Social is all about."

Signature dishes
"Social biscuits": a happy meeting of a drop biscuit and cornbread served with cane syrup butter and house pickles; smoked brisket rubbed with a cinnamon-coffee blend; Southern "ramen": smoked ham hock broth, soy, and ginger, ladled over egg noodles, topped with pulled pork, jalapeño shrimp cake, roasted mushroom, benne seed, and egg.

What we say
Gilbert cooks food that reminds him of his parents, his mother, a St. Augustine, Florida, native and one of seven siblings; his father from Chicago who passed on his love for barbecue. Through food, Gilbert aims to tell a history lesson, one that values compassion and people. Some temporary employees have participated in a local work-release program. One woman was so successful, they hired her on permanently. "Working with programs like that, it lets people know, if you've gone through some things, you can still work hard and show discipline and willingness to learn", Gilbert says.

Gilbert's Southern Kitchen + Bar

Duval

What
Modern Southern barbecue & seafood

Who
Kenny Gilbert, chef/owner

When
Lunch & dinner, Tuesday to Sunday

Address
831 First Street North, Jacksonville Beach, Duval, FL 32250

+1 904 372 0444

gilbertssouthern.com

Bookings
Website, OpenTable.com

Price guide

What they say
"We're bringing worlds together."

Signature dishes
Smoked conch dip with seasonal vegetables, assorted crackers, and datil pepper hot sauce; alligator rib gumbo: smoked and braised Cypress Creek Farm alligator ribs with okra, tomatoes, sassafras, garlic rice, and scallions; smoked brisket, with black bean crumble, watermelon radish, and cornbread crumble.

What we say
Of Gilbert's four restaurant properties, three are in Jacksonville Beach. He bet big on the coastal community to spread the word on Southern cuisine – his take on the food he grew up eating; inspired by global travels, culinary training, and an urge to expand what it means to cook food from this region. He's fond of Congaree + Penn, an independent rice farm just outside of the city, and Eddie Chaser Seafood, where he sources whole shrimp. Atlantic Farm's hydroponic setup gives Gilbert scarlet mustard greens he can't stop talking about.

But part of being all-in in a place is seeing where you can make a difference. Gilbert has made a point to hire employees in transition, decent people who are rebounding from hard times, and perhaps some poor choices. He prioritizes training and development because he wants to promote from within, to offer people a career if they want it. His outlook reaps unexpected benefits. A recent hire had worked under a chef that Gilbert trained a while back. "It was like the guy had already worked for me".

The Columbia

Hillborough

What
Iconic Spanish-Cuban

Who
Richard Gonzmart, fourth-generation caretaker

When
Lunch & dinner, daily

Address
2117 East 7th Avenue, Tampa, Hillborough, FL 33605

+1 813 248 4961

columbiarestaurant.com

Bookings
Phone, website, OpenTable.com, walk-ins

Price guide

What they say
"Our restaurant features food and family, history and heritage. Our food is prepared with love and served with pride. It's not just business, it's personal. We are committed to sustainability. All of our seafood is either wild-caught or farmed in ways that consider the long-time viability of the species and the well-being of the waters. We buy all natural, wild-caught Gulf of Mexico shrimp from Carson Kimbrough in Bon Secour, Alabama, a former shrimp boat captain."

Signature dishes
Spanish bean soup with garbanzo beans, smoked ham, chorizo sausage, and potatoes in chicken and ham broth; Columbia's Original '1905 Salad®' with iceberg lettuce, julienned baked ham, Swiss cheese, tomatoes, olives, grated Romano, and garlic dressing; chicken and yellow rice Valenciana: original recipe with bone-in chicken, green peppers, onions, tomato, smoked ham, hearts of palm, garlic, herbs, and Valencia rice.

What others say
"The Columbia is the oldest restaurant in Florida and the oldest Spanish eatery in the United States ... But [it] is more popular than ever, and perhaps the colorful neighborhood's most enduring symbol."

-Larry Olmsted, *USA Today*

What we say
The Columbia is a community stalwart - their contributions illustrate how successful restaurant groups can be powerful advocates. Through their Community Harvest program, they donate five percent of guest checks - more than two million dollars. For more than ninety years they've bought from the same family-owned companies - La Secunda Central Bakery, Naviera Coffee Mills, and Sunny Florida Dairy.

Ghee Indian Kitchen

Miami

What
Modern, local, vegetable-centric Indian

Who
Niven Patel, chef/owner

When
Lunch & dinner, Tuesday to Saturday

Address
8965 Southwest 72nd Place, Miami, FL 33156

+1 305 968 1850

gheemiami.com

Bookings
OpenTable.com, phone

Price guide

What they say
"Our number one focus was to create a business model that takes care of my people. That to us is sustainability. We can talk about supporting local farms and businesses, but if we're not creating great jobs we're not going to last. It's all about our employees and our people. We built a great team that believes in what we're doing and this gets conveyed to our guests."

Signature dishes
Pakora with seasonal vegetables from the restaurant's garden and tamarind chutney; vegetable *poriyal* with fresh coconut, carrots, beets, lentils, green chilis, garlic, and lemon; *gulab jamun* with hibiscus meringue, coconut water, simple syrup, white chocolate, whipped cream, and pistachios.

What we say
To understand Niven Patel's philosophy, you must first understand this: He put a farmer on the payroll. The half-acre called Rancho Patel is a backyard garden where Ghee Indian Kitchen sources the majority of its produce. Things were going so well, Patel decided to hire Brendan Sutton as a full-time farmer. "We can grow things that other farmers in Miami aren't growing", Patel says. "We can still support them, but we can now grow specific to what we need for certain dishes". Like taro leaf, a crop from Gujarat, India, where his parents are from. Sutton is developing an additional two acres about ten miles from the restaurant. Patel can't wait. "It's going to triple our volume for the growing season".

Joe's Stone Crab

Miami

What
104-year-old, family-owned restaurant specialising in seafood, stone crabs & steaks

Who
Stephen Sawitz, owner

When
Tuesday to Sunday, hours change seasonally

Address
11 Washington Avenue, Miami Beach, FL 33139

+1 305 673 0365

joesstonecrab.com

Bookings
Walk-ins

Price guide

What they say
"We consider ourselves as a pillar of the community - we donate to local charitable events and source some produce from local vendors. Gender equality is valued here, as is maintaining a diverse workforce with people from varied backgrounds."

Signature dishes
Stone crab claws with mustard sauce; hobo grouper bake roasted in lemon butter with brussel sprouts, tomato, onion, and green beans; fried chicken.

What others say
"Devotees give two claws up to this century-old South Beach institution - ranked Miami's Most Popular eatery - for the magnificent sweetness of its heavenly stone crabs."

Zagat.com

What we say
In an ever-developing South Beach scene, it's nice that some traditions remain. Stone crab claws with mustard sauce are the main draw - served with hefty sides like creamed spinach, hash browns, or grilled vegetables - though there's plenty to satisfy in the delicacy's off-season, too. Joe's Stone Crab uses free-range chicken and ethically-raised beef to ensure animals are treated fairly. Finish your meal with a tart slice of key lime pie, baked fresh every day. If you're on the move, order something from Joe's Take Away next door.

Stiltsville Fish Bar

Miami

What
Chef-driven Florida fish house

Who
Jeff McInnis & Janine Booth, chefs, Grove Bay Hospitality Group, partners

When
Dinner, daily, lunch Monday to Friday, weekend brunch

Address
1787 Purdy Avenue, Miami Beach, FL 33139

+1 786 353 0477

stiltsvillefishbar.com

Bookings
OpenTable.com

Price guide

What they say
"We wanted to make sure we serve locals local fish, and do it at an affordable rate. We want to give the public what they need."

Signature dishes
Trigger fish; hog snapper; blue runner.

What we say
Daily deliveries from local fishers set the menu here, where customers can get fresh, direct seafood in a luxe environment. McInnis, who grew up in the Panhandle, remembers the days of getting twenty-five-cent oysters and ten-dollar fish dishes. Stiltsville doesn't reach quite that far back into nostalgia, but the idea of having access to fresh product from local people remains. When the restaurant's opening day was impacted by a hurricane - from Key West and upward north, fishmongers were out of business - Booth and McInnis hired fishermen to wait tables, process fish, and cook. Eventually they were able to help get fifteen boats back out on the water; most of those vendors still supply the restaurant today.

El Siboney Restaurant

Monroe

What
Home-style Cuban cuisine, made from scratch

Who
Julio Delacruz, owner

When
Lunch & dinner, daily

Address
900 Catherine Street, Key West, Monroe, FL 33040

+1 305 296 4184

elsiboneyrestaurant.com

Bookings
Walk-ins

Price guide

What they say
"We're a small restaurant with a big heart. Everybody knows everybody and everyone is welcome. Our staff has been the same for the last fifteen or twenty years. Our local customers are the best in the world. They not only come for the great food, but also to get away from the daily hustle in the Keys. This place belongs to them."

Signature dishes
Marinated pulled pork with rice, beans, and plantains; mojo-marinated churrasco skirt steak with onion and parsley; whole fried yellowtail snapper with lemon juice, spices, and crispy tostones.

What we say
It is easy to feel the trappings of tourism as a visitor in Key West. But gems like El Siboney, named for Cuba's, remind that island paradise is also home to many. Traditional Cuban cuisine has been beloved and taken seriously here since 1984. Under new ownership from 2004, entrée plates continue to sizzle, marked with heaping mounds of beans and rice. Seafood comes from local fishers and produce that can't be sourced locally typically ships from Miami. Daily specials seem straight from grandma's kitchen - lima bean soup mid-week, or oxtails on Saturday. Much of the staff has been around for at least fifteen years, giving the team a shorthand that's entertaining to observe. Get cozy and speak up - it's often loud, just like any feel-good family dining room ought to be.

Buccan

Palm Beach

What
New American melting pot

Who
Clay Conley, chef/owner

When
Dinner, daily

Address
350 South County Road,
Palm Beach, FL 33480

+1 561 833 3450

buccanpalmbeach.com

Bookings
Phone, OpenTable.com

Price guide

What they say
"We're passionate about our people, our food and our ingredients. We treat our staff as well as we treat our guests. We have a good culture and people are happy here."

Signature dishes
Hamachi *tiradito*: a sashimi, based on a Peruvian dish; squid ink orecchiette with handmade Italian sausage, bright white wine, butter, Calabrian chili, and thinly sliced Turks and Caicos conch; and Florida-inspired version of *moqueca* (Brazilian seafood stew).

What we say
From slow-cooked *moqueca* made with Florida red snapper, local coconut porridge and rock shrimp, to his bright and minty octopus tabouleh atop a layer of hummus, Chef Clay Conley makes clear he likes to toy with tradition. It's easy to play when the bounty of southern Florida is your toolbox. Buccan keeps a garden with six raised beds in rotation, all twelve to fifty feet each. The kitchen composts, and what they can't grow is purchased from local farmers.

The Regional Kitchen & Public House

Palm Beach

What
Regional Southern-inspired cuisine

Who
Lindsay Autry, chef/partner

When
Lunch & dinner, daily, Sunday brunch

Address
651 Okeechobee Boulevard,
West Palm Beach, FL 33401

+1 561 557 6460

eatregional.com

Bookings
Website, OpenTable.com

Price guide

What they say
"One thing I'm the most passionate about is the sourcing of ingredients."

Signature dishes
Tomato pie with cheese, herbs, and caramelized onions; Florida sea trout or speckled trout with buttermilk, and cornmeal butter and green tomato slaw; carrot cake with cream cheese frosting.

What we say
Autry blends her native North Carolina sensibility and affinity for Mediterranean-style cooking with the Florida bounty. Find fried chicken thighs brined in sweet tea right next to Florida snapper ceviche, with *leche de tigre* and Jasper tomatoes, alongside a bucatini parade of country ham, crushed chili, garlic, and Parmesan.

She's developed a strong relationship with Kai Kai Farm in Stuart, Florida, where the beautiful produce she sources there include special-requested okra and black-eye peas. Autry "puts them up" - Southern vernacular for preserving the food for later in the year. Her restaurant is a member of Seafood Watch and works with veteran local fishmongers. Pastry Chef Sarah Sipe does the No Kid Hungry Chef Cycle, a 300-mile ride, where a portion of sales from the dessert menu helps fund the organization.

301

Georgia

Little Tart Bakeshop

Atlanta

What
French-inspired, seasonal pastry, delicious coffee & light, vegetable-driven lunch & brunch

Who
Sarah O'Brien, baker/owner

When
Breakfast, brunch & lunch, daily

Address
437 Memorial Drive Southest, Atlanta, GA 30312, plus other locations - see website

+1 404 348 4797

littletartatl.com

Bookings
Walk-ins

Price guide

What they say
"We are passionate about pastry. We strive every day to become better bakers and cooks by choosing to work with thoughtfully sourced and ethically produced ingredients, by paying intense attention to every step of our baking process, and by being good community members through exemplary service to our customers and to our staff alike."

Signature dishes
Croissant: soft in the middle, buttery, sweet, malty, light and layered; galette: mixed with Carolina Ground rye flour with seasonal fruit filling; quiche with house-made local crème fraîche, local free-range eggs, seasonal vegetables, and local cheese.

What others say
Semifinalist: Outstanding Baker 2016, 2017, 2018.

James Beard Foundation

What we say
From airy *gougères* to buttery *kouign-amann*, O'Brien's guiding light shines through - using the best ingredients grown by community farmers in a fulfilling work environment designed for stable careers. With ninety percent of the bakery's produce being sourced locally, customers can count on local milk, honey, peanut butter, and cheese. Compostwheels picks up the food waste, which goes to farmers' fields. The bakeshop is also community-minded and organizes a citywide "cookie grab" to benefit Planned Parenthood Southeast, which has raised $26,000 over the past two years.

B's Cracklin' Barbecue

Atlanta

What
Whole hog Southern barbecue

Who
Bryan Furman, pitmaster/owner

When
Lunch & dinner, Tuesday to Sunday

Address
2061 Main Street Northwest, Atlanta, GA 30318

+1 678 949 9912

bscracklinbbq.com

Bookings
Walk-ins

Price guide

What they say
"The cracklin' in our cornbread comes from the skin of the hog. We mix it with our cornbread mix. I learned how to make it from my grandmother, Susie Furman. They are called 'Hoe Cakes'."

Signature dishes
Pork ribs cooked over a blend of hickory and cherrywood coals; hash and rice: a take on traditional South Carolina stewed hog's head meat dish; fried cracklin' cornbread.

What we say
That pitmaster Furman raises multiple heritage pork breeds in Southern Georgia is just the first indication of the knowledge and commitment that drives the menu at B's Cracklin' Barbecue. The barbecue is celebrated for its depth of flavor, and that richness the comes from the fat of the heritage breed pigs. His pit-smoking skills don't stop with pork. Chicken and beef brisket are on the menu too, as are freshly made vegetable sides ranging from stewed collard greens to vegetable slaw sourced from local growers.

Bread & Butterfly

Atlanta

What
All-day café & restaurant serving French-inspired fare

Who
Billy Allin, chef/owner & Kristin Allin, owner

When
Breakfast, lunch & dinner, daily

Address
290 Elizabeth Street, Suite F, Atlanta, GA 30307

+1 678 515 4536

bread-and-butterfly.com

Bookings
Phone, walk-ins

Price guide

What they say
"This is a place where you can drop by any time of the day, eat, drink, and relax. We're less a destination, more a place to take a load off."

Signature dishes
Tomato soup with puff pastry; "burger *Americain*": brioche bun, high-quality ground beef with gruyère cheese, caramelized onion, grain mustard, and aïoli, served with frites; and omelette du jour, often served with Parmesan, and a side of mixed green lettuces.

What we say
Inspired by the fictional insect from Lewis Carroll's *Through the Looking-Glass*, Bread & Butterfly hopes guests flitter into a Parisian wonderland during their meal.

It's easy to forget you're in Inman Park, the posh Atlanta neighborhood teeming with artisan shops and restaurants, and not a cozy brasserie in France. But the Allins, along with longtime beverage director Jordan Smelt, succeed in taking cues from the City of Lights without losing their Southern sense of self.

Smelt's wine list cascades from Champagne to Rhône, domaine selections that pair beautifully with recipes seemingly cut from a time-worn French cookbook. Find soft scrambled eggs with cold-smoked trout from Sunburst Farms in North Carolina, or cauliflower soup deepened with charred green garlic, just picked from an Atlanta farmers' market.

Miller Union

Atlanta

What
Fresh, local ingredients, embracing the seasons

Who
Steven Satterfield, chef/owner, & Neal McCarthy, general manager/owner

When
Dinner Monday to Saturday, lunch Tuesday to Saturday

Address
999 Brady Avenue Northwest, Atlanta, GA 30318

+1 678 733 8550

millerunion.com

Bookings
Phone, Resy.com

Price guide

What they say
"We serve well-considered seasonal dishes in a relaxed environment. We are passionate, and proud of the ingredients that we source."

Signature dishes
Field pea and boiled peanut salad with roasted pepper, tomato, ricotta, and mint; farm egg baked in celery cream with grilled bread; vegetable plate featuring dishes like roasted beets and roasted okra with tomato and sautéed greens, or farro with snap peas and celery; house-made ice cream sandwiches.

What others say
"South Georgia native Steven Satterfield bares the heart of his region in dishes like field pea and peanut salad or pan-roasted chicken with creamed rice."

-Bill Addison, *Eater*

What we say
Satterfield's menu breathes Georgia harvest - to dine here throughout the year is to embrace every season in its own particular expression. Being so closely tethered to local land has meant developing deep relationships with farmers. Taste the care and integrity on the plate from producers like Riverview Farms for pastured pork, White Oak Pastures for pastured poultry, Joyce Farms for grass-fed beef, and the hit parade of Crystal Organic, Woodland Gardens, and produce delivery start-up The Turnip Truck for a range of vegetables and fruits.

Ticonderoga Club

Atlanta

What
American tavern, welcoming & inclusive

Who
David Bies, chef, Regan Smith, accounting, Greg Best, management, Paul Calvert, beverage & Bart Sasso, creative director

When
Dinner Thursday to Tuesday, brunch Sunday

Address
99 Krog Street Northeast, Atlanta, GA 30307

+1 404 458 4534

ticonderogaclub.com

Bookings
Website, walk-ins

Price guide

What they say
"We are committed to providing a warm, welcoming environment for our guests. We are passionate about sharing only the food and drink we love. We trust that in an inviting space and with exemplary service we will be able to turn our guests on to all sorts of new cuisine and delicious beverages. In short, that they'll love it because we love it."

Signature dishes
Snapper ceviche with *aji amarillo*, tiger's milk, and whole, wild-caught American red snapper; Ipswich clam roll; vegan noodle bowl.

What we say
Because Ticonderoga Club is a small restaurant, they nixed the walk-in refrigerator to create more dining space. It makes for coveted seating at peak times, but allows the team to receive fresh produce and proteins every business day. "There is no stockpiling at the Club", they tell us. Full-time employees at the Club keep to a forty-hour work week, and staff are guaranteed an hourly minimum so even on a rare quiet night, no one ever works for nothing. Tips are shared with kitchen staff because they are equally valued members of the team. "We believe that in order for a career in the service industry to be sustainable, we have to take care of our people so that they can find honor and balance in restaurant work".

Twisted Soul Cookhouse & Pours

Atlanta

What
Comfort food & food memories

Who
Deborah VanTrece, chef/ owner

When
Lunch & dinner, Tuesday to Saturday, brunch Sunday

Address
1133 Huff Road Northwest #D, Atlanta, GA 30318

+1 404 350 5500

twistedsoulcookhouse-andpours.com

Bookings
Phone, website

Price guide

What they say
"We believe that all cultures have a soul food and we use our restaurant to bring cultures and food together. I am passionate about food that brings comfort."

Signature dishes
Hoisin oxtails with vegetable fried rice, ginger-shallot roasted bok choy; grilled duck wings with sweet potato hash browns and bourbon-peach preserves; harissa lamb ribs with dandelion greens, cucumber, tomato, mint relish, and grit croutons.

What others say
"VanTrece remains at the top of Atlanta's dining scene, winning numerous local awards for her updated takes on globally influenced soul food inspired by her travels around the world."

-Sara Ventiera, *Zagat*

What we say
Born to a Midwest family, Chef Deborah VanTrece says she understood sustainability - especially using the whole animal - quite early. As a chef, she takes care to learn about the food she procures and how it was cultivated. "I think it is a responsibility of all chefs to care what fuels the body", she says.

VanTrece cofounded a women-led dinner series called The Cast Iron Chronicles, where she and her colleagues aim to debunk the myths of African-American soul food through dining and conversation. The series addresses racial inequality and gender representation in the culinary industry and received national attention, including an invitation to bring the series to the James Beard House in New York City.

The Grey

Chatham

What
Port-city southern food

Who
John O. Morisano, managing partner, & Mashama Bailey, chef

When
Dinner, Tuesday to Sunday

Address
109 Martin Luther King Jr Boulevard, Savannah, Chatham, GA 31401

+1 912 662 5999

thegreyrestaurant.com

Bookings
Resy.com

Price guide

What they say
"We're passionate about being a team and providing our guests with a complete experience."

Signature dishes
Salted fish toast: Mediterranean-style cured fish on grilled heritage grain levain with green garlic, garlic, and herbs; country captain: roasted curried chicken with almonds and currants; crab and spring pea pasta: fresh lump crab meat with bottarga, pickled peppers, and scallions served on linguini.

What others say
Winner, 2017 Restaurant of the Year
Eater

What we say
The menu, reflective of the American South's port cities and the African, French, Spanish, and Native influences that seasoned the cultural melting pot. The building, formerly a Greyhound bus station, art deco-inspired and designed to evoke movement. But the team, led by Bailey and Morisano, capture the real spirit of this place. The yard out back is a community space that hosts a monthly benefit where profits go to charity. Bailey serves as chairperson of the Edna Lewis Foundation and Morisano is a board member - the organization celebrates African-American cooking in Southern food and educates about the historic role of black foodways. Every staff member can participate in a health care plan broadly subsidized by the restaurant and employees can contribute to a retirement plan.

home.made

Clarke

What
Seasonal, reimagined regional cuisine

Who
Mimi Maumus, chef/owner

When
Lunch & dinner, Tuesday to Saturday, brunch Saturday

Address
1072 Baxter Street, Athens, Clarke, GA 30606

+1 706 206 9216

homemadeathens.com

Bookings
Email info@homemadeathens.com

Price guide

What they say
"We try to bring out the best in our ingredients and the best in our workers. Employing people can be rewarding when the relationship has a good balance and an understanding that we're all trying to do the very best that we can."

Signature dishes
Georgia peach salad with pickled dahlia root, arugula, rye-soaked pecans, cottage cheese, and dahlia vinaigrette; New Orleans hot chicken: fried chicken with hot sauce, beignets, and pickled okra; smoked pork shoulder ham with boiled peanut cassoulet, seared baby collards with hot pepper mash, and pickled magnolia blossoms.

What others say
"[Mimi Maumus is an] innovative thinker and chef grounded in the place she loves."

-John T. Edge, *The Local Palate*

What we say
Maumus pulls inspiration from everywhere she can. Often, that means asking farmers for lesser-known wild, native foods. "I make a color-changing lemonade made from the fragrant, grape soda-scented flowers of the kudzu vine". She sources uncommon items like nasturtium capers, magnolia flowers, kudzu flowers, and smilax shoots.

home.made spotlights local breweries like Creature Comforts and Terrapin, and bean-to-bar chocolate producer Condor Chocolates. Let Us Compost takes their waste. "We try to cook leaf to stem to root - to showcase parts of plants that people would otherwise scrap".

The restaurant works with local nonprofits like the Immigrants Rights Coalition and Athens Pride. They support the biannual journal Crop Stories, which explores the farmer-to-consumer relationship in the American South, one crop at a time.

Seabear Oyster Bar

Clarke

What
Neighborhood bar & restaurant serving sustainable seafood

Who
Patrick Stubbers, Noah Brendel & Peter Dale

When
Dinner, daily

Address
297 Prince Avenue, Suite 10, Athens, Clarke, GA 30601

+1 706 510 8327

seabearoysterbar.com

Bookings
Walk ins

Price guide

What they say
"We support as many oyster farms as possible. We care about our oceans and the bounty they provide for us - we ensure that what we are sourcing is being farmed or harvested by like-minded individuals."

Signature dishes
Taiwanese-style pancake with Maine rock crab, radish, local micro greens, and sesame vinaigrette; seared okra with tomato, roasted garlic aïoli, and Old Bay seasoning; New England clam chowder.

What others say
"I still can't get over chef Patrick Stubbers's pillowy Parker House rolls drenched in brown butter and sprinkled with raw sugar and sea salt. Or his crispy, briny, deep-fried clam strips. Or the icy Negroni slushies that go down just a little too easy."

-Ashlea Halpern, *Condé Nast Traveler*

What we say
Check the chalkboard for daily oyster and raw bar offerings, all sustainably sourced. They support the University of Georgia-Athens Shellfish Research Laboratory through donations and help fund Oyster Roast for a Reason. Part of the university's team is creating brood stock to help launch the state's first oyster hatchery. Shucked shells often see another life - whether back on the coast for habitat, in the hands of local artisans, in garden pathways or driveways, or as chicken feed supplement. They also direct event proceeds to The Giving Kitchen, an Atlanta organization that provides emergency grants to restaurant workers, and support *Crop Stories* by Andre Gallant that celebrates food-focused storytelling.

Arepa Mia

DeKalb

What
Traditional Venezuelan cuisine in Southern surroundings

Who
Lis Hernandez, founder/chef/owner

When
Lunch & dinner, Tuesday to Sunday

Address
10 North Clarendon Avenue, Suite A, Avondale Estates, DeKalb, GA 30002

+1 404 600 3509

arepamiaatlanta.com

Bookings
Walk-ins

Price guide

What they say
"When it comes to my restaurants, I'm most passionate about my cooking, doing it with fresh ingredients and having a friendly atmosphere. I want to make you feel like you're in Venezuela."

Signature dishes
Arepa pabellón: grilled cornmeal patty filled with twelve-hour roasted beef, black beans, sweet plantains, and *queso año*; *Cachapa pernil*: corn dough pancake brimming with slow-roasted pork in mojo sauce, cilantro sauce, and Guayanés cheese; *Empanada pollo la catira*: fried corn flour turnovers stuffed with chicken, cheddar, grilled onions, and bell peppers, served with *Nata a Venezuelan* and *guasacaca*, a cilantro-parsley sauce seasoned with onion and garlic.

What others say
"Atlanta needed a captivating introduction to Venezuelan food, and this is it."

Atlanta magazine

What we say
Arepas are fundamental to Venezuelan cuisine and with Chef Liz Hernandez's expertise, they've become fan favorites in Atlanta, too. Her cornmeal flour patties, crunchy on the outside, piping hot and filled with meats, seafood, or vegetables, are recipes she learned and evolved from her mother, who taught Hernandez the arepa-making business in their native country.

Hernandez's menu is deceiving in its simplicity - countless hours go into the flavorful fillings of her corn-based dishes - wash them down with locally made beer, fresh sangria or house-made fruit drinks. She supports thoughtful producers like White Oak Pastures and Riverview Farms who value organic, sustainable, hormone-free methods of raising meat. Vegetarians and vegans have plenty to choose from, and the menu is gluten free.

Chai Pani

DeKalb

What
Indian street food

Who
Meherwan Irani, chef/owner

When
Lunch & dinner, daily

Address
406 West Ponce de Leon Avenue, Decatur, DeKalb, GA 30030

+1 404 378 4030

chaipanidecatur.com

Bookings
Walk-ins

Price guide

What they say
"We make Indian food fun, approachable, and representative of the breadth and diversity of cuisine in the subcontinent. We are trying to change the perception of Indian food in America. The best compliment we ever received was from an Indian gentleman who said that Chai Pani made him proud to be an Indian!"

Signature dishes
Kale *pakoras*; sloppy Jai; corn *bhel* with corn, coriander, mint, cucumber, tomato, and salad tossed in cumin-lime dressing.

What others say
"Kudos to Meherwan Irani, who sticks to his spicy central and south Indian roots at Chai Pani restaurant in Decatur. Locals crowd the colorful space for street snacks, ranging from okra fries and puffed flour crisps stuffed with potatoes, onions, and cilantro to a humorously named "Sloppy Jai," lamb hash simmered with tomatoes and ginger and served on a bun. Even kale haters will happily eat their greens once Irani gives them the fritter treatment."

Atlanta magazine

What we say
Meherwan Irani, chef and owner of Chai Pani, honors pan-Indian cuisine for mostly American palates. The restaurant brings a festive energy to sharing regional variations of Indian street food (many dishes can be made vegan and gluten-free). Irani interprets his native country through fresh eyes, delighting visitors with food that's lush with storytelling and soul. The restaurant also partners with a local nonprofit once a month to raise awareness and donate ten percent of the day's sales to the organization.

Kimball House

DeKalb

What
Fulled by humility, hospitality & passion for the crafts

Who
Bryan Rackley, Miles Macquarrie, Jesse Smith and Matthew Christison, co-owners

When
Dinner, daily, lunch Sunday

Address
303 East Howard Avenue, Decatur, DeKalb, GA 30030

+1 404 478 3502

kimball-house.com

Bookings
Walk-ins, website, Reserve.com

Price guide

What they say
"We use great products across the board, sourcing from small, organic farmers each week. But goddamn, those kitchen guys like to cook with butter!"

Signature dishes
Raw oyster bar; snapper crudo with carrot, radish, lime, coriander, and elderberry; pan-seared grouper, kohlrabi, cucumber, and garlic scape.

What others say
Semifinalist: Outstanding Bar Program.

James Beard Foundation

What we say
So many star attractions - prized cocktails, drinks served in antique glassware; upscale, southern brasserie food; raw oysters with pitch-perfect notes (Island Creek from Duxbury Bay, Massachusetts, "kings of the cape, kapow!"). They partner with Love is Love at Gaia Gardens, who manage the adjacent restaurant garden. The kitchen and bar staff harvest items for dishes, and time in the garden before service adds a touch of balance.

Heralded as the best oyster bar in the Atlanta area, they partner with Oyster South. Their support contributes to the development of southern oyster aquaculture, encouraging oyster farms to help improve water quality and add biodiversity.

The Georgia Department of Natural Resources will collect the restaurant's spent oyster shells - about one million - to be placed along the Georgia coast for an artificial reef-building project. "Hopefully our shell pile will be someday be the habitat of many wild oysters and other sea life", says co-owner Bryan Rackley.

The Farmer & The Larder

Glynn

What
Mixed-use culinary event space

Who
Matthew Raiford & Jovan Sage, owners

When
Lunch Wednesday to Sunday

Address
1523 Newcastle Street, Brunswick, Glynn, GA 31520

+1 912 342 7700

farmerandlarder.com

Bookings
Walk-ins, website

Price guide

What they say
"Good food and community go hand in hand. So we are extremely passionate about growing our food, and connecting locally with food purveyors who are doing the same."

Signature dishes
Stoneground grits with smoked collards, mustard, turnip, kale greens, caramelized onions, and cremini mushrooms; porterhouse pork wrapped in bacon with garlic confit fingerling potatoes; cast-iron cobbler with seasonal fruit jams and sweet cream biscuit crust.

What we say
Raiford and Sage keep this farm-restaurant-events space constantly humming. Located on the coast of Georgia and just twenty-nine miles from the Florida state line, they're the recipients of an often nine-month-plus growing season. Employees work one weekly shift on the farm. They're near zero percent food waste by using all food scraps for compost and chicken maintenance, and getting creative with byproducts. During apple season, they make apple butter, and use the peels for apple vinegar.

Raiford has known his fishmonger, Frank Owens at City Market, his whole life. His nana bought fish and Georgia wild-caught shrimp from Owens' grandfather. Raiford relies on Jon Jackson at Comfort Farms in Milledgeville, Georgia, for ethically raised pork and rabbit, and Chad Hunter of Hunter Farms in Bluffton, Georgia, for grass-fed beef. The couple also offers cooking classes where participants learn to ferment kombucha and begin to compost.

311

Kentucky

610 Magnolia

Louisville

What
A modern approach to the Southern table by Chef Edward Lee

Who
Edward Lee, chef

When
Dinner Wednesday to Saturday

Address
610 West Magnolia Avenue, Louisville, KY 40208

+1 502 636 0783

610Magnolia.com

Bookings
Email 610@610Magnolia.com, phone

Price guide

What they say
"We take a modern approach to the cuisine of the South that is inclusive of all the influences and cultures that surround us in Louisville. We believe in the food we cook and the commitment we have made to try and better our community and staff everyday."

Signature dishes
Beef pastrami and pickled tongue with kimchi remoulade and pickled mustard seeds; poached rockfish with barley dashi broth and low country spelt with pickled ginger; and KY fried quail with sorghum glaze, kale grits, and lemon butter.

What we say
Chef Edward Lee is constantly evolving what Southern food can be at his tasting menu restaurant 610 Magnolia in Louisville. A Korean-American chef, born and raised in New York City, Lee infuses his cooking with his heritage in dishes like beef pastrami and pickled tongue with kimchi remoulade, while his adopted home in the South inspires recipes like KY fried quail with sorghum glaze and kale grits.

His menu is served as four-or six-course options and is built around ingredients sourced from local farms like Foxhollow, which raises cattle in open air in Kentucky. Meanwhile, summer produce may be sourced as locally as the restaurant's garden and year-round, the entire team helps tend to an 800-square foot on-site greenhouse.

The team is also invested in training the next generation. Through The LEE Initiative, they provide mentorship for female chefs in Kentucky.

610

Garage Bar

Louisville

What
Wood-fired pizzas & Southern specialties in a former auto-service garage

Who
Richard Sible, executive chef

When
Dinner, daily, lunch, Friday, weekend brunch

Address
700 East Market Street, Louisville, KY 40202

+1 502 749 7100

garageonmarket.com

Bookings
OpenTable.com, phone, walk-ins

Price guide

What they say
"We're most passionate about using local, responsibly sourced ingredients to create quality food to serve to our community. We also try to serve our community in other ways by incorporating civic engagement and charitable giving. We run a program called +Love, which highlights a local non profit every month on our menu to spread awareness and raise donations from guests - which we match dollar-for-dollar."

What others say
"Garage Bar's brick oven pizzas are on a rapid ascent to legendary status."

-Nancy Miller, *Courier Journal*

Signature dishes
Pepperoni pizza with house-made pepperoni, and local bison and pork; country ham and cheese boards with local bread, honey and carrot marmalade and red-eye aïoli; cheeseburger with pasture-raised beef and local tomatoes and pickles.

What we say
On a nice day in Louisville, the team at this converted auto service garage raises up the large side door, allowing sun to flood into the restaurant. Grab a seat inside or outdoors at one of the many picnic tables. No matter where you sit, the brick oven pizza is in order here with topping options like house-made pepperoni with meat raised in the nearby town of Goshen, sweet corn and *fior di latte*, or Kentucky-grown mushrooms that are paired with potatoes. A local cheese plate is a good start, but for carnivores, the ham-tasting is a must. Either way, a visit to Garage Bar comes highly recommended.

Lilly's Bistro

Louisville

What
A café reflective of the seasons & the farmers it supports

Who
Kathy Cary, owner/executive chef

When
Lunch & dinner, Tuesday to Saturday

Address
1147 Bardstown Road, Louisville, KY 40204

+1 502 451 0447

lillysbistro.com

Bookings
Website, OpenTable.com, walk-ins

Price guide

What they say
"Since growing up on a farm, my philosophy has always been to support local. To this day, I am proud to still have a garden at the farm where I grew up. I have watched our farmers multiply in our region over the past twenty-five years."

What others say
"If you ever see a list of Louisville's best restaurants that doesn't include Lilly's Bistro, please do us a favor and disregard it ... Kathy Cary should be known throughout the land. She opened her beloved Lilly's Bistro in 1988, sourcing all of her produce from local farmers and purveyors (whatever they couldn't provide, she grew herself) ... Cary has been nominated for the James Beard Foundation's Best Chef Southeast multiple times."

-Keith Pandolfi, *Saveur*

Signature dishes
Prawns and grits; lamb meatballs; chargrilled Spanish octopus.

What we say
Louisville doesn't sound like a seafood destination, but the presence of a UPS shipping hub means Lilly's Bistro has access to the freshest sustainable seafood. The restaurant also sources fair trade chocolate, coffee, and olive oil, but is best known for the proteins and produce it purchases from local farmers. Executive Chef Kathy Cary is passionate about "seasonal ingredients that inspire me and my chefs to create exceptional new menu items".

Mayan Cafe

Louisville

What
A casual, authentic Mayan restaurant that primarily uses farm-to-table sourcing

Who
Bruce Ucán & Anne Shadle, owners

When
Lunch Monday to Friday, dinner Monday to Saturday

Address
813 East Market Street, Louisville, KY 40206

+1 502 566 0651

themayancafe.com

Bookings
Phone, website, Yelpreservations.com

Price guide

What they say
"We support our employees by providing predictable and consistent work schedules, and we encourage local food entrepreneurs by functioning as an ideal testing ground for emerging sustainable or local products. We are a small restaurant, so meeting our demand is manageable for many small or new operations, such as local coffee, biodegradable takeout containers, and Kentucky silver carp. Our most recent connection has been to a new company that imports heirloom corn from Oaxaca, Mexico."

Signature dishes
Tok-sel lima beans roasted with ground pumpkin seeds; *salbutes*: a Yucatán-style taco; *huevos motuleños*: fried tortilla with chorizo, fried plantains, and *queso fresco*.

What others say
"Long before eating local was a hashtag, Chef Bruce Ucán was simply cooking food in the way he knew best - calling on his Mayan heritage as a platform for displaying the bounty of the land that surrounded him."

-Dana McMahan, *Courier Journal*

What we say
The beloved Mayan Cafe is especially attentive to dietary restrictions and health concerns, creating sauces without garlic and onions and swapping out whipping cream for coconut milk to make its menu more accessible. Whatever your dietary restrictions, there's bound to be something for you at this eclectic restaurant.

MozzaPi

Louisville

What
Millers, bakers & pizza makers; locally sourced & delicious

Who
Tom Edwards, chef

When
Breakfast & lunch, Tuesday to Friday, weekend brunch

Address
12102 La Grange Road, Louisville, KY 40223

+1 502 890 4832

mozzapi.com

Bookings
Phone

Price guide

What they say
"The mission of MozzaPi is to create food and experiences that bring joy to people's days. We seek to create an environment of respect, appreciation, abundance, and gratitude. This means constantly ensuring that our pizzas, baked items, stone-milled flour, and educational experiences are always memorable and unique. We chose Italian grain dishes as our foundation because we believe they make beautiful platforms for sustainability. We use freshly-milled Kentucky wheat and durham for our pizza and pasta. Pasta provides a platform for our farm-to-table ingredients. Kentucky beef and pork raised by responsible caretakers makes for delicious spaghetti and meatballs."

Signature dishes
Scones; pizza; pasta.

What others say
"Edwards' passion is apparent in both the space he has crafted and the pizza he has spent years perfecting."

-Lindsey McClave, *Louisville Courier Journal*

What we say
Step into MozzaPi and feel like you're going back in time to a gothic mill in a sleepy river town. MozzaPi was built from the ground up by owner Tom Edwards and his family, but feels timeless. Tom is somewhat of a renaissance man and not only built this spectacular structure, but also acts as chef, miller, baker, and pizza maker. Oh yeah, and he roasts his own coffee, too. Tom and his team focus on excellence in sourcing. They are a sustainable gathering place by design. We love that they offer their parking lot every Saturday in the summer to host Louisville's only organic farmers' market.

Proof on Main

Louisville

What
Modern American restaurant located in the artistic 21c Museum Hotel

Who
Mike Wajda, executive chef

When
Breakfast, lunch & dinner, daily

Address
702 West Main Street, Louisville, KY 40202

+1 502 217 6360

proofonmain.com

Bookings
Phone, OpenTable.com, walk-ins

Price guide

What they say
"We take the same approach to food as we do to the art on our walls, with brushstrokes of contemporary flair against a backdrop of southern cuisine. 21c owners Laura Lee Brown and Steve Wilson have their own 1,000-acre farm east of downtown, and they collaborate with Chef Mike Wajda. Preserving the farmland of Kentucky and bringing heritage foods back to the table are among our greatest passions."

Signature dishes
Spring onion soup with ramps and Calabrian chili; roasted beets, with labneh, sorghum vinaigrette, juniper za'atar spice; whole roasted duck, with Barr Farms carrot, Louismill grains, and Urfa spice.

What others say
"Dining at Proof on Main can feel like an out-of-body experience. Situated on Museum Row inside the boutique 21c Museum Hotel, the restaurant's art-dappled space is as exciting and fresh as the creative Southern food being served."

-Lauren Matison, *Travel + Leisure*

What we say
Proof on Main is engaged in numerous programs helping to change the food industry and promote sustainability. They recently joined the #stopsucking movement to eliminate plastic straws and help clean up the oceans. Their menus change often with farmers and foragers of the Ohio River valley delivering produce to ensure they get the freshest possible ingredients year-round. Veering from their farm-to-table peers, they serve a mix of ingredients; a fusion of sorts. This artistry is an adornment to serious southern cuisine that celebrates locally grown and milled grits, southern sorghum, and cast-iron cornbread.

Red Hog Artisan Butcher

Louisville

What
A whole animal butcher shop & adjoining restaurant supporting local farmers

Who
Robert Hancock & Katherine Garrett, owners

When
Lunch & dinner, Tuesday to Saturday

Address
2622 Frankfort Avenue, Louisville, KY 40206

+1 502 384 0795

redhogartisanmeat.com

Bookings
Walk-ins

Price guide

What they say
"The day at Red Hog Artisan Butcher starts long before the shop opens. Chef and co-owner Bob Hancock starts every day by focusing his attention on his heritage hogs, custom-mixing their feed and delivering it to the farm in Oldham county where his mulefoot, red wattles, and crossbred animals reside. Supporting the local farming community that we are proud to be a part of ourselves is of the highest importance to Red Hog."

Signature dishes
Kentucky ham: charcuterie featuring Spanish-style cured ham served and pimiento cheese; dry-aged and cold-smoked beef burger; fresh pork chop.

What we say
Sustainability is one of the reasons Robert Hancock and Katherine Garrett - affectionally known as "Bob" and "Kit" - created Red Hog. They are passionate about butchering whole animals, as the process allows for minimal waste. Caring for both the animal and the land is a huge part of their farming and butchering philosophy. They are drastically reducing their carbon footprint by traveling small distances to source their animals. The triad of operating as a butcher shop, restaurant, and farm also promotes sustainability in all cycles of the food chain. The non-animal waste from the restaurant goes right back to the farm to feed the pigs. Full circle.

Doodles Breakfast & Lunch

Fayette

What
Decade-old daytime restaurant housed in a converted gas station

Who
Melissa Jackson, owner

When
Breakfast & lunch, Tuesday to Saturday

Address
262 North Limestone Street, Lexington, Fayette, KY 40507

+1 859 537 8935

doodleslex.com

Bookings
Website

Price guide

What they say
"Locally sourcing as many of our ingredients as possible is what drives us. We source our about 450 pounds of bacon a month from Garey Farms in Paris, Kentucky. We buy all of our eggs - about 800 a month - from Clark Family Farms here in Lexington, and our vegetables are grown about one-and-a-half miles north of us at North Farm. Our house coffee is roasted specifically for us by Lexington's oldest roaster, Lexington Coffee and Tea."

Signature dishes
Biscuits and gravy; hot brown strata; Johnny cakes.

What we say
The official motto of Doodles is "comfort food with a conscience", which speaks both to the restaurant's dedication to buying from community members - a lengthy list of local purveyors anchors its website - and also to welcoming them in as guests. Doodles demonstrates its neighborliness by offering a range of items appropriate for people with various dietary restrictions, and by energetically supporting youth sports teams and organizations in the area.

Commonwealth Bistro

Kenton

What
Locally sourced & inspired by our region's past, served with Kentucky hospitality

Who
Chris Burns, chef/co-owner; Tess Burns, co-owner

When
Dinner Tuesday to Sunday

Address
621 Main Street, Covington, Kenton, KY 41011

+1 859 916 6719

commonwealthbistro.com

Bookings
Website

Price guide

What they say
"Our vision for our business is that it grows to be sustainable and successful, that it can add value to the community fabric, and allow us to invest in our employees. That the model we are building can not only grow business, but can also help other restauranteurs build success. And that we can best serve our guests and tell the story of Kentucky and local food producers."

Signature dishes
Kentucky-fried rabbit with buttermilk biscuit, creamed collard greens, and Biz Baz sauce; sugar-cubed Kentucky beef carpaccio with green tomato *mostarda*, vinegar cream, and nasturtium; salted honey pie with Carriage House Farms honey and cornmeal crust.

What we say
Chef and co-owner Chris Burns celebrates the cuisine of Ohio and Kentucky on his menu at Commonwealth. He transforms classic dishes like fried rabbit, barbecued mutton and burgoo through skilled cooking and commitment to using quality local ingredients. That dedication to craftsmanship is just one of the seven core values that he and his co-owner, Tess Burns, developed with their staff to fulfill Commonwealth's mission to embrace the restaurant's community. This husband and wife team support their staff with a wellness program and continuing education opportunities. They define community beyond geography, and are mindful of how they and their staff engage their diverse community of guests, teammates, farmers, and fellow entrepreneurs.

The Farmstand Market & Cafe

Union

What
A farm-to-table restaurant, bar & market

Who
Tricia Houston, chef/owner

When
Lunch & dinner, Tuesday to Saturday

Address
9914 Old Union Road, Union, KY 41091

+1 859 817 1134

thefarmstandmarket.com

Bookings
Facebook

Price guide

What they say
"We source locally to every extent we can, from raised beds out front to farmers bringing it right to me."

Signature dishes
Deviled eggs; grilled vegetable wrap; lard crust pies baked by local pastry outfit Pie Bird Pies.

What others say
"The Farmstand Market & Cafe's striking barn-red color hints at its all-in commitment to locally grown, farm-fresh food ... Look for cafe items like spring pea falafel and buttered radishes to showcase the season's harvest."

-Grace S. Yek, *WCPO*

What we say
Tricia Houston's approach to sustainability stresses the embrace of misshapen vegetables that less environmentally minded kitchens might shun. "I take less than perfect", she says. Her philosophy also extends to customer feedback: "Just troll our Facebook page: all the comments are there - good, and bad". An accepting attitude is paramount in Houston's region of Kentucky, where seafood is only sold frozen and farmers aren't accustomed to dealing with small restaurants. So Houston has made changes where she can, buying only eco-friendly packaging, serving only sodas made with cane syrup and ordering the best ingredients she can get from food service companies. "Sysco and US Foods offer organic, free-range choices", she says. "Who knew?"

321

Louisiana

Cochon

New Orleans

What
Southern Cajun food inspired by Louisiana

Who
Donald Link & Stephen Stryjewski, chefs/co-owners

When
Lunch & dinner, daily

Address
930 Tchoupitoulas St., New Orleans, LA 70130

+1 504 588 2123

cochonrestaurant.com

Bookings
Phone, website

Price guide

What they say
"We deliver consistently great food and service and honor the techniques our co-owner Donald Link learnt from around the world, while using the base of his food knowledge from growing up in Louisiana. We have a local system of at least forty farms and producers that we have grown over the years, and we are always looking for and using sustainable products and practices."

Signature dishes
Gumbo; oven-roasted redfish "fisherman style"; rabbit and dumplings.

What others say
"Just about any food lover who has spent any time in New Orleans over the last two years has been to this irresistible restaurant, and has responded with the kind of swoon typically reserved for the front rows at an Obama rally."

-Frank Bruni, *The New York Times*

What we say
In their boisterous, no-linen warehouse space, chefs and co-owners Donald Link and Stephen Stryjewski honor Louisianna's Cajun roots, focusing on traditional, authentic flavors with a pork-forward sensibility through a vast network of local suppliers, cultivated by an in-house farmer liaison. They buy whole animals and have seeded new farms, developing custom-growing cycles to ensure success for the farmers' and supply for their restaurants.

Cochon thrives on a philosophy of equality and fairness - all members of the staff receive health insurance. And outside of the kitchen, they established the Link Stryjewski Foundation in 2015 to address youth issues in New Orleans, including mentorship programs, job training, head start and music initiatives.

Compere Lapin

New Orleans

What
Robust dishes that meld flavors of the Caribbean with Italian technique & Louisiana ingredients

Who
Nina Compton, chef/owner

When
Lunch & dinner, daily, weekend brunch

Address
The Old No. 77 Hotel & Chandlery, 535 Tchoupitoulas, New Orleans, LA 70130

+1 504 599 2119

comperelapin.com

Bookings
Phone, website, OpenTable.com

Price guide

What they say
"It's important to support local growers and it gives us the opportunity to have incredible produce at times of the year that aren't available elsewhere. Our menu highlights these amazing products, along with Chef Nina Compton's Caribbean roots and the Italian techniques she was trained with."

Signature dishes
Curried goat with sweet potato gnocchi; conch croquettes with pickled pineapple tartar sauce; dirty rice arancini with sour orange *mojo*.

What others say
"[Nina] has been crushing it with this sexy combination of bayou and Caribbean, all with the flair that only she can provide."

-Nilou Motamed, *Food & Wine* magazine

What we say
Discovering New Orleans cuisine through the eyes of this Caribbean daughter, now a James Beard Award "Best Chef" winner, feels like unpacking a treasure chest. Chef Nina Compton pulls together surprising and delightful flavor combinations, and intertwines various regional cuisines - like collard greens with creole spices - all with cohesive effect. "I love seeing customers' reactions when they try my food and can see the inspiration behind every dish", she says. "It's a great feeling and we've developed such a loyal following". The dining room is art-filled and energetic, making the experience as playful as the chef herself.

MOPHO

New Orleans

What
A true neighborhood restaurant mixing Southeast Asia & Southeast Louisiana

Who
Michael Gulotta, chef/partner

When
Lunch & dinner, daily

Address
514 City Park Avenue, Suite F, New Orleans, LA 70119

+1 504 482 6845

mophonola.com

Bookings
Phone, website
OpenTable.com

Price guide

What they say
"We are passionate about being a neighborhood restaurant that continues to innovate and, in doing so, we keep our regular customers engaged and excited. We have signature dishes that have been on the menu forever, that our locals love and depend on, but even those change slightly through the seasons to reflect what our farmer friends are growing. This extends to our cocktail and drink menus as well."

Signature dishes
Coconut and corn *laksa* with bacon and blue crab; pepper jelly braised Florida clams with annatto beignets; MOPHO *som tam.*

What others say
"[Gulotta is] turning out awesome, Delta-inspired Vietnamese food - like pho with oxtail and mustard greens - in a casual strip-mall restaurant that explores the seafood traditions around both Southeast Asia and the American South."

Food & Wine magazine

What we say
Come for the Saturday night pig roasts, where Gulotta prepares local hogs on the patio served with pickles and roti, and you'll immediately find your way back for the funky flavors of Southeast Asia made with South Louisiana seafood, meats, and produce, some grown on spare lots in the Lower Ninth Ward. Thursdays are "the night of the vegetables", while Tuesdays they're raising funds for a local cause.

As founding members of the #FairKitchens movement, MOPHO is working to lower levels of burn out, drug and alcohol abuse, and harassment in kitchens. And, partner Jeffrey Gulotta is a mentor for Liberty's Kitchen, teaching at-risk youth restaurant and life skills.

Mosquito Supper Club

New Orleans

What
A Cajun restaurant that seeks to redefine what it means to feed people

Who
Melissa M. Martin, chef/owner

When
Dinner Thursday to Saturday

Address
3824 Draydes Street, New Orleans, LA 70115

+1 504 517 0374

mosquitosupperclub.com

Bookings
Exploretock.com

Price guide

What they say
"We choose a tasting format for our restaurant. One seating, served family style. Strangers have to talk to each other. We are not open every day of the week so the restaurant has time to breathe. We try to buy locally first and always natural. I am passionate about running a small business based around sustainability, that is not wasteful, that brings together the best a community has to offer."

Signature dishes
Shrimp okra gumbo; shrimp *boulettes*; blackberry dumplings and ice cream.

What others say
"When the New Orleans chef Melissa Martin began craving a slower pace and deeper connections - to her coastal Louisiana roots, food, and the people she cooks for - she started Mosquito Supper Club, a wildly popular weekly ticketed dining experience."

-Logan Ward, *Garden & Gun*

What we say
With just three seatings each week, Mosquito Supper Club is an intimate, community building, dining experience. Chef and owner Melissa Martin uses her menu to celebrate the fishing industry, as well as the incredible products to be found in South Louisiana. The focus is on a healthy menu that leaves guests feeling full but great. There is no meat served, only seafood, with crab coming from families like The Higgins in Lafitte, Louisiana, who run a successful and impossibly tiny operation despite hurricanes, floods, regulations, and more. "Food has to tell a story for me. I believe in seeing history and a community in every plate", Martin says.

Gabrielle Restaurant

New Orleans

What
Small family owned & operated restaurant offering modern Louisiana cuisine & cocktails

Who
Greg Sonnier, chef/co-owner & Mary Sonnier, co-owner

When
Dinner, Tuesday to Saturday

Address
2441 Orleans Avenue, New Orleans, LA 70119

+1 504 623 2344

Facebook.com

Bookings
Phone

Price guide

What they say
"We originally opened in March 1992, but were shuttered by Hurricane Katrina in August 2005. We reopened in September 2017 after being closed for twelve years. We are most passionate about providing a cultural dining experience for our customers. We cook from scratch using techniques that we learned from the master of Louisiana cookery, Chef Paul Prudhomme. We use every part of the animal by making our own sausages and pâtés, and we source local fish and seafood on a daily basis."

Signature dishes
Smoked quail gumbo; slow roasted duck with orange sherry sauce; apple upside-down bread pudding with vanilla bean sauce.

What others say
"Greg Sonnier's cooking is something else. It sits at the intersection of Cajun and Creole ... It's a style few local chefs still embrace."

-Brett Anderson, *The Times-Picayune*

What we say
Despite a twelve-year hiatus, the current Gabrielle Restaurant is a familiar and comforting space where Chef Greg Sonnier is cooking food in a way that preserves the culture of Louisiana. By sourcing local produce and maintaining long-lasting relationships with fishermen and farmers, the Sonniers have rooted themselves deeply into their local community. Whether feeding their regulars, or providing food for charity fundraisers, the Sonniers always aim to do right by their neighbors. "[Our return] has been humbling and we are so happy that our customers have welcomed us back", Mary Sonnier says.

Pêche

New Orleans

What
Seafood restaurant based on simple wood-fired techniques

Who
Donald Link, Stephen Stryjewski & Ryan Prewitt, chefs

When
Breakfast, lunch & dinner, daily

Address
800 Magazine Street, New Orleans, LA 70130

+1 504 522 1744

pecherestaurant.com

Bookings
Phone, walk-ins, Reserve.com

Price guide

What they say
"Pêche is part of a large local restaurant group that can provide farms with enough business to sustain good farming practices and a good income. We're passionate about using sustainable fresh seafood while supporting our local fisheries with an understanding of how it affects the environment."

Signature dishes
Whole grilled fish with salsa verde; local oysters on the half shell; daily selections of crudos.

What others say
"Pêche is the realization of a modest but still visionary vision: a traditional Louisiana seafood restaurant that owes little to any particular style of restaurant that has come before. Its chef and co-owner, Ryan Prewitt, is not prone to wild experiments. Whatever thought process goes into Peche's food is concealed beneath a veneer of simplicity."

-Brett Anderson, *Times Picayune*

What we say
The heady scent of live-fire that fills this airy space alights from the main cooking source - a wood-fired oven overseen by chef/partner Ryan Prewitt and his team, who practice techniques inspired by those found in South America, Spain, and the Gulf Coast. Dishes are brought to life with the help of local producers who Prewitt knows on a first-name basis. The chef is also involved with the Gulf Coast Seafood Alliance, which advocates for the sustainability of seafood in the region. All of this equates to a remarkable dining experience, and proves Pêche's community-minded mission.

Seaworthy

New Orleans

What
An oyster bar set in an old creole cottage in New Orleans

Who
Daniel Causgrove, executive chef

When
Dinner, daily, weekend brunch

Address
630 Carondelet Street, New Orleans, LA 70130

+1 504 930 3070

seaworthynola.com

Bookings
Website, OpenTable.com

Price guide

What they say
"We are proud of the local oysters that we offer and passionate about the development of off-bottom culturing methods along the Gulf coast. There are so many upsides, including better flavor and size of the oyster, the health of our aquatic ecosystem, and healthier margins for our farmers. We source oysters from Grand Isle, Louisiana and the area surrounding Bayou la Batre, Alabama, having developed relationships with the farmers themselves."

Signature dishes
Amberjack rillette with ancho chili oil and toasted baguette; BBQ cobia collar with *gochujang* compressed squash, fried onion, and Kewpie mayo; UGA Siberian sturgeon caviar.

What others say
"This seafood hub at the Ace Hotel specializes in raw oyster, caviar, lobster rolls and sustainable Gulf bounty, along with low proof (and boozier) drinks."

-Gwendolyn Knapp and Nora McGunnigle, *Eater New Orleans*

What we say
This oyster-focused seafood room elevates the humble bivalve, as well as underutilized cuts and appropriately managed species. Executive Chef Daniel Causgrove coaxes big flavors from bycatch and sustainably harvested products - and it's best to experience that during the family style "Crew Mess" meal on Tuesdays. Behind the scenes, they recycle oyster shells; buy from local produce farms; offer multiple vegan and vegetarian options, and occasionally practise yoga as a team.

Toups' Meatery

New Orleans

What
New Orleans restaurant featuring updated, sophisticated takes on Cajun rustic cookery

Who
Isaac Toups, chef/owner & Amanda Toups, co-owner

When
Lunch & dinner, Tuesday to Saturday

Address
845 North Carrollton Avenue, New Orleans, LA 70119

+1 504 252 4999

toupsmeatery.com

Bookings
Phone, website, OpenTable.com

Price guide

What they say
"This restaurant really is a glimpse into my 'id'. It's all about the family roots I have in Louisiana, the rustic cooking I grew up with, and the modern approach I like to add to each of my dishes. If tradition and innovation had a baby, this would be it. It's Cajun at its essence, but I love adding my own unique and sophisticated twist to it. I truly love sharing a piece of my family history with each and every diner and nothing is better to me than seeing full bellies and smiling faces walk out after a meal."

Signature dishes
Authentic cracklins; confit chicken thighs with chicken liver and cornbread dressing; double-cut pork chop with Cajun dirty rice and cane syrup *gastrique*; gulf seafood *couvillon*.

What others say
"Work in the right fine dining kitchens and you learn the precision and restraint to amplify the qualities great products have to offer. Grow up in the right Cajun household, and you learn the rough-and-tumble aspects of rustic cooking, with its alchemic need to wring maximum reward from lower-born staples. Combine those two realms and you end up with Toups' Meatery."

-Ian McNulty, *Gambit*

What we say
Inside the airy, utilitarian Toups' Meatery, you'll find an appreciation for the simplicity of Cajun fare (cracklins and beer), a commitment to local sourcing, and a love for all things meat, from the sausage and offal-packed meatery board to the hulking dry-aged ribeyes.

Willa Jean

New Orleans

What
Southern inspired bakery & restaurant

Who
Kelly Fields, chef/owner

When
Breakfast, lunch & dinner, daily

Address
611 O'Keefe Avenue,
New Orleans, LA 70113

+1 504 509 7334

willajean.com

Bookings
Walk-ins, phone, OpenTable.com

Price guide

What they say
"The mission of Willa Jean is to secure the future. We work daily to ensure the future of our brand, our business, each of our employees, our guests, our farmers, and our community. We strive to all continue to grow.

"Our biggest effort and focus in sustainability is with our employees. [We] ensure a sustainable longevity for their chosen careers through a healthy work-life balance, mentorship, support, and even physical, mental, and emotional health. We have also created a foundation, 'Yes Ma'am', to create community, leadership, and mentorship opportunities for women in the restaurant and hospitality industry."

Signature dishes
BBQ shrimp toast with grilled sourdough, *burrata*, gulf shrimp, and nola-style BBQ sauce; crawfish and grits with crawfish tails, *etouffee* gravy, grits, and poached egg; roasted beets with local greens, pistachio, citrus, and local goat cheese dressing.

What we say
Intelligentsia Coffee with a splash of local dairy. Fresh biscuits with jam or sausage gravy. A hanger steak with a fried egg for dinner. Willa Jean, a brick-walled all-day bakery and café, serves all of this, along with a side of community involvement, in New Orleans. Sourcing locally, and from small-scale producers, Fields' menu showcases produce and seafood from the region, such as collards, shrimp, crawfish, strawberries, and even beer - an effort to support local businesses. And they work with employees to promote professional and personal growth through mentorship and leadership training.

329

Maryland

Preserve

Anne Arundel

What
A casual spot with a focus on pickling & fermentation

Who
Michelle Hoffman, co-owner

When
Lunch & dinner, Tuesday to Sunday, weekend brunch

Address
164 Main Street, Annapolis, Anne Arundel, MD 21401

+1 443 598 6920

preserve-eats.com

Bookings
Website, Exploretock.com

Price guide

What they say
"We work hard to create a family atmosphere at the restaurant and this is shown in many ways. We pick up a percentage of health insurance for our staff, everyone gets one week of paid vacation, and we have a three percent labor-of-love charge added to each check to help support a good wage for our staff."

Signature dishes
Coffee-glazed beef with hasselback potatoes and ham-hock relish; griddled mushroom cake with baby carrots, oyster mushrooms, pickled ramps, and preserved lemon vinaigrette; pulled-to-order mozzarella over house-made sourdough bread.

What we say
There's always blue catfish on the menu at Preserve, a certified-green eatery in Annapolis, Maryland. It's a clean-tasting fish, not muddy at all, and takes to all manner of preparation. But that's not why Preserve serves it. It's a species invasive to Chesapeake Bay, and eating it promotes balance in the local environment. As for the rest of the menu, it is shaped by bounty from local farmers and co-ops, not to mention the sous chef's foraging trips. But everything that exits the kitchen is unified by a common theme: On each plate, diners will find something pickled, preserved, or fermented - the unctuous pork braised in house-made sauerkraut is a prime example.

What others say
"Many plates are meant to be shared - pimiento cheese, chicken skins with pickle dip - a lovely approach until you fight for the last bite."

-Ann Limpert, Anna Spiegel, Jessica Sidman, and Cynthia Hacinli, *Washingtonian* magazine

Atwater's

Baltimore

What
Neighborhood sandwich shop using seasonal, local ingredients

Who
Ned Atwater, owner

When
Breakfast & lunch, daily, dinner Monday to Saturday

Address
529 East Belvedere Avenue #1, Baltimore, MD 21212, plus other locations - see website

+1 410 323 2396

atwaters.biz

Bookings
Walk-ins

Price guide

What they say
"We change the world with wonderful handcrafted food for Baltimore and beyond. We are passionate about providing our community with a healthy option, while supporting local farmers and craftsmen."

Signature dishes
Chilled gazpacho with corn, black beans, and avocado; free-range chicken salad sandwich with golden raisins, Granny Smith apples, cranberry, basil mayonnaise, and lettuce on seven grain and flax bread.

What we say
Atwater's has been a low-key soup-and-sandwich mainstay in Baltimore for years, and now spans six locations across the area. Its success proves that high-quality seasonal produce - much of it from the company's own kitchen farm - can make for a lasting business model. The same can be said for Atwater's dedication to paying its staff a fair wage. In 2018, owner Ned Atwater publicly pressed state lawmakers to raise the minimum wage to $15 by 2023. "Our staff are on the front lines of our survival and steady growth over the years in a tough industry", he told *The Baltimore Sun*. "When you pay employees a decent wage, they stick with you and grow with you. Lower turnover saves money and time in hiring and training costs. More experienced staff are also more efficient and productive, and they provide the best customer service".

Maggie's Farm

Baltimore

What
New American neighborhood spot supporting local farms

Who
Dana Inches & Abdul Saeed, co-owners

When
Dinner Wednesday to Saturday, weekend brunch

Address
4341 Harford Road, Baltimore, MD 21214

+1 410 254 2376

maggiesfarmmd.com

Bookings
Phone, walk-ins

Price guide

What they say
"It is very important to support local family farms and companies in Baltimore, and we do our best to do so. One of the ways we do this is by sourcing our seafood from a local supplier."

Signature dishes
Falafel platter with homemade Syrian-style hummus, *baba ganoush*, and *fattoush*; fried Brussels sprouts with dried cranberries, pistachios, and red wine *gastrique*; mussels with apple cider, tart apples, shallots, white wine, bacon, and heavy cream.

What others say
"After you've had a meal at Maggie's Farm, summer trips to Maryland won't just be for blue crab anymore."

-Lauren Matison, *Travel + Leisure*

What we say
In this cozy, red-hued dining room in northeast Baltimore's leafy Lauraville neighborhood, farm-to-table dining is down to earth and accessible. Co-owner Abdul Saeed, who took over the space last year and also helms the kitchen, has infused the menu with dishes from his Syrian heritage, including a tempting falafel platter piled high with crisp *fattoush* salad. Much of the grass-fed meat and fresh produce come from local farms, and ninety percent of the beers on offer - including suds from local outfits The Brewer's Art and Terrapin Beer Co. - are brewed in Charm City.

Woodberry Kitchen

Baltimore

What
Spike Gjerde's trailblazing restaurant committed to sourcing entirely from the Mid-Atlantic

Who
Spike Gjerde, chef/owner

When
Dinner, daily, weekend brunch

Address
2010 Clipper Park Road, Baltimore, MD 21211

+1 410 464 8000

woodberrykitchen.com

Bookings
OpenTable.com

Price guide

What they say
"Our goal is to create meaningful and measurable change within our local food system - to wholly support thoughtful food production in the Mid-Atlantic and to help ensure a future for its farmers and watermen."

Signature dishes
Butcher's flatbread with *lomo*, fish pepper sausage, *krakowska*, browned onion, and herb salad; raw scallops with ramps, nasturtium, mint, puffed rice, bronze fennel, sorrel, and cucumber; crab and rigatoni with ramp-peanut pesto, asparagus, bacon, and nasturtium pesto.

What others say
"Spike Gjerde is to Baltimore what Alice Waters is to California: a purist who pledges allegiance to a region and can't seem to serve an inferior dish. Smoked fluke dip served with spelt crackers, a chopped salad rethought with scrapple croutons, egg noodles draped with slow-cooked lamb and pretty-as-a-peach peach pie all taste like blue-ribbon winners."

-Tom Sietsema, *The Washington Post*

What we say
When Woodberry Kitchen opened more than a decade ago, its pernickety attention to detail and obsessive adherence to local and sustainable ingredients helped put Baltimore's culinary scene in the national spotlight. It's still doing just that, drawing diners in droves to its rustic mill building every night, with the wood-fired oven built from old Baltimore street bricks. All of the breads are baked on-site with locally grown and milled grains. But such virtue must be underwritten by truly exceptional cuisine, and Woodberry indeed delivers. From the crab cakes to the rhubarb tart, there's little not to love here.

Addie's

Montogomery

What
Seasonal-driven American restaurant & raw bar

Who
Jeff Black, chef/owner

When
Lunch Monday to Saturday, dinner, daily, brunch Sunday

Address
12435 Park Potomac Avenue, Potomac, Montogomer, MD 20854

+1 301 340 0081

addiesrestaurant.com

Bookings
OpenTable.com

Price guide

What they say
"When sourcing ingredients, we look locally. This approach started at the original Addie's in the late 1990s, when our owners Jeff and Barbara Black first opened the modest eatery in a small cottage on Rockville Pike. Early on, Brett Grohsgal of Even Star Organic Farms knocked on the back door with trays of fresh heirloom tomatoes bursting with flavor in hand. We were hooked, and from then on sought to source from the best local purveyors."

Signature dishes
"The seafood tower": rotating menu of small plates like Maryland blue crab salad dabbed with basil pesto and grilled local oysters swathed in garlic chili butter; grilled pork chop with English pea emulsion, herbed spaetzle, baby turnips, and orange and fennel gastrique.

What others say
"Warning: The biscuits that start a meal can ruin your appetite if you're not careful. The bread also underscores a truth: lard and butter make life better".

The Washington Post

What we say
At Addie's, nestled in an airy, window-filled space in the Park Potomac complex, seafood is the main attraction. Design-your-own tiered towers come in three sizes, each packed with offerings ranging from fried oysters and grilled octopus to lemon-spiked ricotta tortellini.

Sustainable seafood, hand-picked by the Black Restaurant Group's fishmongers, shines in dishes like pan-seared rockfish glazed with sweet-sour tamarind and mussels bathed in coconut milk, lemongrass, and basil. But carnivores will be pleased, too, with a meaty Allen Brothers ribeye for two.

333

Mississippi

Saint Leo

Oxford

What
Wood-fired Italian cooking in Oxford, Mississippi

Who
Emily Blount, owner

When
Lunch & dinner, Wednesday to Monday

Address
1101 East Jackson Ave, Oxford, MS 38655

+1 662 380 5141

eatsaintleo.com

Bookings
Email events@eatsaintleo.com

Price guide

What they say
"We aim to raise the expectations for good food in Mississippi. We pride ourselves on caring for our employees, our suppliers, our customers, our natural environment and our community. Thoughtfulness and respect permeate all of the tangible aspects of the business, from farmer interactions to our handcrafted tables. Our intention is that our attention to detail will always reflect the sense of belonging and community we aim to nurture by taking care with all things."

Signature dishes
Farinata (chickpea pancake made with rosemary, cooked in an iron skillet in the wood-fired oven); assorted pizza (Neapolitan-style dough topped with house-made mozzarella and ricotta from a local organic dairy); seasonal *crostata*.

What others say
2018 Best Restaurant, Mississippi.

Southern Living

What we say
Sourcing first from Mississippi Hill Country and the Delta regions, Saint Leo counts farmers like Native Son in Tupelo and Home Place Pastures in Como as close allies. Seafood here comes from the Gulf and about one-third of the wine list is biodynamic. Blount is especially motivated by her staff, who she aims to recognize for their individual skills and talents, while supporting gender equity as a main priority in the restaurant.

One of Blount's broader concerns is to impact hunger in the United States. She actively supports nonprofit No Kid Hungry in a state where one in four children doesn't get enough food. "I am powerfully compelled to advocate for real change", she says.

Big Bad Breakfast

Oxford

What
Quaint café giving proper respect to the most important meal of the day

Who
John Currence, chef/founder

When
Breakfast, lunch & dinner, daily

Address
719 North Lamar Boulevard, Oxford, MS 38655

+1 662 236 2666

bigbadbreakfast.com

Bookings
Walk-ins

Price guide

What they say
"Every morning we serve families, old friends catching up, business meetings, and students on their way to school. We love being a place for you to gather together and fuel up for the coming day."

Signature dishes
Breakfast "crumble": crumbled buttermilk biscuit, with grits, tomato gravy, bacon, poached eggs, and green onions; "cathead" chicken biscuit - nicknamed regionally for its size - crispy fried chicken with cheddar, and sausage gravy on a black pepper buttermilk biscuit; Creole omelet with shrimp, andouille, onions, tomatoes, cheddar, topped with tomato gravy, and green onions.

What we say
Too often, breakfast doesn't get the care and attention it should. By way of his menu, Currence shows that Southern breakfast can be comforting and good, and equally deserving of thoughtful ingredients as dinner.

Biscuits, jellies, sausage, and bacon are made in-house (the bacon is a thing to remember: leftover pepper mash from Tabasco hot sauce production is blended with dark brown sugar, then cured before smoking).

Healthier menu options are in the mix - think *brûléed* grapefruit, stone-cut oats by Anson Mills, or egg whites served with sweet potato hash. Big Bad Breakfast features its own breakfast blend of coffee roasted by Royal Cup, serves their own smoked meats sourced from the Fatback Pig Project in Eva, Alabama, and gets their grits from Original Grit Girl, also in Oxford.

City Grocery

Oxford

What
Local fare, Southern style, since 1992

Who
John Currence, chef/owner

When
Lunch & dinner, Monday to Saturday, brunch Sunday

Address
152 Courthouse Square, Oxford, MS 38655

+1 662 232 8080

citygroceryonline.com

Bookings
Phone, Resy.com, walk-ins

Price guide

What they say
"Providing the greatest guest experience with food is where our passions lie. As Chef John Currence says: 'Whether I'm cooking for my family, friends, guests at the restaurant, or my four-year-old daughter, I get the same charge out of it. There's a reason I've been doing this my whole life. It's a passion; it's not a job to me. Cleaning is work, but I never look at cooking like that.' We use this philosophy in the kitchen to create beautiful, creative dishes made from exceptional, local ingredients."

Signature dishes
Shrimp and grits with mushrooms, garlic, scallions, white wine, lemon juice, and Big Bad Bacon; Home Place Pastures pork belly with garlic polenta, charred cabbage slaw, and pork jus; oyster toast with cherry tomato confit, horseradish aïoli, and fresh herbs.

What we say
Repeat, regular diners are in high supply at this university town landmark, but newcomers get the red carpet welcome, too. From fried soft shell crab, to pan-roasted Mississippi redfish and chili-glazed rib tips, there's no wrong way to go about a good meal at City Grocery. Staff follow Gulf Wild updates to track fish sourcing and Chef Currence is an active community member who helps raise funds for the health, well-being, and education of local children.

Snackbar

Oxford

What
Globally influenced, French-inspired bistro in North Mississippi

Who
John Currence, owner & Vishwesh Bhatt, chef

When
Dinner Monday to Saturday

Address
721 North Lamar Boulevard, Oxford, MS 38655

+1 662 236 6363

snackbaroxford.com

Bookings
Phone, Resy.com, walk-ins

Price guide

What they say
"We tell our story through the food we cook and seek to create a wonderful guest experience. We support Smart Catch, No Kid Hungry, Move On Up Mississippi, the Southern Foodways Alliance, and the Yoknapatawpha Arts Council."

Signature dishes
Hoppin' John *chaat* with lady peas, puffed rice, tomatoes, bacon, and chili-sorghum dressing; catfish fried in black-eyed pea grits with garam masala succotash and okra-tomato chutney; Mississippi Gulf Coast *cioppino*.

What others say
"It's food rooted in the Southern past, while also pointing to where the South is going ... it's people like Vish Bhatt who keep the taste of the American melting pot ever evolving."

-Maria Godoy, *npr*

What we say
It's always a good idea to see what Bhatt has cooking at Snackbar, a key pillar of John Currence's restaurant group. The menu feels like the crew is having fun: fried boudin balls of pork and rice sausage, Gulf shrimp with roasted eggplant in *nuoc cham* sauce, and every Monday, the daily special of red beans and rice.

Bhatt trains his staff on why they source from producers like Two Brooks Farm and Native Son Farm, and, when possible, introduces his team to the growers whose sustainable practices yield great food. Bhatt can sometimes be found teaching cooking classes to high school students and is passionate about raising awareness for underrepresented chefs from minority backgrounds.

339

North Carolina

French Broad Chocolates

Asheville

What
We make awesome chocolate, crafted with love & served with gratitude

Who
Jael & Dan Rattigan, co-creators

When
Lunch & dinner, daily

Address
10 South Pack Square, Asheville, NC 28801

+1 828 252 4181

frenchbroadchocolates.com

Bookings
Walk-ins

Price guide

What they say
"We are passionate about building connections to the source of our food, and honoring our farmers and producers by sharing their story as a part of our own. We have cultivated a deep passion for cacao by visiting our cacao farms, meeting our farmers, and learning how cacao is processed at origin. Connections formed around chocolate change people for the better."

Signature dishes
Highland Mocha Stout cake; dark chocolate ice cream; chocolate bonbons made with local beer.

What others say
"French Broad Chocolate Lounge serves the sweet stuff in all its forms: bars, cakes, truffles, cookies, ice cream, mousse, brownies, and - perhaps best of all - hot and melted. I took a place in line not suspecting that my opinion of chocolate was about to be altered forever."

-Sarah Maeillano, *The Washington Post*

What we say
An international leader in the sustainable production of chocolate, French Broad Chocolates supports its Southern Appalachian community by buying and preserving local ingredients, helping area farmers, feeding residents in need through the Downtown Welcome Table initiative and contributing to the cleanup of the river for which the company is named. Not only do they make incredible chocolate that will send guests back time after time, they make the community better, too.

Hole Doughnuts

Asheville

What
Donuts made to order in an open kitchen using organic, local, seasonal ingredients

Who
Hallee Hirsh & Ryan Martin, co-owners/operators

When
Breakfast & lunch, Wednesday to Monday

Address
168 Haywood Road, Asheville, NC 28806

+1 828 774 5667

hole-doughnuts.com

Bookings
Walk-ins

Price guide

What they say
"The question we ask ourselves before we make every decision is: 'Will this create joy for ourselves and others?' This applies to everything, including the environment we create with our employees and customers, the relationships we create with farmers and distributors, and how we choose to grow (or not grow) our business."

Signature dishes
Seasonal donuts made with freshly picked flowers, fruit, or herbs, such as honeysuckle, juneberries, and *tulsi*; drip coffee; local grass-fed milk.

What others say
"A doughnut is a doughnut is a doughnut, unless that doughnut happens to be ... from Hole in Asheville, NC. In that case, you're dealing with something else entirely."

-Alex Delany, *bon appétit*

What we say
Not only do their donuts deliver on flavor and provenance of ingredients, but Hole Doughnuts pays attention to all steps in the food chain, including paying a living wage, giving their non-GMO rice bran oil to a biofuel company in their area, and composting all of their coffee grounds. They've chosen not to offer straws or plastic utensils, and they pay special attention to produce that wouldn't otherwise sell.

Step into Hole Doughnuts for pure and modest joy. They are the donut shop of your southern whistle stop imaginings. The donuts are made with organic, stoneground, local flour, and they only offer four flavors at any given time. Don't miss their sesame, almond, cinnamon version, which looks savory, but delivers the goods to any well-worn sweet tooth.

HOLE
7:30 AM to 2 PM
...OR UNTIL WE SELL OUT
CLOSED TUESDAY

OWL Bakery

Asheville

What
Small bakery with sourdough breads, laminated pastries, seasonal fare, coffee & tea

Who
Susannah Gebhart & Maia Surdam, owners

When
Breakfast & lunch, Tuesday to Sunday, dinner Thursday to Saturday

Address
295 Haywood Road, Asheville, NC 28806

+1 828 785 1770

owlbakery.com

Bookings
Walk-ins

Price guide

What they say
"OWL owners Susannah and Maia met because of a shared interest in oral history and Appalachian foodways. We see our bakery as a place of community education and discovery. For example, we used our space to teach the historical significance of colonial-era 'election cakes'. After two years of being open, we offer regular workshops that focus on the craft of baking, as well as other topics such as the history of bread and beer."

Signature dishes
Fruit danish; upside-down rye pound cake with peaches and basil; sourdough toast with soft-boiled egg and greens.

What we say
We like how this women-owned business takes the simplicity of the menu and delves in deep. At all levels, they're making decisions with careful consideration, from sourcing ingredients to customer engagement to handling food waste, and they are helping to create a stronger food landscape.

They always use organic flours that are grown and milled in North Carolina, and they laminate their dough with organic butter that comes from grass-fed cows. Their pastry cream flavors and fruit toppings rotate based on seasonal availability, and they choose taste pairings that compliment one another and aim to provide a sense of discovery. Honeysuckle-strawberry danish, anyone?

HomeGrown

Asheville

What
A diner with a locally sourced, affordable, ever-changing menu of comfort food

Who
Miki Loomis, owner

When
Breakfast, lunch, & dinner, daily

Address
371 Merrimon Avenue, Asheville, NC 28801, plus other locations - see website

+1 828 232 4340

slowfoodrightquick.com

Bookings
Walk-ins

Price guide

What they say
"Locally grown and sourced food is the cornerstone of our restaurant. We take that a step further with our commitment to our local community and dedication to various nonprofits. HomeGrown is a green-certified restaurant and we take that very seriously, composting pre and post-consumer, minimizing our impact in cooking practices, and being highly conscientious of the purchases we make. We are also living-wage certified and take care of our people. This isn't an easy industry, but we do our very best to make sure HomeGrown gives back to the community who supports us and that we support the folks that make HomeGrown."

Signature dishes
Fried chicken; sautéed sesame greens; fried sliced tomatoes with basil.

What others say
"Some restaurants are darlings of the national press. Others are local haunts, jealously kept from the public. For much of HomeGrown's eight years serving a comfortable Southern menu of mostly local food, it's been the latter."

-Mackensy Lunsford, *Asheville Citizen Times*

What we say
Acknowledged as a local-foods leader in a community that takes local food seriously, HomeGrown now has two locations offering a chalkboard menu hailed by residents and visitors alike. While the restaurant is known for its natural, cage-free, small-farm-raised chicken, fried in GMO-free canola oil from North Carolina, it also strives to serve healthier options, such as trout from a sustainable local farm that feeds their fish a diet containing no mammal byproducts.

Foothills Butcher Bar

Asheville

What
Restaurant, bar & butcher shop

Who
Casey McKissick, owner

When
Lunch & dinner, daily, Sunday brunch

Address
697 Haywood Road, Unit E, Asheville, NC 28806

+1 828 417 7081

foothillslocalmeats.com

Bookings
Phone

Price guide

What they say
"We're passionate about providing 'honest meat'. We buy big pieces of meat with no added hormones or antibiotics from small, local family farms. Then, our butchers and chefs turn these quality ingredients into delicious meals. We take great pride in working only with farmers we know and trust. We're passionate about establishing Foothills Butcher Bar as a cornerstone of the community, where multiple generations feel welcome and seen. And since we're passionate about simplicity and transparency, they can count on being served only the finest products."

Signature dishes
Carolina-style hot dog; classic cheeseburger; beef tallow fries.

What others say
"The folks at Foothills Meats have served the Asheville community custom-cut meats for years. Now they use the same top-quality meat at ... Foothills Butcher Bar. Chef Joe Penton prepares sensational snacks like ranch-barbecue chicharrones and house-made Slim Jims and hoop cheese, ... burgers, hot dogs, rotating daily meatballs and insane beef-tallow fries."

Food Network

What we say
Pioneers in the carnivorous category of the local food movement, Foothills Butcher Bar has lately opened two modest restaurant locations in which to further express its food philosophy. It's based on the word "simple", according to owner Casey McKissick. In other words, Foothills Butcher Bar strives not to muck up the planet with practices that rely on chemicals instead of craftsmanship, or by creating food waste. Leftovers that can't be transformed into menu specials are made into compost or pet treats. Now that's conscious dining.

Cúrate

Asheville

What
Asheville's only traditional Spanish tapas bar & vermuteria

Who
Katie Button, executive chef/ co-owner

When
Lunch & dinner, Tuesday to Sunday

Address
13 Biltmore Avenue, Asheville, NC 28801

+1 828 239 2946

heirloomhg.com/curate

Bookings
Reserve.com

Price guide

What they say
"We want to make sustainable product choices, but we are also passionate about maintaining a work environment where our staff feels supported. We want each and every job in the restaurant to be a job that allows people to balance their lives and their families with their work. We strive to offer benefits that take care of our employees, and are living wage certified by Just Economics, a local group that calculates those metrics for our area."

Signature dishes
Vegetable paella, made from scraps including mushroom stems and tomato skins; fried squid sandwich with wild-caught American squid and shrimp-shell aïoli.

What we say
A two-time James Beard Foundation award nominee, Chef Katie Button has upheld the culinary standards she absorbed in the kitchen at elBulli while raising the bar for sustainability in western North Carolina. At the terrifically cosmopolitan Cúrate, the honey drizzled over salt cod fritters, the beef in the *albondigas*, and the egg accompanying the *ensaladilla rusa* all come from local producers. So do the plates on which they're served; a local potter came up with new colors to enhance the restaurant's aesthetic. Don't miss this forward-thinking, unique restaurant next time you're in the area.

Crook's Corner

Chapel Hill

What
Serving New Southern Cuisine since 1982

Who
Gene Hamer, owner

When
Dinner Tuesday to Sunday, brunch Sunday

Address
610 West Franklin Street, Chapel Hill, NC 27516

+1 919 929 7267

crookscorner.com

Bookings
OpenTable.com

Price guide

What they say
"We use a great deal of seasonal produce sourced locally and have a great group of local farmers and suppliers. We obtain a lot of our seasonal produce from local farmers who are often at our farmers' market on Wednesday and Saturdays. We are passionate about not just our cuisine and produce, but our patrons, our staff, our funky building, and our patio and gardens."

Signature dishes
Soft-shell crabs; shrimp and grits; honeysuckle sorbet.

What others say
"This restaurant has trained many of the South's top toques. Current chef, Bill Smith, is an expert at dishes with ethereal, rustic ingredients, such as honeysuckle sorbet made from flowers he collects on bike rides."

-Matt & Ted Lee, *Travel & Leisure*

What we say
Chef Bill Smith took over the kitchen at Crook's Corner in 1993, two years after the death of the restaurant's founding chef, Bill Neal. Smith's allegiance to Neal's legacy and personal interpretations of Southern cuisine have earned him two nominations for the prestigious James Beard Best Chef Southeast title, but he's perhaps known within the Southern culinary community for his abiding concern with the welfare of his workers. Politically, Smith is an outspoken supporter of human rights, especially the plight of immigrants. He's also an enthusiastic student of Latino culture in a region grappling with fast-changing demographics, and helps bring together the state's diverse communities through his dishes.

Honeysuckle Tea House

Chapel Hill

What
Open-air teahouse with herb gardens & berry farm

Who
Alisa Wilcher, chief operating officer of East West Organics

When
Breakfast, lunch, & dinner, Thursday to Sunday, hours change seasonally

Address
8871 Pickards Meadow Road, Chapel Hill, NC 27516

+1 919 903 9131

honeysuckleteahouse.com

Bookings
Website, email info@ honeysuckleteahouse.com

Price guide

What they say
"Honeysuckle is about bringing people together in mind, body, and spirit. We demonstrate our strong focus on healthy living through our love of teas and grown-on premises herbs and berries."

Signature dishes
Coconut matcha latte made with coconut milk; blackberry fig Darjeeling, available iced or hot; and *tulsi* chai, featuring *tulsi* grown on the farm.

What we say
Honeysuckle is sophisticated about tea, but its operators take pride in allowing customers to experience the simpler side of life on their pesticide-free property.

"We want to provide a safe place for people to be together and to just be themselves", Alisa Wilcher says. "To allow kids to run and get back to nature and get dirty and to eat their way through our berry fields. To let people hang out in the hammock garden and just reconnect with their breath and just take a beat and enjoy the world around us. This is what Honeysuckle means to me".

Lantern

Chapel Hill

What
A Chapel Hill restaurant showcasing Asian flavors created with North Carolina ingredients

Who
Andrea Reusing, chef/owner

When
Dinner Monday to Saturday

Address
423 West Franklin Street, Chapel Hill, NC 27516

+1 919 969 8846

lanternrestaurant.com

Bookings
Phone, OpenTable.com

Price guide

What they say
"We're passionate about creating a great place for our employees to work, supporting and collaborating with our local ranchers, farmers, and fishermen, and offering a warm and welcoming environment to our guests."

Signature dishes
Pork and chive dumplings; Japanese pot on fire; buttermilk panna cotta.

What others say
"It seems that everyone who comes to Chapel Hill loves Lantern, from writers like John Grisham to rock bands playing at the Cat's Cradle club. 'We go out of our way to eat at Lantern when we're on tour,' says Ira Kaplan, the frontman for Yo La Tengo."

Food & Wine magazine

What we say
Lantern is a longtime backer of transparency in food systems, particularly in the case of seafood, which plays an outsized role in the charming restaurant's award-winning dishes. When customers order steamed black drum, they can be sure it was caught wild off the Carolina coast - and didn't travel to New York City and Atlanta before returning to Chapel Hill, thanks to the work of partner purveyor Locals Seafood. Lantern advocates for responsible sourcing at other restaurants in the Southeast and beyond through its work with Monterey Bay Aquarium's Chefs for Fish program, the James Beard Foundation's Smart Catch program, and Good Food 100.

Fullsteam Tavern

Durham

What
A plow-to-pint brewery & tavern brewing & cooking with Southern ingredients

Who
Sean Lilly Wilson, owner

When
Lunch & dinner daily

Address
726 Rigsbee Avenue, Durham, NC 27701

+1 919 682 2337

fullsteam.ag

Bookings
Walk-ins

Price guide

What they say
"We're tireless advocates for the local farm and the Southern wild. Truly local beer and food fosters community and deepens our connection to the land. For example, we brewed a Baltic Porter, Farm's Edge: Brumley Forest, with foraged black walnuts, sassafras, and hickory nuts - all collected on land protected from development and open to the public for wandering. For the beer's release, we made a handheld pie with local sorghum and black walnuts. This beer and pie pairing shined a light on a new 600-acre public land that people might not otherwise know about. Our mission is to connect people to the land and to one another - beer and food are by-products."

Signature dishes
Beaufort shrimp salad roll with chili vinegar slaw; pork belly sandwich with black garlic barbecue sauce; pimento cheese with *aji amarillo* and pickled pepper jelly, served with locally made crackers.

What we say
Fullsteam is a consistent voice for progress in North Carolina. The company actively supports the Durham Living Wage campaign, led opposition to a state law barring transgender individuals from bathrooms, and underwrites NC Craft Brewers Guild scholarships for women and people of color.

Pure Pizza

Mecklenburg

What
Farm-to-plate pizzeria

Who
Juli Ghazi, owner

When
Lunch & dinner, Monday to Saturday, brunch Sunday

Address
1911 Central Avenue, Charlotte, Mecklenburg, NC 28205

+1 980 430 1701

purepizzaclt.com

Bookings
Phone

Price guide

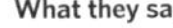

What they say
"We begin with a desire to make a healthy pizza. Our passion for great food, blended with an intention to create something that's good to our bodies and to the Earth, landed us in this place where we've combined both. The result? A pizzeria serving up the most delicious handcrafted menu with local, sustainable and/or organically sourced ingredients and zero waste going into our landfills."

Signature dishes
Salads with hydroponic greens; pizza with organic grains.

What others say
"Pure Pizza is just that - pizza made from the simplest ingredients, including a revolutionary sprouted ancient grain crust and farm fresh vegetables. Try the margherita or chorizo pizza topped with shaved radishes, tomatoes, fresh tomatoes, cilantro, and a squeeze of lime. Not to mention, the side of spicy honey they serve for dunking pizza crust is spot on..."

Thrillist

What we say
Pure Pizza has forty seats in its dining room, but no televisions - and not a single trash can. Customers are asked to scrape food into a compost collector, and toss unwanted packaging into a recycling bin. "Food waste is one of the largest culprits in our landfills, so we are proud to say nothing from our restaurant occupies any space within any landfill", owner Juli Ghazi says, adding, "all of our kitchen grease is turned into biodiesel fuel".

Rose's Noodles, Dumplings and Sweets

Durham

What
Serving food influenced by East Asian cuisine, with North Carolina ingredients

Who
Justin & Katie Meddis, owners

When
Dinner, Wednesday to Saturday, lunch, daily

Address
121 N. Gregson Street, Durham, NC 27701

+1 919 797 2233

Bookings
Walk-ins

Price guide

What they say
"We use North Carolina ingredients to produce dishes that embody the strong food cultures from across the Pacific that we find awe inspiring. We are passionate about consistency. We want people that come in regularly to always know that the food and the service they receive will consistently be great. That takes a lot of work, from sourcing the best ingredients, to preparing them in a way that highlights the flavours."

Signature dishes
Ramen bowl with local pork and chicken bones cooked overnight; house-made tofu with avocado and house-made XO sauce; ice cream sandwiches.

What we say
Rose's Noodles, Dumplings and Sweets is a must-visit for the ramen alone. Juicy and packed full of flavor, it's guaranteed to satisfy - as are the other dishes (don't miss dessert). But there's more than just delicious food at this Durham location. Roses's prides itself in using local produce, bought from farmers' markets and local farms, or collected from their own front yard. All fish is sourced sustainably, and other small acts - such as composting and participating in the program Green to Go, which promotes reusable food containers - help this restaurant lower its carbon footprint.

What others say
"The shrimp and corn gyoza I ordered recently at Rose's Noodles, Dumplings & Sweets were exceptional, the shrimp in the filling chopped into pieces large enough that you could appreciate their snappy texture as well as their briny-sweet flavor."

-Greg Cox, *The News & Observer*

Garland

Wake

What
Locally sourced pan-Asian restaurant in downtown Raleigh

Who
Cheetie Kumar, chef/owner

When
Lunch Wednesday to Friday, dinner Tuesday to Saturday

Address
14 West Martin Street, Raleigh, Wake, NC 27601

+1 919 833 6886

garlandraleigh.com

Bookings
OpenTable.com

Price guide

What they say
"As at least half our menu is vegetable-driven; we hear from a lot of diners that they feel like they can eat at Garland often without feeling 'heavy' afterwards. Our food has its roots in humble cultures so the reliance on 'richness' is just not really a part of who we are. We don't 'mount' our sauces in butter. We rely on either long cooking for braising meats, or quick cooking for vegetables to keep them fresh, vibrant and nutritious."

Signature dishes
Smashed salt-roasted new potatoes with fresh fenugreek and green onion purée; asparagus with green alliums, roasted oyster mushrooms and sticky rice; fish with wilted braising greens and puffed rice salad.

What others say
"Although the menu at Garland is pan-Asian, it draws specifically from Kumar's Indian heritage and the cooking style she learned from her mother, prepared with ingredients she sources from North Carolina farmers."

-Hannah Hayes, *Southern Living*

What we say
Kumar takes a minimalist approach to seasoning, making sure every spice strikes a decisive pose, but doesn't stint on charitable work. Garland hosts upward of fourteen annual fundraisers for children, women and civil rights; works with the Interfaith Food Shuttle to raise awareness of food insecurity, and donates its food scraps to farmers for compost. This is a restaurant to get behind - and you won't be sorry you did.

Poole's Diner

Wake

What
A modern diner in downtown Raleigh with re-imagined comfort food

Who
Ashley Christensen, chef/owner

When
Dinner, daily, weekend brunch

Address
426 South McDowell Street, Raleigh, Wake, NC 27601

+1 919 832 4477

ac-restaurants.com

Bookings
Walk-ins

Price guide

What they say
"Poole's has been a part of the community of downtown Raleigh for over seven decades. Our daily mission is to create a space that feels comfortable and accessible. In our menu, we try to tap into the things that help people connect through food, and our service philosophy is about making a seat at the table for everyone."

Signature dishes
Hook's three-year aged pimento cheese; bibb lettuce salad with red wine vinaigrette; "royale", a Sunday-only burger seared in duck fat, topped with cheese and served open-faced on toasted brioche.

What others say
"Christensen aims to elevate everything she touches, up to and including her customers, who feel in the moment that, yes, this is what food should taste like - loved, respected, realized. And this exquisite visceral contentment is about nothing so much as it is Christensen, who infuses every dish not just with impeccably balanced flavor but also her decency.

-Allison Glock, *Garden & Gun*

What we say
Poole's is widely admired for its integrity, which drives everything from its sourcing decisions to employee management methods. Chef and owner Ashley Christensen believes business and community go hand-in-hand. "Being involved in various local non-profits taught me how to use my voice as a chef. I often tell our team that hospitality is a relationship, not a transaction - so being active members of our community is one of the most important parts of what we do as hospitality professionals".

355

South Carolina

FARM

Beaufort

What
Small-plates café inspired by seasonal produce & global traditions

Who
Brandon Carter, Josh Heaton & Ryan Williamson, partners

When
Lunch & dinner, Tuesday to Saturday

Address
1301 May River Road, Bluffton, Beaufort, SC 29910

+1 843 707 2041

farmbluffton.com

Bookings
Website

Price guide

What they say
"We thoughtfully source everything we use in the restaurant and take great care in nurturing relationships with all sorts of purveyors. We will do whatever it takes to get the best. Sometimes that means foraging chanterelles in the woods. Sometimes that means making a drive out to a farm ourselves. We are hands-on from start to finish, sometimes working directly with farmers to select seed varieties for the upcoming season. We are quality driven, but we work with what/who is around us first to see if our needs can be met by a local provider."

Signature dishes
Daily crudo; panzanella salad; grilled quail *diavolo*.

What others say
"There is absolutely zero corner cutting going on at FARM and the best part for you, the consumer, is that the final product is always delicious."

-Jesse Bianco, *Eat It and Like It*

What we say
After twenty months in business, Bluffton's first restaurant to mimic the sourcing habits of restaurants in bigger cities to the north (Charleston) and south (Savannah) had gone through nineteen menus. In its effort to compete with those culinary capitals, FARM is constantly revising dishes to reflect what is unique to its location, such as May River oysters and ripe fruit from customers' trees, bartered for restaurant credit. A highly seasonal menu means dishes are always changing, giving foodies the perfect excuse to return to FARM again and again.

The Glass Onion

Charleston

What
A locally focused, all-natural restaurant that champions Southern food

Who
Chris Stewart, chef

When
Lunch & dinner, Monday to Saturday

Address
1219 Savannah Highway, Charleston, SC 29407

+1 843 225 1717

ilovetheglassonion.com

Bookings
Resy.com

Price guide

What they say
"Everything is sourced from as close to home as we can find, and our menu changes daily. Our mission is to serve only humanely raised meats, which are hormone and antibiotic free. We're also members of South Carolina's sustainable seafood initiative, and have gone to great lengths to remove all high-fructose corn syrup from the restaurant."

Signature dishes
Okra beignets; Carolina gold rice; buttermilk custard.

What others say
"This sweet restaurant in West Ashley serves up all the Southern classics, from fried green tomatoes to pimento cheese and grits, but makes everything with local ingredients. The grits come from nearby Edisto Island, and much of the produce is sourced from Johns Island."

-Angela Fleury, *AFAR*

What we say
The Glass Onion is eight generations in the making. Its endearing menu reflects chef/owner Chris Stewart's deep Alabama roots, although his current relationships with local farmers account for the fresh ingredients he uses to pay tribute to his culinary heritage. Stewart is an inveterate supporter of Lowcountry fishermen and farmers, an allegiance he expresses through dishes such as pan-roasted fish with tomatoes, prepared with a sophistication that can come as a surprise in The Glass Onion's comfortable dining room.

Basic Kitchen

Charleston

What
Lifestyle-driven food & drink in historic downtown Charleston

Who
Ben Towill, owner

When
Brunch, daily, dinner Monday to Saturday

Address
82 Wentworth Street, Charleston, SC 29401

+1 843 789 4568

basickitchen.com

Bookings
Resy.com

Price guide

What they say
"The goal of Basic Kitchen is simple: use seasonal, local produce, and the best ingredients to create food that's nourishing and delicious, giving eaters tons of energy to pursue the things they love. We're big into diverse flavors and are inspired by dishes from around the world."

Signature dishes
Tempura cauliflower with buffalo sauce and a side of cashew ranch; brown rice bowl with seasonal vegetables, legumes and "magic green sauce"; "Conscious Cowboy" plate: local chicken and ginger sausage with cauliflower grits, spinach, hash browns, and two local farm eggs.

What others say
"Basic Kitchen stands apart from the crowded dining landscape for the way it fills a notable void with healthful, nourishing, local fare - the kind of food you crave and could eat every single day."

-Laura Neilson, *Vogue* magazine

What we say
Customers at Basic Kitchen can't help but participate in the restaurant's mission to strengthen its community, protect the planet, and advance good health through food - especially if they order the beet burger. The wholesome patty is constructed from the pulpy remains of root vegetables pressed for juice, a delicious and nutritious tactic for reducing food waste.

Basic's juice bar also produces a monthly cleanse program, consistent with owner Ben Towill's belief that Basic Kitchen is "a lifestyle rather than just a restaurant." It holds monthly Boot Camp & Brunch sessions, with a boot camp session in the parking lot followed by brunch at the restaurant.

Wild Olive

Charleston

What
An Italian restaurant that treats the Lowcountry as a lost region of Italy

Who
Jacques Larson, executive chef

When
Dinner, daily

Address
2867 Maybank Highway, Johns Island, Charleston, SC 29455

+1 843 737 4177

wildoliverestaurant.com

Bookings
Resy.com

Price guide

What they say
"We are most passionate about highlighting the wonderful bounty of the Lowcountry, whether from the area's farm community or watermen who live and work on Johns Island."

Signature dishes
Bruschetta with whipped ricotta and fried corn; local clams in spicy lemon caper *zuppetta*; ravioli with pistachios, spring onions, double-roasted beets, lemon butter, and local goat's cheese.

What others say
"Local growers first avoided Jacques Larson, who cooks strictly authentic Italian food at Wild Olive, outside Charleston in Johns Island, but he proved an avid buyer of local pork, tomatoes and greens. 'Some farmers around here thought my food was strange at first, but now they drop off escarole on the way to church,' he said."

-Julia Moskin, *The New York Times*

What we say
Wild Olive, a green-certified restaurant, meets its responsibility to the sea by never serving seafood on a trusted environmental group's watch list; meets its responsibility to the land by purchasing local, organic, and grass-fed meat, and meets its responsibility to the air with pollution-fighting measures such as recycling. But the restaurant is best known around Charleston for the work it does on behalf of community members. Larson is the chef chair of an event which annually raises upward of $350,000 to combat food insecurity.

The Obstinate Daughter

Charleston

What
A Lowcountry restaurant on Sullivan's Island

Who
Jacques Larson, executive chef

When
Lunch & dinner, daily

Address
2063 Middle Street, Sullivan's Island, Charleston, SC 29482

+1 843 416 5020

theobstinatedaughter.com

Bookings
Resy.com

Price guide

What they say
"We are most passionate about celebrating the rich cuisine and history of the Lowcountry and giving our guests an honest taste of our region. We are passionate about working along sustainable lines and placing a premium importance on sourcing as much as we can locally."

Signature dishes
Geechie frites with local grits fried and trimmed to look like French fries; Lowcountry shrimp roll; SC strawberry salad.

What others say
"Dishes are freshly sourced, creative, beautifully conceived and executed, the ambiance comfortably chic. With both the kitchen and bar laser-focused on quality, there are no disappointments here."

Travel + Leisure

What we say
The Obstinate Daughter, one of just three Green Restaurant Certified businesses in South Carolina, sources three-quarters of its ingredients from local producers. It also returns all of its spent oyster shells to South Carolina waterways in order to nourish oyster beds, and composts all of its organic waste. But beyond those environmentally friendly initiatives, the restaurant is best known locally for its respectful attitude toward employees; support of programs combating food insecurity, and reliably terrific pizzas and pastas showcasing seafood from nearby fishing grounds.

Swamp Rabbit Cafe & Grocery

Greenville

What
A bakery, café, grocery store, pizza shop, wholesaler & butchery

Who
Mary Walsh, owner

When
Breakfast, lunch & dinner, Monday to Saturday, lunch Sunday

Address
205 Cedar Lane Road, Greenville, SC 29611

+1 864 255 3385

swamprabbitcafe.com

Bookings
Email will@swamprabbitcafe.com

Price guide
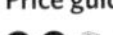

What they say
"We are ridiculously and ambitiously local. We process more than 100 invoices each week because we buy from that many different farmers. Our entire business revolves around local food. We love our farmers so much that we've even employed them during the off-season."

Signature dishes
Wood-fired pizza with locally-milled flour; roast beef sandwich with local grass-fed beef; egg, cheese and bacon sandwich with local eggs.

What others say
"Step inside the Swamp Rabbit Cafe & Grocery on a Wednesday morning and the place feels alive. The smells of fresh-brewed coffee and just-baked bread hang delightfully in the air. Customers push through the door, some going straight to the produce room in back and others to the café in front, all with a sense of familiarity. There is a feeling of intimacy and community here that is unmistakable. People speak to one another and discuss work and kids over fresh-made scones."

-Lillia Callum-Penso, *The Greenville News*

What we say
At first, Swamp Rabbit Cafe & Grocery opened as a cafe, bakery, and grocery, to make up for the lack of places in the immediate area to buy fresh vegetables, meat, and bread. Over time it evolved to include a butchery, wood-fired pizza, and wholesale - they now distribute farm-fresh fruits and vegetables to other area restaurants. On top of that, they offer prepared food and cooking classes to popularize plentiful local foods, such as eggplant and kohlrabi. Don't miss their delicious pizzas and sandwiches.

Motor Supply Co. Bistro

Richland

What
A prime mover in the upscale dining scene in Columbia with a chef-driven menu

Who
Eddie Wales, owner & Wesley Fulmer, executive chef

When
Lunch & dinner, Tuesday to Sunday

Address
920 Gervais Street, Columbia, Richland, SC 29201

+1 803 256 6687

motorsupplycobistro.com

Bookings
OpenTable.com

Price guide

What they say
"The main goal at Motor Supply is to make people happy. Owner Eddie Wales takes pride in providing a positive experience for all guests and enjoys finding a diverse and vibrant crowd filling the seats - from executives on a business lunch to young professionals celebrating great accomplishments, hipster bar diners searching for the freshest fare to travelers visiting Columbia for the first time. Wales' hope is that eating at Motor Supply can be the highlight of someone's day."

Signature dishes
Seared black grouper with rutabaga and butterbeans; rabbit over corn pudding, flat iron steak with Carolina Gold rice grits and pickled persimmons.

What others say
"In his impressively small kitchen at Motor Supply, coppa and pork legs hang for curing below a shelf of a dozen artisanal vinegars; kimchi ferments nearby. The daily rotating dinner menu might feature plates of yellowfin tuna, seared and placed onto a bed of crispy endive and tonnato. It's the perfect balance between tart, salt, and sweet. Many of (Chef Wes) Fulmer's creations have a Thai-inspired twang of acid and herb, although you can also order redfish and heirloom grits that were milled in town - and you won't regret it."

-Chandra Gowri, *Food & Wine* magazine

What we say
Motor Supply Co. carved out a space in Columbia for culinary ambition when it opened in 1989, and has since expanded its vision of excellence to include leadership in the revival of heirloom ingredients and the reduction of food waste.

Juniper

Saluda

What
An unexpectedly unique restaurant in the South Carolina Midlands

Who
Brandon Velie, chef/co-owner & Jeanne Velie, co-owner

When
Lunch Thursday to Tuesday, dinner Thursday to Saturday

Address
640 East Main Street, Ridge Spring, Saluda, SC 29129

+1 803 685 7547

facebook.com

Bookings
Phone

Price guide

What they say
"Our food philosophy is to take Southern favorites and put our own fun and creative spin on them, using local and seasonal products and keeping it simple. But we are most passionate about the details. This not only includes the quality of ingredients, but also the way our customers and employees are treated. We strive for excellence every day, every shift, every plate."

Signature dishes
Shrimp and grits; barbecue quail with rice, flash-fried collards, and mustard sauce; house salad with local greens and Clemson University blue cheese dressing.

What others say
"For Brandon Viele, the co-owner of Juniper restaurant in Ridge Spring, sustainability is inspiring experimentation with local ingredients for dishes on the restaurant's dinner menu."

-Susan Ardis, *The State*

What we say
When the Velies talk about buying locally, they mean food within walking distance - the couple sources red meat from a farm just down the road. But their definition of responsible restaurateurs isn't limited to what they take in; Juniper is also thoughtful about what it puts out. A portion of profits goes toward dinners for veterans and multiple children's charities, soda tops go to Ronald McDonald House, meat scraps go to a pig farmer, and vegetable scraps go to an employee's pet goat.

361

Tennessee

Capitol Grille

Nashville

What
A day restaurant featuring refined Southern cuisine

Who
Derek Brooks, executive chef

When
Breakfast, lunch & dinner, daily

Address
231 6th Avenue North, Nashville TN 37219

+1 615 345 7116

capitolgrillenashville.com

Bookings
OpenTable.com

Price guide

What they say
"We are passionate about our local farmers and purveyors, especially our own farms. We feature our own Glen Leven Farm as well as ten local farmers within a forty-mile radius. All of our seafood is wild, line-caught and from reputable suppliers. We also change our menu seasonally to help use different products throughout the year and do our part for lowering the burden on specific offerings."

Signature dishes
Onion bisque; confit hot chicken; fresh garden pasta.

What we say
Set inside the historic Hermitage Hotel in downtown Nashville, Capitol Grille brings the Southern tradition of farm-inspired cooking to its tables. The team, led by Chef Derek Brooks, combines history and tradition on its impressive menu. The hotel is deeply committed to both local farming and land preservation, as evidenced by their partnership with The Land Trust for Tennessee, which over ten years has resulted in more than $800,000 donated by hotel guests, which has helped to directly preserve 85,000 acres of land. On the plate, you can taste that commitment in flavorful ribeyes and filets, and garden-harvested salads and side dishes.

City House

Nashville

What
An Italian influenced restaurant that's been open over ten years

Who
Tandy Wilson, chef/owner

When
Dinner Wednesday to Monday

Address
1222 4th Avenue North, Nashville, TN 37208

+1 615 736 5838

cityhousenashville.com

Bookings
Resy.com

Price guide

What they say
"City House is a neighborhood restaurant. To be a neighborhood restaurant, you have to be a part of your community. You can't just be that place in the neighborhood that people want to come to - you can't just take. You have to give back. And that means you have to work with the people around you. We have our own mill and grow organic, biodynamic corn that's raised under the finest principles that then produces some really great meals. We work with the stuff that comes from our lakes and waterways, like trout and catfish. These are the things that determine our menu. We set our morals and way of operation and then we create the best menu we can from that."

Signature dishes
Sour corn cake with turnip green, and smoked tomato; belly ham pizza with mozzarella, *Grana Padano*, oregano, and chili; bread gnocchi with rabbit sugo, parsley, and *Grana Padano*.

What we say
White stucco walls marked by bits of exposed brick. Utilitarian furnishings. And yet, warmth spreads through City House, thanks to the open kitchen's wood-fired oven, and a family-like hospitality - a vibe that comes from Chef Tandy Wilson and his staff, many of whom have been on since opening day. Italian by way of the South, Wilson's food is marked by locality and simplicity. House-milled grits. Slow-cooked pork *sugo*. Dishes that show off the region - and show a deep commitment to the community.

Fin & Pearl

Nashville

What
Fresh seafood restaurant committed to sustainable sourcing & eco-friendly operations

Who
Tom Morales, owner

When
Breakfast, lunch & dinner, daily

Address
211 12th Avenue South, Nashville, TN 37203

+1 615 577 6688

finandpearl.com

Bookings
Resy.com

Price guide

What they say
"Our mission is to create a sustainable, Earth-friendly seafood restaurant in both our practices and buying strategies, while communicating with our customers honestly and with 100 percent transparency. We hope to inspire others to embrace these simple tenets through our culinary efforts and a kind, hospitable attitude."

Signature dishes
Wild caught fresh catch; Rapa Nui Tuna Poke with scallion, avocado, cucumber, edamame, seaweed, *furikake*, sesame soy, and wontons.

What others say
"Fin & Pearl has created a restaurant experience all of its own ... While [its] sourcing might vary, quality dishes are always guaranteed."

-Genevieve Moore, *Sophisticated Living Magazine*

What we say
This fresh seafood-focused restaurant, where you'll find gumbo, ceviches, a full raw bar, po'boys, and daily fresh catch specials, commits firmly to a zero-waste mission. This is drilled into every facet of the business, from the use of an ORCA machine for aerobic digestion of food waste, to their sustainably sourced custom-made furniture. A Blubar Water System for filtered water eliminates the recycling and transportation needs of bottled water and they utilize Restaurant Technologies' services to recycle cooking oil.

EiO & The Hive

Nashville

What
A community doing its best for people & the planet

Who
Jennifer Masley, owner/founder

When
Breakfast, lunch & dinner, daily

Address
5304 Charlotte Avenue, Nashville, TN 37209

+1 615 942 7031

eioandthehive.com

Bookings
Walk-ins

Price guide

What they say
"We care about the well-being of people and our planet. We want to create a positive community using healthy food and artisanal products as a vehicle - connecting local farmers with local families, and creating awareness around sustainability. By creating in-house sustainability systems and sourcing and using responsibly sourced design materials and products, we believe we can create positive changes. Communication and education are the keys for any successful change - and no greenwashing allowed."

Signature dishes
Sustainably sourced salmon with local spring pea purée, corn, and black-eyed peas; coconut curry bowl with chickpeas, bok choy, sweet potatoes, cauliflower, and golden raisins; and vegan flapjacks made with toasted pecan, hemp seeds, maple roasted butternut squash, orange, and banana.

What we say
Inside this bright, cozy, all-day cafe, you'll find healthy food and drinks, community, and a mindful dining experience. Customizable grain bowls, salads, and tapas selections, which are all thoughtfully labelled as vegan, vegetarian, lacto or gluten free, provide the edible base.

The space also plays host to free community events, Sunday morning yoga, and dinner and conversation with health experts. Local, artisanal products, such as books, juices, herbs, and supplements, fill their retail shelves, so that you may incorporate their mission into your own daily routine. "The Hive is our community", explains founder Jennifer Masley. "Just like bees have an intimate network of roles and responsibilities necessary to keep them happy and healthy, we as humans need this, too".

Henrietta Red

Nashville

What
Restaurant & oyster bar with a regional seafood & seasonal vegetable driven menu

Who
Julia Sullivan, chef/partner

When
Dinner Tuesday to Sunday, weekend brunch

Address
1200 Fourth Avenue, North., Nashville TN 37208

+1 615 260 9993

henriettared.com

Bookings
Walk-ins, OpenTable.com

Price guide

What they say
"I feel strongly that local businesses should add value and interest to a city, so we work hard to ensure that our food and service are among the best here in Nashville, and to bring something unique and fun to the table. I'm also passionate about creating a healthy workplace - we do what we can to make working here sustainable and beneficial to the employee."

Signature dishes
Diverse selection of up to eighteen varieties of raw oysters; Poppy's caviar with sour cream, scallion vinaigrette, and Tennessee paddlefish caviar; cauliflower steak.

What others say
"This is a place that serves Jell-O shots at the bar and monkey bread for brunch without a hint of irony, even if they are both upscale versions. Very clearly, [Julia] Sullivan and [Allie] Poindexter have created a restaurant around their personal expressions of food and place."

-Steve Cavendish, *Nashville Scene*

What we say
This bright, lively neighborhood restaurant elevates everything great about Nashville dining. Chef Julia Sullivan sources sustainably - seafood, local meat and dairy, produce, natural and organic wines - and also grows herbs and flowers on the patio garden, all to produce a delightful menu of shareable small and large plates.

Behind the scenes, they compost food and oyster shells, take field trips to area farms, and Sullivan produces panels on food and business to offer transparent conversation. A now essential restaurant, Henrietta Red is truly bettering its own community.

Husk Nashville

Nashville

What
Husk works to reimagine what Southern food is, utilizing Southern ingredients

Who
Sean Brock, executive chef

When
Lunch & dinner, daily, weekend brunch

Address
37 Rutledge Street, Nashville, TN 37210

+1 615 256 6565

husknashville.com

Bookings
Phone, Resy.com

Price guide

What they say
"If it doesn't come from the south it doesn't come through the door and if it isn't grown seasonally we don't serve it. All of our poultry, beef, pork, and fish are raised by compassionate and passionate farmers who care deeply about their animals. And our commitment to serving only southern ingredients drastically reduces our carbon footprint. Our menu is constantly changing. We are continually inspired to find new ways to utilize the bounty of produce that is available to us here. More often than not, it is the ingredient that fosters the idea."

What others say
"Quite simply, Brock has a relentless mind working to preserve the historical foodways of the South. Oh, he also happens to know how to cook. Like nobody else."

-Jim Myers, *The Tennessean*

What we say
With its hyper-regional focus and passion for ingredients, plain and simple, Husk Nashville brings the cuisine of the Cumberland River Valley to new heights - but also remains grounded in its efforts of sustainability and seasonality.

They source herbs, flowers, and produce from the gardens that surround the restaurant and utilize nearly 100 percent of all of ingredients. What they don't serve they pickle, preserve, or conserve for later use.

This year, the thought-leaders made the decision to stop purchasing wild ramps with the bulbs attached, since that practice is devastating for the once abundant allium - a commitment that others will surely follow.

Josephine

Nashville

What
Modern American farmhouse restaurant

Who
Andy Little, chef

When
Dinner, daily, weekend brunch

Address
2316 12th Avenue South, Nashville, TN 37204

+1 615 292 7766

josephineon12th.com

Bookings
Phone, walk-ins, OpenTable.com

Price guide

What they say
"The goal at Josephine is to provide a remarkable dining experience while maintaining a sense of place and ease of going out. We do our best to source from producers who provide a great work environment, are constantly pointing staff toward new educational experiences, and doing demos to help educate our community about food. As we are buying what we can from local producers we are impacting their economies and reducing the impact on the environment. We are always looking at ways to reduce food waste and, when the seasons allow it, vegetables make up a large part of the Josephine menu."

Signature dishes
Nashville hot scrapple; whole chicken with kale and crispy potatoes; warm seasonal cobbler with ice cream.

What we say
Working closely with local suppliers, Chef Andy Little and the team at Josephine bring Pennsylvania Dutch cuisine to the upper south. Inside a candlelit, convivial room, Little embraces his roots through his dishes (the hot scrapple says it all), as well as his new home with strong partnerships in the Nashville community.

"We are very dedicated to buying produce from boutique growers, thus helping them explore different products", Little says. For example, the restaurant is involved with an urban farmer who is growing heirloom seeds from the Pennsylvania Dutch area where Little grew up, in hope of bringing some of these flavorsome crops to Middle Tennessee.

Margot Café

Nashville

What
French-inspired restaurant serving a local, seasonal menu that changes daily

Who
Margot McCormack, chef/owner

When
Dinner Tuesday to Sunday

Address
1017 Woodland Street, Nashville, TN 37206

+1 615 227 4668

margotcafe.com

Bookings
Phone

Price guide

What they say
"We have driven the now-passé farm-to-table movement here in Nashville for over seventeen years. We have introduced seasonal, fresh dining to this community and made it absolute. At the same time, we herald our growers, value our staff, and welcome our guests. Our passion is serving the freshest food in a comfortable environment with integrity and care. We have no glass ceiling and mentor women and men alike. We also look for diversity in our staff as well as our customer base. We participate in more than a dozen charity fundraisers every year that benefit everything from hunger to homelessness to aid to schools."

Signature dishes
Local strawberries with English peas, ricotta *salata*, hazelnuts, scallions, lemon poppyseed dressing; fried soft-shell crabs with chilled cucumber and avocado purée, watercress, radish, shaved carrots, and preserved lemon; pan-roasted chicken with pistachio basmati rice, marinated feta, cilantro, and mint.

What we say
Chef Margot McCormack writes out a menu each day using what can be found locally to craft plates that tend to put vegetables front and center. McCormack's dedication to farmers goes further: she sits on the board of the Nashville Farmers' Market and hosts a fundraising dinner to support one farmer each year. She encourages purveyors to deliver produce in baskets, so that they're presented as works of art. "We care so very deeply about everyone involved in the making of a simple meal", she says.

Lockeland Table

Nashville

What
Neighborhood restaurant focusing on relationships between community, environment, staff & family

Who
Cara Graham, owner, & Hal Holden-Bache, chef/owner

When
Dinner Monday to Saturday

Address
1520 Woodland Street, Nashville, TN 37206

+1 615 228 4864

lockelandtable.com

Bookings
Phone, walk-ins

Price guide

What they say
"We are not a restaurant that only focuses on local but it's where we start. We are passionate about being a positive business in our community. We practice seasonal cooking in the kitchen and bar, give thought to our sourcing practices, and give back to our local community in a way that hopefully inspires others to do the same.

"We are a ninety percent trash-free restaurant. We recycle all glass, cardboard, plastics, aluminium, paper, and oil. We also compost. We have changed our buying strategies in order to compost as many things as possible, including straws made from corn, to-go containers made from sugar cane pulp, unbleached paper products, and more. We also have gardens in the back that we use for herbs, onions, peppers, tomatoes, carrots, turnips, and radishes, which we utilize year-round."

Signature dishes
Chicken liver pâté with smoked peach preserves; Porter Road Butcher New York strip with chimichurri; vegan farmers' plate.

What we say
Behind a brick storefront, Lockeland Table is a true neighborhood restaurant where a wood-fired pizza oven anchors the kitchen, familiar faces gather in the bar and lounge, and the nightly "community hour" raises funds for the nearby public school. Children are welcome, and so is conversation, be it catching up with neighbors or more meaningful chats about an often broken food-supply system. Through partnerships with local farms, Lockeland Table aims to stimulate the local economy and reduce its carbon footprint.

The Barn at Blackberry Farm

Blount

What
A James Beard Award-winning restaurant offering multi-course menus of Foothills Cuisine

Who
Cassidee Dabney, executive chef

When
Dinner, daily

Address
1471 West Millers Cove Road, Walland, Blount, TN 37886

+1 865 984 8166

blackberryfarm.com

Bookings
Email outsidedining@blackberryfarm.com

Price guide

What they say
"The Barn at Blackberry Farm celebrates the natural rhythms of East Tennessee and showcases seasonal flavors. Our menus showcase what is growing fresh in the garden that day, allowing us to share a taste of what is happening on the farm, and in our region, in real time. There are elements grown or foraged on our land in every dish that we serve. We are passionate about every dish that we serve being thoughtful and purposeful. There is intent behind the choices we make, how we pair flavors, and the care that is put into crafting the final presentation on the plate. Here, the sense of place and connection to the land is really important and we use our dishes to share that with our guests."

Signature dishes
Field greens and bolts; toasted grains and seeds with beef broth, smoked butter, cured beef, and radishes; spring mushroom salad with morel mushrooms, pea shoots, *verjus*, and pecans.

What we say
Under the helm of executive chef Cassidee Dabney, The Barn at Blackberry Farm remains one of the most coveted destination dining spots in the United States.

Using high-level techniques to produce a constantly changing menu, Dabney's team crafts dishes that are creative, exciting, and unexpected. They're often vegetable forward, too, thanks to Chef Dabney's root-to-leaf approach, making the meals here nutritional yet still comforting and filling. What doesn't go on the plate is reused, recycled, or composted on the farm.

Main Street Meats

Hamilton

What
Local butcher & charcuterie shop with a kitchen & bourbon bar

Who
Erik Niel, chef

When
Lunch & dinner, daily

Address
217 East Main Street, Chattanooga, Hamilton, TN 37408

+1 423 602 9568

mainstreetmeatschatt.com

Bookings
Walk-ins

Price guide

What they say
"We are a local butcher shop and restaurant that specializes in Old World butchery and charcuterie techniques. We pair that with a kitchen and bar that feature the seasons, and all the local bounty we have to offer."

Signature dishes
MSM burger with fresh ground beef; MSM dry-aged steaks; butcher's charcuterie with five charcuterie selections, made in-house or sourced from local and regional favorites.

What we say
This butcher shop and kitchen, whose sister restaurant Easy Bistro & Bar is another Chattanooga institution, keeps a tight focus on local animals, produce, and regionally produced goods. They source animals as close to them as they can, choosing ethically raised pork and beef that are hormone and antibiotic free, and fed non-GMO feed when possible.

Beyond its attention to expert butchery, Main Street Meats remains committed to its community by co-sponsoring the seasonal dinner series Scenic City Supper Club with its sister restaurant, which is designed to foster camaraderie among the culinary and hospitality professionals in Chattanooga. They also host multiple school groups for educational sessions every year.

What others say
"A restaurant with a butcher shop - or is it a butcher shop with a restaurant? - is always a winning combination. Main Street Meats ... specializes in meats that have been processed in-house, like andouille made with pork from Knoxville-based Southern Natural Farms and various steak cuts from Lake Majestik Farms just 45 miles away in Flat Rock, Alabama."

-Lia Picard, *Tasting Table*

Knox Mason

Knox

What
A small, neighborhood restaurant & bar featuring regional Appalachian cuisine

Who
Matt Gallaher, executive chef/owner

When
Dinner daily, weekend brunch

Address
131 South Gay Street, Knoxville, TN 37902

+1 865 544 2004

knoxmason.com

Bookings
Phone, OpenTable.com

Price guide

What they say
"I'm passionate about investing in my staff and partnering with local farmers to help grow each others' businesses. We rely heavily on local farmers and our Market Square Farmers' Market. In peak growing season, we do an economic study and have found that we spend seventy percent of our food dollars on local and regional farms."

Signature dishes
Kilt greens salad, sautéed in Benton's bacon vinaigrette with toasted homemade bread and poached Circle V. Farm egg; Sweetwater Valley pimiento cheese with house-made wicked pickles and Fanatic beer bread; fresh pork rinds with bourbon barrel-smoked paprika and Tennessee sunshine hot sauce.

What others say
"For many Knoxville diners, Matt Gallaher will forever be the man who brought pork rinds to fine dining ... Gallaher's food, whether it's his take on Southern classics or classic Italian, is vibrant, intense, and satisfying to both eye and appetite."

Knoxville Mercury

What we say
The centerpiece of Matt Gallaher's buzzing, shotgun space is the open kitchen, where seats at the counter offer a glimpse of the chefs who are advancing Appalachian cuisine with dishes like deviled eggs with chow chow and black-eyed pea hummus. Even cocktails are mixed with local spirits. Gallaher's efforts to source locally means farmers like cattle grower John Mitchell can increase output and profits. He's also on the board for the city's farmers' market, and in summer works with underprivileged elementary school children, showing them how to cook "real" food.

Andrew Michael Italian Kitchen

Memphis

What
Memphis restaurant innovative Italian cooking rooted in Southern tradition

Who
Andrew Ticer & Michael Hudman, chefs/owners

When
Dinner Tuesday to Saturday

Address
712 West Brookhaven Circle, Memphis, TN 38117

+1 901 347 3569

andrewmichaelitaliankitchen.com

Bookings
Phone, walk-ins, OpenTable.com

Price guide

What they say
"We're most passionate about recreating the experience of eating in our grandmothers' kitchens - that feeling of really great food, boisterous and lively conversation, and being taken care of with an open heart. We source a majority of our ingredients from farms within a seven-hour drive. [And] we're extremely connected to our hometown. We strive to invest in the personal and professional growth of our staff. We send back of house employees on stages around the country and the world, with two of our chef de cuisines spending a month in Italy to better understand the food we are trying to create. We also provide stipends and scholarships to our front of house team members looking to further their professional development."

Signature dishes
"Andrew Michael Breakfast": a playful version of breakfast for dinner; Maw Maw's ravioli with gravy; *chiatara* with greens, ham hock, and cornbread *panna gratta*.

What we say
Family is the driving theme at this East Memphis mainstay. Set inside a ranch with a patio out back, the restaurant gives guests a taste of the Italian cooking, and family camaraderie, both chefs grew up with. They cook from their grandmothers' recipes, and Michael's father still makes the gravy for all of the restaurants. The chefs now own multiple restaurants in Memphis and beyond, but their firmly planted roots can be found here, at the original.

373

Virginia

The Ivy Inn Restaurant

Charlottesville

What
Fine dining through a contemporary, locally-minded lens

Who
Angelo Vangelopoulos, chef/owner

When
Dinner, daily

Address
2244 Old Ivy Road, Charlottesville, VA 22903

+1 434 977 1222

ivyinnrestaurant.com

Bookings
Phone, OpenTable.com

Price guide

What they say
"Important virtues at The Ivy Inn include shopping at my local farmers' market, investing in local growers, and cooking foods with regional relevance and history."

Signature dishes
Rag Mountain trout with asparagus, peas, wild mushrooms, Carolina rice, and ramp butter; pork rib chop with andouille-braised greens and bacon-wrapped potato terrine; spinach and ricotta ravioli with mushroom Bolognese, tomato, basil, and Parmesan cheese.

What others say
"Hailed by some of his peers as Charlottesville's best chef, Angelo Vangelopoulos is surely one of the town's most hospitable. Every Easter for the past four years, he has roasted a goat in the restaurant's garden as a post-shift thank-you to his staff and their families. The party has grown from an initial 50 guests to 250 or so last year, because his peers in the industry started showing up for the feast. 'We used to have leftovers,' jokes Vangelopoulos, whose attendees one holiday included José Andrés and his tribe."

-Tom Sietsema, *The Washington Post*

What we say
Virginia native Angelo Vangelopoulos has been at the helm of this forty-five-year-old Charlottesville classic since 1995, and ever since has led the charge for local and sustainable ingredients. Some of the best dishes reflect Vangelopoulos's Greek heritage, on full display in a lamb-two-ways entrée, which, in addition to a mustard-crusted rack, features a two-bite *gyro* pita stuffed with ground lamb, tangy homemade yogurt, and aged feta cheese.

Market Table Bistro

Loudoun

What
Family-owned restaurant serving seasonal fare

Who
Jason Lage, chef/owner & Rebecca Dudley, owner

When
Lunch Tuesday to Friday, dinner Tuesday to Saturday, weekend brunch

Address
13 East Broad Way, Lovettsville, Loudoun, VA 20180

+1 540 822 3008

markettablebistro.com

Bookings
Phone

Price guide

What they say
"We're most passionate about the quality of food and the importance of knowing where your food comes from and how it is raised or grown."

Signature dishes
Mac 'n' cheese with two kinds of cheddar blended with classic béchamel sauce; charcuterie with house-made sausages, pâtés, head cheese, rillettes, and schmaltz.

What others say
"Young ramps are super tender, possessing a subtle garlic/onion taste. Lage offers them simply prepared: lightly fried in a tempura batter and served with soy sauce aged in Kentucky bourbon barrels, along with fresh ginger. The dish was an instant hit - a treasured rarity a diner can't find just anywhere."

-John McNeilly, *Loudoun Now*

What we say
There are 140 laying hens, four beehives, an array of turkeys and pigs, and rows upon rows of produce at Fairbrook Farms, the sprawling ten-acre operation that supplies a major chunk of the ingredients at nearby Market Table Bistro. Both are owned by Jason Lage and Rebecca Dudley, which helps ensure that the restaurant's origin-specific cuisine and inventive, locally inspired cocktails remain exactly that.

Lage, also the restaurant's chef, supplements Fairbrook's bounty with ingredients from more than 100 local farms and his own foraging expeditions in the Virginia woods. The results are magnificent, with dishes like pillowy sweet potato gnocchi draped in nettle pesto and delicate quiche packed with spring mushroom, wild ramps, and aged cheddar. Every bit of food waste is composted or fed to the chickens at Fairbrook.

Hunter's Head Tavern

Frauquier

What
Traditional English pub with not-so-traditional, farm-fresh ingredients

Who
Sandy Lerner, owner/farmer

When
Lunch & dinner, daily

Address
9048 John S Mosby Highway, Upperville, Frauquier, VA 20184

+1 540 592 9020

huntersheadtavern.com

Bookings
Phone, OpenTable.com

Price guide

What they say
"Sandy Lerner fought a large list of organizations, many led by the big cartels who don't want middle-sized farms to flourish, but in spite of their attempts, she survived and has developed a great farming model. When problems occurred, she often consulted farming guides from more than one hundred years ago, when everyone farmed organically."

Signature dishes
Rosemary-brined grilled pork chop with brown mustard sauce; superfood salad with tossed garden greens, farm-raised heritage-breed turkey, legumes, quinoa, beets, and sunflower seeds; brined and baked Ayrshire chicken.

What others say
"The restaurant is a bit of merry, old England in rural Virginia, rustic in its evocation of the corner pub ... But it retains its connection to the farm: This may be the only neighborhood bar on the planet where the burger you're served, for $14.50, comes from an animal that was grazing in the fields a mile or so away a few weeks earlier."

-Charles Passy, *The Wall Street Journal*

What we say
Nearly every ingredient on this modest English pub's menu - think shepherd's pie, bangers and mash, bubble and squeak - comes from nearby Ayrshire Farm, which is certified organic and humane. Both restaurant and farm are owned by tech giant Sandy Lerner, a cofounder of Cisco Systems and the cosmetics company Urban Decay, who's made sure that the chicken, turkey, pork, and beef are all hardy, deeply flavorful heritage breeds.

The Restaurant at Patowmack Farm

Loudoun

What
Earth-to-table tasting menu in a greenhouse setting

Who
Beverly Morton Billand, owner

When
Dinner Thursday to Saturday, weekend brunch

Address
42461 Lovettsville Road, Lovettsville, Loudoun, VA 20180

+1 540 822 9017

patowmackfarm.com

Bookings
Phone, website, OpenTable.com

Price guide

What they say
"Menu planning at The Restaurant at Patowmack Farm requires a walk to the field, inspiring thoughts of what the menu may have to offer."

What others say
"At this votive-lit greenhouse in northern Loudoun County, many ingredients on Tarver King's multi-course prix fixe menu are grown or foraged in the fields and forest surrounding the farm. Each course has a tale (printed on a card left behind by your server), yet the experience is more adventure than tutorial. Plates are sometimes not plates at all - maitake mushrooms 'grow' on a small log."

-Ann Limpert, Anna Spiegel, Jessica Sidman, and Cynthia Hacinli, *Washingtonian* magazine

What we say
It's difficult to say what might spring forth from the kitchen at The Restaurant at Patowmack Farm. The tasting menu here changes weekly, based on whatever looks good in the eatery's surrounding fields, home to one of the first certified-organic farms in the state of Virginia. But you can reliably anticipate that Chef Tarver King's showstopper cuisine will be fresh and thoughtful, inspired by the history of this corner of Virginia and the many peoples who've lived here. That might mean house-cured ham smeared with house-made mustard, roasted cornmeal dolloped with crème fraîche and a dribble of sassafras root-spiked molasses, or even a toasted fennel custard ringed with red wine-flavored meringue. As far as ingredients go, everything not grown on-site comes from local organic growers.

Field & Main

Frauquier

What
Farm-to-table dining over an open flame

Who
Neal & Star Wavra, owners

When
Dinner Thursday to Monday, weekend brunch

Address
8369 W. Main Street, Marshall, Frauquier, VA 20115

+1 540 364 8166

fieldandmainrestaurant.com

Bookings
Phone, website

Price guide

What they say
"We're most passionate about relationships - with the farmers and artisans that provide us with the food and drink we feature, with our patrons, and with our team. What makes us distinctive is the building that houses our restaurant. It was built in phases over time since 1790, with the main portion being built about 1830 for the purpose of being a restaurant. So it is gratifying to take an old building in a small town and render it functional and relevant by returning it to its original purpose."

Signature dishes
Ember-roasted whole rockfish with soy sauce and olive olive; grilled *porchetta* with pickled ramps and foie gras sauce; buffalo-style pig ears with ribboned celery with blue cheese crumble.

What others say
"Our newest country obsession is this Federal-era restaurant ... We'd happily travel for a host of small plates such as crunchy Buffalo-style pig ears."

Washingtonian magazine

What we say
The beating heart of this seasonally-focused gem is the ten-foot-wide hearth reminiscent of colonial times. The dishes prepared over the rollicking flames are deliciously primal, but nonetheless refined. Almost everything, from the produce and meat to the wine and beer, is local, helping to support the larger community and reduce the restaurant's environmental footprint. Be sure to visit on a night with the Seedlings program, which Field & Main kickstarted in 2017. The initiative invites local students to prepare and serve a three-course meal, learning about each step along the way.

Milton's

St. Paul

What
Elevated, Appalachian-inspired "greasy spoon" with heirloom ingredients

Who
Travis Milton, chef/co-owner

When
Lunch & dinner, Tuesday to Saturday, lunch Sunday

Address
3025 4th Avenue, St. Paul, VA 24283

+1 276 738 3041

cheftravismilton.com

Bookings
Walk-ins, phone

Price guide

What they say
"We are most passionate about creating true economic development in the Appalachian region through its foodways. We work alongside Appalachian Sustainable Development to help give farmers in the local region access to Heirloom Seeds for growing. We also grow our own produce and host talks with local educational institutions to help foster local workforce development."

Signature dishes
Hickory King hominy porridge with creasy greens, mulefoot hog *lardo*, and Tennessee Mountain black truffle; Virginia peanut smoked chicken with shuck bean dashi, radish, and yellow tomato preserves; *koji*-crusted pork cutlet with greasy beans, chanterelle butter, wild mushrooms, and goosefoot.

What others say
"Travis Milton could still be cooking at a top-flight restaurant in Richmond. Instead, he's at the edge of the Virginia coalfields, just past his childhood home at Castlewood."

-Joe Tennis, *The Washington Times*

What we say
A leading advocate for the long-underappreciated cuisine of Appalachia, Chef Travis Milton made a name for himself in Richmond's high-end restaurants. But he felt strongly that his new venture, Milton's, had to be in his hometown, the modest Virginia coal-mining town of St. Paul. The meat-and-three joint - anchored by heirloom local vegetables, whole-hog pits behind the restaurant, and an intense adherence to seasonality - opened in early 2018 in St. Paul's first boutique hotel, the Western Front. Come for modern interpretations of classic Appalachian fare, including specialties like chicken-fried bacon dressed with pickled onions and okra.

379

West Virginia

Hill & Hollow

Monongalia

What
Elevated Appalachian cuisine with global accents

Who
Alegria Ohlinger & Marion Ohlinger, co-owners

When
Dinner Monday to Saturday

Address
709 Beechurst Avenue, Morgantown, Monongalia, WV 26505

+1 304 241 4551

hillandhollowwv.com

Bookings
Phone

Price guide

What they say
"We are primarily farm-to-fork, proudly Appalachian-centric, unapologetically modernist, and progressively globalist. We feel that Appalachia is deeply misunderstood, and there is no better way to introduce who we really are than through a modern Appalachian culinary vernacular, one that is rooted in tradition and yet aware of and involved with the world around us."

Signature dishes
Frosted leek brûlée with alfalfa-steamed catfish scrapple, hog maw headcheese, creamed corn smut, and smoked tomato powder; house-made venison sausage with mayhaw leather, cider reduction, hothouse basil, and malted vinegar dust; willowbark-smoked duck wings with homegrown rocoto pepper, bluegill bagoong, rutabaga, ramp *jangaiji*, and goat butter.

What we say
Appalachian cuisine steps into the spotlight in this Morgantown standout encamped in the historic Seneca Center, a former glass factory on the National Register of Historical Places. The majority of the ingredients are locally or regionally sourced from small-scale farms, fisheries, and foragers, while nearly every egg comes from owners Alegria and Marion Ohlinger's very own chickens. Local ingredients often translate to familiar fare, but always with a twist, like chilled heirloom tomato soup zinged up with cucumber-ginger salsa or fresh biscuits slicked with warm sweet chili butter. The restaurant boasts nearly zero food waste; anything that can't be reused becomes animal feed or compost.

Via Carota (p. 464)

The Northeast

Connecticut	385
Delaware	389
Maine	391
Massachusetts	399
New Hampshire	413
New Jersey	417
New York	423
Pennslyvania	479
Rhode Island	487
Vermont	491

385

Connecticut

Dining Room at The White Hart

Litchfield

What
The White Hart Inn is a landmarked, historic building dating from 1806

Who
Annie Wayte, chef/partner

When
Breakfast & lunch, daily, dinner Friday & Saturday

Address
15 Under Mountain Road,
Salisbury, Litchfield,
CT 06068

+1 860 435 0030

whitehartinn.com

Bookings
Phone, walk-ins

Price guide

What they say
"A good restaurant does more than offer quality food and beverages - it enhances its local community. Our job is to make our guests feel valued and welcome, regardless of whether they've come in for a beer or an overnight stay. With respect to the food, we start, and occasionally end, with the quality of our ingredients. Our approach to cooking is simple, emphasizing bold, vibrant flavors and mostly free of any need to show off. Of course, the simpler the dish, the harder it is to pull off. Food is about our customers; it's a way of making people happy."

Signature dishes
Local greens with Dijon-shallot vinaigrette and croutons; Moroccan chicken with roasted carrots, orange, and olives; Scotch egg with house-made chorizo and garlicky aïoli.

What others say
"The restaurant alone is worth the trip."

-Jane Beiles, *The New York Times*

What we say
Wild ingredients - including ramps, mushrooms, pine, dandelions, violas, and lambs quarters - foraged by Chef Annie Wayte and her team, along with a waste-nothing, nose-to-tail approach are part of what makes The White Hart Inn's simple yet distinctive cuisine so special. Inn guests mingle with locals in Wayte's chic yet unpretentious Dining Room; her more casual Tap Room; and General Store and Cafe, where locally-roasted coffee, homemade jams, and maple syrup are on offer alongside local vegetables and flowers. Add this thoughtful and interesting destination to your list.

Ore Hill & Swyft

Litchfield

What
A modern tavern serving wood-fired, farm-driven pizzas

Who
Joel Viehland, chef/owner & Audra Viehland, owner

When
Dinner Tuesday, lunch & dinner, Wednesday to Sunday

Address
3 Maple Street, Kent, Litchfield, CT 06757

+1 860 592 0404

orehillandswyft.com

Bookings
Resy.com, website, phone, walk-ins

Price guide

What they say
"Many of the seasonally changing toppings for our pizzas at Swyft come from nearby Rock Cobble Farm, including the milk and cream we use to make the ricotta for our pizzas. Crisped to perfection in a Pavesi oven from Naples, Italy, our pizzas reflect our conviction that simplicity requires the most attention to detail. We are committed to developing practices to move the restaurant towards a zero-waste presence."

Signature dishes
Baby back ribs with *guanciale* XO sauce and Swiss chard *furikake*; Swyft burger with 100 percent grass-fed beef from heritage Randall cattle; pizza with mozzarella stretched in-house.

What we say
In an eighteenth-century post-and-beam house, Chef Joel Viehland - a James Beard semifinalist who formerly manned stoves at Copenhagen's Noma and NYC's Gramercy Tavern - is wowing folks from near and far with his all-in-one pizza and fine dining restaurant.

At Swyft, Neapolitan-style wood-fired pizzas are topped with everything from fresh clams, pancetta, and lemon to asparagus, caper berries, and dried heirloom tomatoes. (The dough is prepared using natural sourdough from a thirty-year-old starter and five artisanal flours.) Viehland's skin-to-seed approach means skins from roasted peppers are dried and ground into a dry rub for pork ribs, and spent kelp and bonito flakes from his dashi are folded into a nettle *furikake* seasoning.

Next door at Ore Hill - coming soon - ingredients like finger limes and yuzu figure into a more refined experience, but one that is equally unpretentious and inviting.

Miya's

New Haven

What
The world's first sustainable sushi restaurant

Who
Yoshiko Lai, Bun Lai, Ted Lai & Mie Lai, chefs

When
Dinner Wednesday to Saturday

Address
68 Howe Street, New Haven, CT 06511

+1 203 777 9760

miyassushi.com

Bookings
Email mlyassushi@gmail.com

Price guide

What they say
"Miya's strives to help make the world a better place through plant-based sushi/sustainable seafood-based sushi/invasive species-based sushi/nutrition-optimized recipes. We use the technique of sushi as a medium to explore what it means to be human. Food creates some of our most powerful memories; it can conjure up images and feelings of country, home, friends, and family. In our recipes, ingredients from disparate cultures are combined, symbolizing what is possible when people of the world live in harmony with one another."

Signature dishes
Sushi Salaam: roasted eggplant, avocado, smoked jalapeño vegan cashew cheese, za'atar; Weeds of Change: medley of sushi made from weeds that are medicinal herbs; Sakura Sashimi: beet-infused frozen lionfish sashimi.

What we say
You won't find freshwater eel, fake crab, or long line-caught tuna on Miya's revolutionary, ever-changing sustainable sushi menu. Instead, Chef Bun Lai channels his commitment to sustainability into exceptionally delicious but paradigm-shifting creations made with destructive invasive species like lionfish, Asian carp, Chesapeake Bay blue catfish, feral pigs, and a plethora of weeds too. Come by with friends and try the family-style dinner, which is the quintessential Miya's experience.

389

Delaware

The Blue Hen

Sussex

What
Beach town eats in a fine dining setting

Who
Chris Bisaha & Joe Baker, owners, & Julia Robinson, chef

When
Dinner, daily

Address
33 Wilmington Avenue, Rehoboth Beach, Sussex, DE 19971

+1 302 278 7842

thebluehenrehoboth.com

Bookings
Phone, walk-ins

Price guide

What they say
"Using fresh, local, sustainable, quality products in all things is our goal. We use seasonal produce from local farms and only fresh and local crabmeat and soft-shell crabs."

Signature dishes
Brined and battered fried chicken with bacon-braised collards, macaroni and cheese, and honey hot sauce; potato gnocchi with spring vegetables, shaved ham, leek cream, and Parmesan cheese; deviled eggs with curried egg yolks, lobster, and chives.

What we say
Chef Julia Robinson defies the sandy-footed beach restaurant stereotype at The Blue Hen, a blue-and-white fine dining establishment just a few blocks from the surf in Rehoboth Beach. Although on the menu you'll find Mid-Atlantic classics like fried soft-shell crab, here served with in-season ramps and pickled chili, this is not a strictly Mid-Atlantic restaurant. Nor is it strictly a seafood restaurant, although you'll find charred octopus and succulent mussels. Rather, this is a restaurant that serves, well, whatever Robinson feels like cooking. That might mean a delicate Wagyu beef crudo awash in yuzu aïoli, or meaty brisket swathed in beet-infused barbecue sauce. Regardless of how you define this spot, a James Beard Foundation semifinalist for best new restaurant in 2018, diners are sure to walk away happy.

391

Maine

Solo Italiano

Portland

What
An authentic Northern Italian restaurant specializing in handmade pastas & homemade plates

Who
Paolo Laboa, chef/owner, Mercedes Laboa, owner & Jesse Bania, wine director/owner

When
Dinner, daily

Address
100 Commercial Street, Portland, ME 04101

+1 207 780 0227

soloitalianorestaurant.com

Bookings
Phone, walk-ins, OpenTable.com

Price guide

What they say
"Using top-quality imported ingredients where necessary, while sourcing the freshest fish from the sea and meat and produce from our local lands, we soulfully aim to offer an Italian experience that lets Maine's ingredients sing."

Signature dishes
Sfoglia di Capesante: Maine celery root with honey and scallops; *Pansotti al Sugo di Noci*: seasonal farm greens and local ricotta stuffed into handmade "pouch" pasta; *Pesce alla Ligure*: locally-caught fish with hydroponic cherry tomatoes, locally-cultivated mushrooms and farm parsnips in winter/spring or new potatoes in summer/fall.

What we say
It's no wonder Paolo Laboa says that Maine, more than anywhere else he has lived outside his native Genoa, Italy, feels most like home. Solo Italiano practically sits on the edge of the sea, in Portland's historic Old Port, and just steps away from the wholesaler he visits every morning to handpick his seafood for the day. Organized from antipasti to secondi, Solo's Ligurian menu changes daily, though Laboa's silky handkerchief pasta, tossed in the bright herbaceous basil pesto that won him the 2008 Genova Pesto Championship, is a mainstay and not to be missed. From crudo to handcrafted pastas and fish and meat mains, Laboa takes inspiration from his hero farm suppliers, cooking with a micro-seasonal and nose-to-tail mindset that produces some of the best Italian cuisine this side of the pond.

Drifters Wife

Portland

What
Serving a new seasonal menu nightly along with an entirely natural wine list

Who
Orenda & Peter Hale, owners & Ben Jackson, chef

When
Dinner Tuesday to Saturday

Address
59 Washington Avenue, Portland, ME 04101

+1 207 805 1336

drifterswife.com

Bookings
Website, walk-ins

Price guide

What they say
"We are passionate about serving real wine; wine that is grown organically (no synthetic chemicals or pesticides), hand-harvested, made with wild yeasts with nothing added except minimal sulfites, if that. The food menu is a true daily snapshot of the world around us, highly seasonal and a reflection of our local environment. The driving inspiration to our cooking is seasonality, which requires us to use plants and animals local to our climate and region as much as possible. For instance, when local diver scallops are in season, they will certainly be on the menu."

Signature dishes
Fiddlehead Ferns with cured Atlantic mackerel, Parmigiano, and breadcrumbs; pork shoulder with celery root, morel cream, and stinging nettles; hake with braised lentils, razor clam salsa verde, aïoli, and *agretti*.

What we say
Seasonality and locality drives the small but studied menu that changes daily at Drifters Wife. Simple-sounding dishes, such as soft shell crab with chickpeas, ramps, and a fried duck egg, remain stamped in your memory long after you've enjoyed them via a combination of perfectly procured ingredients and Chef Ben Jackson's unexpected touches and thoughtful techniques. Paired with his cuisine are is the stunning natural wine selection courtesy of owners Orenda and Peter Hale's, poured by the bottle and glass. Pick up a bottle to take home from their adjacent wine shop, Maine & Loire.

Fore Street

Portland

What
Maine restaurant founded on local, seasonal, sustainable seafoods, meats, wild foods & producers

Who
Dana Street, Victor Leon & Sam Hayward, partners

When
Dinner, daily

Address
288 Fore Street, Portland, ME 04101

+1 207 775 2717

forestreet.biz

Bookings
Phone, OpenTable.com, walk-ins

Price guide

What they say
"Our passion is for seeking out the best raw foods from Maine's fisheries, farms, and forests, and preparing them in ways that bring guests to an appreciation of our state's unique agriculture, food ways, and culture. We are passionate about the integrity, values, and professional growth we strive to instill in our staff. We ask our fishmonger for full information on fishing methods, marine locations, compliance with management requirements, and health of stocks. We avoid purchasing from fisheries where overfishing or unethical practices are known."

Signature dishes
Wood oven-roasted Maine mussels with garlic almond butter; summer flounder filet with ramps and spring herbs; two cuts of Maine farm lamb with asparagus and morels.

What we say
In Sam Hayward's high-ceilinged, brick-walled, wooden beam-clad warehouse space overlooking Portland's historic Old Port district and the glistening wharf beyond, New England's finest seafood, meats, game, and vegetables cook over hardwood and applewood fires. The open kitchen, on view from every copper-top table in the main dining room, sports a wood-burning oven, grill, and turn-spit, where Hayward and his team cook a daily changing menu inspired by bounty collected from four-season farms, woodland foragers, dayboat fishers, shellfish gatherers, and nearby pastures. Hayward, revered as a pioneer of the Portland dining scene, is a master of robust, fuss-free fare. Make reservations ahead, or get to the restaurant at 5pm sharp for a spot on the evening's walk-in wait list.

Tandem Coffee + Bakery

Portland

What
A great little café where the coffee & baked goods share an equal place in the spotlight

Who
Will & Kathleen Pratt, owners, & Briana Holt, baker

When
Breakfast & lunch, daily

Address
742 Congress Street, Portland, ME 04102

+1 207 805 1887

tandemcoffee.com

Bookings
Walk-ins

Price guide

What they say
"While we may sell great coffee (roasted by us) and amazing baked goods (made by us), it's the overall experience of the place that we think is our most important product. We are passionate about our vibe and our community. The first line in our company mission is 'Tandem is a community of family and friends '. We hope that this is felt by employees, customers, tourists, and any other person who walks through our doors."

Signature dishes
Rhubarb hibiscus pie; loaded buttermilk biscuit with house-made jam; maple-parsnip scone with brown butter-maple glaze.

What others say
"At the heart of it is pastry genius Briana Holt's altar of sweets: thick slices of moist chocolate-malt cake, insane coconut-almond cream pie, and flaky-beyond-belief biscuits, slathered with butter and jam. They're sweet, they're salty, they're everything. Even a little cute."

–Peter Frank Edwards, *bon appétit*

What we say
Personality and charm. Warmth and welcome. A super hip, former gas station vibe, with expert baristas prepping superlative house-roasted coffees and spinning everything from Link Wray to Bach. Go for pastry goddess Briana Holt's irresistibly decadent and creative spins on classic home-baked goods. Stay for sumptuous lunchtime sandwiches. The house-made almond milk (sweetened with dates) and turmeric oatmeal with coconut milk and cacao nibs are loved by insiders, young and old. And the "coffee + vinyl" subscription might just be the coolest gift ever.

Nīna June

Knox

What
A restaurant on the coast of Maine serving Mediterranean food with local ingredients

Who
Sara Jenkins, chef/owner

When
Dinner, Tuesday to Saturday

Address
24 Central Street, Rockport, Knox, ME 04856

+1 207 236 8880

ninajunerestaurant.com

Bookings
Phone, walk-ins, or OpenTable.com

Price guide

What they say
"My menu changes a little every day to reflect the ever-varying seasonal range of local ingredients. I don't manipulate ingredients much and am just as likely to serve a perfect piece of fruit for dessert as anything else. I am a firm supporter of ROC United and prominently display the poster advocating for room at the table for everyone. I have a hole in my heart over Syria and, both here and at my NYC restaurant, have put on dinners to benefit and bring awareness to the situation."

Signature dishes
Mixed local green salad with ingredients that change nightly; pasta *chitarra* with lemon butter and Maine crabmeat; pork Milanese with local micro-greens.

What we say
At this Mediterranean-style trattoria overlooking picturesque Rockport harbor, Sara Jenkins turns an expertly curated selection of local and artisanal ingredients into gorgeous simple dishes that are at once familiar and unique. A Roman-style soup might feature rich, nutty chickpeas from a small Italian artisan producer, while a plate of beets, celery, and lovage with a yogurt dressing is composed of vegetables and dairy from farms merely minutes away. Local beer, produced with local grains, along with Maine-made vodka, rum, and gin complement a beautiful wine list that includes many naturally produced offerings. Jenkins' off-season cooking classes, and cookbooks, *Olives and Oranges* and *The Four Seasons of Pasta*, allow you to take a bit of the experience home.

Nebo Lodge

Knox

What
Nebo Lodge is a farm-to-table restaurant & inn located on North Haven island in Maine

Who
Chellie Pingree, owner & Amanda Hallowell, chef

When
Hours change seasonally

Address
11 Mullins Lane, North Haven, Knox, ME 04853

+1 207 867 2007

nebolodge.com

Bookings
Walk-ins, phone, email
info@nebolodge.com

Price guide

What they say
"Our menu is based entirely on what is available locally - mostly on the island itself, from island fishermen, and mainly at our farm - and we are unafraid to run out of a menu item or change the menu daily to maintain our core value of eating what is grown and raised on our doorstep. We have always prized 'ugly' vegetables and try as often as possible to show them in their natural states. We will turn arugula with holey leaves into pesto - or even serve it and explain to our diners that that is what local, organic greens sometimes look like."

Signature dishes
Fried green tomatoes with chive dressing; spicy pork belly banh mi with quick pickles, smoked sea salt butter, and sriracha; fresh herb and edible flower salad with champagne vinaigrette.

What we say
At a rambling nine-room inn on Penobscot Bay, Chef Amanda Hallowell serves stunningly simple yet fine-tuned fare. Dinners - at both the inn and family-style barn suppers at Nebo's sister property, Turner Farm - are rustic feasts replete with ingredient-driven dishes that tell the story of the season and the island's "makers". Whether tender greens with fresh cheese and many herbs, or a local line-caught fish with a simply flavored mayonnaise and lemon, everything is alive with flavor, prepared and served with exceptional skill along with warmth, grace, respect, and care.

Primo

Knox

What
Farmhouse restaurant on five acres with two greenhouses, extensive gardens, livestock & bees

Who
Melissa Kelly, chef/owner

When
Dinner Wednesday to Monday, hours change seasonally

Address
2 Main Street, Rockland, ME 04841

+1 207 596 0770

primorestaurant.com

Bookings
Website, Reserve.com

Price guide

What they say
"Farm-fresh organic food, made by hand and wood-fired is our passion. Our eggs, vegetables, and meat are all raised on our property, and we supplement with ingredients from other local small businesses and farms. Our family atmosphere is warm, friendly, and proud. We have a serious recycling program at Primo; it is a full-circle kitchen. Any food waste is recycled to our pigs and chickens. We dehydrate, can, and pickle our garden's bounty."

Signature dishes
Farmer Salad: backyard egg, house bacon, lemon Parmesan dressing; whey-brined pork chop; rhubarb *crostata*, buttermilk gelato.

What others say
Winner: Melissa Kelly, Best Chefs in America Northeast.

James Beard Foundation

What we say
In an old Victorian house on a hill in mid-coast Maine, Chef Melissa Kelly tends to extensive vegetable gardens and raises pigs, bees, ducks, and chickens that help supply her kitchen with many of the exquisite ingredients she uses to turn out her equally exquisite fare. Reserve ahead for The Parlor Room, where crisp-fried chicken livers, local apple salads, homemade pastas, and wood-fired fish and grass-fed meats sparkle alongside stunning ocean and farm views. Start with a seasonal cocktail that changes with the gardens' offerings. And don't miss the house-made charcuterie, which "rivals any in the US" according to *bon appétit*.

The Lost Kitchen

Waldo

What
Farm-to-table restaurant located in a historic grist mill

Who
Erin French, chef/owner

When
Dinner Wednesday to Saturday

Address
22 Mill Street, Freedom, Waldo, ME 04941

+1 207 382 3333

findthelostkitchen.com

Bookings
Walk-ins

Price guide

What they say
"We insist on letting the ingredients of the season write the menu. Our produce comes from a tight radius. There is nothing more heartwarming then having one of our servers come to your table with a prepared platter of food that she grew from seed, helped prepare in the kitchen, and served on a plate, to then have the satisfaction of watching the fruits of her labor be enjoyed. For us, this is full-circle feeding. You cannot make good food without good ingredients."

What others say
"The restaurant has turned tiny Freedom ... into an unlikely dining destination ... People come from nearby Winslow and Waterville, but also from every time zone, to eat here."

–Devra First, *The Boston Globe*

What we say
In a hydropower grist mill in the tiny rural town of Freedom, Maine, lies The Lost Kitchen, a restaurant that takes reservations by postcard only, which Erin French proudly says, "keeps our dying post office in our tiny community relevant and open." French is also proud to employ local farmers, who not only supply her with exquisite heirloom produce, but often work second shifts at the restaurant, where stress is low and wages are fair. Her hyper-seasonal cooking is straightforward, yet nuanced, welcoming and extremely personal. Think chilled golden beet and buttermilk soup in summer, or black sea bass with summer beans and bee balm bread salad.

399

Massachusetts

Cultivar

Boston

What
Hyper-seasonal restaurant inspired by our diverse New England landscape

Who
Mary Dumont chef/co-owner & Emily French Dumont, co-owner

When
Lunch & dinner, daily, weekend brunch

Address
1 Court Street, Boston, MA 02108

+1 617 979 8203

cultivarboston.com

Bookings
OpenTable.com

Price guide

What they say
"In the community of chefs, we utilize referrals and share sources with young chefs coming up to keep the cycle going. There are no good secrets out there. Sharing is the only way to preserve the stories of our purveyors. We choose only traceable seafood, often from fishermen that deliver their catch themselves. We also promote education for our staff and fundraising for sustainable organizations that are both local and nationally recognised."

Signature dishes
Squid ink with Calabrian chili and foraged sea beans; chicken with yakitori-grilled vegetables and heirloom grains; rooibos tea-marinated duck breast with quinoa, sugar snap peas, braised radish, and lemon verbena.

What we say
In acclaimed Chef Mary Dumont's upscale yet earthy space, nature and culture align. Chandeliers resemble tree branches; a Japanese *kokedama* garden hangs from the ceiling; and tender salad greens, vibrant fresh herbs, and edible flowers come from Dumont's onsite hydroponic farm – a shipping container-turned-indoor garden that produces vegetables year-round, utilizing less than five gallons of water per day.

Dumont's ingredient-driven new American menu celebrates wild seasonal gems, such as ramps, stinging nettles, and favas; highlights ancient grains, like einkorn and rye; and thoughtfully makes use of punchy flavors, like XO sauce, smoked olive oil, and *verjus*. Driven by an insatiable curiosity, Dumont lives by Andy Warhol's quote, "the world fascinates me", a sentiment that is clearly reflected in her gorgeous cuisine and the sensitivity that drives her business choices.

Island Creek Oyster Bar

Boston

What
An iconic oyster bar where seafood unites farmer, chef & diner

Who
Jeremy Sewall, chef/owner

When
Dinner, daily, weekend lunch

Address
500 Commonwealth Avenue, Boston, MA, 02215, plus other locations - see website

+1 617 532 5300

islandcreekoysterbar.com

Bookings
OpenTable.com

Price guide

What they say
"We strive to provide the highest-quality farmed oysters to consumers and acclaimed chefs alike, with an emphasis on education around sustainable aquaculture practices. Simple seafood is our main passion. We print our menu on the day based on what is caught locally; we buy our lobsters from Maine and visit the fish pier daily to find what is best. Having Island Creek Oyster as a partner gives us access to the freshest oysters that you can get."

Signature dishes
Lobster roe noodles; monkfish schnitzel with mustard spätzle, bacon, and brown butter cauliflower.

What others say
"Three reasons Island Creek Oyster Bar [was] an early hit: It has a big space that's fun to be in, a restaurateur who knows how to make a lot of people happy even when the place is packed, and a chef who knows both how to get good fish and how to best show off its flavor."

-Corby Kummer, *Boston* magazine

What we say
Go for the oysters - regional stars from Duxbury, Massachusetts to Muscongus Bay, Maine, Charlestown, Rhode Island, and more, share the spotlight - stay for the daily fish selections and infamous lobster roe noodles, tossed with grilled lobster, braised short rib, oyster mushrooms and pecorino. Whatever you choose from Chef Jeremy Sewall's gorgeously crafted menu, you can't go wrong. Seafood-focused offerings are balanced with vibrant salads and vegetable-forward sides. Pair oysters with a regional beer; a cheekily crafted cocktail, bubbles by the bottle or glass, or a hand-selected spirit, served by the ounce.

Saloniki Greek Restaurant

Boston

What
A Greek sandwich shop serving pitas, plates & salads from a local, scratch kitchen

Who
Jody Adams, Eric Papachristos, & Jon Mendez, partners

When
Lunch & dinner, daily

Address
181 Massachusetts Avenue, Cambridge, MA 02139, plus other locations - see website

+1 617 266 0001

salonikigreek.com

Bookings
Walk-ins

Price guide

What they say
"We started Saloniki so that everyone could taste the flavors of Greece in a fun, energetic atmosphere. We want to source the best possible ingredients and, staying solely in the Greek flavor profile, cook the best possible food we can. We are proud of the care and attention with which we treat our food, starting with sourcing locally through vendors and purveyors we know and trust, so that we can offer the highest quality food in a very casual setting. We also strive to empower people in our community by offering a career path without extensive prior experience."

Signature dishes
"The Herc": braised honey-garlic Maine pork shoulder with spicy whipped feta, secret sauce, greens, tomato, onion, Greek fries, spicy slaw, and fresh herbs on a just-made pita; zucchini feta fritters; baked-to-order pita.

What we say
Jody Adams - who has long garnered national star status in the fine dining arena - co-launched Saloniki Greek as a platform to express the bold, bright flavors of Greece at an accessible price point, and to much applause. The James Beard Award-winner brings a health-conscious mindset to Greek street food with a menu of brown rice bowls and salads that are customizable with proteins like spicy lamb meatballs or honey-braised pork shoulder. Best of all, there's no extra sugar or oil added. Do stay for dessert, though - sweets include fried-to-order *loukoumades*, Greek yogurt with jammy toppings, and, of course, house-made Greek cookies.

Superfine Food

Essex

What
A relaxed joint serving crave-able comforts upgraded with the best ingredients

Who
Matthew Gaudet, chef/partner

When
Lunch & dinner, Tuesday to Sunday

Address
25 Union Street, Manchester-by-the-Sea, Essex, MA 01944, plus other locations - see website

+1 978 526 0964

superfinefood.com

Bookings
Walk-ins

Price guide

What they say
"Our motto is: common food done uncommonly well. Our dishes are crave-able and delicious counterpoints to common American fast food, and are at once indulgent and health-conscious."

Signature dishes
Fonzarelli pizza with asparagus, pecorino, sunny egg, and preserved lemon; vegan tahini caesar with tofu, spicy broccoli, cucumbers, carrots, pears, lemon tahini, and pistachios; fried chicken sandwich with miso slaw, bread and butter pickles, and white barbecue sauce.

What others say
"Gaudet's first cooking job was at Chez Henri and it was there, he says, that he learned how a griddle could get the outside crunch and inside 'melty cheese thing.' The Reuben is fabulous."

-Sheryl Julian, *The Boston Globe*

What we say
At Superfine Food, the menus are familiar at first glance - pizzas, salads, crispy chicken sandwiches, and the like. A deeper look quickly reveals these old standbys are tweaked by a chef with a deft hand, who knows a thing or two about using robust, bright, and healthful ingredients to make what's old new again, and irresistibly so. Pizzas, topped with vegetables like roasted kale and fresh asparagus, along with local cheese and meats, are made with a slow-fermented dough and cooked, as Chef Matthew Gaudet says, "till the bottom has a perfect leopard print, no blond spots, and stays horizontal when you hold it up". Salads are vibrant and savvily dressed. Fun sweets include dessert cups - s'mores, sundae, or seasonal fruit - milkshakes, and more.

The Kirkland Tap & Trotter

Middlesex

What
Award-winning chef meets monster wood-fire grill & fires up... everything!

Who
Tony Maws, chef/owner

When
Dinner, daily, brunch Sunday

Address
425 Washington Street, Somerville, Middlesex, MA 02143

+1 857 259 6585

kirklandtapandtrotter.com

Bookings
Phone, website

Price guide

What they say
"We're a 'go-to' neighborhood restaurant serving really tasty locally sourced food prepared with love and passion on our monster wood-fired grill. If local tomatoes aren't in season, we don't serve them, even on our burger. This initially created angst for guests and media, but now people understand what we're doing and maybe, just maybe, think twice before using out-of-season tomatoes at home!"

Signature dishes
Grilled local asparagus with anchovy vinaigrette; grilled swordfish with ramp salsa verde and *freekeh* tabbouleh; smoked mackerel salad with pea greens, radishes, and labneh.

What we say
Tony Maws landed top nods from the James Beard Foundation, *Food & Wine*, and more with his first restaurant, Craigie on Main, where his dishes reflected a French-inspired refined rusticity and nose-to-tail style. At The Kirkland Tap & Trotter, the fare is more relaxed, with robust flavors that showcase Maws' interest in global cuisine. Fried chicken wings are showered with green chilies and pepitas; the chicken is *chermoula*-spiced; and a harissa aïoli accompanies a tasty lamb burger. Alongside classic cocktails are KT&T conflations like The Uncle Monty (Pimm's No. 1, Montenegro, orange, lemon and a Scotch rinse), and a great beer list featuring local and regional offerings. At brunch, beet hummus, *labneh*, celery-root tabbouleh, and rye toast make up Maws' Israeli meze plate, and a KT&T corned beef hash is topped with a fried egg and spicy kimchi. Order a side of grilled pork belly for the table.

The Market Restaurant

Essex

What
Seasonal restaurant with daily-changing menu based on the best that local farms & fishermen provide

Who
Nico & Amelia Monday, chefs/owners

When
Dinner Wednesday to Monday, weekend brunch, hours change seasonally

Address
33 River Road, Gloucester, Essex, MA 01930

+1 978 282 0700

themarketrestaurant.com

Bookings
Phone, website, Resy.com

Price guide

What they say
"We are most passionate about creating a sense of place and community through our restaurant, and sharing healthy, vibrant, and delicious meals with our guests. Our farmers grow such beautiful produce; we love to let the ingredients speak for themselves. Every time we write the menu, we're constantly assessing how to make the best of each and every ingredient, whether it's using all parts of an animal, or making use of the less 'pretty' ingredients."

Signature dishes
Heirloom and cherry tomato salad with Romano beans, fresh herbs, and red wine vinaigrette; handmade ricotta ravioli with green garlic *brodo*, cherry tomatoes, and Parmesan; gently cooked halibut with seasonal accompaniments.

What we say
Nico and Amelia Monday met as cooks at Alice Waters' Chez Panisse, before getting hitched and returning to Amelia's seaside childhood stomping grounds of Gloucester, Massachusetts, to open two dream restaurants of their own. At The Market, daily dinner and brunch menus reflect the bounty of local produce, meat, fish, and cheeses, with local shellfish (including lobster, clams, mussels, and oysters) heavily featured. Linger over a simple plate of fresh oysters with mignonette and lemon, or a chilled lobster and grapefruit salad with endive, pickled shallots, and a crème fraîche dressing, while you watch the burning colors of a streaking sunset over the glimmering waters of Lobster Cove, where the restaurant hovers over the water on stilt-like pilings. The dynamic wine list offers organic, biodynamic, and natural selections.

Oleana

Middlesex

What
Fresh ingredients, homegrown vegetables, flavorful spices with an emphasis on Turkish cuisine

Who
Ana Sortun, executive chef/co-owner

When
Dinner, daily

Address
134 Hampshire Street, Cambridge, Middlesex, MA 02139

+1 617 661 0505

oleanarestaurant.com

Bookings
Reserve.com

Price guide

What they say
"We represent the Mediterranean diet, creating rich flavors from spices and vegetables without a lot of heavy fats, like butter and cream. We have a lot of vegetarian options on offer. We adore the flavors of the eastern Mediterranean and have helped bring them to the mainstream. We use as much of our own produce as possible, grown on Siena Farms which owner Ana Sortun's husband owns."

Signature dishes
Fatteh: caramelized onion with romanesco, crispy mushrooms, pine nuts and yogurt; baked shells with nettles, green garlic butter, yogurt and poppy seed; char with spring-dug parsnip, currants, pine nuts, and sorrel labneh.

What we say
Ana Sortun has been a pioneer in both farm-to-table cookery and the celebration of Middle Eastern and Turkish cuisine for over two decades. Her vivid flavors, aromatic spices, and commitment to the freshest ingredients - many straight from her own family farm and others nearby - have made Oleana a front runner in the Boston food scene. The menu dazzles with twenty meze to choose from - think spinach falafel with tahini sauce, beet yogurt, and cress, or a lamb and grape leaf tart with cumin, orange, orzo, and spicy feta - and equally enticing main dishes. For dessert, don't miss the pine nut *sarma*, with cocoa halva butter, date ice cream, and chocolate breadcrumbs.

Mezze Bistro + Bar

Williamstown

What
Contemporary seasonal American cuisine supporting independent farmers using sustainable practices

Who
Nancy Thomas, founder/proprietor

When
Dinner, daily

Address
777 Cold Spring Road, Williamstown, MA 01267

+1 413 458 0123

mezzebistro.com

Bookings
Phone, OpenTable.com

Price guide

What they say
"We are so fortunate to live in a region that respects the land, honors the importance of agriculture, and supports the talented and hard-working people who produce our food. The ingredients that are made available to us are nothing short of inspiring. Most of all, the building of strong relationships with our farmers and food makers, our team, and our guests is what makes us get up and go to work every day. Our kitchen team's foraging efforts keep sustainability as a top priority. We realize that we need to leave certain elements behind in order for those delicious wildcrafted foods to be there again the following year."

Signature dishes
Young Asian salad greens with brown rice miso vinaigrette; hen of the woods mushrooms with spring parsnip purée, confit pigtails, and egg yolk; New Bedford scallops with native corn, leeks, and chanterelles.

What we say
In a sustainably renovated nineteenth-century building overlooking Sheep Hill in historic Williamstown, Massachusetts, proprietor Nancy Thomas, Chef Nick Moulton, and team serve a welcoming menu of contemporary bistro fare that reflects the four seasons, the ever-changing bounty of local Berkshire produce, and Mezze's own kitchen garden and wild foraging efforts. Vegetables are a springboard for almost every dish on the menu, and are especially highlighted in small dishes, like raw asparagus with hazelnuts, crowdie, and Calabrian chili. Seasonal gems, like strawberries from The Berry Patch, might star in a chilled soup with radish tops and farm-fresh yogurt.

deadhorse hill

Worcester

What
American seasonal restaurant featuring local produce & outstanding coffee

Who
Jared Forman, chef/owner

When
Lunch & dinner, Tuesday to Sunday, weekend breakfast, lunch Monday

Address
281 Main Street, Worcester, MA 01608

+1 774 420 7107

deadhorsehill.com

Bookings
Email
jared@deadhorsehill.com

Price guide

What they say
"We want to take the intimate connection we have with the people that grow, raise, and make the food we prepare, and share that local tale with our guests. We pride ourselves in sourcing the most beautiful products from local farms run by people who have become our friends. We take those products and respect them and treat them with care."

Signature dishes
Spaghetti and ramp *aglio e olio*, with pecorino and house-dried local chilies; Chimney Hill Farm *porchetta* with Chinese chives, kumquats, smoked soy sauce, and dried Hachiya persimmons.

What others say
"Forman's dishes were a blissful matrimony of taste, texture and presentation - his Fluke Crudo serving as a prime example. The crudo lined one half of a small porcelain bowl in an arc of flesh and petals to form a bohemian flower crown fit for the likes of Frida Kahlo or a neo-hippie festival girl."

-Sanrda Rain, *Worcester Magazine*

What we say
With an adventurous but studied hand, Jared Forman and his team turn local bounty into sumptuous, accessible, season-driven dishes that make choosing from his menu a welcome torture. Small plates dress shellfish from local waters with umami-forward flavors, and the rest of the land and sea menu follows suit. By day, deadhorse hill serves "plates", salads, and sandwiches stacked with goodies like fried green tomatoes, pistachio pesto, and fresh mozzarella. Not to be missed.

Woods Hill Table

Middlesex

What
Pasture-to-plate restaurant featuring modern American cuisine

Who
Charlie Foster, chef,
Jason Doo, manager &
Kristin Canty, owner

When
Dinner Tuesday to Saturday, brunch Saturday

Address
24 Commonwealth Avenue,
Concord, Middlesex,
MA 01742

+1 978 254 1435

woodshilltable.com

Bookings
Website, Reserve.com

Price guide

What they say
"By investing in raising our own animals and supporting local farmers and fisheries, we create a framework for what we are serving, and we are constantly striving to communicate that story to our guests. By focusing on seasonality, sustainability, and supporting local economies, we know what products are right to use at a given time, and this frees us to focus on creatively utilizing those ingredients and showcasing their inherent beauty. To offset the energy required to maintain and run both a functional farm and full-service restaurant, we've installed banks of solar panels that help power both facilities."

Signature dishes
Crisp pork belly confit with Island Creek oysters and poached in prosciutto consommé; chicken breast roulade with maple-glazed thigh confit, buttermilk, and spring legumes; seventy-two-hour smoked beef brisket with sunny-side-up quail eggs, tallow-fried wholewheat spaetzle, and ramps.

What we say
Kristin Canty is not just a farm and restaurant owner, she's also a filmmaker, known for the much-lauded documentary *Farmageddon*. At Woods Hill Table - awarded three stars for three years running by the Sustainable Restaurant Association and best overall restaurant finalist 2017 - cattle are 100 percent grass-fed, legumes and grains are soaked for easier digestion, and cheeses are local and raw.

Chef Charlie Foster's beautifully crafted modern American fare is cooked with healthy fats: organic sunflower oil, olive oil, grass-fed, organic butter, and tallow. Even desserts - think spring-dug parsnip cheesecake with oat crumble, mint, and pineapple sorbet - are thoughtfully delicious seasonal celebrations.

413

New Hampshire

Black Trumpet

Portsmouth

What
A restaurant & wine bar located in a historic building overlooking Portsmouth Harbor

Who
Evan Mallett, chef/owner

When
Dinner, daily

Address
29 Ceres Street, Portsmouth, NH 03801

+1 603 431 0887

blacktrumpetbistro.com

Bookings
Website, OpenTable.com, Reserve.com

Price guide

What they say
"Our passion for the bounty of local food, coupled with the knowledge that our servers bring to the table, makes us unique in the arena of farm-to-table restaurants. It is a vital part of our mission that our guests receive not only a great dining experience but also, if they seek it, education about all the food sources we hold sacred. A local farmer and I co-founded a company called Abundance that makes soup out of farm waste - blemished and unmarketable produce that would otherwise go to the compost pile. The mission is simple: to bridge the gap between organic agricultural surplus and the food insecurity in our region."

Signature dishes
Braised spring dug parsnips with lamb *salpicon* and chard; mountain paella with Maine rabbit, snails, chicken meatballs, peppers, leeks, and mushrooms; rhubarb oat crisp with honey crème fraîche.

What we say
With a studied global influence, a humble intelligence, and extreme care, Chef Evan Mallett and his team offer an extraordinary dining experience that defines modern coastal New England cuisine. Local vegetables - many grown in Mallett's heirloom teaching garden - and day-boat fish, fresh from local Maine waters, where Mallett sources all of his catch, are seasoned with a palette of flavors that ranges from Morocco and Mexico to India and beyond. Views of the majestic Piscataqua River, among the many points of pride in this historic seacoast city, are as enchanting as the meal itself.

Franklin Oyster House

Portsmouth

What
Modern local oyster house with full menu & bar

Who
Matt Louis, chef/owner

When
Dinner, daily

Address
148 Fleet Street, Portsmouth, NH 03801

+1 603 373 8500

franklinrestaurant.com

Bookings
Website

Price guide

What they say
"Celebrating the local New Hampshire oyster farmers and community is our passion. New Hampshire oysters are still not well-known. We are helping to get the word out that they are delicious, sustainable, and right in our own backyard. We get most of our fish through a program called, New England Fishmongers. It arrives just hours after being caught and everything is caught by rod and reel only, which is rarely done these days. We recycle 100 percent of our oyster shells through the Coastal Conservation Association, where the shells are put through a composting process, then added back to Great Bay to help fuel a healthy ecosystem and promote future oyster growth."

Signature dishes
Oysters on toast with whipped pork belly and sambal mayo; fish tacos with cilantro, lime, and house-made queso; chicken ramen with invasive green crabs and house-made rye noodles and kimchi.

What we say
Raw oysters, served in their purest form, get top billing on Chef Matt Louis' menu, each one listed with its point of origin and distance from the restaurant. Louis and his team are intent on making sure their guests feel welcome and have a great time. For those who don't do bivalves, there are easy-going dishes like fish tacos, ramen, and fried rice with fresh crab, shrimp, smoked mussels, and grapefruit *nuoc cham*. Pull up a beer, a glass of wine, or one of Franklin's ingenious cocktails, and enjoy.

Moxy

Portsmouth

What
Modern American tapas restaurant with a focus on the history, culture & foodstuffs of the region

Who
Matt Louis, chef/owner

When
Dinner, daily

Address
106 Penhallow Street, Portsmouth, NH 03801

+1 603 319 8178

moxyrestaurant.com

Bookings
Website, Reserve.com

Price guide

What they say
"Our motto is: if it doesn't grow here naturally, we don't use it. We have our own farm that, during the season, eighty percent of our produce comes from, and we are out working on it and harvesting ourselves. Rabbits, pigs, goats, and lambs are sourced direct from local farms, and our seafood is all locally caught and mostly underused species. We are focused on education efforts and make a point to get staff involved in sustainability-based projects, such as whole animal butchery."

Signature dishes
Hasty pudding *frites*; "Something to Snack On": crispy kale chip and seedy savory granola mix; "New England Dinner 2.0": corned beef brisket with napa cabbage, crispy potatoes, maple mustard, and pickled root vegetables.

What we say
Matt Louis has won many awards and been a James Beard Foundation Best Chef Northeast finalist for multiple years. He and his team turn out inventive modern tapas: plates built for sharing, using hyper-local ingredients with a nod to traditional New England flavors.

Try a dish of crispy Rhode Island calamari with piccalilli before diving into lacquered pork belly bites with radish and pickled rhubarb. Add a side of *patatas* Portsmouth with spicy tomato and herbed sour cream, and perhaps a Portsmouth rarebit, with anadama bread, beer cheese sauce, caramelized onions, apple, and pickled beets. Drinks include a wide array of lively cocktails, a mostly local beer list, and terrific wines from the region and beyond.

Vida Cantina

Portsmouth

What
Restaurant celebrating modern Mexican cuisine using adventurous flavors & local ingredients

Who
David Vargas, chef/owner

When
Dinner, daily, lunch Friday to Sunday

Address
2456 Lafayette Road, Portsmouth, NH 03801

+1 603 501 0648

vidacantinanh.com

Bookings
Reserve.com

Price guide

What they say
"We bring a Mexican heritage and appreciation for local seasonal New England product to every plate. As an entire staff, we are participating in a seacoast commute smart program that encourages us to cut down on fuel emissions by carpooling, using public transportation, or biking to work."

Signature dishes
Tacos; vegan jackfruit "*carnitas*"; steak *plato* (steak cooked sous vide for two days and served with avocado radish salsa, Ibarra *mole* powder, and *epazote* brown butter).

What we say
What was once a Friendly's is now David Vargas's colorful modern cantina, where local ingredients are used to make fresh, boldly flavored Mexican fare. The tortillas for double-wrapped tacos are especially good, made with locally grown flint corn that Vargas and his staff mill by hand. Tucked inside those tacos you might find tasty cubes of pork belly confit topped with Cotija cheese and a spicy mango habanero salsa, or mezcal-battered fried fish with Vargas's Baja slaw. Vegan, vegetarian, and gluten and dairy-free options are plenty. Cocktails lean heavily to tequila and mezcal-based offerings, dressed up with showy flavors that make choosing a challenge. Try El Matador: mezcal with sweet vermouth, grapefruit shrub, and lemon, or the Smoke Show: blend of mezcal, fresh chilies, and Cointreau with a chili-salt rim.

Stages at One Washington

Strafford

What
Nine-seat kitchen table restaurant serving progressive New England cuisine

Who
Evan Hennessey, chef/owner

When
Dinner Wednesday to Saturday

Address
1 Washington Street #325, Dover, Strafford, NH 03820

+1 603 842 4077

stages-dining.com

Bookings
Website, OpenTable.com

Price guide

What they say
"We serve a constantly evolving tasting menu of ten to twelve courses that consists of ingredients from the farm and from our walks outdoors. Our menu reflects what we feel best represents New Hampshire right now. We source rod and reel-caught fish from one fishing vessel, of which we know the captain very well. If they can't fish due to weather, then we don't serve fish until they can."

Signature dishes
Cabbage with cow's heart and dashi; mushrooms and mint; carrots with coffee and duck egg.

What we say
At this tiny nine-seater, you'll experience a ten to twelve-course tasting menu that changes nightly. Clues, loosely describing each dish, are offered on a "menu", which is more like a roadmap you'll follow along as you leave yourself in the artful, capable hands of Chef Evan Hennessey and his crew. A simple-sounding dish, called mushrooms and mint, is a complex yet nuanced creation of foraged juniper wood-smoked mushrooms, briefly cooked with yogurt whey and cabbage juice and seasoned with fresh house-grown mint. A dried mushroom and pine needle broth provides the finishing touch.

If you're lucky enough to land a seat at the bar, you can watch as the chef and his team stage each course, using induction burners, immersion circulators, electric ovens, and one coal/wood-based yakitori grill. Dishes are inspired by the local ingredients available that day, responsibly foraged in the wild and procured from nearby farms and fisherfolk.

417

New Jersey

Brick Farm Tavern

Mercer

What
We focus on terroir & being as sustainable as possible in our "closed loop system"

Who
Max Hosey, executive chef, Jon & Robin McConaughy, owners

When
Dinner Wednesday to Sunday, lunch Friday to Sunday

Address
130 Hopewell Rocky Hill Road, Hopewell, Mercer, NJ 08525

+1 609 333 9200

brickfarmtavern.com

Bookings
Email reservations@brickfarmgroup.com, Tock.com

Price guide

What they say
"At Brick Farm Tavern, we use only animals from our own farm. We also use our own produce first, then outsource from about thirty other local farms that fall within fifty miles of the restaurant so there is no commercial produce coming into the restaurant. You are getting true terroir."

Signature dishes
"Dry land caviar": rye berries with duck confit, fiddleheads, and preserved blackberries; Devon beef tartare with Atlantic seaweed, sea bean, soy shiitake, carrot, and puffed rice.

What others say
"If you care about each aspect of your food - its origin, how it is prepared and where you eat it - Brick Farm Tavern will serve you well."

-Cody Kendall, *NJ.com*

What we say
Brick Farm Tavern goes well beyond the *de rigueur* of farm-to-table dining, doing what many thought couldn't be done in New Jersey. The restaurant runs its own farming operation and all meat served is homegrown. That means the menu changes nightly as whole animals are used up nose-to-tail in flavorful and sometimes unconventional ways by Chef Greg Vassos and his team. There is beef tallow in the fryers - not the refined commercial cooking oil found in even the highest-end restaurants - and solar panels planted strategically around the property. Even during the challenging long winters, when little to nothing grows, the kitchen makes inspired use of root vegetables and all that they preserved at the height of the growing season.

The Farm & Fisherman Tavern

Camden

What
Neighborhood tavern providing sustainable cuisine to the community in a family friendly environment

Who
Josh Lawler & Todd Fuller, chefs/owners

When
Lunch & dinner, daily

Address
1442 Marlton Pike East, Cherry Hill, NJ 08034

+1 856 356 2286

fandftavern.com

Bookings
Phone, OpenTable.com

Price guide

What they say
"We are passionate about the community. This includes our guests who choose to dine with us, our purveyors who have the same sustainable philosophy as us, and our staff and their families who make everything possible. We strive for our food to be accessible, communal, and seasonal. We have always committed to using local farmers, brewers, and distillers."

Signature dishes
Bloody beet salad with yogurt, pistachio, greens, and pan drippings; bread and spreads with smoky hummus, *romesco*, chickpea fries, pickles, and puffed pita.

What others say
"Something special is definitely happening in this restaurant ... They've taken the principles of an approach more common with modern fine dining - scratch cooking, quality local ingredients, micro-seasonality - and creatively reapplied them for the masses."

-Craig Laban, *The Philidelphia Inquirer*

What we say
A strip mall is the last place you'd expect to find a former chef from Dan Barber's famous Blue Hill at Stone Barns, but that's exactly where chef Josh Lawlor has chosen to ply his craft. His dream: taking the kind of local food he worked with at Blue Hill and making it accessible to everyone. His restaurant is a laid-back place where diners enjoy beers and burgers. It just so happens the beer is brewed nearby and the meat is grass-fed and local, too. Though the commitment to ethical food values runs deep, The Farm & Fisherman has a light touch in messaging, letting the food experience speak for itself.

Agricola

Mercer

What
A community eatery that is fresh, down to earth & full of flavor

Who
Jim Nawn, owner

When
Lunch & dinner, daily, weekend brunch

Address
11 Witherspoon Street, Princeton, Mercer, NJ 08540

+1 609 921 2798

agricolaeatery.com

Bookings
Phone, walk-ins

Price guide

What they say
"Seventy-five percent of our menu is sourced within a hundred miles. There is nothing we enjoy more than gathering old friends and new around a big table and serving up a carefully crafted meal. Using fresh local ingredients from our very own Great Road Farm as well as from other neighboring providers, we serve food that brings people together to laugh, share, and celebrate."

Signature dishes
Griggstown Farm roast chicken; maitake mushrooms with grits.

What others say
"When the restaurant opened, longtime Princetonians showed up, likely skeptical. Once they came, however, they kept coming. The buzz has never stopped and big city newspapers have written glowing reviews."

-Rich Fisher, *centraljersey.com*

What we say
"Agricola" is the Latin word for farmer, and the team at this restaurant takes much inspiration from owner Jim Nawn's own farm and the New Jersey growers whose products help make the food here so distinct.

In fact, the restaurant goes beyond the notion of seasonality by talking with their farmers at the time crops are planted so chefs can craft the menu based on what will be coming from the fields. This awareness of the labor that goes into growing food makes the kitchen vigilant about avoiding food waste, saving scraps for stock-making and coming up with creative ways to make typically disposable odds and ends taste delicious. Anything that cannot be repurposed becomes compost to enrich the local soil that produces so many of Agricola's ingredients.

Elements

Mercer

What
Interpretive American cuisine

Who
Steve Distler, owner & Scott Anderson, chef/owner

When
Dinner Tuesday to Saturday

Address
66 Witherspoon Street, Princeton, Mercer, NJ 08542

+1 609 924 0078

elementsprinceton.com

Bookings
Website, OpenTable.com

Price guide

What they say
"The team at Elements seamlessly blends together progressive modernist cooking techniques with a focus on fresh, locally sourced ingredients. Chef Scott Anderson teaches his kitchen staff the importance of collaboration among chefs and local purveyors in order to collectively disrupt traditional kitchen boundaries and allow for unconventional culinary ideas to take root, flourish and move forward."

Signature dishes
Long Island tuna with magnolia; white asparagus with trout roe, woodruff, and pineapple weed; squab with sour cherry, blossoms, and oats.

What others say
"We were off on a wild but carefully plotted journey through Asian, Latin, French and American flavors and techniques. It wasn't a slide show of single images, but an evening's immersion in cross-cultural montages."

-Eric Levin, *New Jersey Monthly*

What we say
Fans of modern fine dining flock to Elements. The dining room is set up with only nine tables, each of which looks in on the laboratory-like open kitchen. Chef Anderson describes his culinary style as "interpretive American" cuisine that ultimately draws out the purest flavors of each ingredient. But under the veneer of artistry lies the hyper-local sensibility you'd expect from a more rustic restaurant. Elements remains as committed to the old-fashioned ideals of local food as it is to its forward-thinking creative mission.

423

New York

al di la Trattoria

Brooklyn

What
A Northern Italian trattoria focusing on simply-prepared seasonal ingredients

Who
Anna Klinger, chef/co-owner & Emilano Coppa, co-owner

When
Lunch & dinner daily

Address
248 Fifth Avenue, Brooklyn, NY 11215

+1 718 783 4565

aldilatrattoria.com

Bookings
Walk-ins, website bookings for 6+

Price guide

What they say
"Neighbors have been coming since we opened in 1998. They come when they're in need of a quick meal during the week and to celebrate a special occasion. We produce as much as possible in house from all the fresh pastas to ice creams and sorbets to *guanciale*, pancetta, vinegar and pickles. Trattoria in Italian means family run restaurant, which is what we still are after twenty years."

Signature dishes
Trippa, a stew of tripe with tomato, served with grilled bread rubbed with garlic; spring salad with blanched vegetables and shavings of pecorino; *saltimbocca all romana*: pork loin pounded paper thin with prosciutto and sage, and crispy crushed potatoes.

What we say
Despite its Brooklyn location, al di la Trattoria's food could easily be mistaken for the fare at a trattoria in Northern Italy. The menu is fresh, simple, and changes its colors throughout the year to fit with the season. Farro during the spring is accompanied by snap peas, radishes, and ricotta *salata*; in the summer, it's paired up with tomatoes, cucumbers, and basil. *Tortelli*, meanwhile, are filled with corn in the summer, roasted squash in the fall, sheep's milk ricotta in winter and peas in spring.

Just like in Italy, many of the house's signatures like those pastas are made in-house. As are the ice creams, sorbets, and a few of the vinegars.

Emma's Torch

Brooklyn

What
A nonprofit restaurant that provides culinary training & job placement services to refugees

Who
Kerry Brodie, founder/director

When
Dinner Tuesday to Sunday, weekend brunch

Address
345 Smith Street, Brooklyn, NY 11213

+1 718 243 1222

emmastorch.org

Bookings
Resy.com

Price guide

What they say
"Our restaurant is dedicated to empowering refugees and survivors of human trafficking through culinary training. We strive to create a community of support where they can learn and grow while learning on-the-job skills. We believe that we can change lives, one delicious dish at a time."

Signature dishes
Black-eyed-pea hummus; pistachio bread pudding; herb roasted chicken with harissa.

What others say
"The newest restaurant in Brooklyn has a mission beyond serving seasonal fare - it doubles as a training program for refugees ... The cuisine is seasonal American and designed to familiarize the students with the flavors and ingredients of their adopted home. Still, there are nods to some of their places of origin in the form of shawarma spice on the lamb shank or a sticky tamarind glaze on the barbecue wings."

-Sarah Theeboom, *Eater New York*

What we say
For refugees, food can be both a connection to home and a gateway to employment in the United States. Kerry Brodie wanted to help make that connection stronger. What she started as a pop-up is now a full-grown restaurant whose mission reaches far beyond putting good food on the plate - the kitchen here is a training space for refugees, those seeking asylum, and victims of human trafficking. To diners, it is a warm neighborhood restaurant that serves approachable, contemporary American fare. This Carroll Gardens restaurant reminds us how profoundly food can drive change.

The Farm on Adderley

Brooklyn

What
A forward-thinking, locally sourced & sustainable farm-to-table restaurant

Who
Jai Chun, owner & Steven Hubbell, chef

When
Dinner, daily, lunch Monday to Friday, weekend brunch

Address
1108 Cortelyou Road, Brooklyn, NY 11218

+1 718 287 3101

thefarmonadderley.com

Bookings
Email reservations@thefarmonadderley.com

Price guide

What they say
"We are passionate about being able to offer our guests a diverse selection of local and sustainable produce. We stick pretty tightly to the seasons. We find it much more exciting for ourselves and the guests as the menu is in constant flux with the comings and goings of product and trying to capture them in their essence."

Signature dishes
Lamb dumplings with local pastured lamb, fried onions, fenugreek, ramps, farmer cheese and fresno chili in a rabbit-tarragon broth with fava beans and scallions; rainbow trout over a bed of parsley root and ramp purée with snow peas, and pickled beech mushrooms, fennel-scented goat's milk pannacotta with poached rhubarb.

What we say
More than a decade in, one of Brooklyn's most beloved farm-to-table restaurants is still going strong in the Ditmas Park neighborhood. The menu changes with the seasons and everything that can be sourced locally hails from farms in New York and Pennsylvania. Those ingredients work their way into dishes like roasted chicken thighs with sunchoke, radicchio with orange, and celery vinaigrette, and farro risotto with English peas.

Dessert should never be missed here. Each month, the team selects one offering as its "sweet givings" dessert and donates the proceeds from it to a charity like GrowNYC and Bike New York.

The Four Horsemen

Brooklyn

What
A Williamsburg restaurant serving creative, seasonal food & low-intervention wine

Who
Nick Curtola, chef, Randy Moon, co-owner

When
Dinner, daily, weekend lunch

Address
295 Grand Street, Brooklyn, NY 11211

+1 718 599 4900

fourhorsemenbk.com

Bookings
Walk-ins, Resy.com

Price guide

What they say
"The Four Horsemen is only a forty-seat restaurant but has over 450 wines on its list along with vintage *amari* and other low-intervention drinks. By low-intervention, we not only refer to the rise of so-called 'natural wines'... but also wines made in ancient ways... that put the grapes and place they represent first and foremost. We feel it is important to offer these wines in conjunction with our food as they were meant to be, to be enjoyed together."

Signature dishes
Chicken wings and liver skewers with *shichimi togarashi*; Montauk fluke with English peas, trout roe, and herb juice; spring garlic sausage with grilled asparagus and morels.

What we say
It's a bit hard to tell if this Williamsburg spot is a wine bar masquerading as a restaurant or the other way around. No matter, it is worthy of a visit for adventurous diners and enophiles alike. Dishes from Chef Nick Curtola like grilled fish collar with a spicy Thai dipping sauce and herb salad, warm house bread with cultured butter, and Sasso chicken prepared two ways, capture one of the more exciting waves in New York's dining scene. Anything goes, as long as it goes with wine. And, there's a great deal of it to choose from: 450 bottles to be exact. Wine neophytes are in good hands with staff who graciously help make sense of the list of natural and low-intervention wines.

The Good Fork

Brooklyn

What
A twelve-year-old restaurant in Red Hook, Brooklyn

Who
Sohui Kim, chef/owner & Ben Schneider, owner

When
Dinner Tuesday to Sunday, weekend brunch

Address
391 Van Brunt Street, Brooklyn, NY 11231

+1 718 643-6636

goodfork.com

Bookings
Resy.com, walk-ins

Price guide

What they say
"The relationships that are formed here is like another family to us. Great dedicated staff that shares your vision, produces service and food that most people will remember and seek out again and again."

Signature dishes
Steak and eggs Korean style; roast chicken with fermented black bean butter sauce; seasonal grilled escarole salad.

What others say
"The food is as inviting as the atmosphere, with standout appetizers from around the world – homemade pork-and-chive dumplings, plump and greaseless; a meaty crab cake, its dryness ameliorated by a lively chili aïoli."

–Andrea Thompson, *The New Yorker*

What we say
There is a unique charm and warmth at The Good Fork. Perhaps it's because wife-and-husband owners Sohui Kim and Ben Schneider built the restaurant themselves, perhaps it's because they managed to revive it after Hurricane Sandy devastated the area, but mostly it's because it's a neighborhood restaurant that makes you feel like a local – even if you aren't one.

Kim's menu disregards any attempt of categorization, serving the dishes she loves like house-made pork and chive dumplings, which should be ordered by every carnivore who comes to The Good Fork, a classic burger, and "steak and eggs Korean style" with kimchi that the team ferments themselves. Proteins and produce come from humane and local sources like Early Girl Farm, while much of the drink offerings are made in the neighborhood.

Greenpoint Fish + Lobster Co.

Brooklyn

What
Sustainable seafood market, raw bar & restaurant

Who
Vinny Milburn, owner & Peter Juusola, general manager

When
Lunch & dinner, daily

Address
114 Nassau Avenue, Brooklyn, NY 11222

+1 718 349 0400

greenpointfish.com

Bookings
Walk-ins

Price guide

What they say
"We believe the long-term viability and future of the world's seafood starts with responsibly managed fisheries, transparency, traceability, and well-informed consumers. We focus on local and seasonal seafood from fishermen and purveyors who care as much about the health of our oceans as we do."

Signature dishes
Fish collar simmered in shrimp curry, serrano peppers, and cilantro; live sea scallop crudo; porgy fish tacos topped with citrus cabbage slaw and chipotle-lime mayo, radishes, and cilantro.

What we say
This pristine white-tiled space in the Greenpoint neighborhood of Brooklyn doubles as a fish market and a restaurant for those who would prefer to have their seafood cooked (or shucked) to order. The team partners with the Monterey Bay Aquarium Seafood Watch to ensure they're protecting the future health of the oceans and seafood businesses like theirs.

From clam chowder and fish tacos to hickory smoked fish pâté and razor clam roti, there's little on the menu that doesn't come from the sea, and there's no meat in sight. Diners are served at a marble bar and a few high tops, so it's best to arrive with a date.

Mettā

Brooklyn

What
Seasonal, locally sourced menu cooked over an open wood-burning fire

Who
Norberto Piattoni, chef

When
Dinner Tuesday to Sunday, weekend brunch

Address
197 Adelphi Street, Brooklyn, NY 11205

+1 718 233 9134

mettabk.com

Bookings
Phone, Resy.com

Price guide

What they say
"We are passionate about preserving ancient culinary traditions that honor the earth and the lives of the plants and creatures that we consume. Sustainability has become a misused, trendy word in the restaurant industry. We are on a mission to stay socially responsible and honest about our practices."

Signature dishes
Whole Acadian redfish with curry verde and herb salad; smoked cabbage with sour corn, horseradish cream, and bottarga; short rib salad with dandelion greens, preserved pickled chili peppers, and anchovy dressing.

What we say
Mettā carefully walks the line between a neighborhood restaurant in the charming Fort Greene section of Brooklyn and a destination for a date night. The cozy space has the feel of an intimate dinner party, with the chefs joining in from behind a bar that separates the dining room from the open kitchen. There, they tend to a wood-fire hearth where chicken is roasted and finished with charred onion jus, whole Acadian redfish is prepared with curry verde, and potatoes are cooked with beef tallow. Vegetables like smoked cabbage with bottarga are celebrated when they are in season and preserved for when they aren't.

The team is also ever-conscious of the carbon emission of running a restaurant, and relies exclusively on renewable energy sources and works with ZeroFoodprint to invest in carbon sequestration initiatives.

Insa

Brooklyn

What
A Korean barbecue restaurant that also hosts private karaoke rooms

Who
Sohui Kim, chef/partner, Ben Schneider, partner & Yong Sup Shin, chef

When
Dinner daily, weekend lunch & dinner

Address
328 Douglass Street, Brooklyn, NY 11217

+1 718 855 2620

insabrooklyn.com

Bookings
Resy.com

Price guide

What they say
"We are most passionate about serving delicious food that is responsibly sourced. Our menu is a playful take on traditional Korean barbecue, and we love to boast that we are one of the very few Korean barbecue restaurants that does not use flavor enhancers. We use meat and produce that is grown with love and a sense of responsibility to the world. Our staff is as cultural and racially diverse as possible with a strong recognition of our own LGBT employees that promote a true sense of teamwork and cooperation within our family of employees."

Signature dishes
Banchan with seasonal produce including fermented kimchi; *Tteokbokki*, house-made "Spam".

What we say
Wife and husband team Sohui Kim and Ben Schneider, who own the equally excellent Good Fork restaurant, built this spacious and playful Gowanus spot as their sophomore effort with sous chef Yong Sup Shin. Drawing on Kim's heritage growing up in Seoul, the restaurant brings a Brooklyn approach to Korean dining. *Banchan*, or small plates that accompany the meal, evolve with the seasons here. But the star of the kitchen is the barbecue, prepared with ethically-raised beef and pork, and sustainable seafood, that's cooked to your liking on the table. Pair it with a bottle of biodynamic, natural, or organic wine.

The restaurant doubles as a karaoke destination with private rooms insulating the sound just behind the dining room. Make sure to set aside extra time after your meal to sing a number or two.

Olmsted

Brooklyn

What
A responsible fine dining restaurant masquerading as a casual neighborhood one

Who
Greg Baxtrom, chef/owner

When
Dinner, daily, brunch Friday to Sunday

Address
659 Vanderbilt Avenue, Brooklyn, NY 11238

+1 718 552 2610

olmstednyc.com

Bookings
Resy.com, email contact@olmstednyc.com

Price guide

What they say
"We are passionate about providing a fine dining experience in a playful unpretentious atmosphere. Our garden is modest so we are at the farmers' market about four times a week."

Signature dishes
Crab Rangoon prepared with house-made ricotta and house-grown kale; carrot crêpe with little neck clams and sunflower shoots; grilled scallops with celeriac, apple, and spicy peanuts.

What we say
There are few respites from the city pavement in New York that are as transportive as Olmsted's backyard garden. Guests are welcome to start their meal with cocktails here and end it with s'mores or soft serve. The space doubles as seating area and functional kitchen garden, where vegetables like kale for the signature crab Rangoon are grown.

Baxtrom, who worked under Grant Achatz at Alinea, changes his menu with the seasons, but the carrot crêpe (which lays delicately over juicy little neck clams is available every evening) shouldn't be overlooked. Other dishes celebrate what the team spots in the market and pair it with torn scallops, broken *uni*, or less popular cuts of meat to boost sustainability and keep the price point affordable for diners.

Roman's

Brooklyn

What
An intimate trattoria serving simple, hearty fare to a clientele of fashion-forward locals

Who
Andrew Tarlow, owner & Frank Reed, chef

When
Dinner, daily, weekend brunch

Address
243 Dekalb Avenue, Brooklyn, NY 11205

+1 718 622 5300

romansnyc.com

Bookings
Resy.com, walk-ins

Price guide

What they say
"Our food philosophy celebrates the craft of traditional Italian handmade foods using products grown and harvested in the Northeast."

Signature dishes
Homemade burrata; handmade pastas.

What others say
"The menu changes daily, and there's a sense that you could come back often and rarely get bored."

-Andrea Thompson, *The New Yorker*

What we say
A sustainable approach to cooking is almost a given at Andrew Tarlow's restaurants. The owner of some of Brooklyn's most beloved neighborhood spots sources produce from local farms, works off green energy, and has worked to link his businesses so that they share resources to reduce waste. Meat comes from the team's whole animal butcher, Marlow & Daughters, bread is baked by the company's She Wolf Bakery, and pastas, which change regularly at Roman's, are made in-house.

Sustainability extends beyond sourcing here. The group is focused on supporting its team and paving a new road for restaurant wages. Tarlow kicked off his Gratuity Free movement at this Fort Greene trattoria in early 2016. Here, servers are part of a revenue-sharing model and the kitchen team is started off at $1 above the minimum wage (with the hopes to increase that number to $2). While Roman's is a neighborhood restaurant, it is more than worthy of a special trip to Brooklyn for a date night.

Runner & Stone

Brooklyn

What
A new American bakery & restaurant specializing in seasonal, handmade bread, pastries & food

Who
Peter Endriss, head baker & Chris Pizzulli, chef

When
Breakfast, lunch & dinner, daily

Address
285 Third Avenue, Brooklyn, NY 11215

+1 718 576 3360

runnerandstone.com

Bookings
Phone, email reservations@runnerandstone.com

Price guide

What they say
"We have deep relationships with local farmers from years of selling alongside them at farmers' markets and are always searching the market for what's delicious. We use (literally) tons of local flour grown in New York State and Vermont, and we make all of our preserves in-house during the individual fruit's season."

Signature dishes
Almond croissant made with vanilla rum syrup; duck pastrami with whole grain beer mustard and house-made pickles; house-made orecchiette with fennel sausage and broccoli rabe.

What we say
Tucked away in the formerly industrial neighborhood of Gowanus, Brooklyn, Runner & Stone doubles as a bakery and restaurant. The space is open bright and early for morning coffee drinkers seeking one of the bakery's excellent croissants or seasonal Danishes. And, it stays open through dinner for those hunting for house-made orecchiette or a fish of the day served with cannellini beans, olive *romesco*, and radishes.

The bakery, which uses locally sourced and milled flour, is one of the strengths of this neighborhood establishment, and loaves like walnut levain, rye ciabatta, and sesame semolina, can be purchased to go. During the summer, consider taking one to Prospect Park, just a mile away, for a picnic.

Sunday in Brooklyn

Brooklyn

What
All-day restaurant in Williamsburg serving a seasonal American menu with a focus on sustainability

Who
Todd Enany, Adam Landsman & Jaime Young, chefs

When
Breakfast, brunch & dinner, daily

Address
348 Wythe Avenue, Brooklyn, NY 11211

+1 347 222 6722

sundayinbrooklyn.com

Bookings
Walk-ins, Resy.com

Price guide

What they say
"We aim to source products as local as possible," says the team. That includes buying much of their produce from a non-profit organic farmers cooperative based in Lancaster, Pennsylvania and fish from nearby sustainable seafood purveyor Greenpoint Fish & Lobster. By-products of the kitchen, like chopped ends of fruit and pepitas, are reused by the talented bar team to make produce-forward cocktails."

Signature dishes
Charred leeks with sour apple, butter, and anchovy; wood-roasted maitake mushrooms with onion vinaigrette; black sea bass crudo with curry leaf, radish, oro blanco, and turmeric.

What we say
Sunday in Brooklyn's laid back vibe and morning through evening hours makes visits to this Williamsburg restaurant feel like you're stopping by the house of a friend, who just happens to be an exceptionally skilled chef. During the winter, wood-burning ovens warm the space, while in spring and summer months, diners are treated to rooftop dining.

Executive Chef Jaime Young, who previously worked at the acclaimed high-end restaurant Atera in Manhattan, brings an upscale approach to his cooking here. The daily brunch is the highlight with offerings like warm oatmeal with goat's milk butter and dried blueberries, a sandwich of spicy cauliflower, clothbound cheddar, sauerkraut and red sambal, and big, fluffy malted pancakes with hazelnut maple praline and brown butter.

abc kitchen

New York City

What
A local, seasonal & market-driven restaurant in the Flatiron neighborhood

Who
Jean-Georges Vongerichten, chef/owner

When
Lunch & dinner daily, weekend brunch

Address
35 East 18th Street, New York, NY 10003

+1 212 475 5829

abchome.com

Bookings
OpenTable.com

Price guide

What they say
"Our atmospheric elements, under ABC Home curation, feature environmentally conscious stories, honoring the preservation of the arts and global sustainability."

Signature dishes
Line-caught tuna sashimi marinated with ginger and mint, finished with chives and cracked black pepper; roasted carrot and avocado salad with crunchy seeds, crème fraîche, and citrus dressing; Skuna Bay salmon in mushroom crust, with mashed potatoes, lemon, and herbs.

What we say
Tucked into the stunning ABC Home & Carpet sits Chef Jean-Georges Vongerichten's first of three "abc" restaurants and in many ways, the original is still the strongest, and the best for a crew of more selective eaters. The restaurant's seasonal menu draws on what's available in the nearby Union Square farmers' market and translates it into dishes like spring pea soup with carrots and mint, house-made pastas, and whole-wheat pizzas.

The restaurant's signature (and much buzzed about) carrot and avocado salad, should always be ordered, no matter the time of day you're dining. Just make sure to plan your meal here, as tables can be hard to come by at peak times.

abcV

New York City

What
Thoughtful vegan & vegetarian offerings inside ABC Carpet & Home

Who
Jean-Georges Vongertichten, chef/owner

When
Breakfast, lunch & dinner, Monday to Friday, weekend brunch

Address
38 East 19th Street, New York, NY 10003

+1 212 475 5829

abchome.com/dine/abcv

Bookings
Reserve.com

Price guide

What they say
"abcV is here to serve, inform and inspire a cultural shift towards plant-based intelligence, through creativity and deliciousness... Our plant-based menu features locally grown produce and wild-foraged items from the tri-state area, along with imported products that celebrate organic and biodynamic agriculture."

Signature dishes
Green chickpea hummus with Thai basil and freshly baked pita or *crudité*; house-fermented sauerkraut with shaved horseradish and dill; market carrots with stone-ground nut and seed butter, chili, and lime.

What we say
One might not expect a high-end home goods store to be a dining destination, but Chef Jean-Georges Vongertichten has made it one. In the third of "abc" restaurants, all of which subscribe to a local and sustainable philosophy of cooking in a stylish setting, he has put produce at the heart of the kitchen.

Healthy living is also at the forefront of the cooking here and is best highlighted at breakfast with a menu that offers sections titled "energizing and fresh" (think vanilla chia or wild blueberry bowls) and "warm and sustaining" (soft-boiled eggs with Danish rye, or freshly steamed tofu with roasted cauliflower snd harissa). Diners who don't have time to sit down for a full meal can take out dishes and cold-pressed juices such as a turmeric elixir, in earth-friendly containers.

Amali

New York City

What
A sustainable Mediterranean restaurant located on the Upper East Side

Who
James Mallios, partner & Dan Ross, chef

When
Lunch & dinner daily, weekend brunch

Address
115 East 60th Street, New York, NY 10022

+1 212 339 8363

amalinyc.com

Bookings
Email kylie@amalinyc.com, OpenTable.com

Price guide

What they say
"Fish [at Amali] must pass our comprehensive safety certification process and be made available to members within twenty-four hours of leaving the boat and being brought on shore. It also must have been caught locally and sustainably with respect to species, the environment, the foodshed and the fishers."

Signature dishes
Spanish octopus *a la plancha* with roasted red pepper, potato, black olive, and jalapeño; roasted Cascun Farm chicken "under a brick" with eggplant caponata and salsa verde; salt-baked dayboat fish with dill, lemon, and oregano.

What others say
Awarded the Snail of Approval certification.

Slow Food NYC

What we say
This Upper East Side Greek and Italian restaurant is fiercely committed to sustainability, something that's best exemplified through their fish program. In order to make it on to the plate at Amali, fish must meet with the team's rigorous standards including not traveling more than 150 miles from the dock where it "landed".

Once in the restaurant, seafood works its way into all arms of the menu with dishes like striped bass with cockles, fava beans, and ramps, and whole roasted fish with fennel potato, and olives.

Dig Inn

New York City

What
A seasonal fast-casual restaurant serving vegetable-forward & sustainably sourced food

Who
Matt Weingarten, culinary director & Adam Eskin, CEO

When
Breakfast, lunch & dinner, daily

Address
70 Prince Street, New York, NY 10012, plus other locations - see website

+1 212 253 7854

diginn.com

Bookings
Walk-ins

Price guide

What they say
"Dig Inn's goal is to change the food system by investing in waste reduction, a sustainable future of farming and a locally-sourced, vegetable-driven menu. Mindful sourcing is our bread and butter - our list of growers includes only those with whom we have direct relationships, and our recipe development process always involves a conversation between chef and grower about what we want to cook and harvest."

Signature dishes
Rescued vegetable salad with produce including parsnips, carrots, beets, and radishes; macaroni and cheese with whole wheat pasta, Jasper Hill cheese, and panko breadcrumbs, cashew kale Caesar salad with spiced nuts and shaved cauliflower.

What we say
With nearly twenty locations, including fifteen in New York City and more on the way, it's easy to navigate yourself to an outpost of this fast-casual chain like its two-story Flagship in Soho. Meals here have ordered at the counter, which helps keep the price-tag ultra-affordable. The team is unwavering in their commitment to supporting the local food system. Vegetables are sourced directly from regional farmers like Rise & Root. Rescued or slightly blemished produce is incorporated into a "rescued vegetable salad" and "a better OJ", using recovered oranges, carrots, and mint, to ensure good food isn't wasted. The menu shifts six times a year to celebrate what's in season.

Agern

New York City

What
A restaurant & bar with Nordic roots, tucked into Grand Central Terminal

Who
Claus Meyer, owner & Gunnar Gislason, chef

When
Lunch Monday to Friday, dinner Monday to Saturday

Address
89 East 42nd Street, New York, NY 10017

+1 646 568 4018

agernrestaurant.com

Bookings
Website

Price guide

What they say
"We like to have our guests leave having had an incredible and unique experience. We want to provide top-notch hospitality, with cuisine that is a little bit different."

Signature dishes
Beef tartare with seasonal accompaniments like ramps and green strawberries; lobster with Nordic pairings of sea buckthorn and barley; endive with preserved blackberries, almonds, and Danish *havgus*.

What others say
"If Grand Central is a cathedral for commuters, Agern is a chapel for indulging the senses. Best to stay put."

-Carolyn Corman, *The New Yorker*

What we say
Grand Central Terminal might not be the first place that comes to mind for a fine dining experience, but Claus Meyer, the co-founder of Copenhagen's acclaimed restaurant Noma, is changing that with Great Northern Food Hall and restaurant Agern.

At Agern, his team, captained by Icelandic chef Gunnar Gislason, serves elegantly plated Nordic-inspired fare. Offerings change with the seasons, but spring items include black bass from a sustainable Brooklyn purveyor finished with radish, watercress, and ocean emulsion, and celeriac ravioli with mushrooms grown in the restaurant's leftover coffee grounds. Those dishes are paired with domestically produced wines, beers, and small-batch liquors.

No matter when you stop by, do not skip the bread and butter. These loaves, baked on-site, are some of the best in the city.

Blue Hill

New York City

What
A restaurant in New York City that is focused on cooking from the whole farm

Who
Dan Barber, chef, David & Laureen Barber, co-owners

When
Dinner, daily

Address
75 Washington Street, New York, NY 10011

+1 212 539 1776

bluehillfarm.com

Bookings
OpenTable.com

Price guide

What they say
"Our goal is to cook more in harmony with the land and create a culture of eating in a way that reflects that."

What we say
Tucked into the garden level of a Greenwich Village townhouse sits Dan Barber's city restaurant - the companion to Blue Hill at Stone Barns, a pioneering restaurant, farm, and agriculture center north of the city. Here, Barber offers equally warm service, and the same focus on exceptional ingredients and sustainability.

Dinner involves a dose of theatre. Ingredients, which may be presented to you before cooking for a version of show-and-tell, are sourced from the restaurant's personal farm and other sustainably minded farms in the area. They are woven into a menu that changes nightly and is offered as part of two tasting options: one of which puts more decision power in the hands of the diner, the other in the hands of the kitchen. No matter the choice, the kitchen will adapt to a diner's preferences.

While meat and fish (from ethical sources like Dock to Dish), are always available, it's the kitchen's care of vegetables that is most exciting here. Prepare to eat your way through the vegetable patch.

Buvette

New York City

What
Inspired by European traditions that honor a history of craft & design

Who
Jody Williams, chef

When
Breakfast, lunch & dinner, daily

Address
42 Grove Street, New York, NY 10014

ilovebuvette.com

Bookings
Walk-ins

Price guide

What they say
"Established in the historic and charming West Village neighborhood in New York, Buvette has been the spot to walk in at any time of day to enjoy an espresso, a lunch with an old friend, or a cocktail at the bar in the early hours of the morning. We hope you're able to join us the next time you're passing through."

Signature dishes
Tartinette with cultured butter and anchovies; roast chicken salad with haricot verts and new potatoes in mustard vinaigrette; brandade de morue: house-cured salt cod whipped with olive oil and potatoes.

What others say
"My go-to is Buvette, the preposterously charming café that makes you feel like you're in Paris, except that the energy and bustle and banter of regulars remind you that you can only be in New York City. I wedge into a seat at the always-full marble-topped bar and my work-bound chest begins to untighten. Maybe it's the glass of Sancerre that the bartender talks me into (not much convincing needed). Or maybe it's the fact that I'm debating between a roast chicken salad with a mustardy vinaigrette or a cloud of custardy scrambled eggs."

-Adam Rapoport, *bon appétit*

What we say
Opened in early 2011 by Chef Jody Williams, Buvette is inspired by European traditions that honor a history of craft and design where each delicious detail evokes a sense of story, place and delight. They are also inspired by the slow food movement and sustainable, organic wines.

Buvette (p. 438)

Café Altro Paradiso

New York City

What
A transportive Italian café with a menu of iterations of regional Italian cuisine

Who
Ignacio Mattos, chef/co-owner & Thomas Carter, co-owner

When
Dinner, daily, lunch Tuesday to Friday, weekend brunch

Address
234 Spring Street, New York, NY 10013

+1 646 952 0828

altroparadiso.com

Bookings
Website

Price guide

What they say
"We have decades of experience but never stop refining our craft and ourselves through constant training, traveling and adjusting. We are passionate about creating ingredient-driven, seasonal dishes."

Signature dishes
Strozzapreti al pesto genovese.

What others say
"Sommelier Thomas Carter and Chef Ignacio Mattos, aka Team Estela, work their magic again—this time at a chic Italian café that's warm, welcoming and completely packed. What's their secret? At Café Altro Paradiso, a buzzing bar and inviting dining room help set the scene; but the real draw is Mattos' honest, straightforward and delicious Italian cooking. Kick things off with a wildly fresh crudo dressed with olive oil, caper berry slivers, parsley and a squeeze of lemon; or a bright fennel salad with Castelvetrano olives and diced provolone. Homemade lasagnette is delicious, tucked with silky trumpet mushrooms, leeks and parmesan. Chicken Milanese is rustic and ample, accompanied by lemon, Dijon, and a salad of radicchio, farro and pine nuts."

Michelin Guide

What we say
Co-owners Ignacio Mattos and Thomas Carter own three restaurants in New York, each one different from the next. At Café Altro Paradiso, you will find a range of delicious pastas, salads, sandwiches and more for lunch. For dinner, don't miss the red snapper with asparagus, egg and parsley or the steak with beets and blue cheese butter - made perfect every time.

Cleaver Counter

New York City

What
A charming organic eatery where the daily menu is driven by the farm

Who
Mary R. Cleaver, owner

When
Lunch & dinner, Monday to Saturday, Sunday brunch

Address
75 Ninth Avenue New York, NY 10011

+1 212 741 9174

cleaverco.com

Bookings
Phone, walk-ins

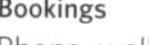

Price guide

What they say
"Our mission is to create beautiful meals and serve delicious food while supporting the regional food and farm economy. Using 'a day's drive from farm-to-table' as a distance guide, we source from smaller, local purveyors, focusing on regenerative agricultural practices, and rely largely on fair trade and organic ingredients for products that do not grow in our region."

Signature dishes
Chicken pot pie made with pastured chicken and a flaky crust; house-made pasta that changes daily; matcha cake with rose whipped cream, yuzu gel, and black tahini.

What we say
The link from farm to restaurant at Mary Cleaver's restaurant, Cleaver Counter, is shorter than most. A long-time caterer and pioneer in local food, Cleaver also owns The Green Table Farm in the Hudson Valley where she and her team raise hogs, pastured poultry, and grow vegetables and flowers. The team shuttles the bounty from the farm to this restaurant in Chelsea Market in Manhattan (the restaurant will relocate to Brooklyn in 2019) ensuring they have the freshest local produce possible.

The menu leans heavily on comfort foods like chicken pot pie and a vegetarian mushroom pot pie with a wholewheat crust. Grilled cheese is made over at lunch with raw milk cheddar and a seasonal chutney. The restaurant practices, meatless Mondays, and there are always vegan options available. No matter what entrée you order, there will be biodynamic or organic wine to pair with it.

Craft

New York City

What
Simply prepared dishes highlighting pristine, seasonal ingredients in a warm, welcoming atmosphere

Who
Tom Colicchio, chef/owner

When
Dinner, daily, lunch Monday to Friday

Address
43 East 19th Street, New York, NY 10003

+1 212 780 0880

craftrestaurant.com

Bookings
OpenTable.com

Price guide

What they say
"Since opening in 2001, we have been dedicated to the art of cooking, and celebrating great ingredients (and their producers) with menus of expertly prepared meat, fish, and produce with seasonality, locality, and community at the core. We partner with local farms to source the freshest ingredients of the season from trusted sources. We write our menus based on ingredients in season each and every day."

Signature dishes
Ricotta agnolotti with asparagus and green garlic; *maccheroni* with suckling pig ragù and fava beans; roasted blackfish with oyster, watercress, and bacon.

What others say
"It's been years since Tom Colicchio first opened Craft to great acclaim, but the easy charms of the celebrity chef and TV personality's downtown institution haven't waned a bit. The room still bustles most nights of the week with stylish types who appreciate the triple threat of cozy décor, elegant fare and a crackerjack service team. As the name suggests, guests "craft" a meal from seasonal, perfectly executed dishes featuring pristine ingredients."

Michelin Guide

What we say
Tom Colicchio's signature restaurant in Flatiron is warm and inviting. The menu here is crafted around what's in peak season that day and available at the city's Greenmarket. No matter the time of the year, the focus of the kitchen is on simple, but not simplistic, fare. Dinner can be ordered à la carte or diners can put themselves in the hands of the kitchen with a tasting menu.

Diner

New York City

What
Housed in an old dining car, Diner serves a seasonally inspired, daily changing menu of comfort food

Who
Andrew Tarlow, owner & Adam Baumgart, chef

When
Dinner daily, brunch Friday to Sunday

Address
85 Broadway, Brooklyn, NY 11249

+1 718 486 3077

dinernyc.com

Bookings
Resy.com, walk-ins

Price guide

What they say
"Our menu is organized around using all parts of an animal, moving from one preparation to another. The dishes work together to support a sustainable program, for example, if we purchase a whole pig, we'll serve schnitzel or house-made sausages on the dinner menu, bacon on the brunch menu, and cure our own ham. We also work with community-based organizations to hire people with significant barriers to sustainable employment."

Signature dishes
House burger made with sustainably sourced meat.

What we say
Housed in a Pullman car from the 1920s that's situated just blocks from the Williamsburg Bridge, Andrew Tarlow's first spot helped usher in an era of sustainably-minded Brooklyn restaurants. There's no formal menu here. Instead, a member of the team comes to each table and describes the offerings while writing a shorthand to help diners remember them on the butcher's paper that blankets the tables. The unpredictability of the offerings is half the fun of dining here. During the spring, dinner might feature beet greens or soft-shell crabs, and brunch buckwheat pancakes and a fried green tomato sandwich. The one constant is the restaurant's iconic burger made from animals butchered in partnership with the team's nearby shop Marlow & Daughters. Much like the hand-written menu, the check at Diner is straightforward.

Dirt Candy

New York City

What
An award-winning fine dining vegetable restaurant on the Lower East Side

Who
Amanda Cohen, chef/owner

When
Dinner Tuesday to Saturday, weekend brunch

Address
86 Allen Street, New York, NY 10002

+1 212 228 7732

dirtcandynyc.com

Bookings
OpenTable.com

Price guide

What they say
"Dirt Candy does for vegetables what Peter Luger's does for steak. There are thousands of restaurants dedicated to seafood, or barbecue, or Italian food, but few that specifically serve vegetables. All we want to do is push vegetables further than they've gone before; to do things with them that no one has ever seen."

Signature dishes
Carrot sliders with carrot confit, carrot juice buns, and carrot-ginger salad; tomato cake with fresh cherry tomatoes, tomato leather, and smoked feta; "eggplant Foster" with cookies and ice cream.

What others say
"Eating at Dirt Candy can be like going to a child's birthday party in a country where all the children love vegetables ... Ms. Cohen is not adapting the vegetarian cuisine of some other culture. She is inventing her own."

-Pete Wells, *The New York Times*

What we say
Dirt Candy Chef Amanda Cohen celebrated the vegetable patch long before veg-forward eating was a trend. At her Lower East Side restaurant, dishes hone in on one vegetable or another, like her kale matzo ball soup, or her addictive fried Korean broccoli that will easily win over any wing-lover. Cohen makes a point to work with vegetables that are available at neighborhood grocery stores, reminding diners that one doesn't need a forager or a trained chef to put vegetables on their plates. She is also an outspoken advocate for her staff. There's no tipping at Dirt Candy; in its place is a profit-sharing program.

Estela

New York City

What
Serving New American food cooked with a personal approach

Who
Ignacio Mattos, chef/co-owner & Thomas Carter, co-owner

When
Dinner Sunday to Thursday, lunch Friday, weekend brunch

Address
47 E Houston Street, New York, NY 10012

+1 212 219 7693

estelanyc.com

Bookings
Website

Price guide

What they say
"We are proud to offer a stimulating environment for our creative, connoisseur and international crowd, celebrating each of our restaurant's neighborhoods and networks, aiming to make them local staples. Our food incorporates the distinct flavors of New York, from the stalls of Chinatown to the bakeries of Brooklyn."

Signature dishes
Summer squash salad.

What others say
"Estela is where you go for some of the most delicious cutting-edge food in town, served with wines that will satisfy quirky naturalists and big-spending bankers alike."

bon appétit

What we say
Dishes at Estela are comprised of local and sustainable ingredients, which evolve seasonally. The Summer Squash Salad uses locally sourced squashes that are at their prime during the warmer months, ensuring this dish is fresh and flavorsome. Located in an intimate space that once housed the Knitting Factory music venue, Estela is a charming addition to downtown Manhattan that features exciting, forward-thinking food.

Flora Bar

New York City

What
A menu which takes subtle cues from its modernist surroundings in the Met Breuer

Who
Ignacio Mattos & Thomas Carter, co-owners

When
Lunch Tuesday to Friday, dinner Tuesday to Sunday, weekend brunch

Address
945 Madison Avenue at 75th Street, New York, NY 10021

+1 646 558 5383

florabarnyc.com

Bookings
Website

Price guide

What they say
"We are most passionate about providing high quality staples for New Yorkers and beyond, inspired by our traveling around the world. We offer top local ingredients, signature dishes and high quality service."

Signature dishes
Lobster dumplings.

What others say
"I know people who, while visiting New York from elsewhere, have dined at Flora Bar. After dessert, they have made reservations to dine there again the following night. The place gets under your skin. There emerges a gnawing need to have those lamb ribs again, and the omelet slathered with caviar, and the oysters spiked with Sichuan mignonette."

-Jeff Gordinier, *Esquire*

What we say
Flora Bar's food philosophy includes ingredient-driven, focused and refined dishes that are seasonal and contain unexpected elements, such as the grilled duck with beets, cherries and basil, or the omelette with hackleback caviar and trout roe. But this is also a community-minded restaurant, with a deep care for the environment. Flora Bar hosts events to support foundations such as the Billion Oyster Project, whose goal is to restore a sustainable oyster population and foster awareness, affinity and understanding of the Harbor by engaging New Yorkers directly in the work of restoring one billion oysters. They also support the The Ali Forney Center, who aids and shelters the LGBT youth in New York by providing mentor services, mental health counseling, medical care, recreational activities for structure and focus, and more.

The Fat Radish

New York City

What
A veg-friendly spot on the Lower East Side that emphasizes local, seasonal ingredients

Who
Nicholas Wilber, executive chef

When
Dinner, daily, weekend brunch

Address
17 Orchard Street, New York, NY 10002

+1 212 300 4053

thefatradishnyc.com

Bookings
Resy.com

Price guide

What they say
"We created a place for like-minded people to come together and share their experiences over good food."

Signature dishes
Celery root pot pie with gruyère and black garlic; fluke crudo prepared with seasonal citrus and herbs; whole roasted hen of the woods mushrooms with juniper butter.

What others say
"Vegetarians, if not vegans, could love it hard."

-Sam Sifton, *The New York Times*

What we say
Entering the dining room at this eight-year-old Lower East Side restaurant, it feels like you have left the city. There are long wooden farm tables with benches on either side, a skylight that allows light to stream in, and plants tucked in here and there. Perenially stylish fellow diners are a clear reminder, however, that you're eating in one of Manhattan's hippest neighborhoods. They're here not just for the people-watching, but the farm-to-table cooking.

The team sources its ingredients, whenever possible, from local and sustainable suppliers like Zone 7, a New Jersey-based farm distributor that connects 120plus sustainable farms with buyers like The Fat Radish. Their bounty, along with meat from ethically minded butcher Heritage Meats and NY-based hydroponic herb-growers like Square Roots, is featured on a menu with dishes like smashed cucumbers in its own natural juice with chives and burnt black garlic, Arctic char with golden tomatoes and pine nut relish, and local-harvest beef with arugula chimichurri.

Graffiti Earth

New York City

What
A Tribeca restaurant that celebrates sustainability, utilizing overlooked vegetables & fish

Who
Jehangir Mehta, chef

When
Dinner Tuesday to Saturday

Address
190 Church Street, New York, NY 10013

+1 212 542 9440

graffitiearthny.com

Bookings
OpenTable.com

Price guide

What they say
"We take sustainability to different spheres from sourcing, to using newspapers as place mats, and all the cutlery, crockery and silverware are hand-me-downs from friends and family. We call ourselves the ER for produce, where we try rigorously to stretch the life, and squeeze every bit, out of every scrap of produce."

Signature dishes
"Caterpillar butterfly soup": coconut soup that uses vegetable scraps of the day; kaleidoscope scallop portobello pâté made with "broken" scallops; Persian toast with second-pressed espresso ice cream.

What we say
Named the most sustainable chef in New York City by Michelin, Jehangir Mehta has made it his mission at this Tribeca restaurant to demonstrate just how environmentally thoughtful a restaurant can be.

The tables in the small space at the Duane Street Hotel are covered with sustainable wares like cloth napkins made from the fashion district's scraps. But the restaurant's sustainability efforts are most clearly seen on the plate. Chef Mehta and his team work to purchase scraps from restaurants like Dirt Candy, bruised produce from local farms, and "broken" scallops that fishermen might not otherwise be able to sell. Those ingredients are celebrated in a menu of coconut soup using daily scraps, scallop brûlée, and an Indian street burger with fingerling potatoes. The team is also working on an initiative to serve the elderly and needy in the restaurant's off hours.

Hearth

New York City

What
Inspired market-driven cuisine with an innate Tuscan influence

Who
Marco Canora, chef/owner

When
Dinner, daily, weekend brunch

Address
403 East 12th Street, New York, NY 10009

+1 646 602 1300

restauranthearth.com

Bookings
Website, OpenTable.com, walk-ins

Price guide

What they say
"Hearth is everything the word implies and more. At our table, market-driven cuisine is uplifted by warm hospitality: good fats are celebrated, whole animals appreciated, and vegetables crowned supreme. But we do more than satiate with signature dishes - we make you a part of our family."

Signature dishes
Fava bean salad with Pecorino Toscano, scallion and grilled bread; "variety burger": bun-less burger made with brisket, chuck, heart, and liver, served with caramelized onions, fontina, and fingerling potatoes; whole chicken with roasted cabbage, chili, and lemon.

What we say
Fourteen years after opening, Hearth remains one of the East Village's best and most welcoming dining options. Walking through the doors on twelfth Street is transportive, the chaos of nearby first avenue fades and diners are treated to thoughtful, seasonal cooking with an Italian lilt.

After a change in Chef Marco Canora's personal diet, the chef revamped the menu in 2012 to reflect his healthful philosophy. Vegetables are served in abundance here, flour and polenta milled in house, and good fats championed. The kitchen, however, doesn't lose sight of an end-of-meal treat, serving sweets like honey-roasted rhubarb and limoncello Napoleon.

What others say
"Chef Marco Canora's seasonal Italian restaurant has become a neighbourhood institution in the fourteen years since it opened. It's the kind of warm, reliable place that's equally great for first dates or dinner with your parents."

-Marguerite Preston, *Thrillist*

Le Bernardin

New York City

What
An internationally acclaimed seafood restaurant

Who
Eric Ripert, chef/owner & Maguy Le Coze, co-owner

When
Lunch Monday to Friday, dinner Monday to Saturday

Address
155 West 51st Street, New York, NY 10019

+1 212 554 1515

le-bernardin.com

Bookings
Website, Resy.com

Price guide

What they say
"The idea of sustainable seafood may be a lofty one but, at least to me, it seems worth the effort if we want to ensure that not only can there be a fish in every sauté pan, but that the fish in the pan is not endangered, is fed naturally, and is treated humanely. While one restaurant alone cannot change the future outcome, collectively we can make a difference."

What we say
For more than three decades, Le Bernardin has served as a temple to exceptional seafood. In recent years, it has increasingly made efforts to weave sustainability into its mission. Chef Eric Ripert and his team research fish and sourcing extensively, at times seeking out a sole fisherman who can provide a fish like cod from a sustainable source. The seafood that's brought in is used in prix fixe and tasting menus for dinner featuring dishes like scallop served with sea beans and bonito butter sauce, and poached halibut with radishes and daikon-ginger dashi. The kitchen recently added a vegetarian tasting menu to their offerings as well.

Fine dining can bring with it waste if chefs aren't thoughtful. Ripert, who is the vice chair of the board of City Harvest, ensures that doesn't happen here. In addition to raising much needed funds, he's overseen the donation of 50,000 pounds of edible food from the restaurant to those in need.

High Street on Hudson

New York City

What
All-day neighborhood restaurant, bakery & café

Who
Ellen Yin, partner & Eli Kulp, chef/partner

When
Breakfast, lunch & dinner, daily

Address
637 Hudson Street, New York, NY 10014

+1 917 388 3944

highstreetonhudson.com

Bookings
Walk-ins, OpenTable.com

Price guide

What they say
"Bread takes center stage here. We make all our bread from grains soourced locally from sourced grains like Castle Valley Mills in Pennsylvania or the Finger Lakes region. Bread is part of our entire concept, from our morning breakfast sandwiches to dinner, so we source as much from local farms as possible!"

Signature dishes
"The Bodega": breakfast sandwich with eggs, cheddar, house-made sausage on a sage black pepper buttermilk biscuit; turkey sandwich with green goddess dressing, lettuce, and tomato on a house-made kaiser roll; handmade smoked paprika *mafaldine* with braised rabbit, peas, and pecorino.

What we say
Originally from Philadelphia, the New York outpost of Ellen Yin and Eli Kulp's restaurant is open from morning to night, providing a respite from the chaos of Manhattan. No matter the hour, each visit should include bread from the exceptional in-house bakery. Whole loaves can be purchased to go, but we recommend sitting down for a breakfast sandwich like "The Forager," prepared with king trumpet mushrooms, sautéed kale, and eggs, or starting a dinner of "chicken in the woods" or vegetarian cauliflower steak, with an order of bread and butter.

Sustainability is front and center with the sourcing of ingredients from Pennsylvania and New York farms. Yin is also on the steering committee for a project called Food250, which aims to set goals for food accessibility, equity, sustainability, and hunger relief for the country's 250th birthday.

What others say
"If I were going to spend the entire day at a single restaurant, it would be High street on Hudson, the cozy West Village space...offers an incredible around-the-clock array of dishes."

Food & Wine, Best New Restaurants

Luke's Lobster

New York City

What
A Maine-bred lobster shack serving the world's best, most sustainable lobster direct from lobstermen

Who
Luke Holden, Ben Conniff & Bryan Holden, partners

When
Lunch & dinner, daily

Address
26 S William Street, New York, NY 10004, plus other locations; see website

+1 646 559 4644

lukeslobster.com

Bookings
Walk-ins

Price guide

What they say
"Our core values are taste, transparency, and purpose. We use only the best ingredients, are vertically integrated, and trace all of our seafood back to the sustainable fishery where it was caught. We're environmentally and economically devoted to our coasts, by supporting sustainable economic models for communities of fishermen and women. Every year we donate a portion of our proceeds to projects that restore harbors, diversify income for coastal communities, and manually clean up trash from local waterways. We only buy seafood from sustainable sources - this means the population is of a healthy, robust size, and management regulations are in place and enforced to ensure that overfishing and environmental damage doesn't occur."

Signature dishes
Lobster roll, made from sustainably-caught lobster from Maine and Canadian harbors; New England clam chowder with fresh-shucked Rhode Island clams; wild blue salad with chilled split lobster tail, organic greens and house-pickled wild Maine blueberries.

What others say
"Luke's Lobster illustrates the benefits of vertical integration, letting the restaurant be part of harvesting, processing and cooking of the key ingredient."

-Janet Morrissey, *The New York Times*

What we say
At Luke's Lobster - a certified B Corp - exceptional lobster, crab, and shrimp are tucked into butter-griddled New England split-top buns, then skillfully seasoned with just the right touch of mayo and lemon butter. A light, tangy poppyseed coleslaw along with bright organic salads, and rich, packed with Maine seafood (clam, and lobster and corn) round out the well-crafted menu.

Le Coq Rico

New York City

What
Chef Antoine Westermann's poultry house serving responsibly raised, sustainably sourced whole birds

Who
Antoine Westermann, chef

When
Lunch Monday to Friday, weekend brunch, dinner, daily

Address
30 East 20th Street, New York, NY 10003

+1 212 267 7426

lecoqriconyc.com

Bookings
Website, Resy.com, walk-ins

Price guide

What they say
"Not a steakhouse, but a 'poultry house'. At Le Coq Rico, poultry takes center stage. Established in 2016 by Chef Antoine Westermann, Le Coq Rico pays tribute to the unique terroir of Northeastern U.S. by offering diverse varieties of responsibly raised and sustainably sourced birds. Combining modern French gastronomy with an Alsatian twist, the experience centers around a selection of heritage breeds including chicken, turkey, duck, goose, quail, and guinea fowl."

Signature dishes
Whole roasted heritage-breed birds; giblets platter with duck liver, apple and heart brochette, glazed wings, roasted chicken liver on horseradish toast, and spiced croquettes; Westermann's *Baeckeoffe:* whole Brune Landaise chicken baked in earthenware with artichokes, dried tomatoes, lemon confit, and Riesling jus.

What others say
"I think I have finally found the perfect restaurant to take people who think they can make a better chicken at home."

-Pete Wells, *The New York Times*

What we say
Chef Antoine Westermann spent a year researching heritage birds in the United States before launching a menu that offers seven different varieties (most of which are locally sourced) including Brune Landaise and Jersey Giant chickens, and Catskill guinea fowl. The birds are poached and roasted, ensuring a tender and juicy flesh and crisp, golden skin, and served with a seasonal salad prepared with greens from regional farms.

Little Park

New York City

What
A seasonal restaurant in Tribeca highlighting organic, sustainable ingredients

Who
Andrew Carmellini, chef/owner

When
Breakfast, lunch & dinner, daily, weekend brunch

Address
85 West Broadway, New York, NY 10007

+1 212 220 4110

littlepark.com

Bookings
Phone, OpenTable.com, walk-ins

Price guide

What they say
"We source everything as locally as possible. We like working directly with small farms. We ask the farmers and purveyors we work with what they have readily available when choosing what to put on our menu. Just because you have the ability to put something on your menu does not always mean that it's the best product."

Signature dishes
Beetroot tartare with horseradish, rye, and smoked trout roe; Long Island squid with new potatoes, ramps, and baby fennel; green fettuccine with smoked mushroom, English peas, and a farm egg.

What we say
Vegetables are front and center at Andrew Carmellini's Tribeca restaurant, Little Park. Situated on the ground floor of the swank Smyth Hotel, the restaurant serves those vegetables from early in the morning - in green juice and heirloom grain porridge with hen of the wood mushrooms - on through lunch and into the evenings.

Dinner offers the best sampling of what's in season with dishes like, rainbow trout with cauliflower, almonds, and blood orange. If you're looking to linger after dinner, wander to Evening Bar, also situated in the hotel, for a nightcap.

Loring Place

New York City

What
A seasonal American restaurant by Chef Dan Kluger located in the heart of Greenwich Village

Who
Dan Kluger, chef

When
Dinner daily, lunch Monday to Friday, weekend brunch

Address
21 West 8th Street, New York, NY 10011

+1 212 388 1831

loringplacenyc.com

Bookings
Resy.com

Price guide

What they say
"Creating seasonal, market-driven dishes that are sourced locally and sustainably while ensuring our guests are always happy and have a great experience while dining with us."

Signature dishes
Wholewheat spaghetti made with house-milled grains, tossed with spinach, Parmesan, basil, and crushed chilies; locally sourced grain salad with ramp rémoulade, English peas, roasted carrots, and lemon; wood-grilled broccoli salad with orange, pistachios, and mint.

What we say
Vegetable-loving New Yorkers were first introduced to Chef Dan Kluger when he put his mark on Jean-Georges Vongerichten's abc kitchen. He has brought the same creativity to vegetable-forward cooking at his first solo project in Greenwich Village. The menu changes with the seasons but the dishes are always created with sharing in mind.

Small plates like sugar snap peas with radishes and roasted beets with ginger, orange, and toasted cashews are case in point. As are wholewheat pizzas, made with wheat that's milled in-house, and topped with ramps, mozzarella, honey, and pickled cherry peppers in the spring. Meanwhile, sustainably farmed seafood like Arctic char is given a smoky touch from a wood-fire grill.

While the dining room is often booked in advance, the large bar here is always open to walk-ins and features cocktails like Lambrusco and rhubarb, and vodka and blood orange made with spirits from local or small-batch artisan producers.

Mayanoki

New York City

What
Sustainable sushi *omakase* focusing on local produce

Who
David Torchiano, co-founder

When
Dinner Wednesday to Sunday

Address
620 East 6th Street, New York, NY 10009

mayanoki.com

Bookings
Resy.com

Price guide

What they say
"Our goal is to convince sushi restaurants in general to serve 100 percent sustainable seafood. We are passionate about respecting the tradition and techniques of sushi, but making it American. We believe that restaurants can help lead the way to solve problems like climate change. Connecting with our customers to change how they think about their food choices when it comes to sushi is at the heart of what we do."

Signature dishes
Oyster in a lemon cup with *ikura* and *shiso*; smoked Arctic char and local blue fish *nigiri*; thirteen to fifteen-course *omakase* highlighting local fish.

What we say
While many of New York's best sushi restaurants regularly purchase seafood that must be flown in from Japan, the team here chose another route. The only sushi restaurant in Manhattan recognized by the Monterey Bay Aquarium Seafood Watch, Mayanoki sources ninety-five percent of its seafood domestically. The fish, which changes with the seasons and availability, arrives before diners as a part of a thirteen to fifteen-course *omakase* offering that's priced at $95 (a steal in Manhattan). Don't be surprised if one or more of those courses uses "trash" fish like raw catfish, which is prepared with thought and care here.

There are plans to add vegan and vegetarian iterations of the menu soon for those who prefer their meal fish-free. And no matter which menu you opt for, there's local wine, beer, cider, and even sake to sip with it.

New Leaf

New York City

What
A charity-minded restaurant in a historical landmark, serving fine food, wine & spirits

Who
Frank Raffaelle, founder/president

When
Dinner, daily, lunch Monday to Friday, weekend brunch

Address
1 Margaret Corbin Drive Fort Tryon Park, New York, NY 10040

+1 212 2568 5323

newleafrestaurant.com

Bookings
OpenTable.com

Price guide

What they say
"We are most passionate about serving honest food with fair prices in a beautiful setting."

Signature dishes
"Greens and grains" made with organic quinoa, local vegetables, and citrus; New York strip steak with mashed potatoes and sautéed broccoli rabe; brioche French toast with local berries, rooftop honey from Brooklyn Grange, and maple-glazed bacon.

What others say
"An imaginative menu is served with an emphasis on seafood, plus seasonal variations like soft-shell crabs in early summer or a minimalist choucroute garni in winter ... Take comfort in eating for a good cause: net profits are donated back to the park for its upkeep and maintenance."

-Stephen Weiss, *New York Magazine*

What we say
Built in the 1930s as a public cafeteria, the building that's home to New Leaf was designed by the Olmsted brothers, the sons of Frederick Law Olmsted. It sits in Fort Tryon Park at the northern tip of Manhattan, making it an ideal spot for a meal before or after a visit to The Cloisters.

Run by COFFEED, the restaurant is charity-minded with seven percent of its revenue donated to the New York Restoration Project and the Fort Tryon Park Trust. The approachable menu offers sustainably, ethically sourced proteins like crab cakes, pan-seared duck breast with vegetable barley and grilled asparagus. During brunch, eggs for classics like eggs Benedict and huevos rancheros come from the rooftop garden at Brooklyn Grange.

Nix

New York City

What
A celebration of vegetarian & vegan cuisine

Who
John Fraser, co-owner/chef, James Truman, co-owner

When
Dinner daily, lunch Monday to Friday, weekend brunch

Address
72 University Place, New York, Ny 10003

+1 212 498 9393

nixny.com

Bookings
OpenTable.com

Price guide

What they say
"Union Square market is our neighbor. We try and stay as close to home as possible. We have a commitment to purchasing firstly from our neighbors and we try to complete the cycle of food by using food trim for our vegetarian family meals and then composting what is inedible."

Signature dishes
Tandoor bread with vegetable dips; jicama with citrus, radicchio, Fresno chilies, and crispy shallots; tandoor-roasted pineapple with tamarind caramel, macadamia nuts, and toasted coconut.

What others say
"The crackle in the air at Nix and other recent meatless restaurants is what you get when you liberate vegetables from vegetarianism. Stripped of ideology, Nix is freed up for hedonic pursuits."

-Pete Wells, *The New York Times*

What we say
Michelin-starred Chef John Fraser and his team are committed to a philosophy that eating a vegetarian meal should be a celebration - not a sacrifice. There are no meat substitutes on the menu at the restaurant, which is just a few blocks south of Union Square. Instead, there are vegetables from the square's iconic farmers' market celebrated in every way possible from a play on *cacio e pepe* with shiitake mushrooms to cauliflower tempura to broccoli-artichoke dumplings. Save room for dessert, where pineapple is brushed with tamarind caramel and roasted in a tandoor oven.

Rouge Tomate Chelsea

New York City

What
Extraordinary, healthy dining experience that supports your total well-being & the environment

Who
Emmanuel Verstraeten, founder/CEO

When
Breakfast & lunch, Monday to Friday, dinner Monday to Saturday

Address
126 West 18th Street, New York, NY 10011

+1 646 395 3978

rougetomatechelsea.com

Bookings
Phone, OpenTable.com

Price guide

What they say
"Our mission is to provide an extraordinary dining experience that supports the total well-being of the individual and the environment. The menu is designed to make it easy to make a choice for health - human and environmental."

Signature dishes
Mushroom tartare with fingerling potatoes and roasted garlic; baked einkorn with roasted fennel and artichoke, confit tomato, and olives; whole-grain *reginetti* with nettle-walnut pesto, *spigarello*, chili, and Parmesan.

What we say
The health of diners and the environment go hand-in-hand at this Michelin star restaurant situated in two carriage houses in Chelsea. Chefs work with dietitians to craft a menu that offers humanely raised meat and fish, but emphasizes plants in dishes like mushroom tartare (in place of steak) and baked einkorn with fennel, artichoke, olive, and Parmesan. The team is mindful to use the entire ingredient: leftover charred pea pods are used to make a broth and stale bread is brined and fermented, dehydrated, and used to make pasta dough.

The environment was also considered when building the space, which opened in late 2016. Wood in the restaurant comes from lumber recovered after Hurricane Sandy struck New York. Look up during your dinner and you'll likely spot window boxes overflowing with greenery or even panels that appear like sun shining through a forest. Those in a rush can stop into the café in the bar room.

Seamore's

New York City

What
A sustainable seafood concept that's happiness driven with a purpose & health-focused backbone

Who
Michael Chernow, founder/president

When
Lunch & dinner, daily

Address
390 Broome Street, New York, NY 10013

+1 212 730 6005

seamores.com

Bookings
Walk-ins, Resy.com

Price guide

What they say
"We want to get to know people and the best way to get to know people is to feed them in a welcoming environment that has a culture of inclusivity. We also want to save the oceans. Sustainability in our sourcing is at the core of what we do."

Signature dishes
Local longfin crispy squid; local curried mussels served with charred bread; seared Acadian redfish tacos.

What we say
Dining at any one of Seamore's five locations gives you the feeling of having left the city for a seaside town. That's especially true at the original location, where two walls are blanketed with windows, allowing sun to stream into the space that's accented with seafoam finishes. On warm days, there's seating outside as well. While there's more than enough trendy details to go around here, owner Michael Chernow hasn't allowed that to detract from a strong core mission of operating a sustainable seafood restaurant. In addition to the regular offerings like fish tacos and lobster rolls, the restaurant offers "daily landings", or fish that's just arrived that can be ordered with sauces like red curry or brown butter miso. And, oyster shells from a raw bar offering are gathered for the Billion Oyster Project, which is working to rebuild oyster reefs in New York's harbor.

PRINT.

New York City

What
A Hell's Kitchen restaurant with the mission: if it's grown in the region, eat it in season

Who
Adam Block, owner, & Gary King, chef

When
Breakfast, lunch, & dinner, daily

Address
653 11th Avenue, New York, NY 10036

+1 630 779 3411

printrestaurant.com

Bookings
OpenTable.com

Price guide

What they say
"We have maintained an organic, slow-food approach since opening. During the growing season we are often able to attain ninety percent fulfillment of local, traceable menu items."

Signature dishes
Farro salad with shaved baby carrots, rainbow radish, purple snow peas, asparagus, and chardonnay vinaigrette; local tuna poke with purple daikon, yellow snow peas sustainable seaweed, and soy chili sauce; Heritage pork chop with English peas, sugar snaps, radishes, preserved lemon, and chili.

What we say
On the far west side of Midtown Manhattan sits the Ink48 Hotel and its restaurant PRINT., one of the few spots in the city that can boast its own dedicated forager. She seeks out local produce, biodynamic wine, and beer from responsible sources. The produce is supplemented by what the team grows on the hotel's rooftop in a repurposed swimming pool.

The menus shift with the seasons, but are long enough for everyone to find something that suits their palate, from wild mushroom dumplings with bok choy, snap peas, kohlrabi, and cilantro, to asparagus flan with truffle butter, and a waffle with bananas, maple syrup, and house-made butter for weekend brunch. Those planning on heading to Broadway should opt for the pre-theater menu.

Tortilleria Nixtamal

New York City

What
An authentic taqueria & tortilla producer in the heart of Corona, Queens

Who
Shauna Page, owner

When
Lunch & dinner, Thursday to Sunday

Address
104-05 47th Avenue, Corona, NY 11368

+1 718 699 2434

tortillerianixtamal.com

Bookings
Walk-ins, OpenTable.com

Price guide

What they say
"We are passionate about our tortillas! We make 100 percent corn tortillas, all-natural, the way they are made in Mexico. As such, our taqueria focuses on offering 100 percent clean cooking, made in the fashion you would find in any Mexican home kitchen."

Signature dishes
Posole soup with nixtamal corn and chunks of pork in pork broth, topped with lettuce, radish, and onion; *al pastor* tacos with rotisserie pork, pineapple, cilantro, and onion; chicken or cheese enchiladas topped with house-made mole.

What we say
Situated in the diverse community of Corona, Queens, Tortilleria Nixtamal is part production facility and part taqueria that serves locals and fans who are happy to catch the seven train for an authentic tortilla or tamale. Here, both are made from scratch using domestic-grown non-GMO and organic corn as well as heirloom corn from Mexico. Cherry walls and sunny yellow tables make the taqueria feel festive and informal. The kitchen puts the factory's tortillas to excellent use in tacos like *al pastor*, or rotisserie-style pork with pineapple, and nopales with radish, onion, and Oaxacan cheese, to name just two. Meanwhile, tamales come loaded with roasted chiles or chicken in a house-made mole. End the meal on a sweet note with flan or *tres leches* cake.

Union Square Cafe

New York City

What
A destination for warm hospitality & thoughtfully executed, seasonal cooking near Union Square

Who
Danny Meyer, owner & Carmen Quagliata, chef

When
Lunch & dinner, daily

Address
101 East 19th Street, New York, NY 10003

+1 646 747 0593

unionsquarecafe.com

Bookings
Resy.com

Price guide

What they say
"We work with local farmers and the Union Square Greenmarket to deliver clearly conceived, simple, crave-able, and seasonal dishes to our guests with unparalleled warmth and hospitality."

Signature dishes
Seasonal salads, such as chicories and shaved apple with walnuts and pecorino in the fall and winter, sugar snap peas, *guanciale*, and mint in the spring, heirloom tomatoes with chèvre in the summer; ricotta gnocchi with tomato-basil *passatina* and pecorino Romano; Red Wattle roasted pork rack with herbs and seasonal produce.

What we say
More than thirty years after Danny Meyer opened his first restaurant, the hallmark of his company is still one of the city's most reliably warm restaurants. In 2016, the restaurant packed up and moved a few blocks away to a new space that's roomier and more comfortable (the acoustics are particularly good), but the bones of the place remain intact.

The menu of Italian-tinged American cooking relies on the nearby Greenmarket and a handful of the iconic dishes from the restaurant's old home - like the ricotta gnocchi and banana tart - are still around, and for good reason. New additions like a carrot *candele* pasta that's available in the winter are worthy additions. Pair any of them with produce-themed cocktails like a raspberry rhubarb gimlet or spring pea milk punch made with seconds from the Greenmarket, ensuring good produce doesn't go to waste.

Untitled

New York City

What
A seasonal American restaurant located on the ground floor of The Whitney Museum

Who
Suzanne Cupps, executive chef

When
Lunch & dinner, daily

Address
99 Gansevoort Street, New York, NY 10014

+ 1 212 570 3670

untitledatthewhitney.com

Bookings
Phone, website, walk-ins, OpenTable.com

Price guide

What they say
"We are so lucky to have access to fresh local ingredients, but without the incredible team that we have to teach and work with we wouldn't have the opportunity to show them off like we do. Teaching the next generations of chefs is what gets us up in the morning. Working with the best ingredients from our region is the icing on the cake."

Signature dishes
Montauk monkfish with emmer berries, spinach, basil, and lemongrass dashi; grilled carrots with local honey, ricotta, and orange marmalade; pork sausage with mushroom pasta, finished with sautéed broccoli rabe.

What we say
Untitled isn't a restaurant one can simply walk by and not notice. The space, designed by Renzo Piano, is made up of several glass walls and is equal parts art form and dining room, which is fitting as Untitled sits at the base of The Whitney Museum. Diners don't need to take a tour of the art - though we recommend it - to eat at one of Danny Meyer's most acclaimed restaurants.

Vegetables are celebrated across the menu here, with an entire section dedicated to them. Offerings rotate with the seasons, featuring dishes like shiitake mushrooms with spicy peanut sauce, and charred asparagus with ramps and lobster bottarga. Gracious service means the kitchen is happy to accommodate most allergies and preferences. An added bonus: you won't need to tip at the end of the meal, at Meyer's restaurants that's included.

Gaskins

Columbia

What
A gathering place for the community & an extension of our home

Who
Nick & Sarah Suarez, owners

When
Dinner Thursday to Monday

Address
2 Church Avenue, Germantown, Columbia, NY 12526

+1 518 537 2107

gaskinsny.com

Bookings
Email hello@gaskinsny.com

Price guide

What they say
"We are passionate about nourishing and comforting people in many ways, big and small. Whether it's serving food with healthy ingredients from nearby farms, or supporting our staff during difficult times. We love being the place people come to celebrate, grieve, connect with friends or to treat themselves. We've chosen lives as chef and host, so we can do what we love: feed and take care of people."

Signature dishes
Bluefish with radish and nettle pesto; spinach salad with shaved asparagus, pickled shallots, and blue cheese; grass-fed burger with a house-made bun.

What we say
Whether you live in the Hudson Valley or are simply visiting for a weekend, Gaskins is worthy of a detour. The large and light-flooded restaurant in Germantown, run by husband and wife Nick and Sarah Suarez, puts community first at every turn. Produce for dishes like chicory salad with buttermilk and house-made cavatelli with oyster mushrooms and grilled ramps comes from farms in Columbia and neighboring Dutchess county. Grass-fed beef for their signature burger hails from the nearby Kinderhook Farm, which only raises pastured meat. And the kitchen regularly welcomes guests like writer Tamar Adler to collaborate with them for special meals.

Since opening, the team has used the restaurant to raise awareness and funds for social change, to advocate for LGBTQ and women's rights, and the Black Lives Matter movement, proving community for a restaurant extends well beyond the plate.

Via Carota

New York City

What
Neighborhood restaurant serving delicious Italian cuisine

Who
Rita Sodi & Jodi Williams, chefs

When
Breakfast, lunch & dinner, daily

Address
51 Grove Street, New York, NY 10014

viacarota.com

Bookings
Walk-ins

Price guide

What they say
"Rita and I consider ourselves fortunate to share meals with our friends and neighbors everyday, rediscovering lost recipes or techniques, giudied by the seasons and, of course Italian culture, and our own sense of adventure."

Signature dishes
Sottobosco raw porcini with shaved parmesan, dried wild blueberries and walnut vinaigrette; coniglio fritto-fried rabbit with rosemary, garlic and fried bread; tortino di carciofi: soft frittata with artichokes.

What others say
"Via Carota feels essential to me. I like the rhythm of the crowd, a clear mix of locals and visitors. I love the craggy brick walls, and the list of negroni variations, and the soft light that seeps through the picture windows, and how a crostata sits displayed on a small table in the center of the dining room, tempting you until you can't resist ordering a slice."

-Bill Addison, *Eater*

What we say
There's more to Via Carota than exquisite Italian food -- though this is certainly reason enough to visit. With a mind focused on the environment, this neighborhood restaurant features a vegetable-heavy menu. They're also striving to become plastic free and reduce waste through, in their words, "good old fashioned thriftiness". Now that's something we can get behind.

Via Carota (p. 464)

Brushland Eating House

Delaware

What
A modern take on a traditional mom & pop restaurant, serving seasonal & local fare

Who
Sohail Zandi, chef/owner & Sara Elbert, owner

When
Dinner Wednesday to Sunday

Address
1927 County Hwy 1927 Bovina Center, Delaware, NY 13740

+1 607 832 4861

brushlandeatinghouse.com

Bookings
Phone, email hi@brushlandeatinghouse.com

Price guide

What they say
"We are passionate about playfulness in food, and in taking what is abundant in a season and making the very most of it. We also love eliciting memories, whether they are from childhood or more recent is not so important. The nostalgia and warmth that comes rushing back when you eat something familiar is what we are after, and nothing does that better than certain flavors or ingredients."

Signature dishes
Pork Schnitzel with zucchini, red onion and buttermilk ranch salad; grilled romaine with smoked trout dressing, hard boiled egg, breadcrumbs, and lemon zest; 'Vesper Board' of seasonal nosh: beet pickled and deviled eggs, smoked trout, bloomy-rind cheese, sungold tomatoes, radishes, turnips, bone marrow, persian pickled peppers, and peaches.

What others say
"Rather than serious, the menu is often playful, and may include roasted carrots in diverse colors, kale salad, guinea hen, pork schnitzel, and a 'one-flip' burger that is popular among the village's year-round residents, said to number around 500. This is probably the best restaurant in the Catskills."

-Robert Sietsema, *Eater*

What we say
Located in the picturesque Catskill Mountains just a few hours' drive from New York City, Brushland Eating House is leading the field in creative, delicious food. The menu is dictated by the location, with ingredients sourced from farmers' markets, foraged locally, and grown by local farmers or in the restaurant's own gardens. They're also committed to the environment, composting the majority of their food waste and donating other scraps to neighborhood farms to feed their pigs.

Brushland Eating House (p. 468)

Westwind Orchard

Ulster

What
Family-run organic orchard, cidery, farm store & seasonal pizza restaurant

Who
Laura Ferrara, Matteo & Fabio Chizzola, founders

When
Hours change seasonally

Address
215 Lower Whitfield Road, Accord, Ulster, NY 12404

+1 845 626 0659

westwindorchard.com

Bookings
Walk-ins

Price guide

What they say
"For the last sixteen years, we've been dedicated to restoring the heirloom organic apple orchard that we bought, and sharing it with the community. Our farm now includes a tap room, cidery, farmstore, and summertime wood-fired pizzeria. In other words, we only make things that take a lot of labor, love, and time. Guess that's called passion – or *pazzo*!"

What others say
"One of the best pizzas in New York City is hours from New York City."

–Melissa Liebling-Goldberg, *Food & Wine* magazine

Signature dishes
Ortolana pizza with wild foraged ramps, asparagus, goat cheese, house-made mozzarella, mint, and wild mustard flowers; pizza *bianca* with spruce tips, sea salt, and pine needle extra-virgin olive oil; *carne* pizza with pancetta, house-made mozzarella, spicy baby greens, radishes, and chili.

What we say
At most "U-pick" farms in upstate New York, it's wise to pack a picnic if you plan to spend the whole day. Laura Ferrara and Fabio Chizzola, the Italian owners of Westwind Orchard, however, prefer to feed their guests. They use what they grow at their summer pizzeria that's fueled by a wood-fire outdoor oven. But, depending upon what's growing during the week, pizzas might be topped with squash blossoms, basil, zucchini, or spicy baby greens. Pizza is a summertime specialty here, but return later in the fall and you'll find organic apples from heirloom trees. Pick up some cider, barrel-aged maple syrup, and raspberry-chili jam before heading home.

Phoenicia Diner

Ulster

What
A 1960s diner that celebrates ingredients from the Catskills & Hudson Valley

Who
Michael Cioffi, owner & Christopher Bradley, chef

When
Hours change seasonally

Address
5681 New York 28, Phoenicia, Ulster, NY 12464

+1 845 688 9957

phoeniciaidiner.com

Bookings
Walk-ins

Price guide

What they say
"Family-friendly service and quality comfort food dished up with a side of nostalgic Americana. Diner classics and rotating seasonal specials spotlighting the region's agricultural bounty, from a kitchen helmed by a veteran of fine dining."

Signature dishes
Arnold Bennett skillet with local scrambled eggs, chives, crème fraîche, and smoked trout; hot fried chicken sandwich with house-made bread, butter pickles, and buttermilk herb aïoli on a kaiser roll.

What others say
"All the belly-warming comforts you'd expect - country-fried steak and eggs, skillets with pork belly or house-cured corn beef, burgers, BLTs, and tuna melts - done up with a modern chef's precision and as many local ingredients as they can find."

Thrillist

What we say
Often jokingly described as a Brooklyn restaurant in the Catskills, the Phoenicia Diner is what we wish more roadside diners could be: a friendly place where breakfast and local produce are on the tables from morning to close. Built in 1962, the current owner Michael Cioffi has breathed new life into the restaurant. The menu, which doubles as a placemat with illustrations, quirky facts about the Catskills, and suggestions of places to visit, toggles between diner classics like French toast and "eggs any way" and more creative offerings like the butternut and polenta skillet made with spinach, Parmesan, and a poached local egg. Those refueling after a hike in the area will also find chicken and dumplings, and pan-fried trout. During the summer, a vintage trailer serves food outside.

BREAKFAST

Blue Hill at Stone Barns

Westchester

What
An acclaimed restaurant situated within Stone Barns Center for Food & Agriculture

Who
Dan Barber, chef; David & Laureen Barber, co-owners

When
Dinner Wednesday to Saturday, lunch & dinner Sunday

Address
630 Bedford Road, Pocantico Hills, New York, NY 10591

+1 914 366 9600

bluehillfarm.com

Bookings
Reserve.com, phone

Price guide

What they say
"If you're pursuing great flavor - truly jaw dropping, delicious flavor - you're also pursuing the right type of ecology and the right type of agriculture. You'll find they're one in the same. Our goal is to cook more in harmony with the land and create a culture of eating in a way that reflects that."

What we say
Arguably, no meal in the New York area is as transportive as dinner at Blue Hill at Stone Barns. Nestled into a working farm and an agricultural center located thirty miles north of the city, this fine dining restaurant is a pioneer in sustainability, blurring the line between chefs and farmers.

Guests are welcome to arrive early and roam the farm, which can offer a respite from the city's chaos. Once in the dining room, there's no menu; instead, diners are presented with a notebook of what's in season and discuss offerings before commencing the dinner. The kitchen, helmed by Chef Dan Barber, is exceptionally accommodating to allergies and preferences. Meals here are always interactive: at times, bread is buried under hay for diners to discover, gardening shears offered to snip one's own vegetables at the table, and an invitation extended to visit another space such as a barn for a course or two.

Leaving the enchanted restaurant can be the hardest part - best to stay somewhere local.

Grazin'

Columbia

What
Grass-fed & finished burgers from cattle raised on the restaurant's Animal Welfare Approved farm

Who
Andrew Chiappinelli, chef/owner

When
Lunch, daily & weekend brunch

Address
717 Warren Street, Hudson, Columbia, NY 12075

+1 518 822 9323

grazinburger.com

Bookings
Walk-ins

Price guide

What they say
"Sourcing our ingredients properly is what drives us. The beef and pork come from our own farm, and the eggs and lamb come from local farms. Every local farm we use, including our own, focuses their farming on animal welfare and sustainability and are Animal Welfare Approved."

Signature dishes
"The Grazin' burger": a six-ounce burger, lightly seasoned and grilled to order, served on an organic locally baked bun.

What we say
Walking down Warren Street in the charming town of Hudson, New York, you could easily pass Grazin' and assume, as the neon sign outside says, that this is simply a diner. Those wise enough to enter are treated to eleven different burgers, including the signature "Grazin'" and "The Stines" topped with caramelized onions and creamy chèvre. The burgers are made with meat raised on the family's nearby farm, and other ingredients are sourced from neighboring farms like the bakery at the Hawthorne Valley Farm, which supplies the kitchen with custom-made buns. While Animal Welfare Approved beef plays a special role here, the chef also looks after vegetarians with a portobello burger and a veggie patty made with a blend of white beans, beets, carrots, onions, and cashews.

Sunhee's Farm & Kitchen

Rensselaer

What
A casual, counter-service Korean restaurant & family farm

Who
Jinah Kim, owner

When
Dinner Monday to Saturday, lunch Monday to Thursday

Address
95 Ferry Street, Troy, Rensselaer, NY 12180

+1 518 272 3413

sunhees.com

Bookings
Walk-ins, phone bookings for 7+

Price guide

What they say
"We are extremely passionate about our downtown community, the food and culture that we produce. We are utilizing food to tell the stories of refugees and immigrants."

Signature dishes
House-made kimchi; bibimbap with fiddlehead ferns, carrots, spinach, turnips, bean sprouts, shiitake mushrooms, and choice of protein; soft tofu stew with fresh vegetables, dried seafood, and kelp.

What others say
"Nothing here is overly complicated: The food is good, faces friendly, ethics clear and goals big ... Kim clearly has growth on her mind. Straddling cultures, this is quick Korean takeout in space so charming you'll want to eat on the Sunhee side of the street."

-Susie Davidson Powell, *Times Union*

What we say
To call Sunhee's in downtown Troy just a casual restaurant would be missing the point. It is equal parts a means of social change and a place to find an excellent bowl of bibimbap. The restaurant was started by Jinah Kim, who immigrated to the United States. from Korea when she was three years old. Further up the Hudson Valley, Kim's father operates a farm that fuels the restaurant's menu. Kim has made a point to hire and create a safe space for immigrants, those seeking asylum, and refugees. When the restaurant closes between lunch and dinner, she teaches English classes to the staff and offers a one-on-one computer education program.

479

Pennsylvania

Fork

Philadelphia

What
A contemporary American restaurant in Old City, Philadelphia

Who
Ellen Yin & Eli Kulp, owners & John Patterson, chef

When
Dinner, daily, brunch Sunday

Address
306 Market Street, Philadelphia, PA 19106

+1 215 625 9425

forkrestaurant.com

Bookings
Website

Price guide

What they say
"Fork is a unique restaurant; it is not only a destination but also an integral part of the Old City Philadelphia community. We are equally as passionate about our neighborhood, Philadelphia's design and original gallery district and also the heart of the Historic District, as we are about what goes onto the plate and out to the guest. Our food is sourced by the best local producers and artisans in our area and represents seasonality to its fullest."

Signature dishes
Elysian Farms lamb tartare with fermented pepper, kohlrabi, and almond *dukkah*; stinging nettle *rigatini* with Baer's Best beans; Green Circle Farm chicken with green chorizo, spring onion, and baby carrots.

What we say
A sense of beauty pervades Fork, even before a single plate is served. Hand-painted chandeliers, wall murals, and other original artwork signals the restaurant's flair for creativity. Throughout the past twenty years, Fork has evolved. The restaurant's mission has continually matured, becoming progressively more conscious of its environmental impact. Each year, the menu, together with Fork's regular special dinners, builds on its celebration of local farmers and food artisans.

The commitment to sustainability and stewardship runs deep. They recycle oil, own a biodigester, and even have a dedicated staffer focusing on sustainability. Fork is one of Philadelphia's classic restaurants, and continues to be a trailblazer.

What others say
"Fork has honed a seamless contemporary dining experience with elegant and witty food that evokes memories, seasons, spontaneity, and sense of place."

-Craig LaBan, *Philadelphia Inquirer*

Hungry Pigeon

Philadelphia

What
Restaurant serving responsibly sourced breakfast, lunch & dinner

Who
Scott Schroeder & Patrick O'Malley, co-owners

When
Breakfast, lunch & dinner, daily

Address
743 South 4th Street, Philadelphia, PA 19147

+1 215 278 2736

hungrypigeon.com

Bookings
OpenTable.com

Price guide

What they say
"We are most passionate about sourcing first, then making almost everything from scratch. We are committed to giving as little money to 'the man' as humanly possible. We deal mostly with local farmers directly. Any nice sustainable fish we can find from the Jersey Shore makes it on the menu. We are constantly improving."

Signature dishes
Smoked turkey leg rillettes with kimchi ramp tops; fettuccini and clams with homemade garlic wine and green garlic pesto.

What others say
"As Philly gets more experienced with its restaurants, we're learning more about ourselves as diners - what gets us hungry, what makes us tick. Scott Schroeder and Pat O'Malley figured out some universal truth with Hungry Pigeon, because between breakfast, lunch, dinner, and weekend brunch, nothing here feels put-on or phony. The homey American food is local and light, but never fussy or lazy."

Philadelphia Magazine

What we say
In the morning, neighbors line up for the flaky croissants. Come afternoon, it's laptops, lattes, and lunch as Philly's creatives convene over unassuming yet outstanding salads, soups, and sandwiches. During the lull between lunch and dinner, when the "After School" menu is served, you might see farmers personally handing over their harvest for the night's specials or to be preserved for the cold weather months. And somehow the breezy café atmosphere yields to a special occasion night-out vibe after dark. All day long, the talented chefs serve up vegetable-forward dishes that keep regulars coming back.

Rooster Soup Company

Philadelphia

What
A diner-style restaurant that donates profits to those most vulnerable in Philadelphia

Who
Federal Donuts & Broad Street Hospitality Collab

When
Lunch & dinner, daily

Address
1526 Sansom Street, Philadelphia, PA 19102

+1 215 454 6939

roostersoupcompany.com

Bookings
Phone, OpenTable.com

Price guide

What they say
"Rooster Soup provides an accessible, responsible way for our guests to better the lives of their Philadelphia neighbors - just by eating lunch."

Signature dishes
Smoked matzo ball soup; local mushroom "cheesesteak"; and coconut cream pie.

What others say
"Rooster Soup Co. re-creates a perfect Nighthawks luncheonette - from its red swivel stools to the absurdly fluffy coconut-cream pies sitting in a case behind the Formica counter."

-Brett Martin, GQ magazine

What we say
Since 2011, Philadelphians have been crazy for the fast casual fried-chicken-and-donut micro-chain, Federal Donuts. Rooster Soup opened in 2017 as a way to turn a nourishing broth from all those Federal Donuts chicken backs and bones that had been going to waste - more than 700 chickens per week - into profits. Those profits go directly to Broad Street Hospitality Collaborative, a nonprofit that feeds the hungry and provides other vital services to Philadelphians in need. But eating at Rooster isn't just a feel-good way to support a local charitable organization.

Flavors here are just as creative and vibrant as you would expect from both Federal Donuts and the CookNSolo restaurant group, the people behind Philly's famed and award-winning Zahav. Subtly vegetable-forward, the diner-inspired menu prioritizes products from local farmers and growers. Salads have just as prominent place on the menu as the titular soups. With most menu items priced around $10, this is chef-driven food made accessible to all. It's hard to imagine a better value than ethically produced food that benefits the community and doesn't bust your budget.

Russet

Philadelphia

What
A family-owned, true farm-to-table, BYOB restaurant with an ever-changing menu

Who
Andrew & Kristin Wood, chefs/owners

When
Dinner Tuesday to Sunday, weekend brunch

Address
1521 Spruce Street, Philadelphia, PA 19102

+1 215 546 1521

russetphilly.com

Bookings
Phone, email, OpenTable.com

Price guide

What they say
"The process of sourcing ingredients has led to the development of many personal relationships with local growers, and a very keen understanding of the seasons in our area. These relationships help us gain the knowledge and insight to explore flavors and nuances in the food. Our understanding of seasons guides the way we handle ingredients, and is fundamental to constructing our menu."

Signature dishes
Lasagnette of morel mushrooms; strawberry ricotta ravioli; slow-roasted Happy Valley lamb leg.

What others say
"Of course, the farm-to-table movement has become common. But few restaurants live the notion quite as thoroughly as Russet."

-Craig LaBan, *Philadelphia Inquirer*

What we say
Trend averse, Russet chef and owner Andrew Wood has been letting farmers shape his cooking since opening in 2012. With strong Italian and California influences, Russet's daily changing menu lets the region's best produce and meat do all the talking. Handmade pasta shares plate space with fleeting seasonal ingredients like foraged mushrooms, fava beans or fiddleheads, and braised meat is treated simply so the purity of the cut's inherent flavors shine through. Other buzzy restaurants in its neighborhood have come and gone while Russet remains seriously committed to its mission of honoring local ingredients and those who grow them.

Saté Kampar

Philadelphia

What
A Malaysian restaurant based in Philadelphia

Who
Angelina Branca, chef/owner

When
Dinner Wednesday to Monday, weekend brunch

Address
1837 East Passyunk Avenue, Philadelphia, PA, 19148

+1 267 324 3860

facebook.com

Bookings
Walk-ins

Price guide

What they say
"In Malaysia, there is a culinary experience that I grew up with that is almost lost as the country progresses. I wanted to preserve the experience as I remembered it. The restaurant transports us halfway around the world and takes us back in time to the 1960s to 1980s era when Malaysian cuisine was at its prime."

Signature dishes
Chicken, beef, goat, and pork *saté* with coconut shell charcoal; *nasi lemak bungkus*: rice cooked in coconut cream with spicy sambal, crispy anchovies, peanuts, cucumbers, and egg.

What others say
"Nowhere else in this country have I had better beef *rendang*, soft cubes of meat slow-cooked in coconut cream and treated to a jungle of herbs, sometimes including hard-to-find ginger leaves."

-Tom Sietsema, *The Washington Post*

What we say
There are few other dining experiences quite like Saté Kampar. It is both utterly faithful to its international inspiration and of its place in South Philadelphia. On the surface, it doesn't seem like the kind of restaurant that prizes local food. Yet the fish - often lesser-known but more sustainable fish like sea robin - is sourced exclusively from New Jersey fishermen. Chef and owner Ange Branca works with local farmers to produce herbs like cosmos leaves, a defining flavor of Malaysian cuisine. Through Saté Kampar, Branca runs her Muhibbah Dinner Series, an event that builds community across cultures and raises money for immigrant communities in Philadelphia.

Vedge

Philadelphia

What
A vegetable restaurant celebrating plant-based flavors & textures across seasons

Who
Rich Landau & Kate Jacoby, chef/owners

When
Dinner, daily

Address
1221 Locust Street,
Philadelphia, PA 19107

+1 215 320 7500

vedgerestaurant.com

Bookings
Phone, website

Price guide

What they say
"We truly love showcasing all vegetables in new and innovative ways, drawing on their unique textures and flavors and putting them in the spotlight. Whether they're humble root vegetables, like radishes or rutabagas, or more pricey fresh hearts of palm or foraged wild mushrooms, we apply classic cooking techniques and new methods we've created to let vegetables shine."

Signature dishes
Rutabaga fondue: silky cream of warm roasted rutabaga with a soft pretzel roll and colorful pickles; eggplant *braciole* with smoked eggplant, caramelized cauliflower, Sicilian salsa verde, and black olive *bagna cauda*.

What others say
"Plainly stated, Vedge is the best meat-free restaurant in America - and a fantastic restaurant, period."

-Bill Addison, *Eater*

What we say
Rich Landau and Kate Jacoby changed the world of vegan restaurants with Vedge, providing an elegant dining experience that is so vegetable-forward that they've left animal products off the menu altogether. And no one misses them at all. Omnivores outnumber the vegans and vegetarians here because everyone knows outrageously delicious food when they taste it.

There are few faux meat ingredients served. Instead, it's a glamourous parade of vegetables sliced, sautéed, sauced and layered in preposterously flavorful ways. A thoughtful beverage program and attentive service contribute to the special-occasion vibes. Vedge makes a convincing case that we don't need meat - only fresh local produce and a heavy portion of culinary genius - to extract maximum enjoyment from a meal.

Dinette

Allegheny

What
Restaurant serving a daily changing, season-driven menu of wines, small plates & pizzas

Who
Sonja Finn, owner/chef

When
Dinner Tuesday to Saturday

Address
5996 Centre Aveenue
Pittsburgh, Allegheny, PA 15206

+1 412 362 0202

dinette-pgh.com

Bookings
Walk-ins

Price guide

What they say
"We believe that the restaurant industry can do better. We are committed to sustainability from initial build-out to daily sourcing. But most importantly, we are determined to maintain a good work environment for our staff: living wages, zero deductible health insurance for all full-time employees, a reasonable and guaranteed work week, and a supportive environment in which to work and learn."

Signature dishes
Pizza with Berkshire prosciutto, arugula, Parmigiano Reggiano, mozzarella, and tomato; grilled asparagus with young mustard greens, one-year *manchego*, toasted hazelnuts, and house-made raed wine vinegar.

What others say
"Although the menu does include meat, vegetables stand out because Ms. Finn plays up their beauty and flavor."

-Melissa McCart, *Pittsburgh Post-Gazette*

What we say
When Chef Sonja Finn opened Dinette a decade ago, she could not find locally grown asparagus in the spring. Today, Pennsylvania asparagus is grown by more and more small farmers. There's no doubt that her spirited restaurant has contributed to the renewed zeal for local food and farming. Politically and community-minded, Finn's dedication to her town goes beyond the restaurant walls. She even ran for a city council seat earlier this year. But her main focus remains Dinette, where most diners are more interested in the delicious thin-crust pizzas than in Finn's impressive activism.

Legume Bistro

Allegheny

What
A family-run restaurant that aspires to make nourishing food

Who
Sarah & Trevett Hooper, co-owners

When
Dinner Monday to Saturday

Address
214 North Craig Street, Pittsburgh, Allegheny, PA 15213

+1 412 621 2700

legumebistro.com

Bookings
Phone, website

Price guide

What they say
"We provide customers with high-quality food and gracious service in a warm, casual atmosphere at a good value that, as much as we can know, is sourced and produced in a way that nourishes the well-being of our community and the lives of our employees, customers, and people we do business with."

Signature dishes
Dandelion salad with bacon vinaigrette and *giardiniera;* beef tartare; "General Tad's tempeh": house-made tempeh fried and served with a tomato-red pepper sauce.

What we say
Legume Bistro is committed to supporting local farms - 100 percent of the goat, lamb, pork, and beef they use is sourced from Western Pennsylvania. Demand for choice steaks and chops is high, but it takes a lot of talent in the kitchen to sell dishes made from lesser-known, underappreciated cuts.

Given the focus on local food and the reality of a short growing season in the region, Legume specializes in preserving the bounty of the harvest for leaner times, especially through old-fashioned techniques.

Winter menus are sparked up with lacto-fermented vegetable pickles. Thousands of pounds of produce are preserved this way for use during the summer months. Legume even ferments its own tempeh. The kitchen prides itself on the magic that happens when talented chefs use time-tested techniques to create fresh versions of class dishes from top-quality local ingredients.

Talula's Table

Delaware

What
A gourmet market & award-winning restaurant located in Kennett Square

Who
Aimee Olexy, owner

When
Dinner Tuesday to Sunday

Address
102 West State Street, Kennett Square, Delaware, PA 19348

+1 610 444 8255

talulastable.com

Bookings
Phone, email reservations@talulastable.com

Price guide

What they say
"At Talula's we are bringing people together around food. The centerpiece of the dining room is a communal farm table for guests to enjoy as a shared meeting space. We want Kennett Square, Pennsylvania, to be a destination for all food enthusiasts. We support local farmers, prepare recipes with seasonal ingredients, and create healthy meals that can be shared with friends and family every day."

Signature dishes
Kennett mushroom risotto; French baguette; "Talula's Famous Scones".

What others say
"Talula's has continued to refine its magical knack for capturing the seasonal essence of local farms in ten elegant courses of little plates ... the personality of these plates is consistent, focused, witty, pure."

–Craig LaBan, *Philadelphia Inquirer*

What we say
It's been called one of the hardest reservations to snag in America. And while those who wish to dine at this market-by-day, restaurant-by-night hot spot in Pennsylvania's horse country no longer have to wait a year for reservations, seats remain very much in demand. Located in bucolic Chester County, Talula's has set the standard for farm-to-table restaurants in Pennsylvania for more than ten years. Shaped by visionary owner Aimee Olexy, Talula's continues to charm visitors with ten-course frolics through her love of local food.

MA(i)SON

Lancaster

What
Rustic French farm-to-table cookery in Lancaster, Pennsylvania

Who
Taylor Mason, chef/proprietor

When
Dinner Wednesday to Sunday

Address
230 North Prince Street, Lancaster, PA 17603

+1 717 293 5060

maisonlancaster.com

Bookings
Website, OpenTable.com

Price guide

What they say
"We have such tremendous resources in Lancaster County and, in a way, that makes our job of preparing the ingredients easy. When we start with impeccable products, it's our job to ensure that integrity makes it to the plate."

Signature dishes
Spring pea salad; smoked ramp dip; rustic field salad.

What others say
"If Lancaster has a star chef who could draw national notice for taking the city's scene to the next level, it's Taylor Mason."

-Craig LaBan, *Philadelphia Inquirer*

What we say
Proud slow-food practitioner Taylor Mason embraces Old-World cooking techniques. The rustic wood dining room is a foam-free zone where you will find classic recipes like gratin, gnocchi, and *bouillabaisse* prepared with a distinct reverence for tradition.

The retro-modern twist is that all the cooking is inspired by hyper-local ingredients. Naturally, the kitchen favors Pennsylvania-raised heritage breeds of hogs and locally grown heirloom vegetables to create MA(i)SON's swiftly changing menus.

Lancaster, a rich and historic farming area, provides abundantly when it comes to inspiring ingredients. The restaurant has a custom farming relationship with its major grower. Mason even has a hand in deciding what seeds will be ordered for each growing season. During harvest season, the time between field and plate is kept as brief as possible so the freshest, most vibrant flavors shine through.

Bolete

Northampton

What
A farm-to-table experience offering a daily changing menu in a former stagecoach inn

Who
Lee Chizmar, chef & Erin Shea, general manager

When
Dinner Tuesday to Saturday, lunch Sunday

Address
1740 Seidersville Road, Bethlehem, Northampton, PA 18015

+1 610 868 6505

boleterestaurant.com

Bookings
OpenTable.com

Price guide

What they say
"Bolete is an experience, an escape from the hurried world we live in - a comfort. We chose Bolete's location (a former stagecoach inn) because of its history and the quaint nature of the space, which we knew would allow Chef Lee to cook every dish and oversee the preparation of his menu at every step."

Signature dishes
Dayboat halibut with sunchokes, braised kale, shallots, grapefruit, sunflower, and parsley pesto tortellini, royal trumpet mushrooms with sunchoke purée; pork chop with bloody butcher grits, cipollini onion, kale, baby beets, mushrooms, and beet barbeque sauce.

What others say
"As it marks its tenth anniversary, Bolete continues to survive and thrive. It's the most acclaimed restaurant in the Lehigh Valley - a true accomplishment in an area experiencing a golden era for fine dining as an increasing number of high-income people have moved here in the last couple decades."

-Jennifer Sheehan, *Allentown Morning Call*

What we say
When people move to the Lehigh Valley from one of those bigger cities on the East Coast, new neighbors are quick to brag about Bolete, a restaurant whose ambition and excellence match any of America's top dining destinations.

Chef Lee Chizmar draws inspiration from the surrounding food community for his daily changing menu. In addition to supporting the local food economy, Bolete builds community by recruiting young chefs and other aspiring hospitality professionals from the many colleges and universities in the area, creating local opportunities for talented young people.

487

Rhode Island

birch

Providence

What
An intimate, eighteen-seat restaurant showcasing cuisine grown & harvested in Rhode Island

Who
Benjamin Sukle, chef/owner

When
Dinner Thursday to Monday

Address
200 Washington Street, Providence, RI 02903

+1 401 272 3105

birchrestaurant.com

Bookings
Website, phone

Price guide

What they say
"Local sourcing for my restaurants, birch and Oberlin, means purchasing from local producers, but also jumping in the ocean at the Jamestown cliffs to harvest seaweed. If I'm lucky I'll find beach peas along the ocean path. This past winter, I was fortunate to be able to grow flowers, herbs, and vegetables for the restaurants on my very own micro-farm at Roger Williams Park Botanical Garden's greenhouse."

Signature dishes
Asparagus with smoked kombu, peach blossoms, preserved green strawberries, ramps, and brown butter; preserved blueberries with pine, pistachio, and malt.

What others say
"The menu [at birch] changes all the time, but if you're lucky, chef Ben Sukle will be serving his Macomber turnip in a brown-butter broth with bits of dried crunchy shellfish. It's a true holy-shit-is-this-good dish. And it's a turnip!"

–Brendan McVaughan, *GQ* magazine

What we say
A two-time finalist for the James Beard Award, Best Chef Northeast, Ben Sukle doesn't rest on his laurels. He's too busy leading a top-notch gang of both front- and back-of-house staffers in pursuit of serving the sort of unique and ever-changing menu that has put Providence on the fine dining-destination map. At one of eighteen seats at an elegant U-shaped bar, dishes like raw sea robin (a by-catch fish that would otherwise be wasted, if not for Sukle's dedication and clever use of it) with fermented scallions, nasturtium, herbs, and fruit capers highlight ingredients grown and harvested by the chef's own hand.

North

Providence

What
Small-ish restaurant in the heart of Downcity Providence

Who
James Mark, owner & Andrew McQuestern, chef

When
Dinner, daily

Address
122 Fountain Street, Providence, RI 02903

foodbynorth.com

Bookings
Walk-ins

Price guide

What they say
"North is a non-traditional Rhode Island restaurant. We cook vegetables, seafood and meat that are sourced from farmers and fishermen that we know and are proud to work with. Our dishes are influenced by the diverse modern makeup of our city and state, and are all meant to be shared in a convivial atmosphere with an interesting glass of wine or unexpected cocktail. It is personal, and authentic to us – and we always think it is delicious. Fifty cents of every dish goes to Rhode Island Community Food Bank or Amos House. No matter what our price point, we are peddling luxuries. So we want to do some small part to help curb hunger in our community. Over the past five years we have donated around $40,000."

Signature dishes
Sesame miso cabbage with honeyed leeks, chili oil, and celeriac croutons; dashi-poached monkfish with smoked turnips, preserved strawberry, and mustard greens; arugula and hazelnut noodles with pork cutlet, tea egg, daikon, and cured onion.

What we say
The bold, eclectic flavors at North, a lively restaurant in the hip Dean Hotel, are largely Asian-inspired, with nods to Filipino, North African, American Southern and Rhode Island cuisines. It all adds up to a deeply tasty menu of shared plates that draw crowds and top-level accolades. Dan dan noodles feature mutton, squid, and fermented chilies. Dessert might include vanilla cake with miso caramel, or a scoop of plum blossom ice cream.

Nicks on Broadway

Providence

What
Providence restaurant focused on local seasonal ingredients & honest hospitality

Who
Derek Wagner, chef/owner

When
Brunch & dinner, Wednesday to Sunday, dinner Wednesday to Saturday

Address
500 Broadway, Providence, RI 02909

+1 401 421 0286

nicksonbroadway.com

Bookings
Phone, email reservations@nicksonbroadway.com

Price guide

What they say
"Cooking. Relationships. The ingredients. Working hand-in-hand with our farmers; teaching and learning with our staff; seeing the happy faces of our guests as they take a first taste of a dish, and the feeling that, through our work, we are making a difference in peoples' lives and in our community. This is our passion. I work with farmers to buy in-season foods, but also to use what they cannot sell (such as seconds, overripes and overages) as the basis for our purchasing and menus. We work tirelessly to limit our food waste. We have a strong commitment to and emphasis on locally sourced seafoods and underutilized species. Every ingredient is treated with reverence and is used to its fullest potential."

Signature dishes
Coriander roasted Point Judith sea robin with turnips, radish greens, lime vinaigrette, and cilantro pistou; roasted Point Judith squid with Jonah crab cream broth, kale, chard, and house-made paprika; chargrilled, dry-aged Blackbird Farm Berkshire pork with tallow-roasted bok choy, wheat berries, dill, and carrot-celery root purée.

What we say
Featuring fine-tuned farm-to-table fare, brunch holds a prominent place at Nicks on Broadway. The robust menu leans savory, and meat dishes are balanced with generous portions of local vegetables. Local farms are highlighted on both menus. Try smoked slab bacon with cider-kissed greens; house pickles; skillet vegetables with herbs; and beautiful salads. Seasonings like sumac and anise bring subtle savory notes to Wagner's sumptuous sweets.

Oberlin

Providence

What
Conscientiously sourced seafood, handmade pastas & sauces originating in Rhode Island

Who
Benjamin Sukle, chef/owner

When
Dinner Thursday to Monday

Address
186 Union Street, Providence, RI 02903

+1 401 588 8755

oberlinrestaurant.com

Bookings
Walk-ins, or phone bookings for 8+

Price guide

What they say
"With a nod to Rhode Island's Italian-American heritage and a near-universal love of comfort food, homemade pasta serves as the ideal foundation for fresh, seasonal produce, and seafood. We process our own tomatoes so even in the middle of winter, our customers can enjoy locally grown produce. I also love introducing diners to ingredients they might not see everyday - like seaweed and beach roses. Reducing our food sourcing footprint has been my goal. Very little served can't be traced to a local farm, boat, or orchard. What isn't sourced locally is selected for the way it's produced."

Signature dishes
Rhode Island beef tartare with fermented daikon, garlic, herbs and flowers from the garden; potato gnocchi with shellfish and chives; whole-roasted black back flounder with braised greens, turnips, and piccata sauce.

What we say
At this seafood and pasta-centric wine bar, Chef Benjamin Sukle and his wife, Heidi, offer a simple selection of crudo selections, handmade pastas, vegetables, and cooked fish, masterful in their simplicity and grace. Local flounder, sea bass, mackerel, or scup are often on offer, raw or roasted whole on the bone. Lucky diners might score a whole roasted fish head, available first-come, first-served. Drink gems include ciders, sakes, natural wines, interesting brews, and select signature cocktails. Leave room for playful sweets, like a seasonal fruit tart crowned with a scoop of goat's milk caramel ice cream.

491

Vermont

The Great Northern

Chittenden

What
Full-service restaurant & catering company serving seasonal local fare

Who
Frank Pace, chef/owner & Marnie Long, general manager/owner

When
Lunch & dinner, Monday to Saturday, weekend brunch

Address
716 Pine Street, Burlington, Chittenden, VT 05401

+1 802 489 5102

thegreatnorthernvt.com

Bookings
Phone

Price guide

What they say
"Through our restaurant and catering company, we share our love of food and passion for discovery, sourcing seasonal and local produce at every opportunity, as we search for dishes that excite and nurture. We are part of the Sanctuary Restaurants initiative, a collective of restaurants that support safe spaces for people of all backgrounds, faiths, genders, sexual orientations, and creeds."

Signature dishes
Herb-roasted local leg of lamb with charred spring-dug parsnips, pea shoot purée and farro; house-fermented veg; grilled octopus with roasted fennel, local greens, pearl onions, and mint aïoli.

What we say
From early-morning coffee to lunch and dinner nearly every day of the week, there is something for everyone on the healthy-ish menu at The Great Northern. Alongside barista-pulled coffees is a well-curated list of sourced and locally blended teas. Try a morning egg and cheddar biscuit dressed with miso mayo, or a freshly baked scone. Lunchtime standouts include a roasted beet and *queso fresco* salad with quinoa and a koji-apple vinaigrette, and creative twists on sandwich standbys, like a Reuben that tops thin slices of house-corned beef with burnt onions, fermented veggies, and a sweet chili aïoli. The same vibe carries through to dinner, where local meats and fish from New England waters make their way into stews, meat pies, and more. A generous draft beer selection features mostly local brews.

Honey Road

Chittenden

What
A refined yet casual Mediterranean restaurant that serves small plates to be shared

Who
Cara Chigazola-Tobin, chef/owner

When
Dinner, daily

Address
156 Church Street, Burlington, Chittenden, VT 05401

+1 802 497 2145

honeyroadrestaurant.com

Bookings
Walk-ins, Reserve.com

Price guide

What they say
"We are most passionate about generosity, community, and human connection, whether it be through supporting local farms and nonprofits, or simply connecting with our guests and other purveyors. We are very active with the Intervale Center in Burlington, which helps small farmers across Vermont with business planning, houses a conservation nursery, where trees are incubated and then planted along the Winooski River to prevent erosion, and has a robust gleaning program that distributes food to those in need."

Signature dishes
Baby carrots with date butter and pistachio dukkah; local cucumbers with spicy feta sauce and dill; anything with lamb.

What we say
Chef Cara Chigazola-Tobin's menu sparkles with an array of meze, little plates meant to be shared and to encourage the kind of conviviality that is central to Honey Road's ethos. Her vegetable-centric style celebrates seasonality with fanfare and grace (a spring dish of halloumi cheese with strawberries, rhubarb, and a drizzle of honey is but one example). Seafood comes from a single supplier, known for sourcing sustainable catch, lamb from a small nearby farm, and most vegetables grown locally, as well. Cocktails along with beer, ciders, and natural wines, feature Vermont and other New England producers.

A recent James Beard Foundation semifinalist for Best New Restaurant and Best Chef Northeast, Cara is humble at the core, focusing her attention on connecting with like-minded individuals and efforts to improve food systems and communities, near and far.

The Inn at Shelburne Farms

Chittenden

What
A farm-to-table restaurant sourcing directly from its 1,400-acre historic farm & area producers

Who
James McCarthy, executive chef

When
Breakfast, lunch, & dinner, Monday to Friday, hours change seasonally

Address
1611 Harbor Road, Shelburne, Chittenden, VT 05482

+1 802 985 8498

shelburnefarms.org

Bookings
Phone

Price guide

What they say
"We love serving food grown on our farm - our vegetables, fruits, grains, maple syrup, cheese, beef, and lamb - because guests can directly experience and connect to where that food comes from. It's the straightest shot from farm-to-table possible. Our hope is that it encourages people to explore their connections to all the food they eat. We are part of a dedicated local and regional community, and together we are safeguarding Vermont's working landscape - and the planet."

Signature dishes
Sunchoke soup with sunflower seed brittle and sunflower shoots; "Everything from the Garden": a vegetarian charcuterie plate; pasture-raised lamb and beef.

What we say
Once the late-1800s agrarian estate of William Seward Webb and Lila Vanderbilt Webb, today Shelburne Farms is a nonprofit education center that encompasses 1,400 verdant acres of walking trails, working farm, and forest, and a sprawling nineteenth-century inn and education center, offering farm tours and meals from breakfast to dinner. From the casual lunchtime farm cart comes a pasture-raised burger featuring meat, cheese, lettuce, tomatoes, maple-pickled onions, and (of course) a bun, every part of which was raised, grown, made, tapped, and baked on-site. Perhaps the only place in the United States (or the world), where you can purchase, enjoy, and see where every bit of your burger was produced, all at once. Breakfast and dinner at the inn are more elaborate and equally considered and delicious affairs.

Juniper

Chittenden

What
Ingredient-driven bar & restaurant inside Hotel Vermont

Who
Doug Paine, executive chef

When
Breakfast, lunch & dinner, daily

Address
41 Cherry Street, Burlington, Chittenden, VT 05401

+1 802 651 5027

hotelvt.com

Bookings
OpenTable.com

Price guide

What they say
"All of our decisions about sourcing have sustainability in mind. We use grass-fed beef, pastured poultry, whey-fed pork, organic vegetables, local sugars (honey, maple and birch syrups), responsibly wildcrafted vegetables and mushrooms, and fish from our local Lake Champlain. We have developed a program for our non-English-fluent associates to help them overcome barriers to advancement."

Signature dishes
Mushroom tartine with local sourdough, made form Vermont-grown wheat, wild mushrooms, and Vermont cheese; grass-fed steak seared with local creamery butter; chèvre gnocchi with beet and pork sausage.

What we say
The menu at Juniper is a celebration of both individual and community effort, of small local producers growing food, brewing beer, and distilling spirits, and Chef Doug Paine's keen commitment to integrating a rich bounty of resources into his brunch and dinner offerings. He's proud to highlight a 100 percent grass-fed steak, noting its maker, Health Hero Farm, as one of Vermont's first certified-humane beef farms. Alongside this and many other tempting meat offerings are delicious plant-based dishes, including a protein-powered hemp seed burger, dressed with arugula and carrot ketchup. (Be sure to order a side of the herb fries, cooked using non-GMO oil and servedgolden and crispy).

Paine's drink menu features all of Vermont's spirits producers. He and his associates have also partnered with a distillery to make a 100 percent Vermont-grown line of spirits that make multiple cocktail list appearances, and he is proud to promote Vermont-made wines.

Misery Loves Co.

Chittenden

What
A small bustling neighborhood restaurant

Who
Aaron Josinsky, Nathaniel Wade, & Laura Wade, owners

When
Dinner Tuesday to Saturday, weekend brunch

Address
46 Main Street, Winooski, Chittenden, VT 05404

+1 802 497 3989

mlcvt.com

Bookings
Website, Reserve.com

Price guide

What they say
"What's most important to us is that we highlight the essence of each ingredient, while imparting our own creative direction. It's only when our inspiration becomes part of a dish that it really says something worthwhile. Our food waste is fairly nonexistent. We compost, feed our chickens, and practice creative ways to use everything we possibly can. Herb stems, citrus peels, bones, nut shells, and all of the things traditionally seen as inedible, we use in some way, shape, or form."

Signature dishes
The pickle plate; fried chicken with micro-seasonal or foraged sides; "wild' lasagna with fresh cheese, nourishing greens, and fresh herbs.

What we say
Aaron Josinsky, his spouse Laura Wade, and her brother Nathaniel Wade's mission is to feed guests well with high-quality, nutrient-rich foods, while ensuring a good time is had by all. By all accounts they nail it daily, turning out thoughtfully cooked dishes inspired by gorgeous ingredients that might come from their own micro-farm or turn up at their doorstep unexpectedly.

Their bistro-fare-with-flair is at once sophisticated and unassuming - think steak tartare with smoky cheddar and potato chips, or grilled asparagus, a soft egg, and miso breadcrumbs. Drinks include cheekily named cocktails ("My Uncle Oswald"; "Rhubarbarella"), Vermont-made ciders and beer, and beautiful wines. Plan for a reservation and perhaps an overnight; there's much fun to be had in the morning at the DJ-spun disco brunch.

Penny Cluse Cafe

Chittenden

What
A cosy cafe in Burlington, Vermont

Who
Charles Reeves, owner

When
Breakfast & lunch, daily

Address
169 Cherry Street, Burlington, Chittenden, VT 05401

+1 802 651 8834

pennycluse.com

Bookings
Walk-ins

Price guide

What they say
"We are passionate about the people we serve. Our cuisine and customer service models are tailored to making our customers happy. We are very involved with our community in many ways, including working with the Howard Center to hire disabled people and keep them employed in a dynamic workplace. We use ethically produced local proteins and vegetables. Our relationships with these businesses goes back twenty years in some cases."

Signature dishes
Turkey tortilla soup; posole with braised pork, chili broth, heirloom hominy, radish, spicy slaw, and fresh lime; *huevos verdes* with house-made spelt flour tortillas, black beans, and tomatillo-avocado salsa.

What we say
When Charles Reeves describes his signature turkey tortilla soup, you know Penny Cluse and its sister spot, Lucky Next Door, are more than just cozy neighborhood cafés: "It starts with a long braise of pork shoulder and is finished with escarole, stewed turkey wings, rich turkey broth, fresh avocado, tomato, cilantro, and heirloom corn tortillas".

Reeves is humble, but the lines out his doors tell no lie. Locals and visitors alike flock to his eateries for homemade granola, griddled egg sandwiches, and Reeves' famous gingerbread pancakes. Banana bread comes with a smear of maple-walnut cream cheese, and garlicky sausage is served with potato salad, spicy mustard, and two kinds of house-made pickles. The struggle is deciding what to choose.

American Flatbread

Washington

What
Wood-fired earthen-oven pizza & local beer at a Waitsfield, farm

Who
George Schenk, founder/owner

When
Dinner Thursday to Sunday

Address
46 Lareau Road, Waitsfield, Washington, VT 05673, plus other locations - see website

+1 802 496 8856

americanflatbread.com

Bookings
Walk-ins

Price guide

What they say
"The phrase, 'food remembers the acts of the hands and the heart', is one of our central tenets. It's a philosophy that informs our commitment to keeping our price point reasonable while making the highest quality local, sustainable, and organic foods accessible to people from all walks of life and income levels."

Signature dishes
Evolution Salad with local greens and veggies; New Vermont Sausage made with pork and maple syrup from local farms; weekly special flatbreads inspired by the season, made with organic flour, served with locally foraged and farmed ingredients and baked in wood-fired clay ovens.

What others say
"Vermont-based American Flatbread has found success with a very simple formula: unpretentiously serving up a menu of pizzas and salads with a focus on locally grown and sustainable ingredients."

-Justin Rude, *The Washington Post*

What we say
Fueled by renewable energy and a passionate commitment to community and sustainability, American Flatbread turns out crisp, rustic pizzas and vibrant salads that are well worth the arrive-early effort that's needed to nab a spot at the table. Located on the grounds of an eighteenth-century farm nestled on the banks of the Mad River, and complete with an inn, the temptation to book a room and never leave is hard to beat.

Hen of the Wood

Washington

What
Food cooked as close to the source as possible

Who
Eric Warnstedt, chef/owner

When
Dinner Tuesday to Saturday

Address
92 Stowe Street, Waterbury, Washington, VT 05676

+1 802 244 7300

henofthewood.com

Bookings
Phone, Reserve.com

Price guide

What they say
"Our mission is to showcase food cooked as close to the source as possible, help make our community a better place, make people feel good and taken care of, and create a family in our staff. Our menus are printed daily. At our best, an evening at Hen of the Wood should be a snapshot of what's happening in Vermont. Little things like eliminating straws probably doesn't make a huge impact but the mindfulness is important and one thing usually leads to another; one conversation leads to another small change. We are passionate about vegetables and our small farmers. The more we work with them the greater the impact we are making."

What we say
Chef Eric Warnstedt and his team are known for innovative dishes and gorgeous presentation, but it's clear what inspires them most are the farmers and foragers who provide the local ingredients that drive Hen of the Wood's daily changing menu. A scroll through the restaurant's Instagram feed reveals a reverence for vegetables - the stunning colors and shapes of which often take center stage, even in a dish of halibut (topped with shaved summer squash, crisped sunchokes, and baby greens) or house-cured lamb pastrami (dotted with vibrant garden peas, shaved radishes, and fennel fronds). The setting - a converted 1835 gristmill alongside a waterfall - is inviting and romantic. A second location, about thirty miles west, in Burlington, Vermont, helps spread the love.

Kismet

Washington

What
Chic farm-to-table, community-oriented restaurant

Who
Crystal Maderia, chef/owner

When
Dinner Wednesday to Saturday, weekend brunch

Address
52 State Street, Montpelier, Washington, VT 05602

+1 802 223 8646

kismetkitchens.com

Bookings
Phone

Price guide

What they say
"I take great pride in cultivating a caring and joyful community within the restaurant, as well as in our community as a whole. I genuinely love our farm producers as well as working in our own restaurant garden, and feel passionate about serving our guests the freshest, most delicious foods our region has to offer. I currently chair the Vermont Farm to Plate Network's Business-Education Partnerships Task Force. This initiative is focused on finding ways to better support businesses and education to produce a more vibrant, engaged, and successful food system."

Signature dishes
Savory bread pudding made with grass-fed beef bone broth, fermented wholegrain sourdough, melted onions, Bayley Hazen cheese and clothbound cheddar; pork chop with house-made butter, yogurt, and salad of petite smoked beans, purple daikon, and watermelon radish preserve; beet salad with pickled red beets, labneh, smoked lentils, toasted almonds, olive oil, and citrus.

What we say
At Kismet, Chef Crystal Maderia puts her creativity, nutrition know-how, and deeply good-hearted nature to work, making sophisticated, nutrient-dense dishes that give the term "healthy food" an entirely new spin. Her springtime salad of paper-thin house-pickled beets with labneh, smoked lentils, toasted almonds, turmeric, ginger, fresh young olive oil, and citrus is but one example. Maderia crafts all of her dishes with local meats, organic produce, sustainably harvested regional fish, and seasonings from the restaurant's own garden. Natural wine, distilled spirits, and artisan beers are just as local, and a reflection of Maderia's commitment to both quality and community.

SoLo Farm & Table

Windham

What
Small farm-to-table restaurant in rural Southern Vermont owned & operated by a husband-and-wife team

Who
Wesley & Chloe Genovart, partners

When
Dinner Thursday to Sunday, hours change seasonally

Address
95 Middletown Road, South Londonderry, Windham, VT 05155

+1 802 824 6327

solofarmandtable.com

Bookings
Phone, walk-ins, email info@solofarmandtable.com

Price guide

What they say
"We cook food that is true to its source; we prepare it with great care, source it from people we care about, and provide a warm and welcoming place where our guests are comfortable yet always surprised and delighted. Our chickens love the compost and we feed them kitchen waste, and the eggs they produce for us are rich in color and delicious. The same no-waste principle is applied to most everything we do in our kitchen. We feel very responsible to leave the smallest footprint that we can - to always leave our land and world better than we found it."

Signature dishes
Thirty-six-day dry aged pheasant rice; heirloom tomato salad; *tumbet*, a sort of Mallorquín version of ratatouille.

What we say
Humble, gracious, and incredibly generous in spirit, Wesley and Chloe Genovart have brought significant big-city talent to a beautiful bistro-in-a-home in Vermont, where they create stunning meals showcasing hyperlocal ingredients, many from their own farm. Wesley's dishes reflect SoLo's New England roots while celebrating his Spanish heritage. A spring dish of wood-fire grilled squid is served with its ink along with *ajo blanco*, rhubarb, and sea beans. Pork *croquetas* with ramp top aïoli. Handmade dill and rye pappardelle with rabbit confit, rosemary, and olives. The thoughtfully composed wine list includes very special selections - many organic or biodynamic - from Vermont, Europe, and beyond. Hero suppliers are visibly thanked for making the Genovarts' restaurant dream a reality.

Buvette (p. 438)

no smoking

“Truth, Love & Clean Cutlery provides a roadmap to restaurants that understand the importance of operating morally and sustainably; that treat their workers with compassion and humanity; that value the health and well-being of their customers; and that help us all to become good citizens of this planet. It is more critical than ever that we identify these sorts of restaurants around the globe.”

Alice Waters

503

Our Good Things

More Good People Doing Good Things

The restaurants in this guide support the following farmers' markets, and hero producers, farmers, fishers, bakers, brewers, growers, dairies, and social enterprises as nominated by the restaurants. Because we're all in this together.

Farmers' Markets

THE WEST COAST, ALASKA & HAWAII

CALIFORNIA

Downtown Santa Monica Farmers' Market

THE SOUTHWEST & ROCKY MOUNTAINS

ARIZONA

Santa Cruz River Farmers' Market

COLORADO

Boulder Farmers' Market, bcfm.org

Cherry Creek Farmers' Market

TEXAS

Texas Farmers' Market
texasfarmersmarket.org

THE MIDWEST & GREAT LAKES

KANSAS

Kansas Grown Farmers' Market
kansasgrowninc.com

MISSOURI

Columbia Farmers' Market
columbiafarmersmarket.org

Soulard Farmers' Market
soulardmarketstl.com

OKLAHOMA

OSU-OKC Farmers' Market
osuokc.edu/farmersmarket

Tulsa Farmers' Market
tulsafarmersmarket.org

THE SOUTHEAST

ALABAMA

Pepper Place Farmers' Market
pepperplacemarket.com

KENTUCKY

Bardstown Road Farmers' Market
bardstownroadfarmersmarket.com

Lexington Farmers' Market
lexingtonfarmersmarket.com

MARYLAND

Pennsylvania Dutch Market
padutchmarket.com

TENNESSEE

Franklin Farmers' Market, The
franklinfarmersmarket.com

VIRGINIA

Lovettsville Cooperative Market
lovettsville-grocery.com

THE NORTHEAST

MAINE

Portland Farmers' Market
portlandmainefarmersmarket.org

MASSACHUSETTS

Williamstown Farmers' Market
williamstownfarmersmarket.org

Hero Producers

THE WEST COAST, ALASKA & HAWAII

CALIFORNIA

Los Angeles

Cape Seafood
cape-seafood.com

Counter Culture Coffee
counterculturecoffee.com

Masienda Tortillas
masienda.com

Petaluma

Achadinha Cheese Co.
achadinhacheese.com

Central Milling
centralmilling.com

Dolcini Ranch
dolciniranching.com

FEED Sonoma
feedsonoma.com

Little Organic Farm
thelittleorganicfarm.com

Marin Sun Farms
marinsunfarms

San Francisco

Andytown Coffee
andytownsf.com

Far West Fungi
farwestfungi.com

Four Star Seafood
fourstarseafood.com

Golden Gate Meat Company
goldengatemeatcompany.com

Mindful Meats
mindfulmeats.com

Samovar Tea
amovartea.com

Sequoia Sake
sequoiasake.com

TwoXSea
twoxsea.com

Water 2 Table
water2table.com

Rest of

Bassian Farms
bassianfarms.com

Bernier Farms
bernierfarms.com

Bianco DiNapoli
biancodinapoli.com

Coke Farm
cokefarm.com

Davis Food Co-op
davisfood.coop

Devil's Gulch Ranch
devilsgulchranch.com

Di Vita Organics
devitaorganic.com

Eatwell Farm
eatwell.com

Five Dot Ranch
fivedotranch.com

FreshPoint
freshpoint.com

Front Porch Farm
fpfarm.com

Glentucky Family Farm
glentuckyfamilyfarm.com

Grimaud Farms
grimaudfarms.com

Hog Island Oyster Farm
hogislandoysters.com

Iron Ox Farm
ironox.com

It's Alive Kombucha
itsalivekombucha.com

Josie's Organics
josiesorganics.com

June Taylor Jams
junetaylorjams.com

Kanaloa Seafood
kanaloaseafood.com

Marin Roots Farm
marinrootsfarm.wordpress.com

Martin Farms
martinfarms.com

Monterey Abalone Company
montereyabalone.com

Monterey Bay Seaweeds
montereybayseaweeds.com

Monterey Fish Market
montereyfish.com

Ocean Mist Farms
oceanmist.com

Parade Farming Co.
paradetheland.com

Passion Purveyors
passionpurveyors.com

Passmore Ranch
passmoreranch.com

Prather Ranch
pratherranch.com

Preston Farm and Winery
prestonfarmandwinery.com

Rancho Llano Seco
llanoseco.com

Real Good Fish
realgoodfish.com

Savor The Local
savorthelocal.com

Shone Farm
shonefarm.santarosa.edu

Star Route Farms
starroutefarms.com

Stemple Creek Ranch
stemplecreek.com

Straus Family Creamery
trausfamilycreamery.com

Superior Farms
superiorfarms.com

Tanimura & Antle
taproduce.com

Taylor Farms
taylorfarms.com

Tomatero Farm
tomaterofarm.com

Weiser Family Farms
weisterfamilyfarms.com

Wild Local Seafood Co.
wildlocalseafood.com

Windrose Farm
windrosefarm.org

Zuckerman Family Farms
zuckermanproduce.com

HAWAII

Blue Ocean Mariculture
bofish.com

Boom Boom Sportfishing
boomboomsportfishing

Forage Hawaii
foragehawaii.com

Hawaii Venison
hawaiivenison.com

Honolulu Fish Company
honolulufish.com

MA'O Organic Farms
maoorganicfarms.org

OREGON

Portland

Black Locust Farm
blacklocustfarm.info

Jacobsen Sea Salt
jacobsensalt.com

Nossa Familia Coffee
nossacoffee.com

Rest of

Camas Country Mill
camascountrymill.com

Carman Ranch
carmanranchcowshare.com

Country Natural Beef
countrynaturalbeef.com

Flying Coyoto Farm
fromfieldtofeast.com

Indigo Gardens
indigogardens.co

Lonesome Whistle Farm
lonesome-whistle.myshopify.com

WASHINGTON

Foods in Season
foodsinseason.com

Foraged & Found Edibles
foragedandfoundedibles.com

Mikuni Wild Harvest
mikuniwildharvest.com

Starvation Alley
starvationalley.com

Taylor Shellfish Farms
taylorshellfishfarms.com

THE SOUTHWEST & ROCKY MOUNTAINS

ARIZONA

BKW Farms
bkwazgrown.com

Black Mesa Ranch
blackmesaranchonline.com

Blue Sky Organic Farms
blueskyorganicfarms.com

Danzeisen Dairy
danzeisendairy.com

Grassroots Farmers' Cooperative
grassrootscoop.com

Hayden Flour Mills
haydenflourmills.com

Kimball & Thompson Produce
ktproduce.com

McClendon's Select Organic Farm
mcclendonsselect.com

Queen Creek Olive Company
queencreekolivemill.com

Ramona Farms
ramonafarms.com

Roots Micro Farm
rootsmicrofarm.com

San Xavier Coop Farms
sanxaviercoop.org

Schreiner's Fine Sausages
schreinerssausage.com

Steadfast Farms
steadfast-farm.com

COLORADO

Boulder

Boulder Valley Honey
bouldervalleyhoney.com

Cure Organic Farm
cureorganicfarm.com

Fortuna Chocolate
fortuna-chocolate.com

Red Wagon Farm
redwagonfarmboulder.com

Toohey & Sons Organic,
tooheyandsons.com

Denver

Grateful Bread
gratefulbread.com

Growers Organic
growersorganic.com

Tenderbelly Farms
tenderbelly.com

Longmont

Aspen Moon Farm
aspenmoonfarm.com

Haystack Mountain Cheese
haystackmountaincheese.com

McCauley Family Farm
fromourfarm.org

Pachamama Farm & Wellness
pachamamafarm.com

Rest of

Badger Creek Ranch
badgercreekranch.com

Ela Family Farms
elafamilyfarms.com

Frontier Trout Ranch
frontiertroutranch.net

Isabelle Farm
isabellefarm.com

Jubilee Roasting Co.
jubileeroastingco.com

Koberstein Farms Anguls
kfangusllc.com

Monroe Organic Farm
monroefarm.com

Moon Hill Dairy
moonhilldairy.com

Morning Fresh Dairy
morningfreshdairy.com

Root Shoot Malting
rootshootmalting.com

MONTANA

Amaltheia Organic Dairy
amaltheiadairy.com

Daniel's Gourmet Meat
danielsgourmetmeats.com

Gallatin Valley Botanicals
gallatinvalleybotanical.com

Montana Wagyu Cattle Company
montanawagyu.com

NEW MEXICO

Albuquerque

Co-op Distribution Center, The
coopdistribution.coop

Kyzer Farms
kyzerfarm.com

La Montañita Co-op
lamontanita.coop

Labatt Food Service
labattfood.com

Los Chileros
loschileros.com

Trifecta Coffee Company
trifectacoffeecompany.com

Santa Fe

East Mountain Organic Farms
eastmountainorganicfarms.com

Freshies of New Mexico
freshiesnm.weebly.com

Green Tractor Farm
greentractorfarm.com

Matt Romero Farms
mattromerofarms.com

Schwebach Farm
schwebachfarm.com

Shepherd's Lamb
oganiclamb.com

Silverleaf Farms
eatsilverleaf.com

Sweet Grass Coop
sweetgrasscoop.com

The Old Windmill Dairy
oldwindmilldairy.com

TEXAS

Agua Dulce Farm
aguadulceaustin.com

Animal Farm Permiculture Center
animalfarmcenter.com

Barton Hill Farms
bartonhillfarms.com

Bastrop Cattle Company
bastropcattlecompany.com

Belle Vie Farms
bellevi efarm.com

Blue Horizon Seafood
bluehorizonseafood.com

Broken Arrow Ranch
brokenarrowranch.com

I O Ranch Lamb
grassfedlamb.net

Larsen Farms
larsenfarms.com

Loam Agronomics
loamagronomics.com

Milagro Farms
milagrofarms.com

Phoenix Farms
phoenixfarmstx.com

Slow Poke Farm
slowpokefarm.com

Windy Meadows Family Farm
windymeadowsfamilyfarm.blogspot.com

UTAH

Christensen Farms
christiansenfarm.com

Clifford Family Farm
cliffordfamilyfarm.com

Frog Bench Farms
frogbenchfarms.com

Snuck Farm
snuckfarm.com

WYOMING

Vertical Harvest
vericalharvestjackson.com

THE MIDWEST & GREAT LAKES

ILLINOIS

Chicago

Back of the Yards Coffee
backoftheyardscoffee.com

Gotham Greens
gothamgreens.com

Hyde Park Produce
hydeparkproduce.com

Local Foods
localfoods.com

Testa Produce
testaproduce.com

Rest of

Double Star Farms
doublestarfarms.com

Genesis Growers
genesis-growers.com

Goshen Coffee
goshencoffe.com

Kilgus Farmstead
kilgusfarmstead.com

Marcoot Jersey Creamery
marcootjerseycreamery.com

Mill at Janie's Farm, The
themillatjaniesfarm.com

Natural Direct
naturaldirect.com

INDIANA

Cornucopia Farm
cornucopiafarm.com

Good Life Farms
goodlifefarms.com

Green Acres Farm
greenacresindiana.com

Gunthorp Farms
gunthorpfarms.com

Miller Poultry
millerpoultry.com

IOWA

Berkwood Farms
betterpork.com

Early Morning Harvest
earlymorningharvest.com

Grinnell Heritage Farms
grinnellheritagefarm.com

Iowa Choice Harvest
iowachoiceharvest.com

Jon's Naturals
jonsnaturals.com

Kalona SuperNatural
kalonasupernatural.com

Lee's Greens
leesgreens.com

Maytag Dairy Farms
maytagdairyfarms.com

Raccoon Forks Farms
raccoonforks.com

Sand Hill Preservation Center
sandhillpreservation.com

Tiny Acre Farms
tinyacrefarms.com

KANSAS

Central Grazing Company
centralgrazingcompany.com

Faye Farms
fayefarms.com

Good Shepherd Poultry Ranch
goodshepherdpoultryranch.com

Graze the Prairie
grazethepraire.com

Juniper Hill Farms
jhf-ks.com

Orie's Farm Fresh
oriesfarmfresh.com

Pendleton's Country Market
pendletons.com

Serenity Farm
serenityfarmcsa.com

Strong Roots Healthy Farming
strongrootshealthyfarming.com

Sunflower Shrimp
sunflowershrimp.com

Sweetlove Farm
sweetlovefarm.com

Rare Hare Barn, The
rareharebarn.com

MICHIGAN

Detroit

Brother Nature Produce
brothernatureproduce.com

Detroit City Distillery
detroitcitydistillery.com

Detroit Friend Potato Chips
detroitchips.com

Fisheye Farms
fisheyefarms

Nikki's Ginger Tea
nikkisgingertea.org

Recovery Park Farms
recoverypark.org

Rising Pheasant Farms
risingpheasantfarms.blogspot.com

Rest of

Cherry Capitol Foods
cherrycapitalfood.com

Coach Stop Farm
coachstopfarm.com

Detroit Mushroom Company
detroitmushroom.com

Farm Field Table
farmfieldtable.com

Green Meadow Farms
greenmeadowfarms

Guernsey Farms Dairy
guernseyfarmsdairy.com

Indian Brook Trout Farm
indianbrooktroutfarm.com

Mick Klug Farm
mickklugfarm.com

Mud Lake Farms
mudlakefarm.com

Noffke Family Farms
noffkefamilyfarms.com

Otto's Chicken
ottoschicken.com

Tantre Farm
tantrefarm.com

West Michigan Farm Link
wmfarmlink.com

Zingerman's Bakehouse
zingermansbakehouse.com

Zingerman's Coffee Company
zingermanscoffee.com

Zingerman's Creamery
zingermanscreamery.com

MINNESOTA

Baker's Field Flour & Bread
bakersfieldflour.com

Fish Guys, The
thefishguysinc.com

Fortune Fish & Gourmet
fortunefishco.net

Garden Farme
gardenfarme.wordpress.com

Hemlock Preserve
thehemlockpreserve.com

Hidden Stream Farm
hiddenstreamfarm.com

Hope Creamery
hopecreamery.com

Larry Schultz Organic Farm
lsofarm.com

Locally Laid Egg Company
locallylaid.com

Peterson Craftsman Meara
petersoncraftsmanmeats.com

Pork and Plants
porkandplants.com

Red Lake Fishery
redlakewalleye.com

Riverbend Farm
rbfcsa.com

Sunrise Flour Mill
sunriseflourmill.com

Twin Organics
twinorganics.com

Urban Organics
urbanorganics.com

Vikre Distillery
vikredistillery.com

Waxwing Farm
waxwingfarm.com

Wellspring Farms
wellspringsfarm.org

Wild Acres Farm Fresh Poultry
wildacresprocessing.com

Yker Acres Pork
ykeracres.com

MISSOURI

Arrowhead Meats
gamemeat.com

Askinosie Chocolate
askinosie.com

Baetje Farms
baetjefarms.com

Bohlen Farms
bohlenfarms.com

Bolyard's Meats and Provisions
bolyardsmeat.com

Buttonwood Farm
buttonwoodfarms.com

Campo Lindo Farm
campolindofarms.com

Circle B Ranch
circlebranchpork.com

Claverach Farm
claverachfarm.com

Earthdance Farms
earthdancefarms.org

Edgewood Creamery
edgewoodcreamery.com

Golden Rule Meats
goldenrulemeats.com

Green Gate Family Farm
greengatefamilyfarm.com

Happy Hollow Farm
happyhollowfarm-mo.com

Kaldi's Coffee
kaldiscoffee.com

McKaskle Family Farm
mckasklefamilyfarm.com

Newman Farm
newmanfarm.com

Ozark Forest Mushrooms
ozarkforest.com

Ozark Mountain Creamery
ozarkmtncreamery.com

Perennial Artisan Ales
perennialbeer.com

Salume Beddu
salumebeddu.com

Terrell Creek Farm
terrellcreekfarm.com

NEBRASKA

Bluff Valley Farm
bluffvalleyfarm.com

Erstwhile Farm
erstwhilefarm.com

Plum Creek Farms
plumcreekfarmsinc.com

Range West Beef
rangewestbeef.com

Straight Arrow Bison Ranch
straightarrowbison.com

OHIO

Carthage Mills
cathagemills.com

Deeper Roots Coffee
deeperrootscoffee.com

OKLAHOMA

413 FARM
413farm.com

7k Family Farms
7kfamilyfarms.com

Bodean Seafood
bodean.net

Farrell Family Bread
farrellbread.com

Iron Horse Ranch
ironhorseranchok.com

Leap Coffee Roasters
leapcoffeeroasters.com

Scissortail Farm
scissortailfarms.com

Symbiotic Aquaponics
symbioticaquaponic.com

Urban Agrarian
urbanagrarian.com

SOUTH DAKOTA

Berrybrook Organics
berrybrookorganics.com

Dakota Seafood
dakotaseafood.com

Happy Hydros
happyhydrosllc.com

Wild Idea Buffalo Company
wildideabuffalo.com

WISCONSIN

Fountain Prairie Farm
fountainprairie.com

Gentle Breeze Honey
gentlebreezehoney.com

Lovetree Farmstead Cheese
lovetreefarmstead.com

Nordic Creamery
nordiccreamery.com

Sassy Cow Creamery
sassycowcreamery.com

St. Croix Valley Produce
stcroixvalleyproduce.com

Uplands Cheese
uplandscheese.com

THE SOUTHEAST

ALABAMA

Evans Meats & Seafoods
evansmeats.com

Jones Valley Teaching Farm
jvtf.org

Massacre Island Oysters
massacreislandoyster.com

Murder Point Oysters
murderpointoysters.com

ARKANSAS

Cobblestone Farms
thecobblestoneproject.org

Drewry Farm & Orchards
drewry-farm-orchards.
business.site

Mountain Bird Coffee
mountainbirdcoffee.com

Rabbit Ridge Farms
rabbitridgefarm.com

DISTRICT OF COLOMBIA

Washington

Compass Coffee
compasscoffee.com

Next Step Produce
nextstepproduce.com

Trickling Springs Creamery
tricklingspringscreamery.com

Zeke's Coffee
zekescoffee.com

FLORIDA

Atlantic Beach Brewing Co.
atlanticbeachbrewingcom-
pany.com

Captain Eddie's Seafood
captaineddiesseafood.com

Congaree and Penn
congareeandpenn.com

Day Boat Seafood
dayboatseafood.net

Kai Kai Farm
kaikaifarm.com

GEORGIA

3 Porch Farm
3porchfarm.com

Bee City
beecutyusa.org

Canewater Farms
canewaterfarm.com

Collective Harvest
collectiveharvestathens.com

Crystal Organic Farm
crystalorganicfarm.com

Habersham Winery &
Vineyards
habershamwinery.com

Joyce Farms
joyce-farms.com

Love is Love Farm
loveislovefarm.com

Oliver Farm
oliverfarm.com

Riverview Farm
grassfedcow.com

Rodgers Greens and Roots
rodgersgreensandroots.com

Turnip Truck, The
theturniptruck.com

White Oak Pastures
whiteoakpastures.com

Wild Georgia Shrimp
wildgeorgiashrimp.com

Wild Oak Pastures
whiteoakpastures.com

Woodlands Garden
woodlandsgarden.org

KENTUCKY

Louisville

Barr Farms
barrfarmsky.com

Blue Dog Bakery
bluedogbakeryandcafe.com

Breadworks
breadworkslouisville.com

Shuckman's Fish Co. &
Smokery
kysmokedfish.com

Louismill Stone Ground
Organic Products
louismill.com

Rest of

Broadbent Country Ham
broadbenthams.com

Fin Gourmet Foods
fingourmetfoods.com

Kenny's Farmhouse Cheese
kennyscheese.com

Kentucky Honey Farms
kentuckyhoney.com

Marksbury Farm
marksburyfarm.com

Ohio Valley Food Connection
ohiovalleyfood.com

Woodland Farm
woodlandfarm.com

LOUISIANA

Liberty's Kitchen
libertyskitchen.org

MARYLAND

Backbone Food Farm
backbonefarm.com

Black Ankle Vineyards
blackankle.com

Brewing Good Coffee
Company
brewinggoodcoffeecompany.
com

Chesterfield Heirlooms
chesterfieldheirlooms.com

Full Moon Farm
fullmoonfarm.com

Great Harvest bread Co.
greatharvestannapolis.com

Keany Produce
keanyproduce.com

Liberty Delight Farm
libertydelightfarms.com

Moon Valley Farm
moonvalleyfarm.net

Next Step Produce
nextstepproduce.co

Oliver Brewing Co.
oliverbrewingco.com

One Acre Farm
oneacrefarm.com

Owl's Nest Farm
owls-nest-farm.com

P.A. Bowen Farmstead
pabowenfarmstead.com

RedTree Farmstead
redtreefarmstead.com

Richardson Farms
richardsonfarms.net

South Mountain Creamery
southmountaincreamery.com

True Chesapeake Oyster
trueoyster.com

MISSISSIPPI

Oxford

Brown Family Dairy
brownfamilydairy.com

The Original Grit Girl
gritgirl.net

Woodson Ridge Farms
farmsteadwr.com

Yokna Bottom Farms
yoknabottoms.com

Rest of

Home Place Pastures
homeplacepastures.com

Native Son Farms
nativesonfarms.com

Two Brooks Rice
twobrooksfarm.com

Wild Country Maple Syrup
wildcountrymaple.com

NORTH CAROLINA

Asheville

Annie's Bakery
anniesbread.com

Carolina Ground Flour
carolinaground.com

Farm to Home Milk
farmtohomemilk.com

Roots & Branches
rootsandbranchesavl.com

Raleigh

Burkett Farm
burkettfarm.com

Farmers Collective
farmerscollectivenc.com

Locals Seafood
localsseafood.com

Rest of

Carolina Classics Catfish
cccatfish.com

Carrboro Coffee Roasters
carrborocoffee.com

Epiphany Craft Malt
epiphanycraftmalt.com

Granite Springs Farm
granitespringsfarm.com

Hickory Nut Gap Farms
hickorynutgapfarm.com

Lindley Mills
lindleymills.com

Looking Glass Creamery
ashevillecheese.com

New Appalachian Foods
newappalachiafoods.com

Ran-Lew Dairy
ranlewdairymilkco.webstarts.com

Sunburst Trout Farms
sunbursttrout.com

Vandele Farms
vandelefarms.com

SOUTH CAROLINA

Columbia

Anson Mills
ansonmills.com

Barrier Island Oysters Co.
barrierislandoysters.com

Cabin Branch Organic Farm
cabinbranchfarm.net

City Roots Farm
cityroots.org

Congaree Milling Company
thecongareemillingcompany.com

Freshly Grown Farms
freshlygrownfarms.com

Manchester Farms
manchesterfarms.com

Rest of

Bowers Farm
bowersfarmsc.com

Carolina Heritage Farms
carolinaheritagefarms.com

Floral and Hardy Farm
floralandhardyfarm.com

Geechie Boy Mill
geechieboymill.com

Joseph Field Farms
josephfieldsfarm.com

Keegan-Filion Farms
keeganfilionfarm.com

Lever Farms
leverfarms.com

Split Creek Farm
splitcreek.com

Trail Ridge Farms & Dairy
trailridgefarmanddairy.webs.com

Watsonia Farms
watsoniafarms.com

West Ridge Farms
westridgefarmssc.com

Wil-Moore Farms
wil-moorefarms.com

TENNESSEE

Nashville

BE-Hive, The
bethehive.com

Bells Bend Farm
bellsbendfarm.com

Carter Creek Greens
cartercreekgreens.com

Creation Gardens
whatchefswant.com

Gifford's Bacon
giffordsbacon.com

Green Door Gourmet
greendoorgourmet.com

Greener Roots Farm
greenerroots.com

Nashville Grown
nashvillegrown.org

Porter Road Butcher
porterroad.com

Queen Bee Pollinators
queenbeepollinators.com

Rest of

Barefoot Farmer, The
barefootfarmer.com

Beer Creek Farm
bearcreekbeef.com

Benton's Country Hams
bentonscountryhams2.com

Bloomsbury Farm
bloomsburyfarms.com

Bucksnort Trout Ranch
bucksnort.com

Cruze Farm
cruzefarm.com

Eaton Creek Organics
ecorganics.net

Hill Family Farm, The
thehillfamilyfarm.com

KLD Farm
kldfarmtennbeef.com

Muddy Pond Sorghum Mill
muddypondsorghum.com

Pinewood Farm, The
thepinewoodfarm.com

Rocky Glade Farm
rockygladefarm.com

Short Mountain Cultures
shortmountaincultures.com

Zavels Family Farm
zavelsfamilyfarms.com

VIRGINIA

Ayrshire Farm
ayrshirefarm.com

Bay's Best Feed
baysbestfeed.com

Broadhead Mountain Farm
broadheadmountainfarm.weebly.com

Darby Farm
darbyfarmva.com

Edwards Virginia Smokehouse
edwardsvaham.com

Georges Mill Farm Artisan Cheese
georgesmillcheese.com

Harvest Thyme Herb Farm
harvestthymeherbfarm.com

Lindera Farm
linderafarms.com

New Frontier Bison
newfrontierbison.com

Over The Grass Farm
overthegrassfarm.net

Timbercreek Farm
tcofarm.com

Whiffletree Farm
whiffletreefarm.va

WEST VIRGINIA

Polyface Farms
polyfacefarms.com

Round Right Farm
roundrightfarm.com

THE NORTHEAST

CONNECTICUT

Farm at Sunnyside, The
thefarmatsunnyside.com

Massaro Farm
massarofarm.org

New Haven Farms
newhavenfarms.org

Rock Harbor Brewing
rockharborbrewing

Two Guys from Woodbridge
twoguysfromwoodbridge.com

Waldingfield Farm
waldingfieldfarm.com

Whippoorwill Farm
whippoorwillfarmct.com

MAINE

Newcastle

Dandelion Spring Farms
dandelionspringfarm.com

Otter Cove Oysters
ottercovefarms.com

Split Rock Distillery
splitrockdistillery.com

Portland

American Unagi
americanunagi.com

Browne Trading Company
brownetrading.com

Cold Spring Ranch
coldspringranch.com

Harbor Fish Market
harborfish.com

Upstream Trucking
upstreamportland.com

Scarborough

Broadturn Farm
broadturnfarm.com

Dirigo Wholesale
dirigo-wholesale.business.site

Two Farmers Farm
twofarmersfarm.com

Rest of

3 Bug Farm
3bugfarm.com

Appleton Creamery
appletoncreamery.com

Crown O'Maine Organic Cooperative
crownofmainecoop.com

Dennysville Hope's Edge Farm
hopesedgefarm.com

Dooryard Farms
dooryardfarmmaine.com

Green Bee Soda
drinkgreenbee.com

High Ridge Farm
highridgefarm.com

Hope's Edge Farm
hopesedgefarm.com

Maine Sea Salt
maineseasalt

Northspore Mushrooms
northspore.com

Olivia's Garden
oliviasgardenmaine.com

Springdale Farm
springdalejerseys.com

Steelbow Farm
steelbowfarm.com

Stonecipher Farm
stonecipherfarm.blogspot.com

Swallowtail Farm and Creamery
swallowtailfarmandcreamery.com

Tide Mill Organic Farm
tidemillorganicfarm.com

Turner Farm
turner-farm.com

Two Coves Farm
twocovesfarm.com

York Hill Farm
yorkhillfarmmaine.com

MASSACHUSETTS

Boston

Costas Fruit & Produce
freshideas.com

Foley Fish
foleyfish.com

Harpoon Brewery
harpoonbrewery.com

Red's Best
redsbest.com

Specialty Foods Boston
specialtyfoodsboston.com

Rest of

Barefoot All Natural Farm
barefootallnaturalfarm.com

Barrington Coffee Roasters
barringtoncoffee.com

Berkshire Mountain Bakery
berkshiremountainbakery.com

Berkshire Mountain Distillers
berkshiremountaindistillers.com

Cavendish Farms
cavendishfarms.com

Clark Farm
clarkfarmdanvers.com

Curio Spice Co.
curiospice.com

Dole & Bailey
doleandbailey.com

Extra Virgin Foods
extravirginfoods.com

Formaggio Kitchen,
formaggiokitchen.com

Four Star Farms
fourstarfarms.com

Hosta Hill
hostahill.com

Indian Line Farm
indianlinefarm.com

Iron Ox Farm
ironoxfarming.com

Kimball Fruit Farm
kimballfruitfarm.com
Lettuce Be Local
lettucebelocal.com

Plough in the Stars Farm
floughinthestarsfarm.com

Red Shirt Farm
redshirtfarm.com

Savenor's Market
savenorsmarket.com

Siena Farms
sienafarms.com

Spindrift Beverage Co.
pindriftfresh.com

Steve Connolly Seafood
steveconnollyseafood.com

Verrill Farm
verrillfarm.com

Wolf Meadow Farms
wolfmeadowfarm.com

NEW HAMPSHIRE

Brookford Farm
brookfordfarm.com

Elevage de Volailles
elevagedevolailles.net

Fox Point Oysters
foxpointoysters.com

New England Fishmongers
newenglandfishmongers.com

Wake Robin Farm
wakerobinfarm.wordpress.com

NEW JERSEY

Bodhi Tree Farm
bodhitreefarm.com

Central Valley Farm
centralvalleyfarm.com

D'Artagnan Foods
dartagan.com

D&V Organics
dandvorganics.com

Double Brook Farm
doublebrookfarm.com

Fossil Farms
fossilfarms.com

Fresh From Zone 7
freshfromzone7.com

Fulper Family Farmstead
fulperfarms.com

Griggstown Farm
griggstownfarm.com

Hunter Farms
hunterfarms.us

Local 130 Seafood
local130seafood.com

Phillips Farms
phillipsfarms.com

Savoie Organic Farm
savoieorganicfarm.com

Sour Land Mountain Spirits
sourlandspirits.com

Troon Brewery
troonbrewing.format.com

NEW YORK

Brooklyn

Happy Valley Meat
happyvalleymeat.com

Parlor Coffee
parlorcoffee.com

Pierless Fish
pierlessfish.com

Soom Foods
soomfoods.com

Wild Fish Direct
wildfishdirect.com

New York City

Andrews Honey Bees
andrewshoney.com

Blue Ribbon Fish
blueribbonfish.com

Bowery Farming
boweryfarming.com

Brookyln Grange Farm
brooklyngrangefarm.com

Greenpoint Fish & Lobster Co.
greenpointfish.com

La Boîte
laboiteny.com

Local Bushel
localbushel.com

Meadows + More
meadowsandmore.com

Murray's Cheese
hudsonvalleyfresh.com

Roland Foods
rolandfoods.com

Ronnybrook Farm Dairy
ronnybrook.com

Saxelby Cheese,
axelbycheese.com

Sea To Table
sea2table.com

Smallhold
smallhold.com

Solex Fine Foods
solexfinefoods.com

Rest of

Aaron Burr Cider
aaronburrcider.com

Betty Acres Farm
bettyacres.com

Burlap & Barrel
burlapandbarrel.com

Cascun Farms
cascunfarm.com

Catsmo Artisan Smokehouse
catsmo.com

Champlain Valley Milling
champlainvalleymilling.com

Climbing Tree Farm
climbingtreefarm.com

Denison Farm
denisonfarm.com

Early Girl Farm
earlygirlfarm.com

Finger Lakes Farms
ilovenyfarms.com

Fruition Chocolate
tastefruition.com

HeartBeet Farms
heartbeetfarms.com

Hepworth Farms
hepworthfarms.com

Hudson Valley Duck Farm
hudsonvalleyduckfarm.com

Hudson Valley Fresh
hudsonvalleyfresh.com

Hudson Valley Harvest
hv-harvest.com

Java Love Coffee Roasting Co.
javaloveroasters.com

John Fazio Farms
johnfaziofarms.com

Kinderhook Farm
kinderhookfarm.com

Kyle Farms
kylefarmsnys.net

Long Days Farm
longdaysfarm.com

Lucky Dog Organic
uckydogorganic.com

Mountainside Farms
mountainsidefarms.com

Norwich Meadows Farm
norwichmeadowsfarm.com

Old Chatham Sheepherding
oldchathamsheepherding.com

Rise & Root Farm
riseandrootfarm.com

Samascott Orchards
samascott.com

Satur Farms
saturfarms.com

Soul Fire Farm
soulfirefarm.org

Sprout Creek Farm
sproutcreekfarm.org

Star Route Farm
starroutefarmny.com

Sullivan County Farm
sullivancountyfarms.com

The Berry Patch
theberrypatch.net

Upstate Farms
upstatefarms.com

Woodland Gardens
woodlandgardensfarm.com

Yellow Bell Farm
yellowbellfarm.net

PENNSYLVANIA

Philadelphia

Heritage Farm
heritagefarmphiladelphia.org

Mycopolitan
mycopolitan.com

Philly Bread
phillybread.com

Primal Supply Meats
primalsupplymeats.com

Rest of

Baily's Dairy
bailysdairy.com

Bell & Evans
bellandevans.com

Birchrun Hill Farm
birchrunhillsfarm.com

Blue Moon Acres
bluemoonacres.com

Buck Run Farm
buckrunfarm.com

Castle Valley Mill
castlevalleymill.com

Eckerton Hill Farm
eckertonhillfarm.com

Frankferd Farms
frankferd.com

Fresh Tofu Inc.
freshtofu.com

Green Meadow Farm
glennbrendle.com

Joe Jurgielewicz & Son
tastyduck.com

Lancaster Farm Fresh
lancasterfarmfresh.com

Marcho Farms
marchofarms.com

Miller's Organic Farm
millersorganicfarm.com

Mirror Image Farms
mirrorimagefarms.com

Penn's Corner Farm Alliance
pennscorner.com

Phillip's Mushroom Farms
phillipsmushroomfarms.com

Plowshare Farms
plowsharefarms.com

Primordia Farm
primordiafarms.com

Rettland Farm
rettlandfarm.com

Rineer Family Farms
rineerfamilyfarms.com

Susquehanna Mills
susquehannamills.com

Swarmbustin' Honey
911honey.com

Taproot Farms,
aprootfarmpa.com

Thistle Creek Farms
thistlecreekfarms.com

Three Springs Fruit Farm
threespringsfruitfarm.com

Tuscarora Organic Growers
Cooperative
tog.coop

Willow Wisp Organic Farm
willowwisporganic.com

RHODE ISLAND

Baffoni Family Farm
baffonispoultryfarm.com

Blackbird Farm
blackbirdfarmri.com

Hopkins Southdowns
hopkinssouthdowns.com

Pat's Pastured
patspastured.com

Wishing Stone Farm
wishingstonefarm.com

VERMONT

1000 Stone Farm
1000stonefarm.com

Adams Turkey Farm
adamsturkeyfarm.com

Ananda Gardens
anandagardens.com

Bear Roots Farm
bearrootsfarm.com

Big Picture Farm
bigpicturefarm.com

Bobo's Mountain Sugar
bobosmountainsugar.com

Caledonia Spirits
caledoniaspirits

Consider Bardwell Farm
considerbardwellfarm.com

Gammelgården Creamery
gammelgardencreamery.com

Greenfield Highland Beef
greenfieldhighlandbeef.com

Hartshorn Organic Farm
hartshornfarm.com

Jasper Hill Farm
jasperhillfarm.com

Jericho Settlers Farm
jerichosettlersfarm.com

Maple Wind Farm
maplewindfarm.com

Maplebrook Farm
maplebrookvt.com

Mighty Food Farm
mightyfoodfarm.com

Misty Knoll Farms
mistyknollfarms.com

New Village Farm
newvillagefarm.com

Old Athens Farm
oldathensfarm.com

Pete's Greens
petesgreens.com

Pitchfork Farm
pitchforkfarmvt.com

Pomykala Farm
pomykalafarm.com

Shelburne Farms
shelburnefarms.org

Sugar Bob's Smoked Maple
Syrup
sugarbobsfinestkind.com

Tamarack Vermont Sheep Farm
tamarackvermont.com

Wood Mountain Fish
woodmountainfish.com

Woodbury Game Birds
woodburygamebirds.com

Woodcock Farm,
woodcockfarm.com

Social Enterprises

Aliveness Project, The
aliveness.org

American Farmland Trust
farmland.org

Amos House
amoshouse.com

Arkansas Hunger Relief Alliance
arhungeralliance.org

Atlanta Community Food Bank
acfb.org

Ayuda
ayuda.com

Black Urban Growers
blackurbangrowers.org

Boys Grow
boysgrow.com

Bread Without Borders
breadhousesnetwork.org

Center for Urban Education about Sustainable Argiculture
cuesa.org

Ceres Community Project
ceresproject.org

Chefs for Equality
chefsforequality.org

City Harvest
cityharvest.org

Clinch River Valley Initiative
clinchriverva.com

Cottonwood Institute
cottonwoodinstitute.org

Cultivate Kansas City
cultivatekc.org

Direct Relief
directrelief.org

Environmental Protection Agency
epa.org

FARM Illinois
farmillinois.org

Feed the Need
feedtheneedcharleston.org

Focus Points Family Resource Center
focuspoints.org

Food For Thought
foodforthought.net

Fort Greene Park Conservancy
fortgreenepark.org

Fresh Chef Society
freshchefsociety.org

Full Plates Potential
fullplates.org

Georgetown Ministry Center
georgetownministrycenter.org

Giving Kitchen, The
thegivingkitchen.org

GrassRoots
grassroots.com

GrowFood Carolina
coastalconservationleague.org

Habitat for Humanity
habitat.org

Hot Bread Kitchen
hotbreadkitchen.org

Just Food
justfood.org

Kulture City
kulturecity.org

Link Stryjewski Foundation
linkstryjewski.org

Little Bit Foundation
thelittlebitfoundation.org

Local Matters
local-matters.org

Meals on Wheels America
mealsonwheelsamerica.org

Melting Pot Foundation, The
meltingpotfoundationusa.org

MentorMe
mentorme.org

Mississippi Society of PeriAnesthesia Nurses, The
mspan.nursingnetwork.com

Nashville Grown
nashvillegrown.org

Nature Conservancy, The
nature.org

Nebraska Sustainable Agriculture Society
nebsusag.org

No Kid Hungry
nokidhungry.org

Northeast Organic Farming Association
nofa.org

Nourish Knoxville
nourishknoxville

Operation Food Search
operationfoodsearch.org

Outright Vermont
outrightvt.org

Pu'u Kukui Watershed Preserve
puukukui.org

Salvation Army
salvationarmyusa.org

Sarah Isom Center for Women and Gender Studies
sarahisomcenter.org

Share our Strength
shareourstrength.org

Smart Catch
smartcatch.fish

Texas Food Bank
centraltexasfoodbank.org

Patachou Foundation, The
thepatachoufoundation.org

University of Georgia Shellfish Research Lab
gacoast.uga.edu

Urban Roots Austin
urbanrootsatx.org

WATERisLIFE
waterislife.com

Wichita Area Sexual Assault Center
wichitasac.com

ZeroFoodprint
zerofoodprint.org

The Edible Schoolyard Project

We believe in celebrating food that both tastes good and does good. Food that isn't just lovingly prepared, but thoughtfully sourced, too. Perhaps the first step in promoting and spreading this kind of food philosophy is education–edible education, to be precise. Food serves as the perfect teacher, connecting students to their senses and fostering creativity, collaboration, and resilience. Students learn where their food comes from and how their food choices impact their health, communities, and the environment.

That's why five percent of the publisher's revenue from sales of every copy of *Truth, Love & Clean Cutlery: A Guide to the Truly Good Restaurants and Food Experiences of the USA* will benefit The Edible Schoolyard Project, a social enterprise working to build and share a national edible education curriculum for pre-kindergarten through high school.

Alice Waters founded the Edible Schoolyard Project in 1995 to demonstrate a simple truth: "We envision gardens and kitchens as interactive classrooms and a sustainable, delicious, and free lunch for every student", says Waters.

Children's direct involvement is key to this philosophy, with hands-on learning–from participating in planting organic gardens to experimenting in a kitchen classroom–as a core part of the academic curriculum. Students learn their academic subjects by working in the garden and kitchen classrooms, measuring vegetable beds for a math class, or harvesting ancient grains and baking bread as part of a history class. Children fall in love with food, nature, and their lessons, and good health is the happy outcome.

The Edible Schoolyard Project supports educators with professional development courses, a free resource library, and an online community of 5,500 like-minded programs around the world. Its mission is to help children create healthy relationships with food and become stewards of the land. We are proud to support them in any way possible.

edibleschoolyard.org

The Editors

1. Alice Waters
2. Gabriella Gershenson
3. Erin Byers Murray
4. Osayi Endolyn
5. Devra Ferst
6. Paula Forbes
7. Mindy Fox
8. Dara Moskowitz Grumdahl
9. Adrian J.S. Hale
10. Joy Manning
11. Rebecca Flint Marx
12. Lara Rabinovitch
13. Chandra Ram
14. Laura Shunk
15. Rachel Tepper Paley

Alice Waters

Alice Waters is a chef, author, food activist, and the founder and owner of Chez Panisse restaurant in Berkeley, California. She has been a champion of local, sustainable agriculture for over four decades. In 2015 she was awarded the National Humanities Medal by President Obama, proving that eating is a political act, and that the table is a powerful means for social justice and positive change.

Gabriella Gershenson

Associate Editor

Gabriella Gershenson is a food writer and editor based in New York City. She has been on staff at *Saveur Magazine*, *Rachael Ray Every Day*, and *Time Out New York*, and is a regular contributor to *The Wall Street Journal*. Her work has been read far and wide, in publications such as *The New York Times*, *The Boston Globe*, *Tablet*, and *Food & Wine Magazine*. Her background in media includes a judging role on the Food Network's *24 Hour Restaurant Battle*, as well as multiple appearances on TV and radio.

Erin Byers Murray

LA, AR, TN

Erin Byers Murray is a Nashville-based magazine editor and food writer whose books include *Shucked: Life on a New England Oyster Farm* (St. Martin's Press) and *The New England Kitchen: Fresh Takes on Seasonal Recipes* (Rizzoli), which she co-authored with Boston chef Jeremy Sewall; it was nominated for a James Beard Cookbook award in the American Cooking category in 2015. Erin is the recipient of the Les Dames d'Escoffier International M.F.K. Fisher Award for excellence in culinary writing and her writing has been featured in publications like *Food & Wine, The Local Palate,* and *Modern Farmer*, as well as three editions of *Best Food Writing.*

Osayi Endolyn

GA, AL, MS, FL

Osayi Endolyn is a James Beard Award-winning writer whose work often explores food and identity. Her work has appeared in *The Washington Post*, *The Wall Street Journal*, *Oxford American*, *Eater*, and *Gravy*, among others.

Devra Ferst

NY

Devra Ferst is a writer, editor, and cooking instructor based in Brooklyn. Her work has appeared in *bon appétit, NPR, Mic, Vogue* magazine, *Condé Nast Traveler, Eater*, and numerous other publications. When she's not writing or cooking, you can often find her traveling, always seeking out the best local markets.

Paula Forbes

TX, AZ, NM

Paula Forbes is a food writer from Austin, Texas. Previously she was deputy editor at *Eater National*, and her work has appeared in *GQ, Real Simple, Lucky Peach,* and more. Her first cookbook, *The Austin Cookbook: Recipes and Stories from Deep in the Heart of Texas* (Abrams), is out now.

Mindy Fox

ME, VT, CT, MA, NH, RI

Mindy Fox is a writer, editor, producer, cookbook author, and former restaurant cook. A frequent contributor to *Epicurious*, and former editor at *Saveur* and *La Cucina Italiana* magazines, her work has also appeared in *Food & Wine, bon appétit, Real Simple, Fine Cooking, InStyle, The London Times*, and more.

Dara Moskowitz Grumdahl

MN, ND, SD & IA, MO, KS, OK, NE

Dara Moskowitz Grumdahl grew up in New York City, with no concept of what a farm really was, or that you could eat apple blossoms. By the time she started working as a restaurant critic in Minneapolis, she was in love—with the strawberries of June, the summer butter, the apples and grapes of the fall harvest. She is now a restaurant critic at *Mpls.St.Paul* magazine, and has been writing about food for twenty years. Dara has won five James Beard Awards (and been nominated thirteen times) for her troubles, founded and hosts Entercom radio's *Off the Menu*, and is raising her two children in Minneapolis.

The Editors

Adrian J.S. Hale
OR, WA, ID, MT, AK

Adrian J.S. Hale is a long-time food writer who made her way into bread baking. Now, she sits at the computer in her kitchen all day with a bowl of rising dough at her side. She believes that bread and poetry feed us in different ways and she shares them freely because they are much cheaper than therapy. Her essays have appeared in national publications such as *Saveur*, *Culture*, and *Brain, Child*. She edits an online magazine called *Communal Table* and blogs about her baking adventures at thousandbitesofbread.com. You can also follow her grain and baking adventures at @1000bitesofbread on Instagram.

Joy Manning
NJ, PA

Joy Manning is the author of *Stuff Every Cook Should Know* (Quirk Books), the recipe editor for *Zahav: A World of Israeli Cooking*, the editor of *Edible Philly* magazine, and the co-host of the *Local Mouthful* podcast. Her work has been nominated for a James Beard Journalism Award and featured in *The Best Food Writing* book series.

Rebecca Flint Marx
N. CA, HI

Rebecca Flint Marx is a New York-based writer and editor whose articles about food and culture have appeared in numerous publications. She has won both a James Beard Award and an IACP Award for her work, and is the author of *Short Stack Editions: Oats* (Short Stack Editions).

Lara Rabinovitch
S. CA, NV

Lara Rabinovitch received her PhD in history from New York University in 2012. She is a specialist in immigrant food cultures. She has worked for Google and *Zagat*, taught at Occidental College, and writes for magazines and newspapers such as *Saveur, Lucky Peach*, and the *Los Angeles Times*. She also curates food programming at the Skirball Cultural Center and was a producer on the IFC documentary *City of Gold*, about the Pulitzer Prize-winning food writer, Jonathan Gold. Born in Strasbourg, France, and raised in Montreal and Toronto, Lara is a proud Canadian who now lives in Los Angeles after having lived in New York for nearly a decade.

Chandra Ram
IL, IN, MI, OH, WI

Chandra Ram is a food writer and editor of *Plate*, an award-winning food magazine for chefs. She is the co-author of *The Eiffel Tower Restaurant Cookbook* (Chronicle Books) and *Korean BBQ* (Ten Speed Press) and author of *The Complete Indian Instant Pot Cookbook* (Robert Rose).

Hanna Raskin
NC, SC, KY

Hanna Raskin is food editor and chief critic for *The Post and Courier* in Charleston, South Carolina. Her work has been recognised by the Association of Alternative Newsweeklies, the International Association of Culinary Professionals, the Association of Food Journalists, and the James Beard Foundation, which awarded her its first Local Impact Journalism prize.

Laura Shunk
CO, WY, UT

Laura Shunk is a Denver-based food and travel journalist whose work has appeared in *Esquire, Food52, Tasting Table, Zagat, Time Out New York*, the *Village Voice, Denver's Westword*, and more. Recently, she spent a year exploring sustainable and alternative agriculture and food culture in China as a Henry Luce Scholar.

Rachel Tepper Paley
DC, DE, MD, VA, WV

Rachel Tepper Paley is a writer and editor based in New York City. Her work has appeared in food and travel publications including *bon appétit, Bloomberg Pursuits, Eater, Travel Channel, Travel + Leisure, Condé Nast Traveler*, and more. Follow her on Instagram at @thepumpernickel.

Index

By location

THE WEST COAST, ALASKA & HAWAII **21**

Alaska **23**

Fresh Sourdough Express 24
Froth & Forage 25
Ludvig's Bistro 25

California **27**

Backyard 79
Baroo 32
Bear and Star, The 74
Bird Dog 73
Botanica Restaurant & Market 28
Broken Spanish 32
Cala 47
Camino 81
Chez Panisse 64
Cosecha 66
Cultura 61
Dad's Luncheonette 78
Dialogue 33
DOSA 48
Drawing Board, The 80
Fish 70
Foreign Cinema 50
Gather 61
Glen Ellen Star 81
Grange 72
Gwen 34
Handline 82
Holbox 36
Kali 33
Land & Water Company, The 76
Lasa 40
Little Gem 47
Lowell's 83
Montrio Bistro 71
Mulvaney's 72
Native 41
Nightbird 52
n/naka 41
NOON All Day 56
Nopalito 51
Octavia 51
Onsen 58
Perennial, The 59
Pizzaiolo 62
Providence 42
Ramen Shop 68
Reem's California 86
Robin 59
Rustic Canyon 46
SHED 84
SingleThread 86
Sorrel 60
Sqirl 46
Taco María 71
Waterbar 60

Hawaii **87**

Kahumana Organic Farm and Café 88
Merriman's 88
Town 89
'Ulu Ocean Grill 89

Oregon **91**

Ava Gene's 96
Bamboo Sushi 92
Farm Spirit 96
Local Ocean Seafoods 100
Lovely's Fifty Fifty 97
Nostrana 97
Seastar Bakery 100
Stacked Sandwich Shop 98

Washington **101**

Burgerville 103
Ursa Minor 102
Whale Wins, The 104
Willows Inn 103

THE SOUTHWEST & ROCKY MOUNTAINS **107**

Arizona **109**

5 Points Market & Restaurant 114
Barrio Bread 115
Brix Restaurant and Wine Bar 113
Cafe Roka 112
FnB 112
Kai Restaurant 111
Pizzeria Bianco 110
Quiessence at the Farm 111

Colorado **117**

Annette 129
Arcana 120
Bin 707 Foodbar 132
Black Cat Bistro 120
Cloverdale Restaurant and Farm 134
Comal Heritage Food Incubator 121
Frasca Food & Wine 118
Fruition Restaurant 128
Kitchen, The 121
Potager 122
Señor Bear 128
Way Back, The 124

Montana **137**

Little Star Diner 138
Masala 139
Montana Ale Works 138

Nevada **149**

Esther's Kitchen 150
Liberty Food & Wine Exchange 150

New Mexico **141**

Campo at Los Poblanos 142
Compound Restaurant, The 146
Farm & Table 144
Fire & Hops Gastropub 145
Grove Cafe & Market, The 144
Roots Farm Café 145
Vinaigrette 148

Texas **151**

Barley Swine 154
Café Momentum 156
Coltivare 157
Dai Due Butcher Shop & Supper Club 152
Eden East 154
Gemma 156
Inn at Dos Brisas, The 160
Rancho Loma 155
Restaurant Gwendolyn 158
Restaurant Mixtli 157

Utah **161**

Communal 165
Copper Onion, The 163
Hell's Backbone Grill 162

Laziz Kitchen 163
Pago 164
Table X 164

Wyoming 167

Persephone Bakery 168
Rendezvous Bistro 168

THE MIDWEST & GREAT LAKES 171

Illinois 173

Baker Miller 174
Blackbird 174
City Mouse 175
Frontera Grill 175
Honey Butter Fried Chicken 176
Lula Cafe 176
North Pond 177
Smyth 177
Uncommon Ground 178
Vie 179

Indiana 181

Bluebeard 182
Cafe Patachou 182
FARMbloomington 183

Iowa 185

Brazen Open Kitchen 188
Harbinger Restaurant 186
HoQ 186
Le Jardin 187
Trellis Cafe 187

Kansas 189

Elderslie Farm 192
Merchants Pub & Plate 190
Public 191
Story 191

Michigan 195

Avalon Breads 197
Granor Farm 197
Grove 198
Lady of the House 198
Luna 199
Salt of the Earth 196
Zingerman's Roadhouse 199

Minnesota 201

Alma 202
Angry Trout Cafe 212
Bachelor Farmer, The 202
Birchwood Cafe 203
Common Roots Cafe 204
Corner Table 205
French Meadow Cafe & Bluestem Bar 206
Heirloom 213
New Scenic Cafe 214
ninetwentyfive 212
Northern Waters Smokehaus 216
Spoonriver 205
Tiny Diner 210
Tongue in Cheek 213

Missouri 217

Black Dirt 218
Bluestem Restaurant 220
Catalpa 228
Farmhaus 223
Farmhouse, The 221
Green Dirt Farm Creamery 227
Harvest 232
Novel 220
Sardella 227
Sidney Street Café 223
Vicia 224
Webster House 222
Winslow's Home 226

Nebraska 233

Grey Plume, The 234
Prairie Plate Restaurant 235
Stirnella Bar & Kitchen 234

North Dakota 237

Pirogue Grille 238
Souris River Brewing 238

Ohio 239

Greenhouse Tavern, The 244
Red Feather 240
Table, The 242

Oklahoma 245

Juniper 250
Ludivine 246
Mary Eddy's Kitchen x Lounge 250
Pritchard, The 248
St. Mark's Chop Room 251

South Dakota 253

M.B. Haskett Delicatessen 254
Parker's Bistro 256

Wisconsin 257

Ardent 262
Braise 259
Driftless Café 260
Forequarter 258
L'Etoile 259

THE SOUTHEAST

Alabama 267

Acre 270
Chez Fonfon 268
Fisher's at Orange Beach Marina 269
Highlands Bar & Grill 268
Johnny's Restaurant 270
Post Office Pies 269
Southern National 271

Arkansas 273

Hive, The 274
Preacher's Son, The 274
Root Cafe, The 276
South on Main 275
Three Fold Noodles + Dumpling Co. 278
Tusk & Trotter American Brasserie 275

District of Columbia 281

Blue Duck Tavern 282
Bresca 283
Centrolina 284
Chaia 283
Cork Wine Bar & Market 285
Dabney, The 285
Ellé 286
Espita 286
Founding Farmers 287
Garrison 288
Kaliwa 288
Kyirisan 289
Rake's Progress, A 282
Salt Line, The 292
Seylou Bakery & Mill 290
Tail Up Goat 293
Timber Pizza 293
Toki Underground 294
Whaley's 294

Florida 295

Buccan 300
Columbia, The 297
El Siboney Restaurant 299
Ghee Indian Kitchen 297
Gilbert's Social 296
Gilbert's Southern Kitchen + Bar 296
Joe's Stone Crab 298
Regional Kitchen & Public House, The 300
Stiltsville Fish Bar 298

Georgia 301

Arepa Mia 308
B's Cracklin' Barbecue 304
Bread & Butterfly 304
Chai Pani 309
Farmer & The Larder, The 310
Grey, The 306
home.made 307
Kimball House 310
Little Tart Bakeshop 302
Miller Union 305
Seabear Oyster Bar 307
Ticonderoga Club 305
Twisted Soul Cookhouse & Pours 306

Kentucky 311

610 Magnolia 312
Commonwealth Bistro 319
Doodles Breakfast & Lunch 319
Farmstand Market & Cafe, The 320
Garage Bar 314
Lilly's Bistro 314
Mayan Cafe 315
MozzaPi 316
Proof on Main 318
Red Hog Artisan Butcher 318

Louisiana 321

Cochon 322
Compere Lapin 322
Gabrielle Restaurant 326
MOPHO 323
Mosquito Supper Club 324
Pêche 326
Seaworthy 327
Toups' Meatery 327
Willa Jean 328

Maryland 329

Addie's 332
Atwater's 330
Maggie's Farm 331
Preserve 330
Woodberry Kitchen 331

Mississippi 333

Big Bad Breakfast 336
City Grocery 336
Saint Leo 334
Snackbar 337

North Carolina 339

Crook's Corner 348
Cúrate 348
Foothills Butcher Bar 347

French Broad Chocolates 340
Fullsteam Tavern 350
Garland 354
Hole Doughnuts 342
HomeGrown 346
Honeysuckle Tea House 349
Lantern 349
OWL Bakery 344
Poole's Diner 354
Pure Pizza 351
Rose's Noodles, Dumplings and Sweets 352

South Carolina 355

Basic Kitchen 357
FARM 356
Glass Onion, The 356
Juniper 360
Motor Supply Co. Bistro 359
Obstinate Daughter, The 358
Swamp Rabbit Cafe & Grocery 359
Wild Olive 358

Tennessee 361

Andrew Michael Italian Kitchen 371
Barn at Blackberry Farm, The 370
Capitol Grille 362
City House 362
EiO & The Hive 364
Fin & Pearl 363
Henrietta Red 366
Husk Nashville 366
Josephine 367
Knox Mason 371
Lockeland Table 368
Main Street Meats 370
Margot Café 367

Virginia 373

Field & Main 376
Hunter's Head Tavern 375
Ivy Inn Restaurant, The 374
Market Table Bistro 374
Milton's 378
Restaurant at Patowmack Farm, The 375

West Virginia 379

Hill & Hollow 380

THE NORTHEAST

Connecticut 385

Dining Room at The White Hart 386
Miya's 387
Ore Hill & Swyft 387

Delaware 389

Blue Hen, The 390

Maine 391

Drifters Wife 394
Fore Street 394
Lost Kitchen, The 397
Nebo Lodge 396
Nīna June 395
Primo 397
Solo Italiano 392
Tandem Coffee + Bakery 395

Massachusetts 399

Cultivar 400
deadhorse hill 410
Island Creek Oyster Bar 402
Kirkland Tap & Trotter, The 403
Market Restaurant, The 404
Mezze Bistro + Bar 408
Oleana 406
Saloniki Greek Restaurant 402
Superfine Food 403
Woods Hill Table 412

New Hampshire 413

Black Trumpet 414
Franklin Oyster House 414
Moxy 415
Stages at One Washington 416
Vida Cantina 415

New Jersey 417

Agricola 420
Brick Farm Tavern 418
Elements 421
Farm & Fisherman Tavern, The 420

New York 423

abc kitchen 432
abcV 432
Agern 434
al di la Trattoria 424
Amali 433
Blue Hill 436
Blue Hill at Stone Barns 476
Brushland Eating House 468
Buvette 438
Café Altro Paradiso 442
Cleaver Counter 444
Craft 446
Dig Inn 433
Diner 447
Dirt Candy 447
Emma's Torch 425
Estela 448
Farm on Adderley, The 425
Fat Radish, The 450
Flora Bar 449
Four Horsemen, The 426
Gaskins 463
Good Fork, The 426
Graffiti Earth 450
Grazin' 478
Greenpoint Fish + Lobster Co. 427
Hearth 451
High Street on Hudson 452
Insa 428
Le Bernardin 451
Le Coq Rico 456
Little Park 456
Loring Place 457
Luke's Lobster 454
Mayanoki 457
Mettā 427
New Leaf 458
Nix 458
Olmsted 430
Phoenicia Diner 474
PRINT. 460
Roman's 430
Rouge Tomate Chelsea 459
Runner & Stone 431
Seamore's 459
Sunday in Brooklyn 431
Sunhee's Farm & Kitchen 478
Tortilleria Nixtamal 462
Union Square Cafe 462
Untitled 463
Via Carota 464
Westwind Orchard 472

Pennsylvania 479

Bolete 486
Dinette 484
Fork 480
Hungry Pigeon 482
Legume Bistro 485
MA(i)SON 486
Rooster Soup Company 482
Russet 483
Saté Kampar 483
Talula's Table 485
Vedge 484

Rhode Island 487

birch 488
Nicks on Broadway 489
North 488
Oberlin 490

Vermont 491

American Flatbread 495
Great Northern, The 492
Hen of the Wood 495
Honey Road 492
Inn at Shelburne Farms, The 493
Juniper 493
Kismet 496
Misery Loves Co. 494
Penny Cluse Cafe 494
SoLo Farm & Table 496

Index

By restaurant name

5 Points Market & Restaurant 114
610 Magnolia 312

A

abc kitchen 432
abcV 432
Acre 270
Addie's 332
Agern 434
Agricola 420
al di la Trattoria 424
Alma 202
Amali 433
American Flatbread 495
Andrew Michael Italian Kitchen 371
Angry Trout Cafe 212
Annette 129
Arcana 120
Ardent 262
Arepa Mia 308
Atwater's 330
Ava Gene's 96
Avalon Breads 197

B

Bachelor Farmer, The 202
Backyard 79
Baker Miller 174
Bamboo Sushi 92
Barley Swine 154
Barn at Blackberry Farm, The 370
Baroo 32
Barrio Bread 115
Basic Kitchen 357
Bear and Star, The 74
Big Bad Breakfast 336
Bin 707 Foodbar 132
birch 488
Birchwood Cafe 203
Bird Dog 73
Black Cat Bistro 120
Black Dirt 218
Black Trumpet 414
Blackbird 174
Blue Duck Tavern 282
Blue Hen, The 390
Blue Hill 436
Blue Hill at Stone Barns 476
Bluebeard 182
Bluestem Restaurant 220
Bolete 486
Botanica Restaurant & Market 28
Braise 259
Brazen Open Kitchen 188
Bread & Butterfly 304
Bresca 283
Brick Farm Tavern 418
Brix Restaurant and Wine Bar 113
Broken Spanish 32
Brushland Eating House 468
B's Cracklin' Barbecue 304
Buccan 300
Burgerville 103
Buvette 438

C

Café Altro Paradiso 442
Café Momentum 156
Cafe Patachou 182
Cafe Roka 112
Cala 47
Camino 81
Campo at Los Poblanos 142
Capitol Grille 362
Catalpa 228
Centrolina 284
Chai Pani 309
Chaia 283
Chez Fonfon 268
Chez Panisse 64
City Grocery 336
City House 362
City Mouse 175
Cleaver Counter 444
Cloverdale Restaurant and Farm 134
Cochon 322
Coltivare 157
Columbia, The 297
Comal Heritage Food Incubator 121
Common Roots Cafe 204
Commonwealth Bistro 319
Communal 165
Compere Lapin 322
Compound Restaurant, The 146
Copper Onion, The 163
Cork Wine Bar & Market 285
Corner Table 205
Cosecha 66
Craft 446
Crook's Corner 348
Cultivar 400
Cultura 61
Cúrate 348

D

Dabney, The 285
Dad's Luncheonette 78
Dai Due Butcher Shop & Supper Club 152
deadhorse hill 410
Dialogue 33
Dig Inn 433
Diner 447
Dinette 484
Dining Room at The White Hart 386
Dirt Candy 447
Doodles Breakfast & Lunch 319
DOSA 48
Drawing Board, The 80
Drifters Wife 394
Driftless Café 260

E

Eden East 154
EiO & The Hive 364
El Siboney Restaurant 299
Elderslie Farm 192
Elements 421
Ellé 286
Emma's Torch 425
Espita 286
Estela 448
Esther's Kitchen 150

F

FARM 356
Farm & Fisherman Tavern, The 420
Farm on Adderley, The 425
Farm Spirit 96
Farm & Table 144
FARMbloomington 183
Farmer & The Larder, The 310
Farmhaus 223
Farmhouse, The 221
Farmstand Market & Cafe, The 320

Fat Radish, The 450
Field & Main 376
Fin & Pearl 363
Fire & Hops Gastropub 145
Fish 70
Fisher's at Orange Beach Marina 269
Flora Bar 449
FnB 112
Foothills Butcher Bar 347
Fore Street 394
Foreign Cinema 50
Forequarter 258
Fork 480
Founding Farmers 287
Four Horsemen, The 426
Franklin Oyster House 414
Frasca Food & Wine 118
French Broad Chocolates 340
French Meadow Cafe & Bluestem Bar 206
Fresh Sourdough Express 24
Frontera Grill 175
Froth & Forage 25
Fruition Restaurant 128
Fullsteam Tavern 350

G

Gabrielle Restaurant 326
Garage Bar 314
Garland 354
Garrison 288
Gaskins 463
Gather 61
Gemma 156
Ghee Indian Kitchen 297
Gilbert's Social 296
Gilbert's Southern Kitchen + Bar 296
Glass Onion, The 356
Glen Ellen Star 81
Good Fork, The 426
Graffiti Earth 450
Grange 72
Granor Farm 197
Grazin' 478
Great Northern, The 492
Green Dirt Farm Creamery 227
Greenhouse Tavern, The 244
Greenpoint Fish + Lobster Co. 427
Grey, The 306
Grey Plume, The 234
Grove 198
Grove Cafe & Market, The 144
Gwen 34

H

Handline 82
Harbinger Restaurant 186
Harvest 232
Hearth 451
Heirloom 213
Hell's Backbone Grill 162
Hen of the Wood 495
Henrietta Red 366
High Street on Hudson 452
Highlands Bar & Grill 268
Hill & Hollow 380
Hive, The 274
Holbox 36
Hole Doughnuts 342
HomeGrown 346
home.made 307
Honey Butter Fried Chicken 176
Honey Road 492
Honeysuckle Tea House 349
HoQ 186
Hungry Pigeon 482
Hunter's Head Tavern 375
Husk Nashville 366

I

Inn at Dos Brisas, The 160
Inn at Shelburne Farms, The 493
Insa 428
Island Creek Oyster Bar 402
Ivy Inn Restaurant, The 374

J

Joe's Stone Crab 298
Johnny's Restaurant 270
Josephine 367
Juniper (Oklahoma) 250
Juniper (South Carolina) 360
Juniper (Vermont) 493

K

Kahumana Organic Farm and Café 88
Kai Restaurant 111
Kali 33
Kaliwa 288
Kimball House 310
Kirkland Tap & Trotter, The 403
Kismet 496
Kitchen, The 121
Knox Mason 371
Kyirisan 289

L

Lady of the House 198
Land & Water Company, The 76
Lantern 349
Lasa 40
Laziz Kitchen 163
Le Bernardin 451
Le Coq Rico 456
Le Jardin 187
Legume Bistro 485
L'Etoile 259
Liberty Food & Wine Exchange 150
Lilly's Bistro 314
Little Gem 47
Little Park 456
Little Star Diner 138
Little Tart Bakeshop 302
Local Ocean Seafoods 100
Lockeland Table 368
Loring Place 457
Lost Kitchen, The 397
Lovely's Fifty Fifty 97
Lowell's 83
Ludivine 246
Ludvig's Bistro 25
Luke's Lobster 454
Lula Cafe 176
Luna 199

M

Maggie's Farm 331
Main Street Meats 370
MA(i)SON 486
Margot Café 367
Market Restaurant, The 404
Market Table Bistro 374
Mary Eddy's Kitchen x Lounge 250
Masala 139
Mayan Cafe 315
Mayanoki 457
M.B. Haskett Delicatessen 254
Merchants Pub & Plate 190
Merriman's 88
Mettā 427
Mezze Bistro + Bar 408
Miller Union 305
Milton's 378
Misery Loves Co. 494
Miya's 387
Montana Ale Works 138
Montrio Bistro 71
MOPHO 323
Mosquito Supper Club 324
Motor Supply Co. Bistro 359
Moxy 415
MozzaPi 316
Mulvaney's 72

N

Native 41
Nebo Lodge 396
New Leaf 458
New Scenic Cafe 214
Nicks on Broadway 489
Nightbird 52
Nīna June 395
ninetwentyfive 212
Nix 458
n/naka 41
NOON All Day 56
Nopalito 51
North 488
North Pond 177
Northern Waters Smokehaus 216
Nostrana 97
Novel 220

O

Oberlin 490
Obstinate Daughter, The 358
Octavia 51
Oleana 406
Olmsted 430
Onsen 58
Ore Hill & Swyft 387
OWL Bakery 344

P

Pago 164

Parker's Bistro 256
Pêche 326
Penny Cluse Cafe 494
Perennial, The 59
Persephone Bakery 168
Phoenicia Diner 474
Pirogue Grille 238
Pizzaiolo 62
Pizzeria Bianco 110
Poole's Diner 354
Post Office Pies 269
Potager 122
Prairie Plate Restaurant 235
Preacher's Son, The 274
Preserve 330
Primo 397
PRINT. 460
Pritchard, The 248
Proof on Main 318
Providence 42
Public 191
Pure Pizza 351

Q

Quiessence at the Farm 111

R

Rake's Progress, A 282
Ramen Shop 68
Rancho Loma 155
Red Feather 240
Red Hog Artisan Butcher 318
Reem's California 86
Regional Kitchen & Public House, The 300
Rendezvous Bistro 168
Restaurant at Patowmack Farm, The 375
Restaurant Gwendolyn 158
Restaurant Mixtli 157
Robin 59
Roman's 430
Rooster Soup Company 482
Root Cafe, The 276
Roots Farm Café 145
Rose's Noodles, Dumplings and Sweets 352
Rouge Tomate Chelsea 459
Runner & Stone 431
Russet 483
Rustic Canyon 46

S

Saint Leo 334
Saloniki Greek Restaurant 402
Salt Line, The 292
Salt of the Earth 196
Sardella 227
Saté Kampar 483
Seabear Oyster Bar 307
Seamore's 459
Seastar Bakery 100
Seaworthy 327
Señor Bear 128
Seylou Bakery & Mill 290
SHED 84
Sidney Street Café 223
SingleThread 86
Smyth 177
Snackbar 337
SoLo Farm & Table 496
Solo Italiano 392
Sorrel 60
Souris River Brewing 238
South on Main 275
Southern National 271
Spoonriver 205
Sqirl 46
St. Mark's Chop Room 251
Stacked Sandwich Shop 98
Stages at One Washington 416
Stiltsville Fish Bar 298
Stirnella Bar & Kitchen 234
Story 191
Sunday in Brooklyn 431
Sunhee's Farm & Kitchen 478
Superfine Food 403
Swamp Rabbit Cafe & Grocery 359

T

Table, The 242
Table X 164
Taco María 71
Tail Up Goat 293
Talula's Table 485
Tandem Coffee + Bakery 395
Three Fold Noodles + Dumpling Co. 278
Ticonderoga Club 305
Timber Pizza 293
Tiny Diner 210
Toki Underground 294
Tongue in Cheek 213
Tortilleria Nixtamal 462
Toups' Meatery 327
Town 89
Trellis Cafe 187
Tusk & Trotter American Brasserie 275
Twisted Soul Cookhouse & Pours 306

U

'Ulu Ocean Grill 89
Uncommon Ground 178
Union Square Cafe 462
Untitled 463
Ursa Minor 102

V

Vedge 484
Via Carota 464
Vicia 224
Vida Cantina 415
Vie 179
Vinaigrette 148

W

Waterbar 60
Way Back, The 124
Webster House 222
Westwind Orchard 472
Whale Wins, The 104
Whaley's 294
Wild Olive 358
Willa Jean 328
Willows Inn 103
Winslow's Home 226
Woodberry Kitchen 331
Woods Hill Table 412

Z

Zingerman's Roadhouse 199

Acknowledgments

We are grateful to everyone who contributed to the making of *Truth, Love & Clean Cutlery*. We would especially like to thank the respective editors: Jill Dupleix, who came on board from the very beginning and adopted the entire project as fairy godmother; Giles Coren who buoyed us throughout with his brilliant writing and generous humour; Jules Mercer for her unfailing commitment and grace which supported us through many a stressful moment; Alice Waters whose integrity and kindness guided us throughout; Gabriella Gershenson who graciously gathered together the US writing team, and Katrina Power, whose indomitable powers of persuasion spanned forty writers in forty-five countries. To them, we are profoundly grateful.

To the contributing regional writers and editors whose words so beautifully captured the restaurants contained here: Amanda Bahl, Carolyn Bánfalvi, Anna Berghe, Vee Bougani, Nelson Carvalheiro, Javier Sánchez Castro, Larissa Dubecki, Lara Dunston, Jody Eddy, Osayi Endolyn, Wolfgang Fassbender, Devra Ferst, Paula Forbes, Mindy Fox, Nicholas Gilman, Daniel Gray, Dara Moskowitz Grumdahl, Adrian Hale, Nigel Hopkins, Lauraine Jacobs, Bethany Kehdy, Lee Tran Lam, Janice Leung-Hayes, Alexander Lobrano, Joy Manning, Josimar Melo, Natashca Mirosch, Martin Morales, Rebecca Flint Marx, Erin Byers Murray, Rachel Tepper Paley, Lara Rabinovitch, Lara Shunk, Chandra Ram, Hanna Raskin, Carlos Reyes, Leonardo Romanelli, Marjorie Ross, Vir Sanghvi, Laura Shunk, Pietro Sorba, Osavi Endolyn, Tara Stevens, Robbie Swinnerton, Mikko Takala, Aylin Oney Tan, Ole Troelsø, Mac van Dinther, Femke Vandevelde, Max Veenhuyzen, Ronit Vered and Samantha Wood. Thank you, these books would not exist without you.

A very special thank you to Dan Barber, Phil Bingley, Liam Fox, Irene Hamburger, Varun Mehra, Cristina Mueller, Andrea Muhlhausen, and Claire Sullivan, for their kind and generous assistance. Thank you also to Andrew Stephen and the team at the Sustainable Restaurant Association.

Words cannot express how grateful we are to be able to work alongside our generous colleagues at Blackwell & Ruth: Cameron Gibb, Stefanie Lim, Elizabeth Blackwell, Nikki Addison, Olivia Hopkinson and Kate Raven; and our wonderful *Truth, Love & Clean Cutlery* team: Karin Reinink, Shelley White, Jane Curtain and Rose Fooks. We couldn't have done any of it without you.

And finally, to the restaurants and food experiences who agreed to be part of *Truth, Love & Clean Cutlery*—thank you. Your passion and care inspired us to create this project and we are truly thankful for your generosity. We hope this book helps celebrate your outstanding efforts to make the world a better place, plate by plate.

Ruth Hobday and Geoff Blackwell
Blackwell & Ruth

B&R.

Blackwell & Ruth
Suite 405 IronBank
150 Karangahape Road
Auckland 1010, New Zealand
blackwellandruth.com

Publisher: Geoff Blackwell
Editor in Chief: Ruth Hobday
Design Director: Cameron Gibb,
Designer & Production Coordinator: Olivia Hopkinson
Publishing Manager: Nikki Addison
Digital Publishing Manager: Elizabeth Blackwell
Truth, Love & Clean Cutlery Membership Manager: Karin Reinink
Truth, Love & Clean Cutlery Coordinator–USA: Shelley White
Truth, Love & Clean Cutlery website developer: Phil Bingley

ISBN: 978-0-473-43224-9
A catalogue record for this book is available from the National Library of New Zealand.
Printed and bound in China by 1010 Printing Ltd
10 9 8 7 6 5 4 3 2 1

Distributed in the USA and Canada by Abrams, an imprint of ABRAMS, 195 Broadway, 9th Floor, New York, NY 10007, USA, abramsbooks.com

Abrams books are available at special discounts when purchased in quantity for premiums and promotions as well as fundraising or educational use. Special editions can also be created to specification. For details, contact: specialsales@abramsbooks.com.

This book is made with FSC®-certified paper and other controlled material and is printed with soy vegetable inks. The Forest Stewardship Council® (FSC®) is a global, not-for-profit organization dedicated to the promotion of responsible forest management worldwide to meet the social, ecological, and economic rights and needs of the present generation without compromising those of future generations.

The images contained in this book have been supplied by the individual restaurants who have provided copyright information where known and are used with permission from copyright © the individual photographers: Blue Hill at Stone Barns exterior–Ira Lippke; Blue Hill at Stone Barns–Jane Nina Sarkhel; Blue Hill parsnip–Andre Baronowski; Blue Hill pizza–Ingrid Hofstra; Handline–Dawn Heumann; Onsen–Grace Sager; Al di la Trattoria–Paul Thorburn; The Salt Line–Greg Powers; Foreign Cinema–Ed Anderson; Lasa–Eva Kolenko; French Broad Chocolates–Katrina Ohstrom; Fish–Marlon Duenas; FARMbloomington–Steve Raymer; Three Fold–Three Fold LLC; Founding Farmer–Ken Fletcher; Hell's Backbone Grill–Sarah Stathas; DOSA–Kassie Borreson; The Whale Wins–Jim Henkins; deadhorse hill–Brian Samuels Photography; Mosquito Supper Club–Jillian Greenberg Photography; The Root Café dish–Luis Vasquez; Botanica Restaurant & Market restaurant interior–Alan Gastelum; Café Altro Paradiso restaurant interior–David Sullivan; Café Altro Paradiso dish–Daniel Krieger; Estela–Tuuka Koski; Chez Panisse restaurant interior–Aya Brackett; Chez Panisse produce–Amanda Marsalis; Buvette waiter–Cerruti Draime; Brick Farm Tavern dish–Robin McConaughy; Brick Farm Tavern interior–Karin Belgrave; Via Carota–Cerruti Draime; Brushland Eating House–Cristian Harder; Rose's Noodles, Dumplings and Sweets–Alex Caterson, The Splinter Group; Agern–Evan Sung; Annette–From The Hip Photography; Driftless Café dish–Russ Viroqua; Fork dish–Steve Legato Photography; Frasca Food & Wine exterior–Megan Swann; Frasca Food & Wine dish–Julia Vandenoever; Gwen staff–Ray Kachatorian; Gwen interior and meat–Wonho Frank Lee; Kyirisan interior–Amber Frederiksen; Pizzaiolo–Paige Green; Solo Italiano–Erin Little; The Land & Water Company–ngiri dish–Carolyn Himes; Vicia kitchen–Kevin Roberts. The publisher cannot accept any responsibility for any unintentional omission in the copyright information provided by the restaurants, however should any copyright holders not be acknowledged here please contact the publisher who undertakes to make all reasonable efforts to include the appropriate acknowledgement in any subsequent editions. Editor photographs: Alice Waters p.10–Amanda Marsalis; Osayi Endolyn–Lucy Schaeffer; Devra Ferst–Martyna Starosta; Gabriella Gershenson–Landon Nordeman; Erin Byers Murray–Danielle Atkins; Chandra Ram–Geoffrey Smith.

Visit us at:
Web: truthloveandcleancutlery.com
Facebook: Truth Love and Clean Cutlery
Instagram: @truthloveandcleancutlery
Twitter: @truthloveandCC